SEVEN SEAS ENTERTAINMENT PRESENTS

Plum Crazy! tales of a tiger-striped cat

jkjc

story and art by NATSUMI HOSHINO VOLUME 2

APR - - 2019

TRANSLATION
Nan Rymer

LETTERING
Laura Scoville

COVER DESIGN
Nicky Lim

PROOFREADER
Katherine Bell
Brett Hallahan

ASSISTANT EDITOR
Jenn Grunigen

PRODUCTION ASSISTANT
CK Russell

PRODUCTION MANAGER
Lissa Pattillo

EDITOR-IN-CHIEF
Adam Arnold

PUBLISHER
Jason DeAngelis

PLUM CRAZY! TALES OF A TIGER-STRIPED CAT VOLUME 2
© Hoshino Natsumi 2008
Originally published in Japan in 2008 by SHONENGAHOSHA Co., Ltd., Tokyo.
English translation rights arranged through TOHAN CORPORATION, Tokyo.

Seven Seas books may be purchased in bulk for promotional, educational, or
business use. Please contact your local bookseller or the Macmillan Corporate
and Premium Sales Department at 1-800-221-7945, extension 5442, or by
e-mail at MacmillanSpecialMarkets@macmillan.com.

Seven Seas and the Seven Seas logo are trademarks of
Seven Seas Entertainment, LLC. All rights reserved.

ISBN: 978-1-626925-48-9

Printed in Canada

First Printing: September 2017

10 9 8 7 6 5 4 3 2 1

P9-DBS-389

FOLLOW US ONLINE: *www.gomanga.com*

READING DIRECTIONS

This book reads from *right to left*, Japanese style.
If this is your first time reading manga, you start
reading from the top right panel on each page and
take it from there. If you get lost, just follow the
numbered diagram here. It may seem backwards at
first, but you'll get the hang of it! Have fun!!

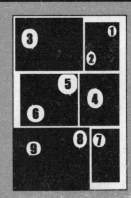

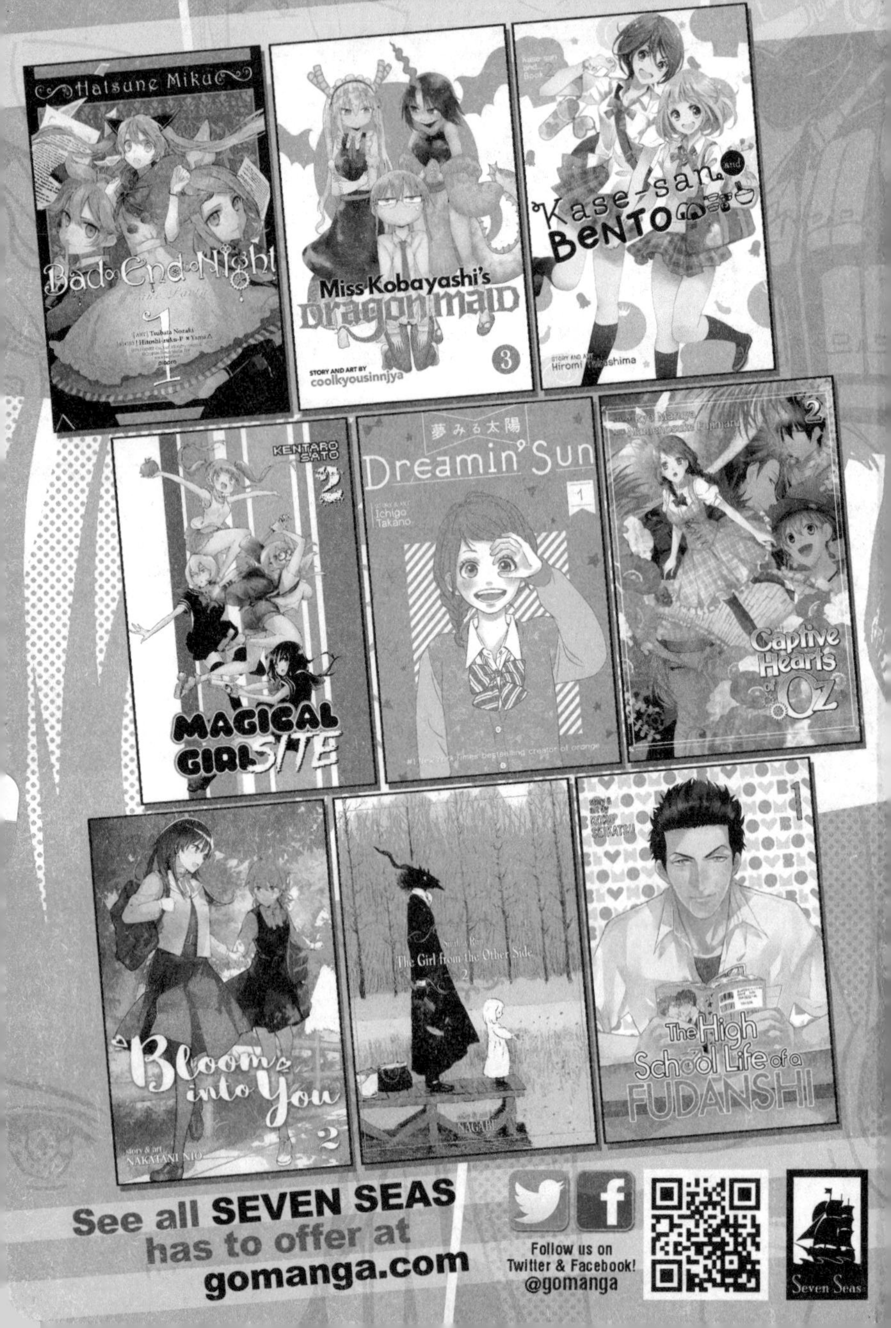
Hatsune Miku
Bad End Night
1
Tsubata Nozaki
Hitoshi-zuku-P x Yama△
Miss Kobayashi's Dragon Maid
3
STORY AND ART BY
coolkyousinnjya
Kase-san and Bento
Hiromi Takashima
KENTARO SATO
2
Magical Girl Site
夢みる太陽
Dreamin' Sun
1
Ichigo Takano
#1 New York Times bestselling creator of orange
2
Captive Hearts of Oz
Bloom into You
2
story & art
NAKATANI NIO
The Girl from the Other Side
2
NAGABE
1
The High School Life of a Fudanshi

Plum Crazy! tales of a tiger-striped cat 2

story & art by
HOSHINO
NATSUMI

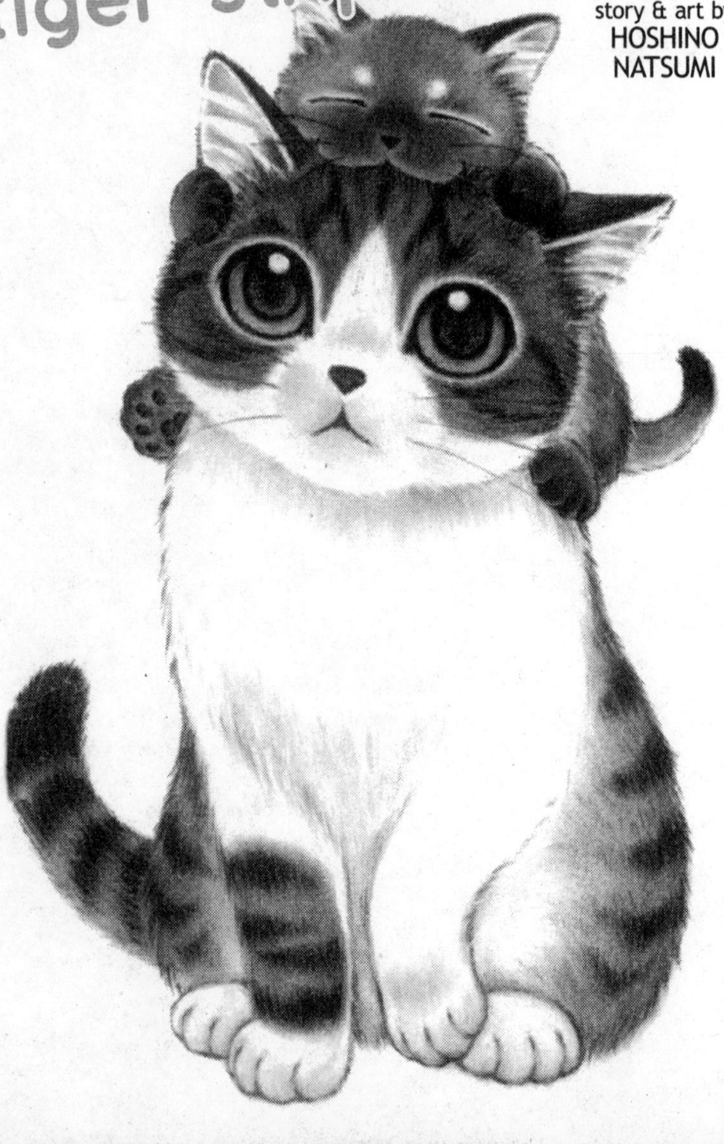

plum Crazy!
tales of a
tiger-striped cat

[KITTEN ARC] PLUM BECOMES THE NAKARAI FAMILY'S CAT

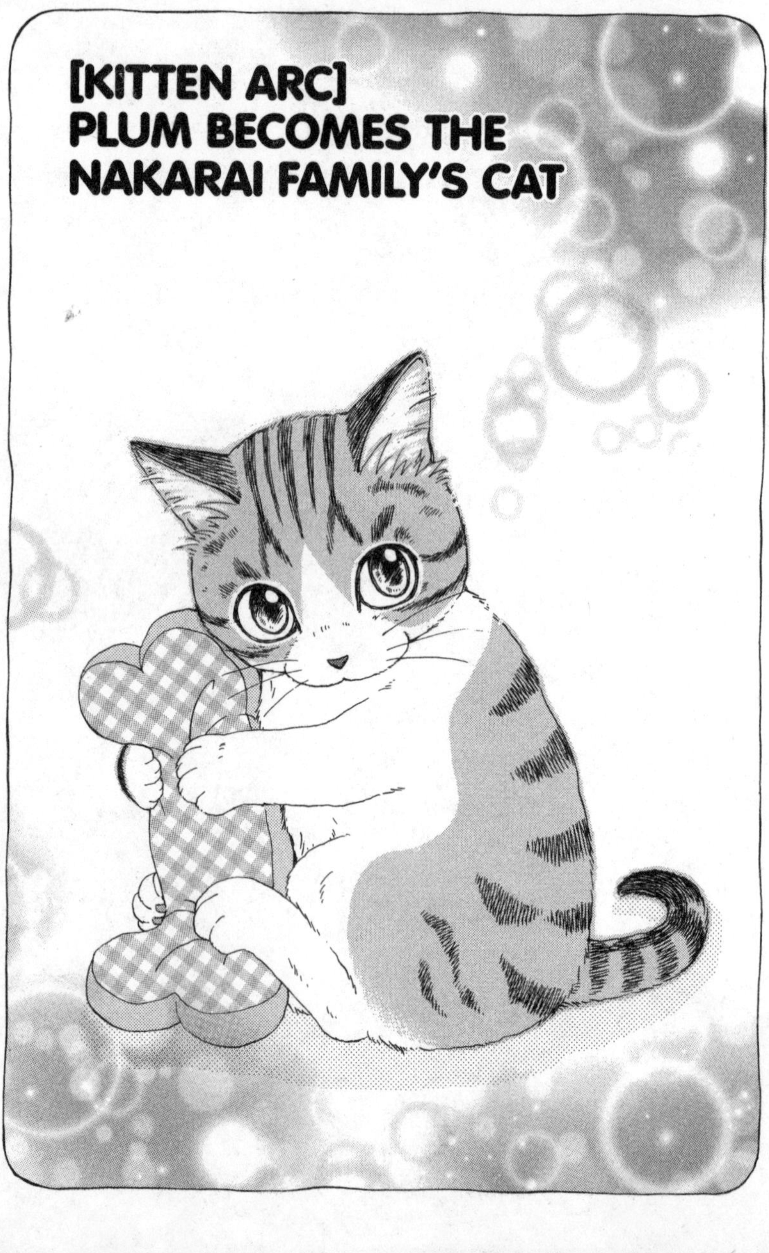

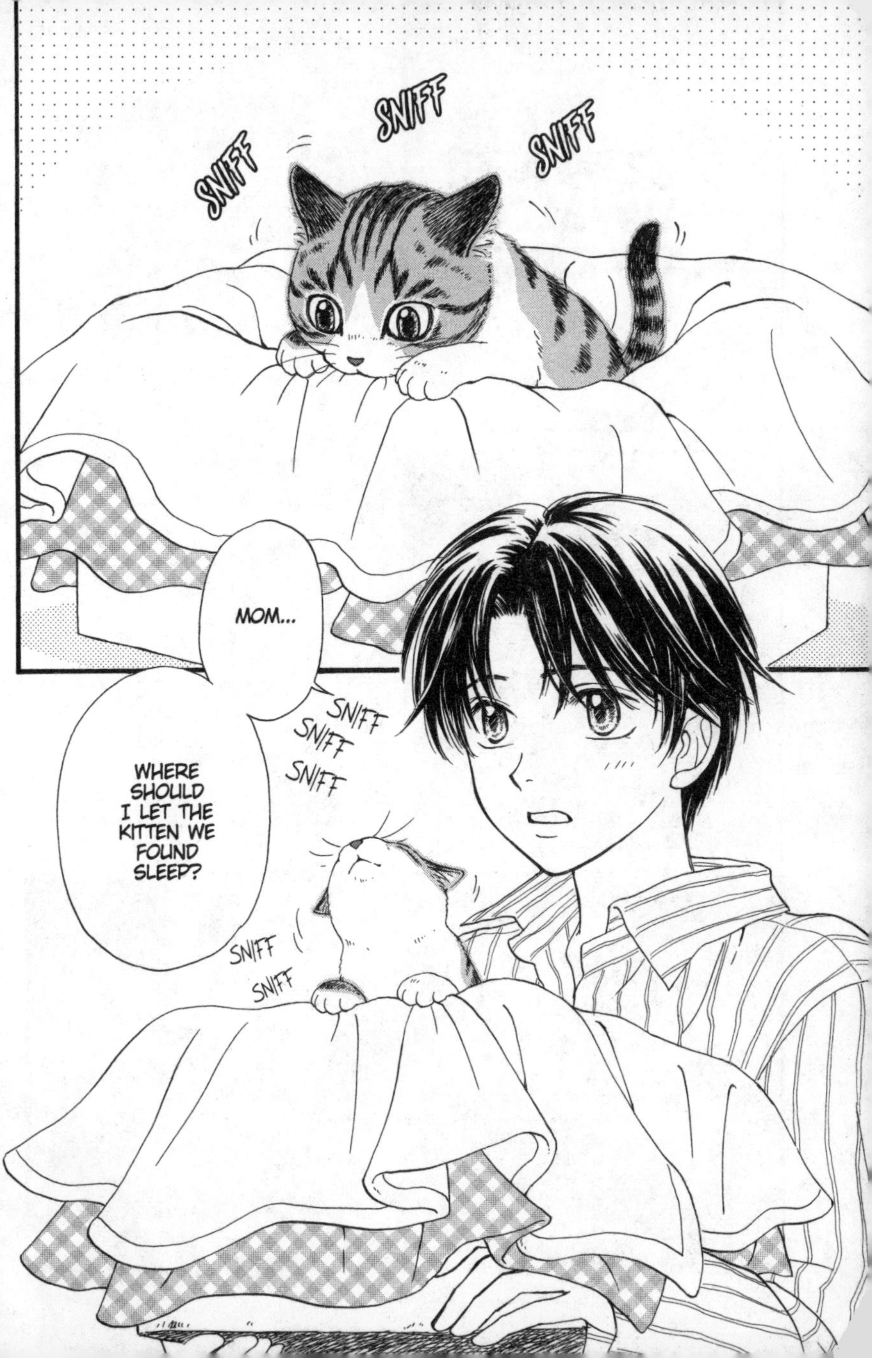
SNIFF
SNIFF
SNIFF
MOM...
WHERE SHOULD I LET THE KITTEN WE FOUND SLEEP?
SNIFF
SNIFF
SNIFF
SNIFF
SNIFF

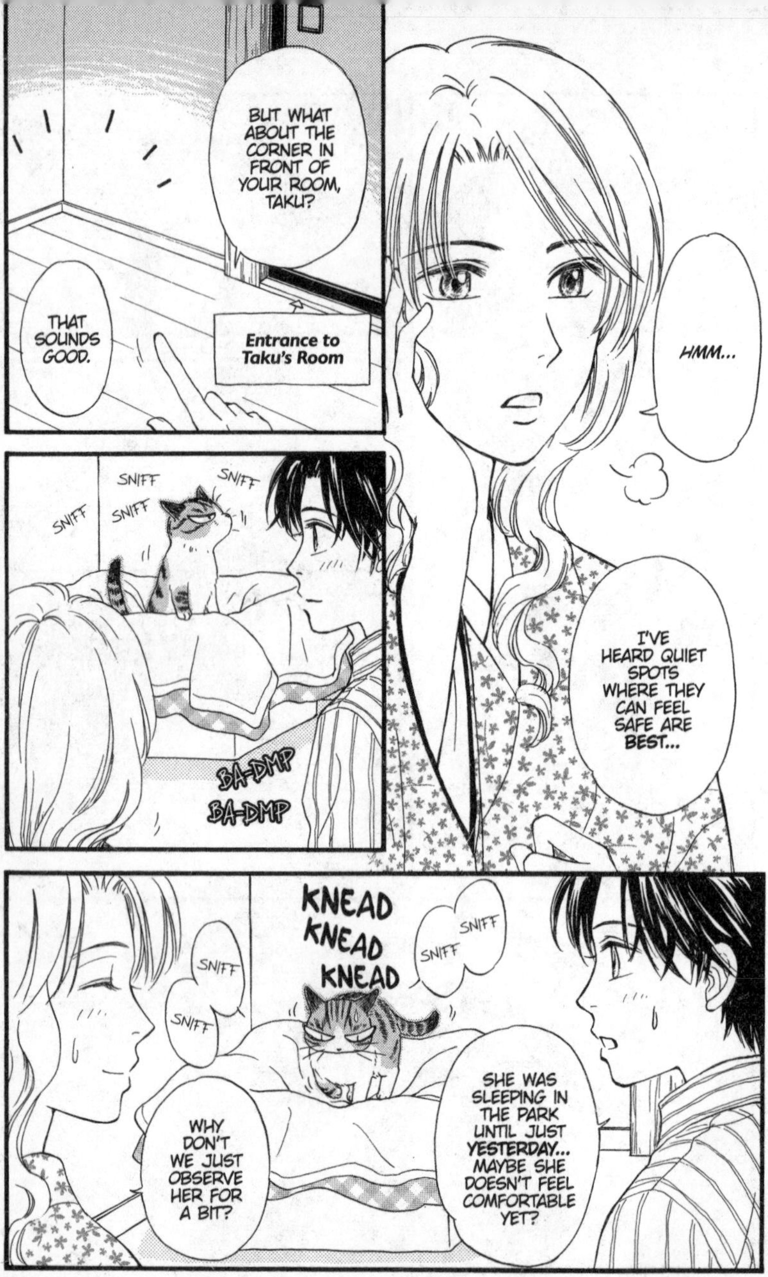
HMM...
I'VE HEARD QUIET SPOTS WHERE THEY CAN FEEL SAFE ARE **BEST**...
BUT WHAT ABOUT THE CORNER IN FRONT OF YOUR ROOM, TAKU?
Entrance to Taku's Room
THAT SOUNDS GOOD.
SNIFF
SNIFF
SNIFF
SNIFF
BA-DMP
BA-DMP
SNIFF
SNIFF
KNEAD
KNEAD
KNEAD
SHE WAS SLEEPING IN THE PARK UNTIL JUST **YESTERDAY**... MAYBE SHE DOESN'T FEEL COMFORTABLE YET?
WHY DON'T WE JUST OBSERVE HER FOR A BIT?
SNIFF
SNIFF

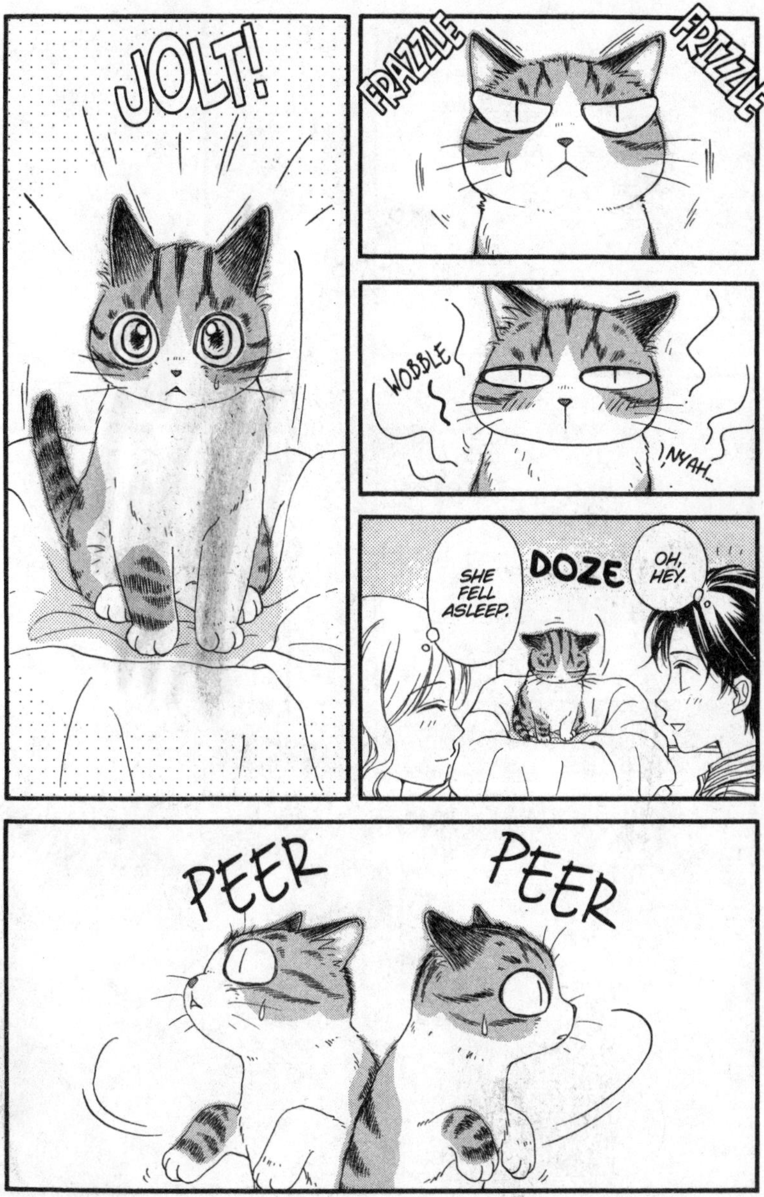
FRIZZLE
FRAZZLE
WOBBLE
NYAH...
OH, HEY.
DOZE
SHE FELL ASLEEP.
JOLT!
PEER
PEER

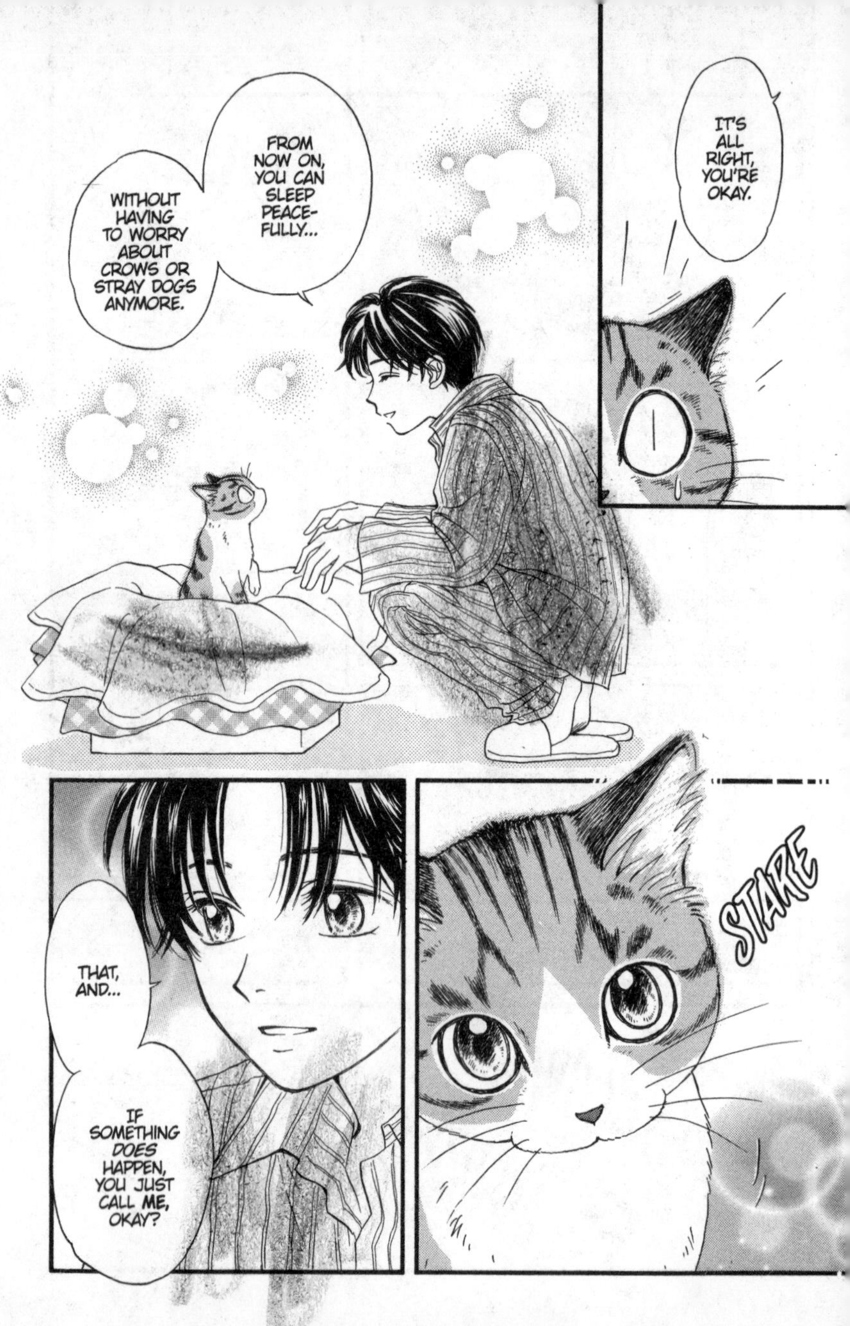
IT'S ALL RIGHT, YOU'RE OKAY.
FROM NOW ON, YOU CAN SLEEP PEACE-FULLY...
WITHOUT HAVING TO WORRY ABOUT CROWS OR STRAY DOGS ANYMORE.
STARE
THAT, AND...
IF SOMETHING *DOES* HAPPEN, YOU JUST CALL ME, OKAY?

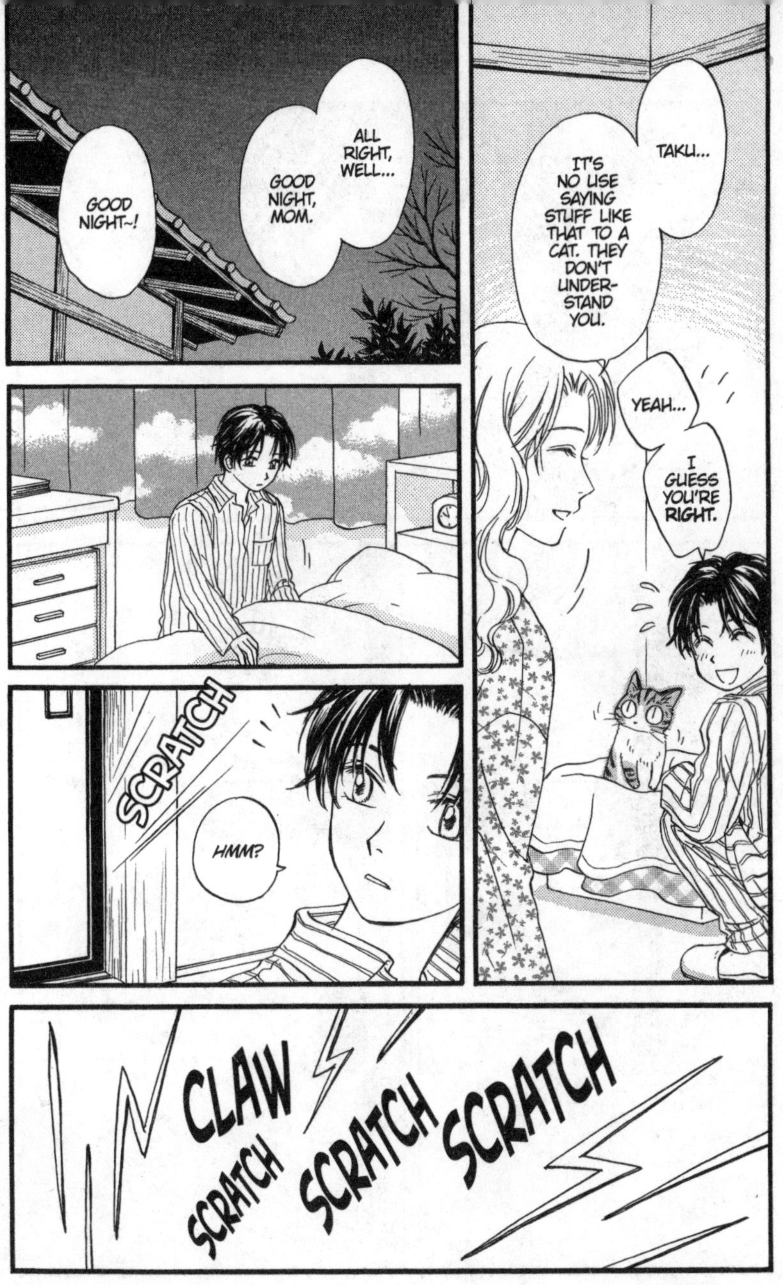
TAKU...
IT'S NO USE SAYING STUFF LIKE THAT TO A CAT. THEY DON'T UNDER-STAND YOU.
YEAH...
I GUESS YOU'RE RIGHT.
ALL RIGHT, WELL...
GOOD NIGHT, MOM.
GOOD NIGHT~!
SCRATCH
HMM?
CLAW
SCRATCH
SCRATCH
SCRATCH

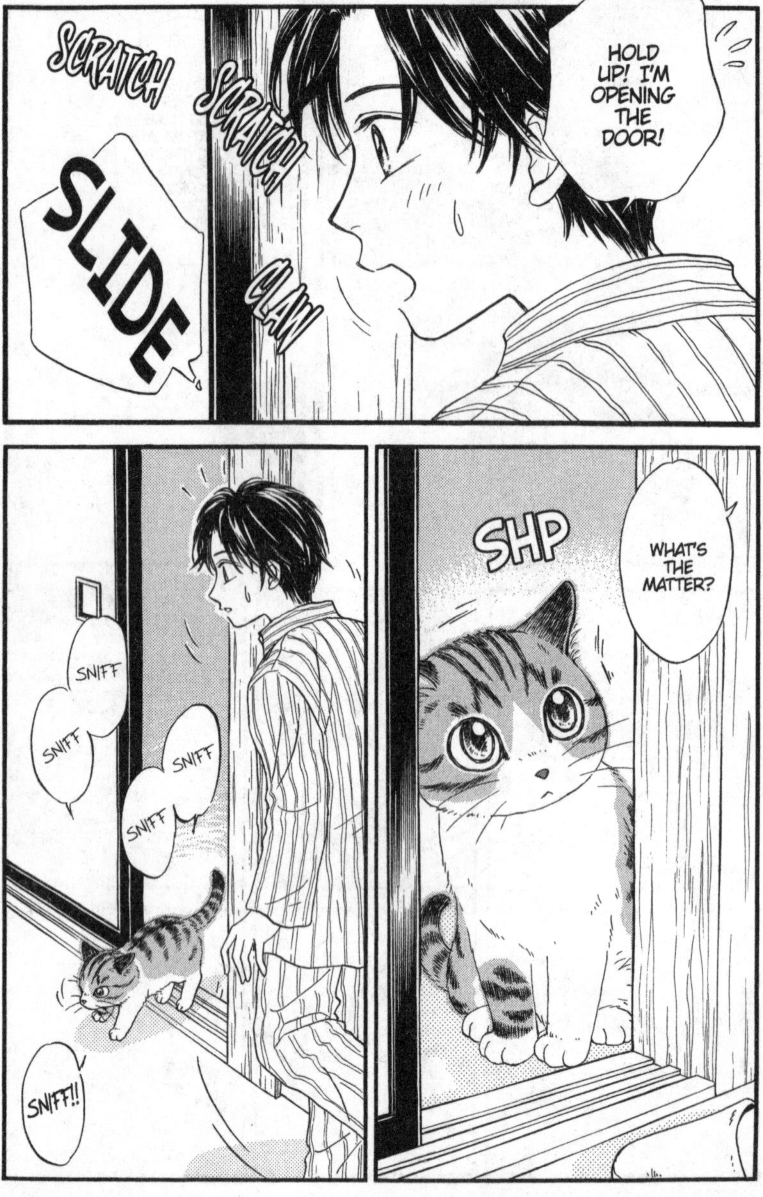
HOLD UP! I'M OPENING THE DOOR!
SCRATCH
SCRATCH
CLAW
SLIDE
WHAT'S THE MATTER?
SHP
SNIFF
SNIFF
SNIFF
SNIFF
SNIFF!!

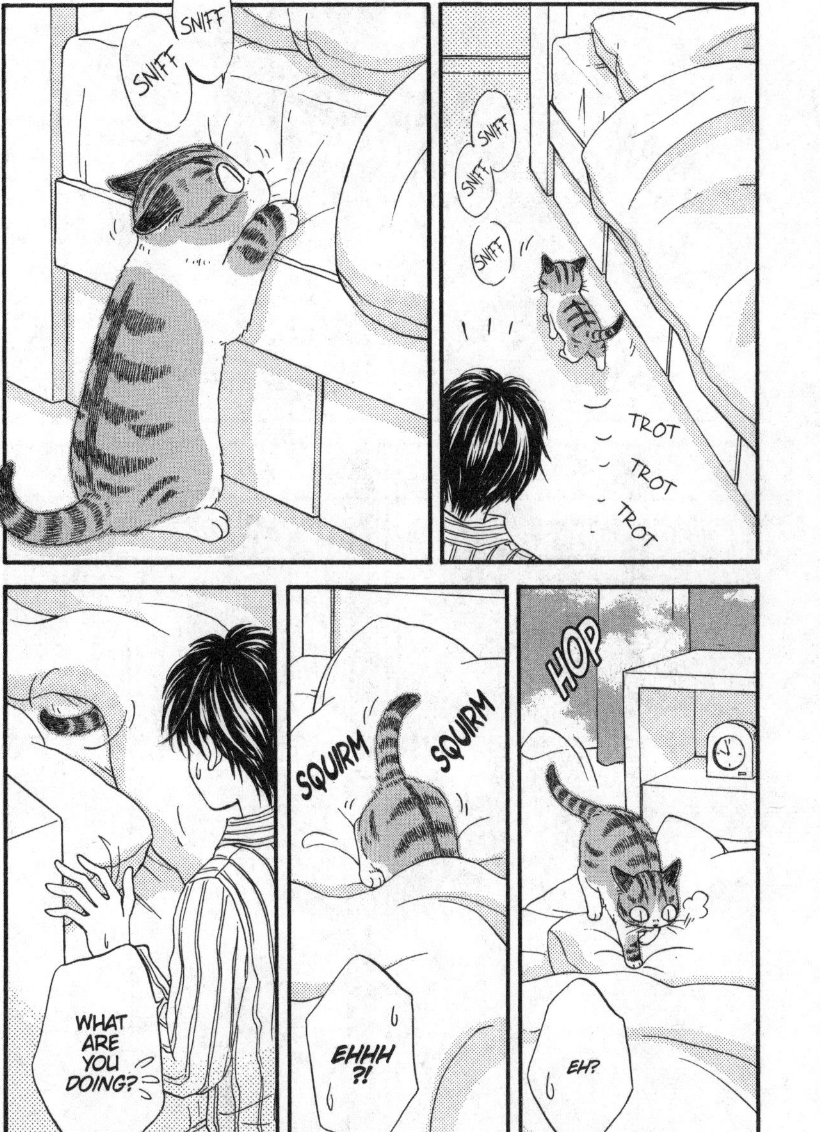
SNIFF
SNIFF
SNIFF
TROT
TROT
TROT
SNIFF
SNIFF
HOP
EH?
SQUIRM
SQUIRM
EHHH ?!
WHAT ARE YOU DOING?

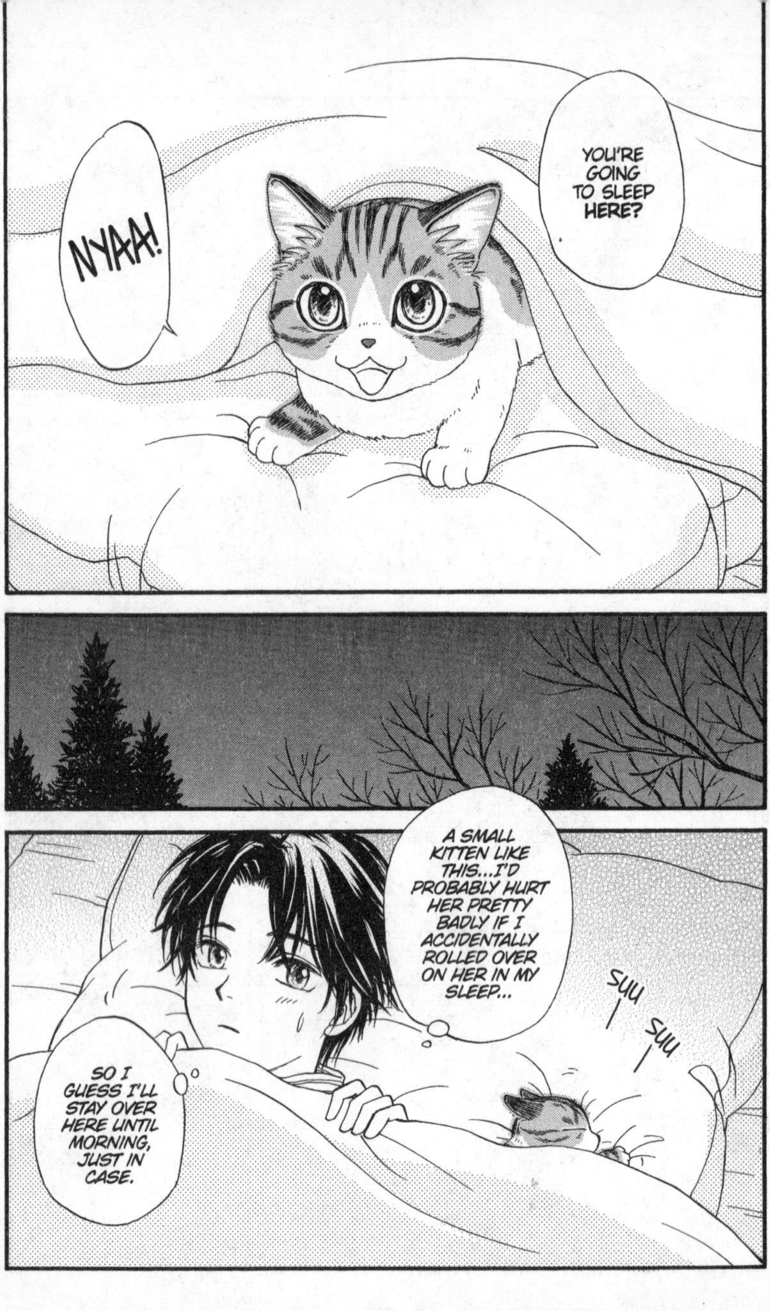
YOU'RE GOING TO SLEEP HERE?
NYAA!
A SMALL KITTEN LIKE THIS...I'D PROBABLY HURT HER PRETTY BADLY IF I ACCIDENTALLY ROLLED OVER ON HER IN MY SLEEP...
SUU SUU
SO I GUESS I'LL STAY OVER HERE UNTIL MORNING, JUST IN CASE.

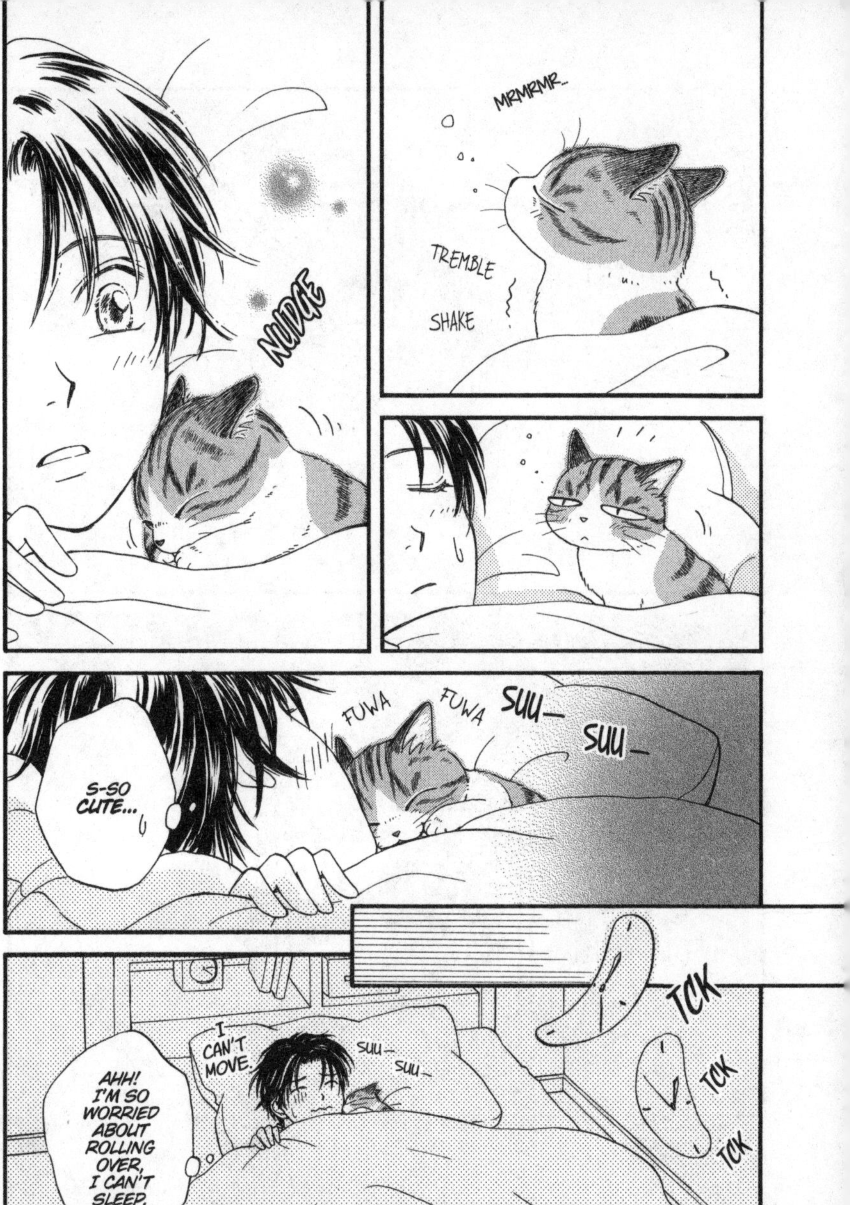
MRMRMR...
TREMBLE
SHAKE
NUDGE
SUU-
SUU-
FUWA
FUWA
S-SO CUTE...
TCK
TCK
TCK
SUU-
SUU-
I CAN'T MOVE.
AHH! I'M SO WORRIED ABOUT ROLLING OVER, I CAN'T SLEEP.

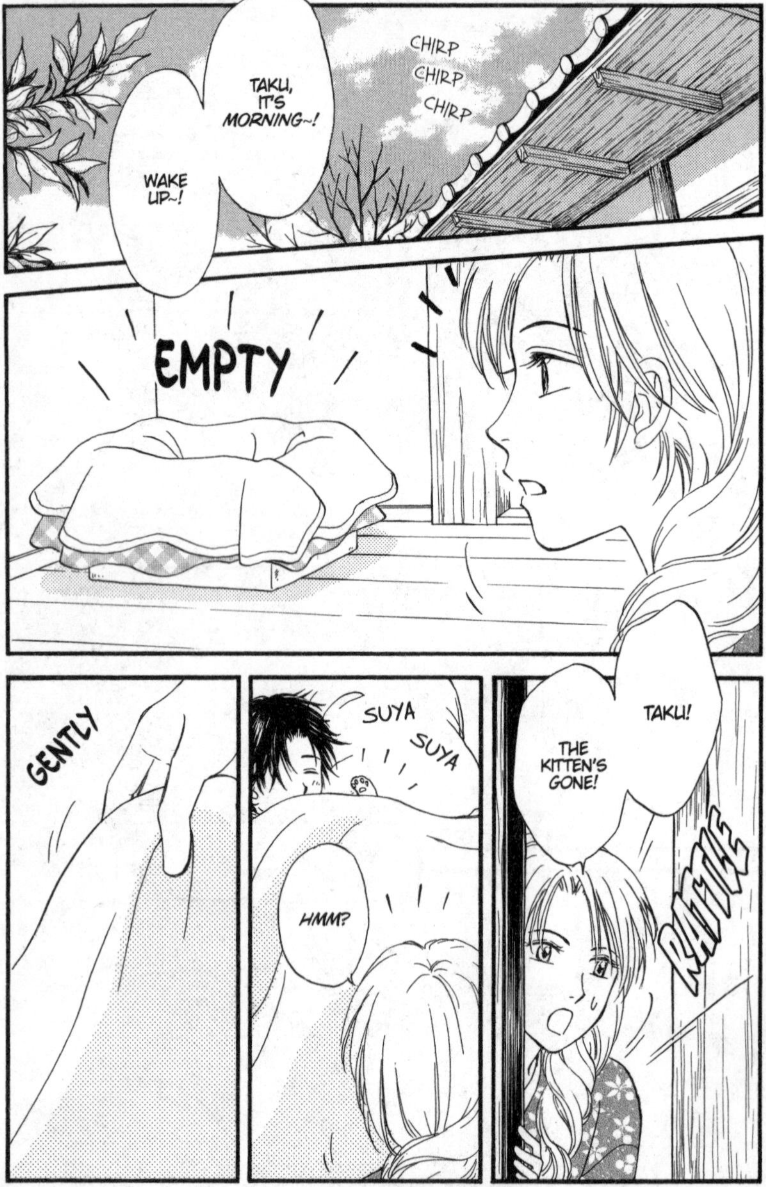
CHIRP
CHIRP
CHIRP
TAKU, IT'S MORNING~!
WAKE UP~!
EMPTY
TAKU!
THE KITTEN'S GONE!
RATTLE
SUYA
SUYA
HMM?
GENTLY

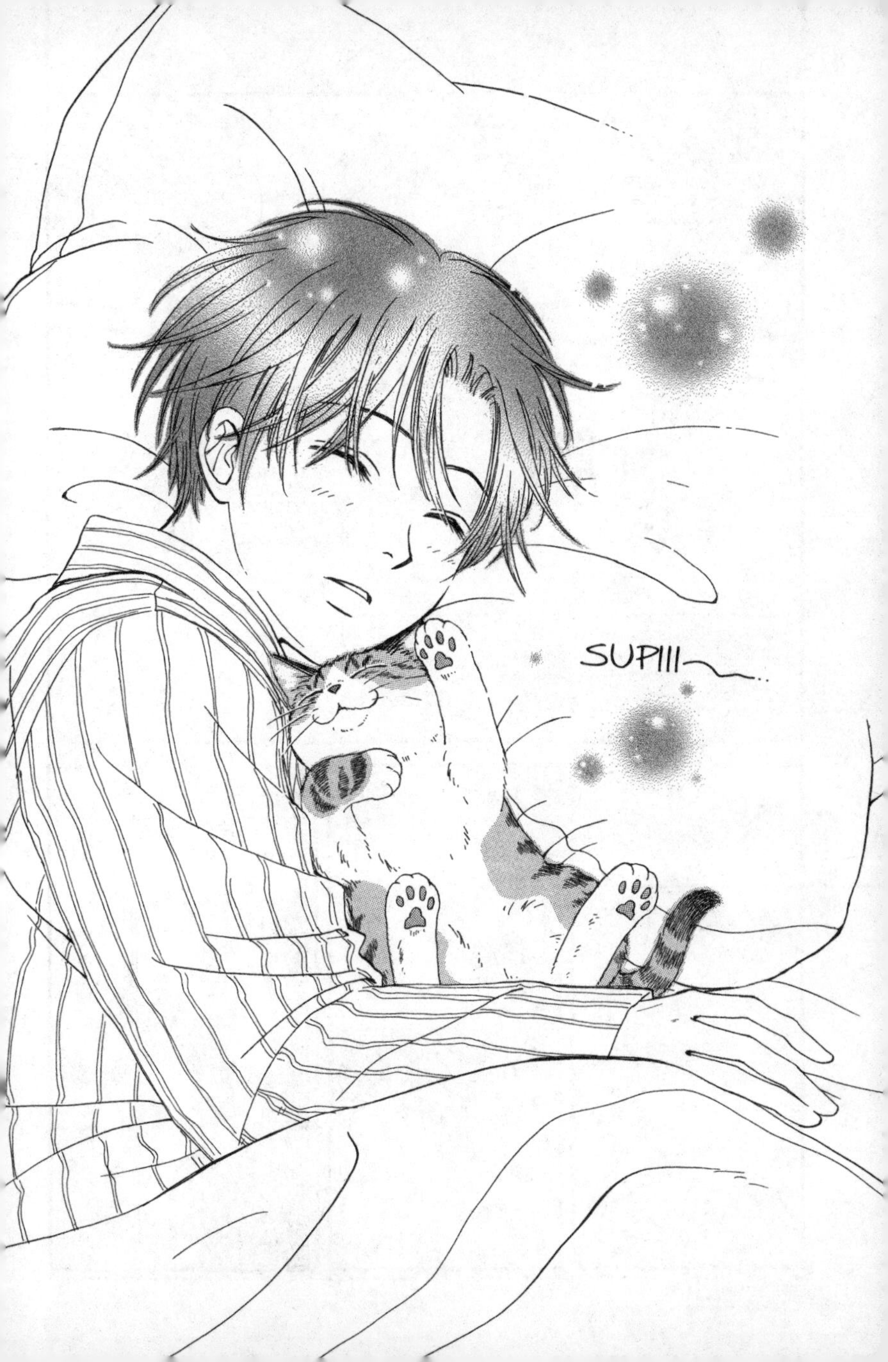
SUPIIII~...

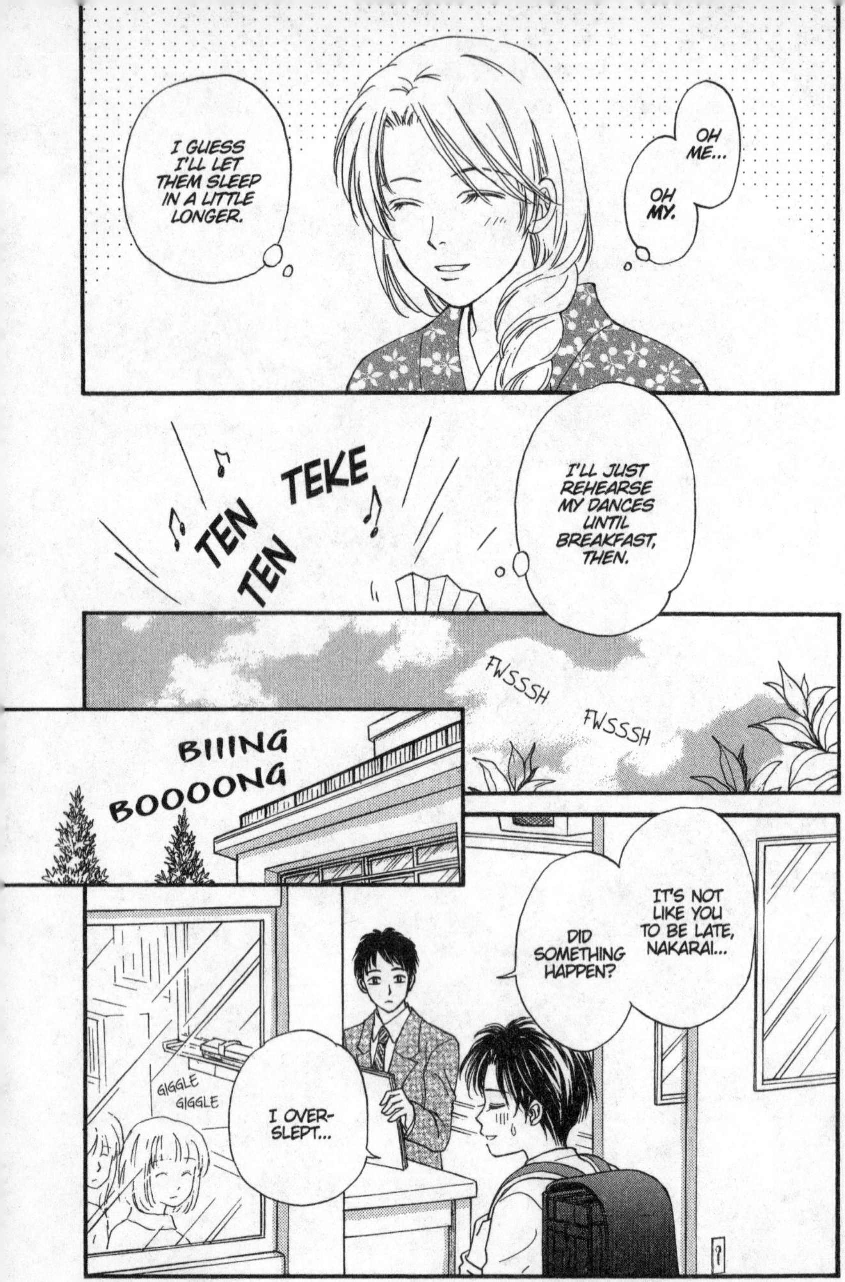
OH ME... OH MY.
I GUESS I'LL LET THEM SLEEP IN A LITTLE LONGER.
I'LL JUST REHEARSE MY DANCES UNTIL BREAKFAST, THEN.
TEN TEKE TEN
FWSSSH
FWSSSH
BIIING BOOOONG
IT'S NOT LIKE YOU TO BE LATE, NAKARAI...
DID SOMETHING HAPPEN?
I OVER-SLEPT...
GIGGLE GIGGLE

The End

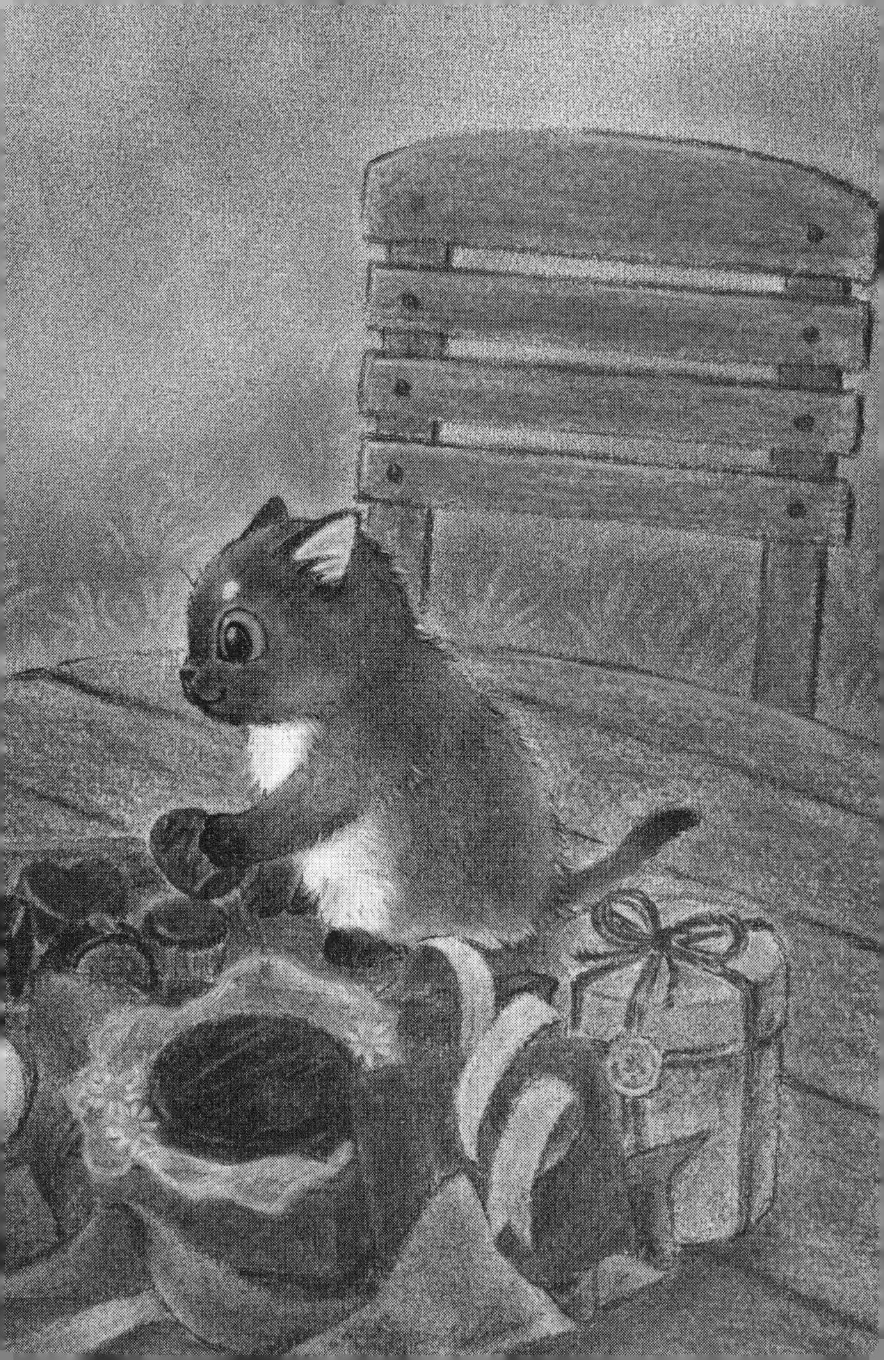

SHORT.5
VALENTINE'S DAY

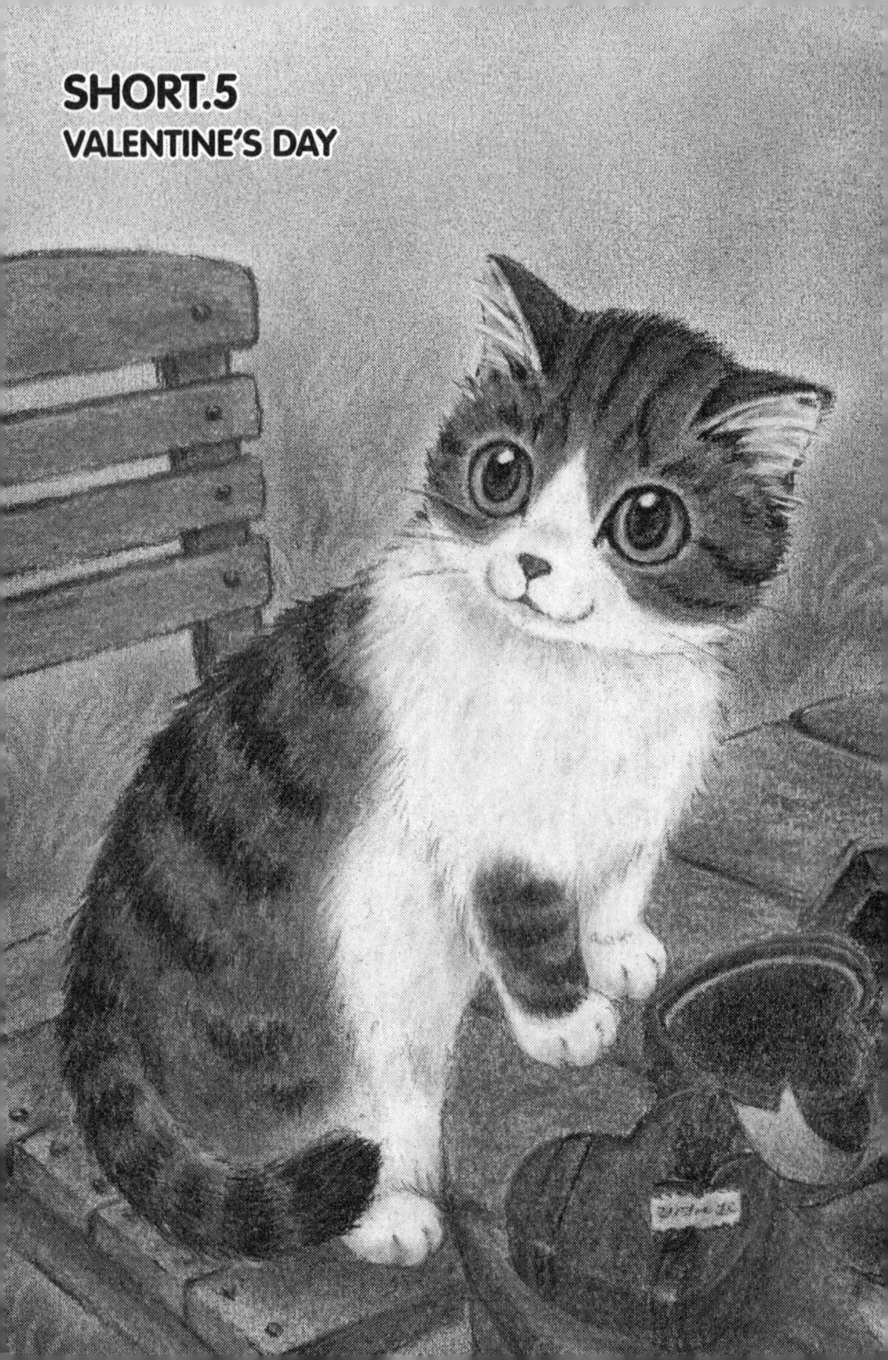

VOLUME 2'S COVER

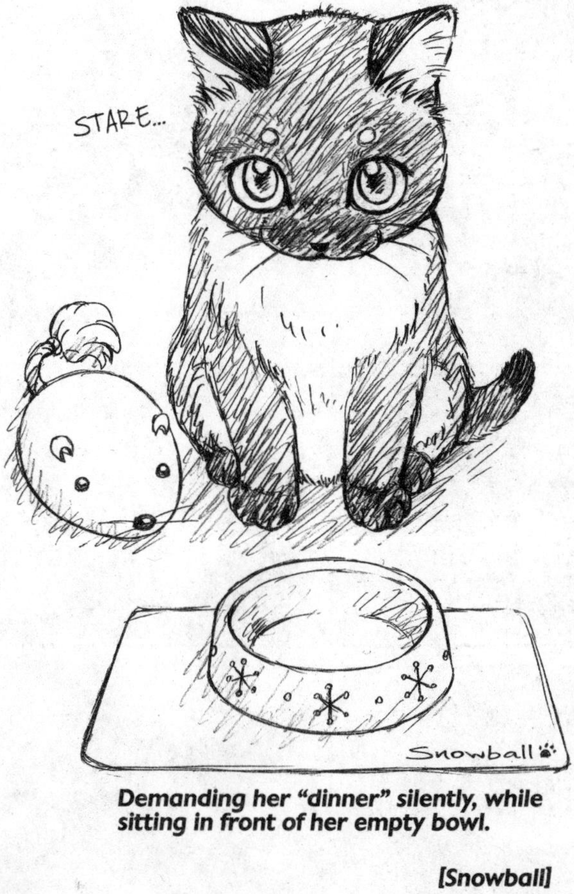
STARE...
Snowball

Demanding her "dinner" silently, while sitting in front of her empty bowl.

[Snowball]

SHORT.5

VALENTINE'S DAY

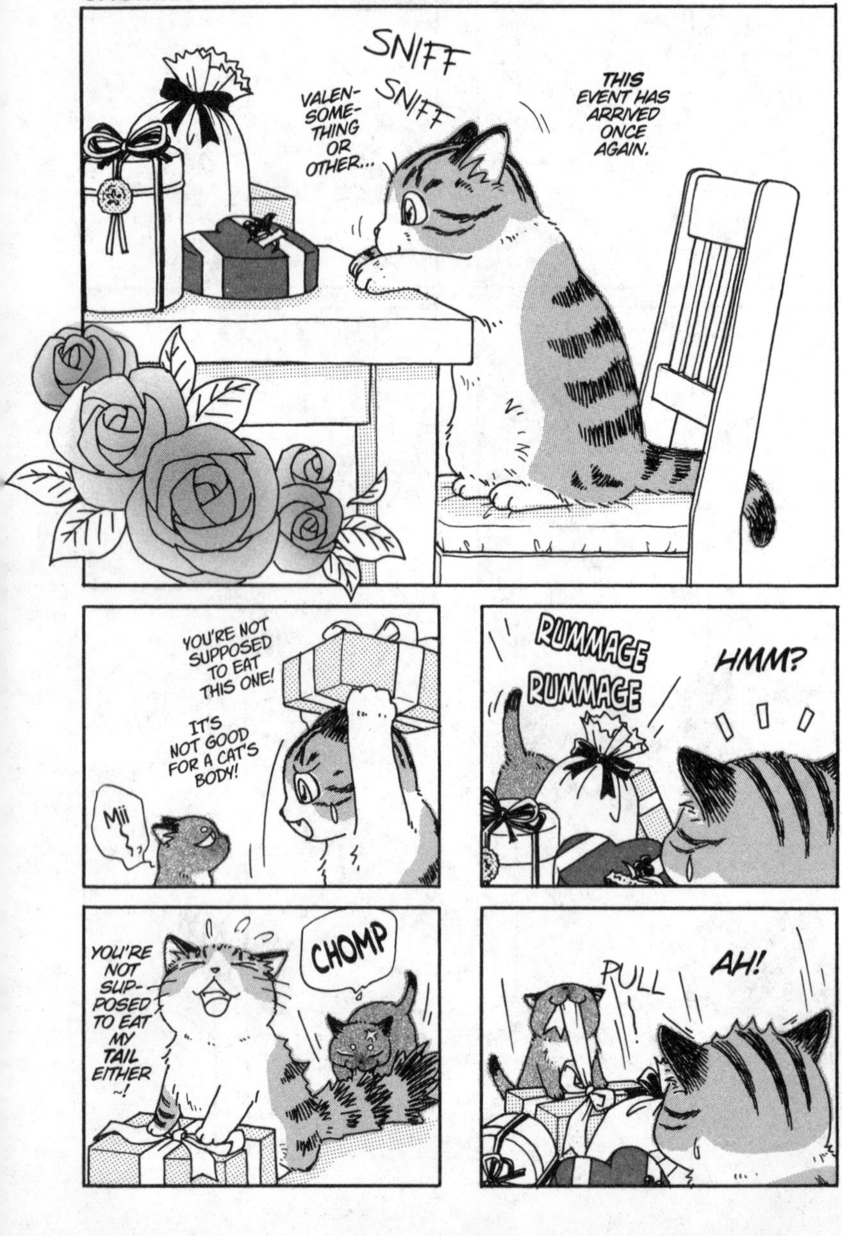
THIS EVENT HAS ARRIVED ONCE AGAIN.
SNIFF
SNIFF
VALEN-SOME-THING OR OTHER...
HMM?
RUMMAGE
RUMMAGE
YOU'RE NOT SUPPOSED TO EAT THIS ONE!
IT'S NOT GOOD FOR A CAT'S BODY!
Mii
AH!
PULL
CHOMP
YOU'RE NOT SUP-POSED TO EAT MY TAIL EITHER ~!

A CAT'S SHALLOW THINKING?

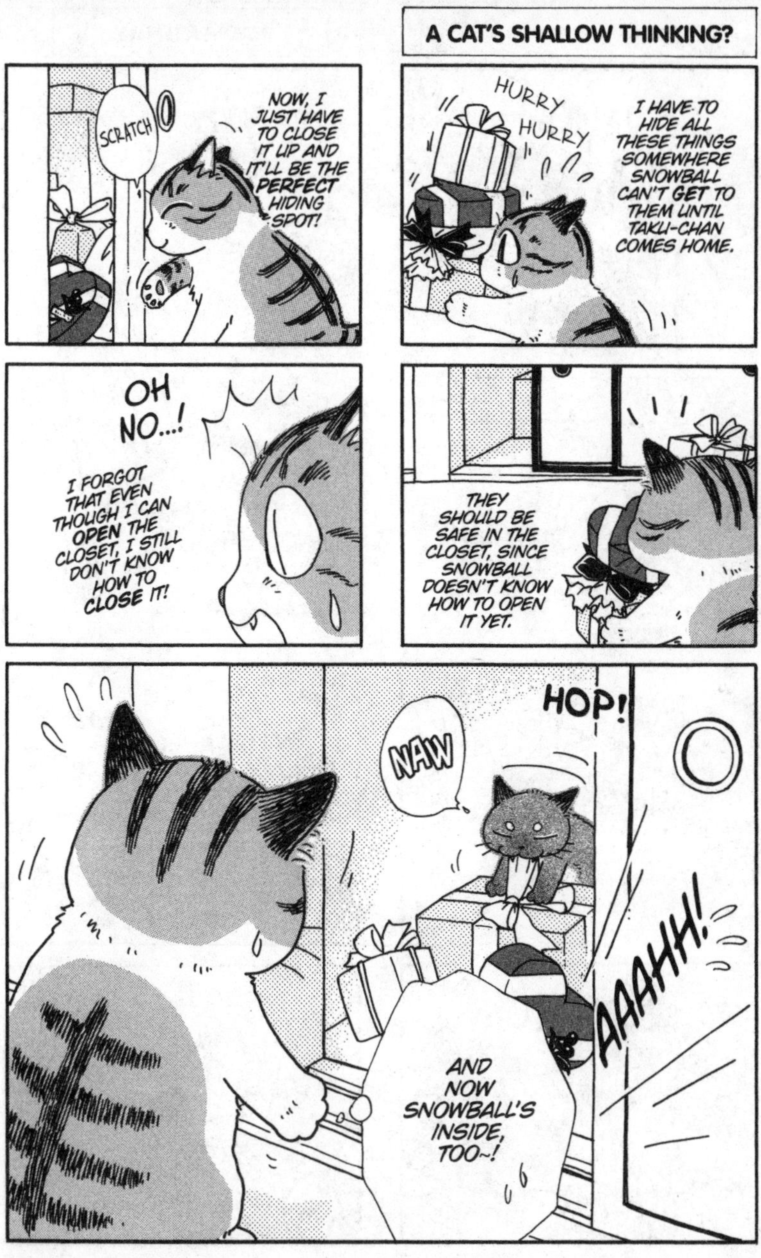
HURRY
HURRY
I HAVE TO HIDE ALL THESE THINGS SOMEWHERE SNOWBALL CAN'T GET TO THEM UNTIL TAKU-CHAN COMES HOME.
THEY SHOULD BE SAFE IN THE CLOSET, SINCE SNOWBALL DOESN'T KNOW HOW TO OPEN IT YET.
SCRATCH
NOW, I JUST HAVE TO CLOSE IT UP AND IT'LL BE THE PERFECT HIDING SPOT!
OH NO...!
I FORGOT THAT EVEN THOUGH I CAN OPEN THE CLOSET, I STILL DON'T KNOW HOW TO CLOSE IT!
HOP!
NAW
AAAHH!
AND NOW SNOWBALL'S INSIDE, TOO~!

INADVERTENTLY...

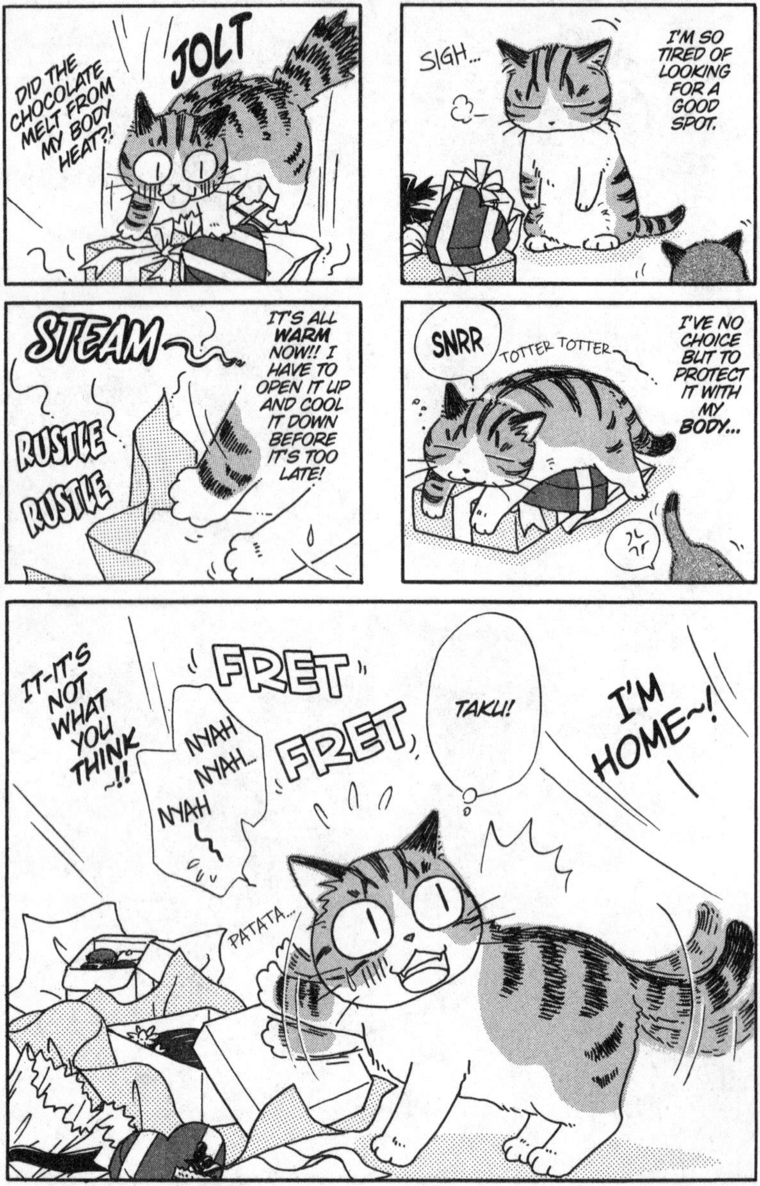

I'M SO TIRED OF LOOKING FOR A GOOD SPOT.
SIGH...
JOLT
DID THE CHOCOLATE MELT FROM MY BODY HEAT?!
I'VE NO CHOICE BUT TO PROTECT IT WITH MY BODY...
TOTTER TOTTER
SNRR
IT'S ALL WARM NOW!! I HAVE TO OPEN IT UP AND COOL IT DOWN BEFORE IT'S TOO LATE!
STEAM
RUSTLE
RUSTLE
I'M HOME~!
TAKU!
FRET
FRET
NYAH NYAH... NYAH
IT-IT'S NOT WHAT YOU THINK~!!
PATATA...

WHAT SNOWBALL WANTS

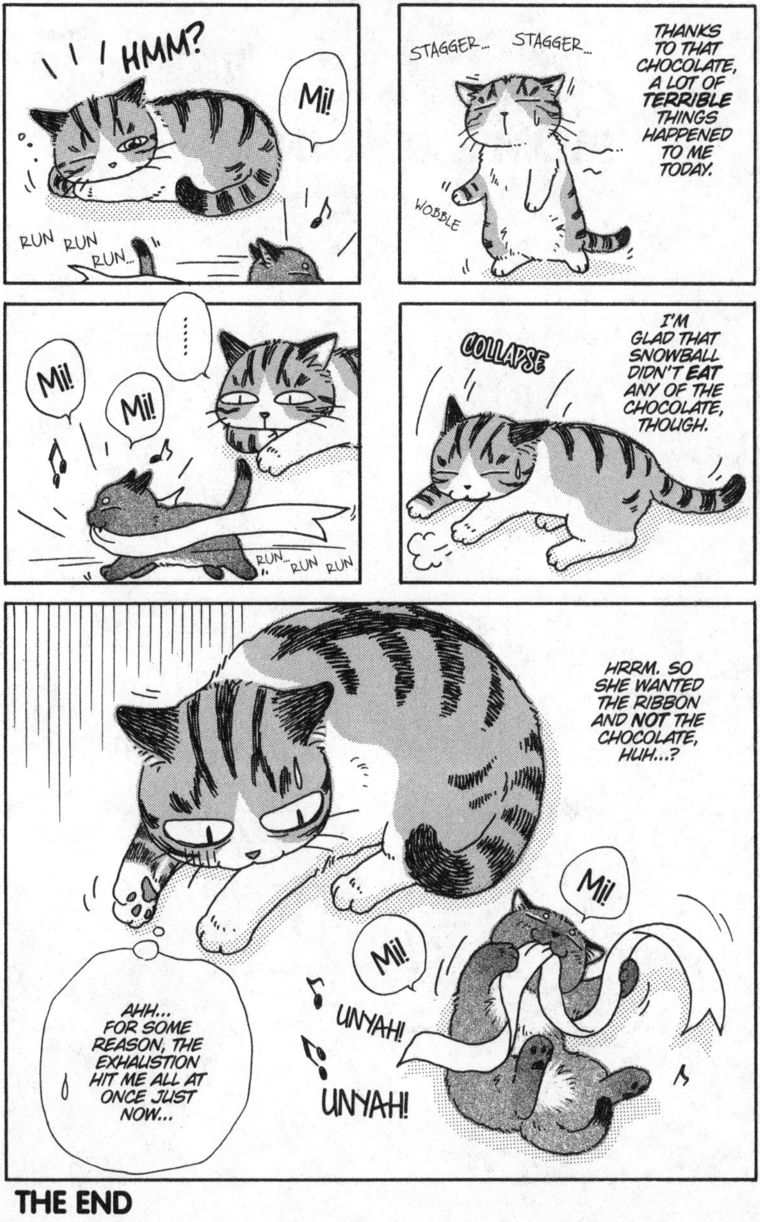
THANKS TO THAT CHOCOLATE, A LOT OF TERRIBLE THINGS HAPPENED TO ME TODAY.
STAGGER... STAGGER...
WOBBLE
Mi!
HMM?
RUN RUN RUN...
I'M GLAD THAT SNOWBALL DIDN'T EAT ANY OF THE CHOCOLATE, THOUGH.
COLLAPSE
......
Mi!
Mi!
RUN... RUN RUN
HRRM. SO SHE WANTED THE RIBBON AND NOT THE CHOCOLATE, HUH...?
Mi!
Mi!
UNYAH!
UNYAH!
AHH... FOR SOME REASON, THE EXHAUSTION HIT ME ALL AT ONCE JUST NOW...

THE END

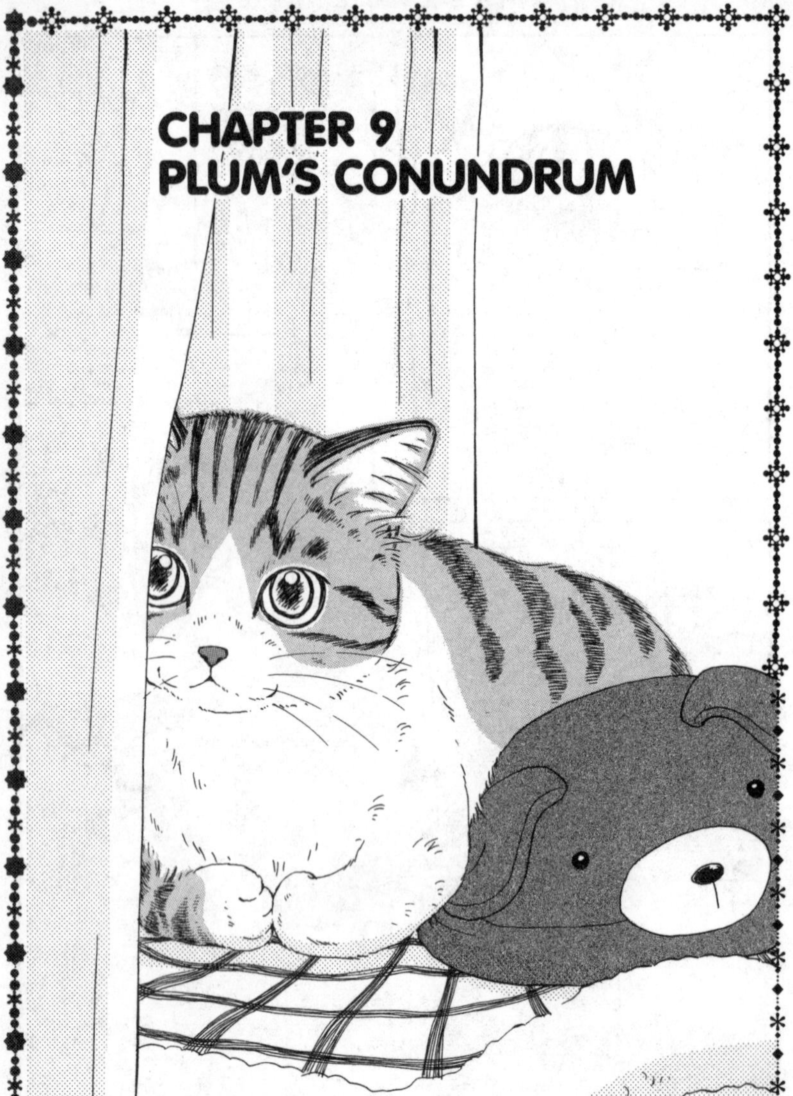
CHAPTER 9
PLUM'S CONUNDRUM

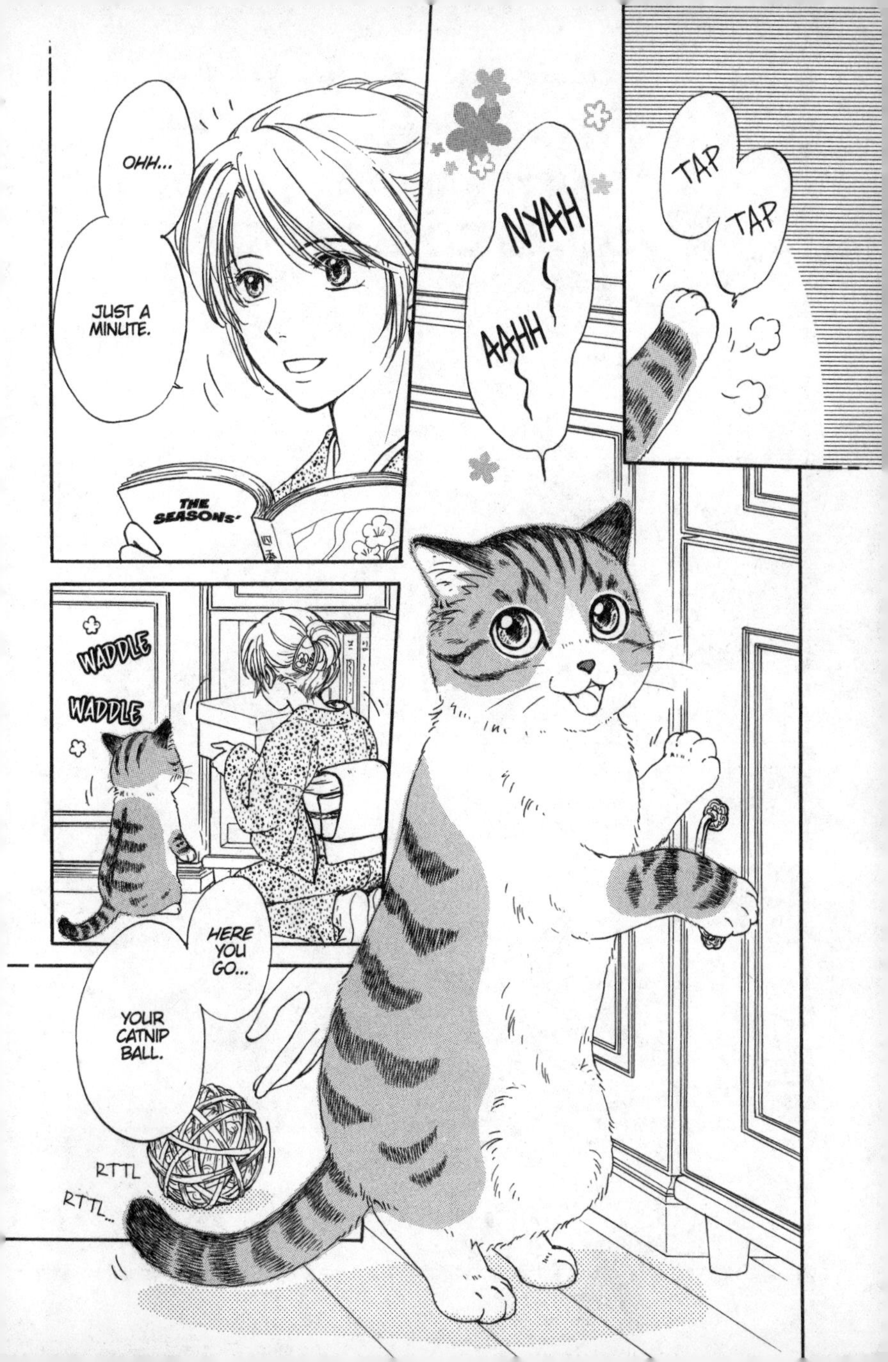
TAP TAP
NYAH AAHH
OHH...
JUST A MINUTE.
THE SEASONS'
WADDLE WADDLE
HERE YOU GO...
YOUR CATNIP BALL.
RTTL RTTL...

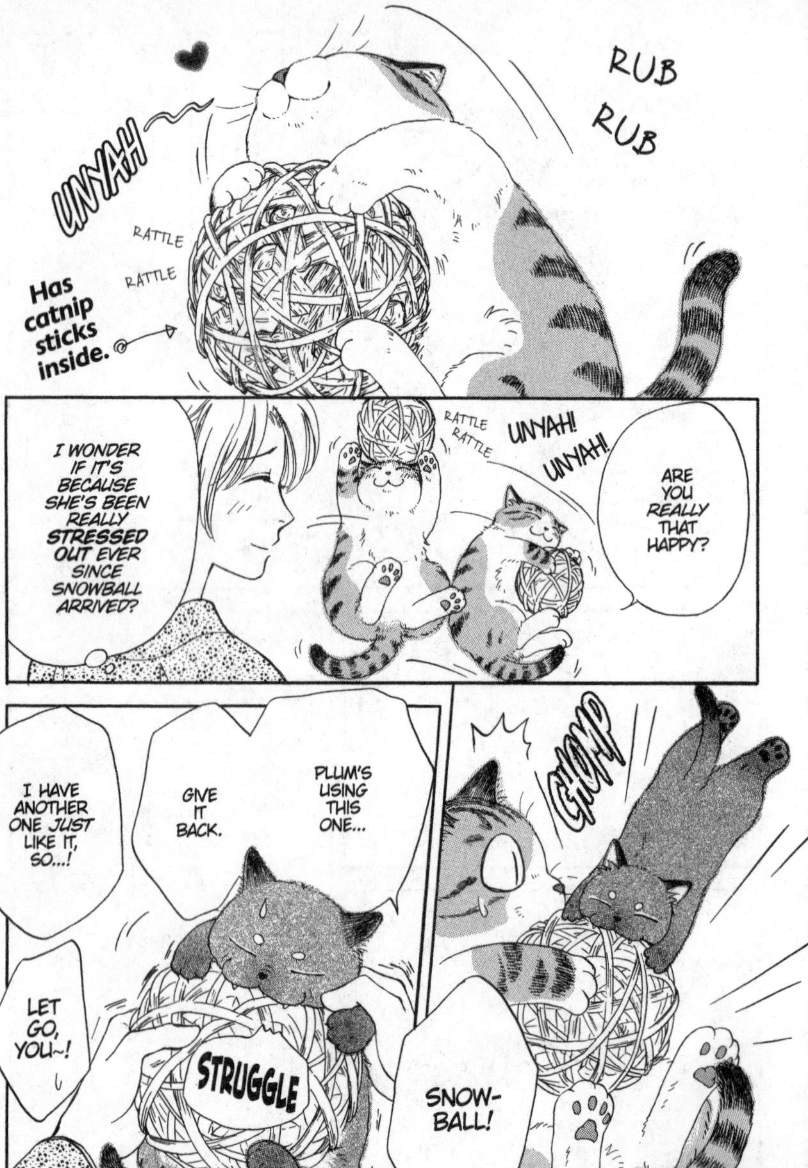
RUB
RUB
UNYAH~~
RATTLE
RATTLE
Has catnip sticks inside.
ARE YOU REALLY THAT HAPPY?
UNYAH!
UNYAH!
RATTLE RATTLE
I WONDER IF IT'S BECAUSE SHE'S BEEN REALLY STRESSED OUT EVER SINCE SNOWBALL ARRIVED?
CHOMP
SNOW-BALL!
PLUM'S USING THIS ONE...
GIVE IT BACK.
I HAVE ANOTHER ONE JUST LIKE IT, SO...!
LET GO, YOU~!
STRUGGLE

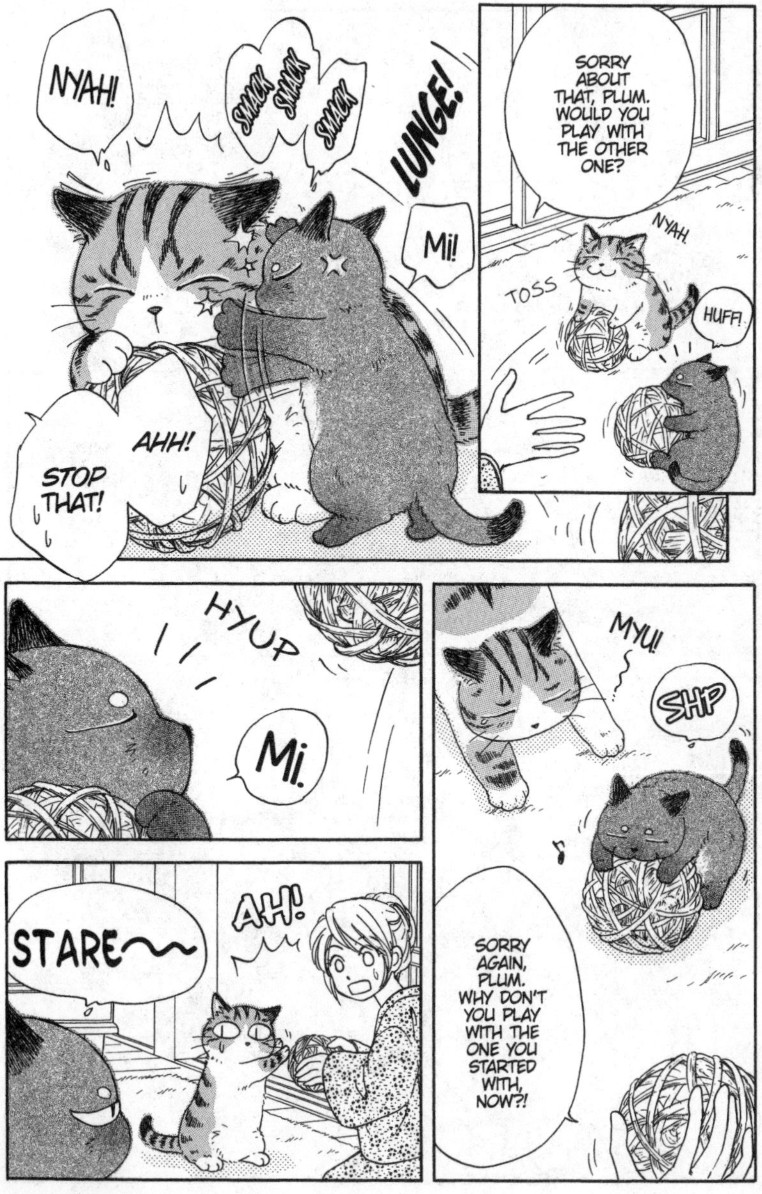
SORRY ABOUT THAT, PLUM. WOULD YOU PLAY WITH THE OTHER ONE?
NYAH.
TOSS
HUFF!
LUNGE!
Mi!
SMACK SMACK SMACK
NYAH!
AHH!
STOP THAT!
MYU!
SHP
SORRY AGAIN, PLUM. WHY DON'T YOU PLAY WITH THE ONE YOU STARTED WITH, NOW?!
HYUP
Mi.
AH!
STARE~~

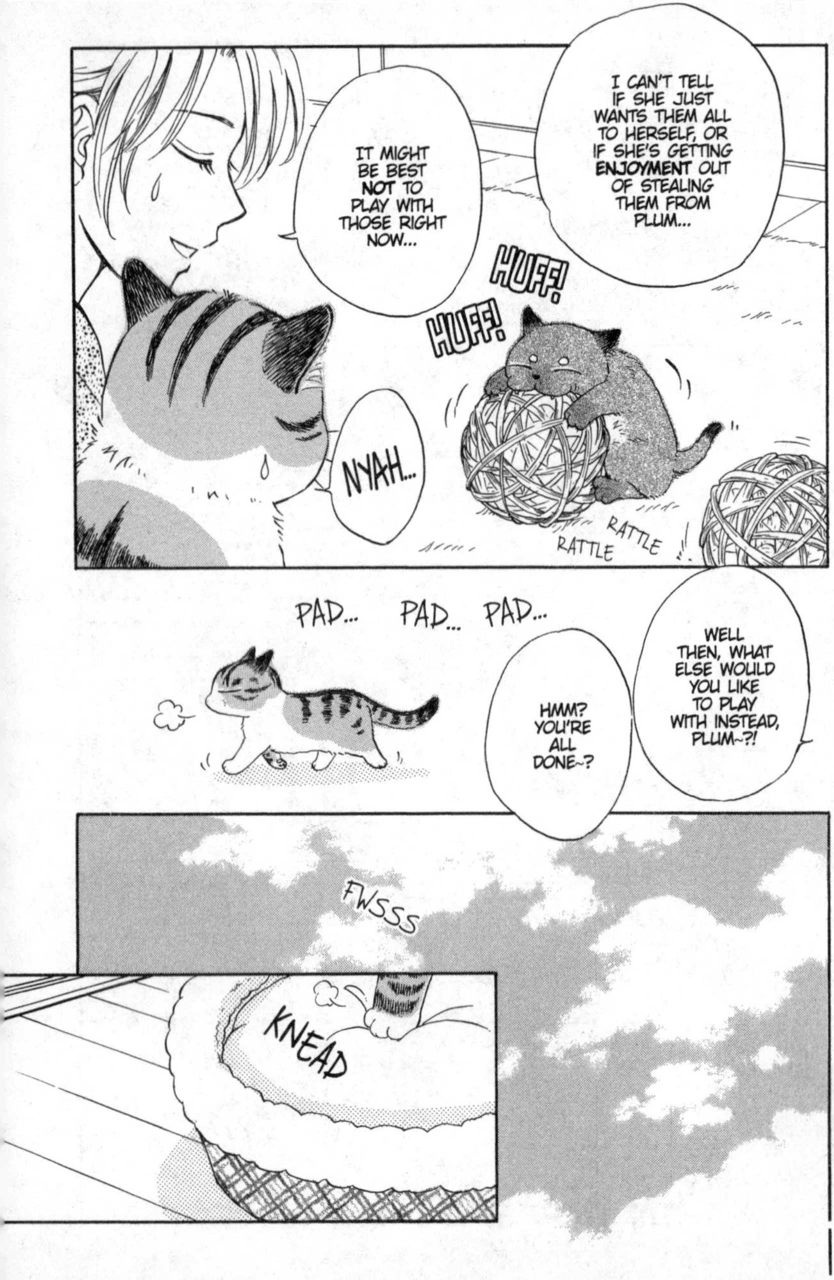
I CAN'T TELL IF SHE JUST WANTS THEM ALL TO HERSELF, OR IF SHE'S GETTING ENJOYMENT OUT OF STEALING THEM FROM PLUM...
IT MIGHT BE BEST NOT TO PLAY WITH THOSE RIGHT NOW...
HUFF!
HUFF!
NYAH...
RATTLE
RATTLE
WELL THEN, WHAT ELSE WOULD YOU LIKE TO PLAY WITH INSTEAD, PLUM~?!
HMM? YOU'RE ALL DONE~?
PAD... PAD... PAD...
FWSSS
KNEAD

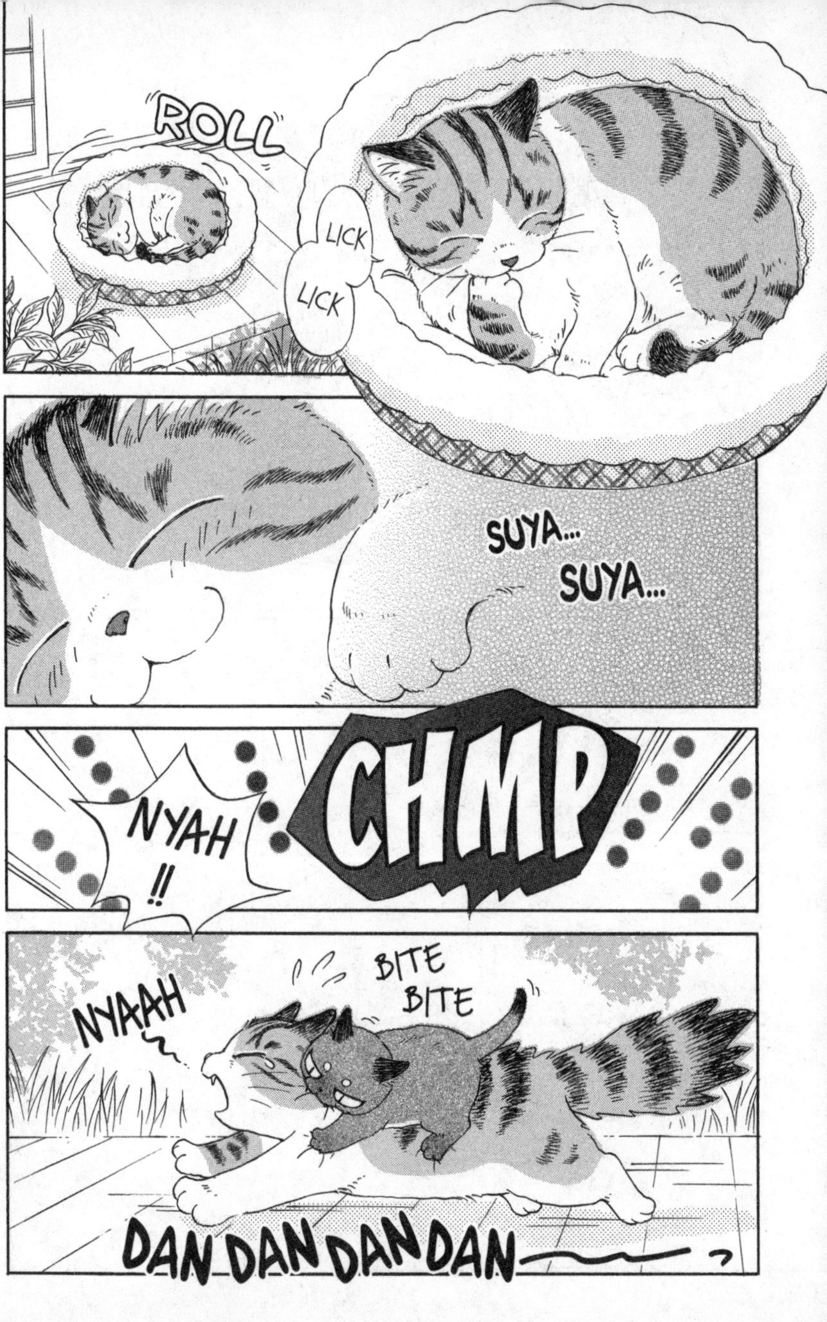
LICK
LICK
ROLL
SUYA...
SUYA...
CHMP
NYAH !!
BITE BITE
NYAAH
DAN DAN DAN DAN

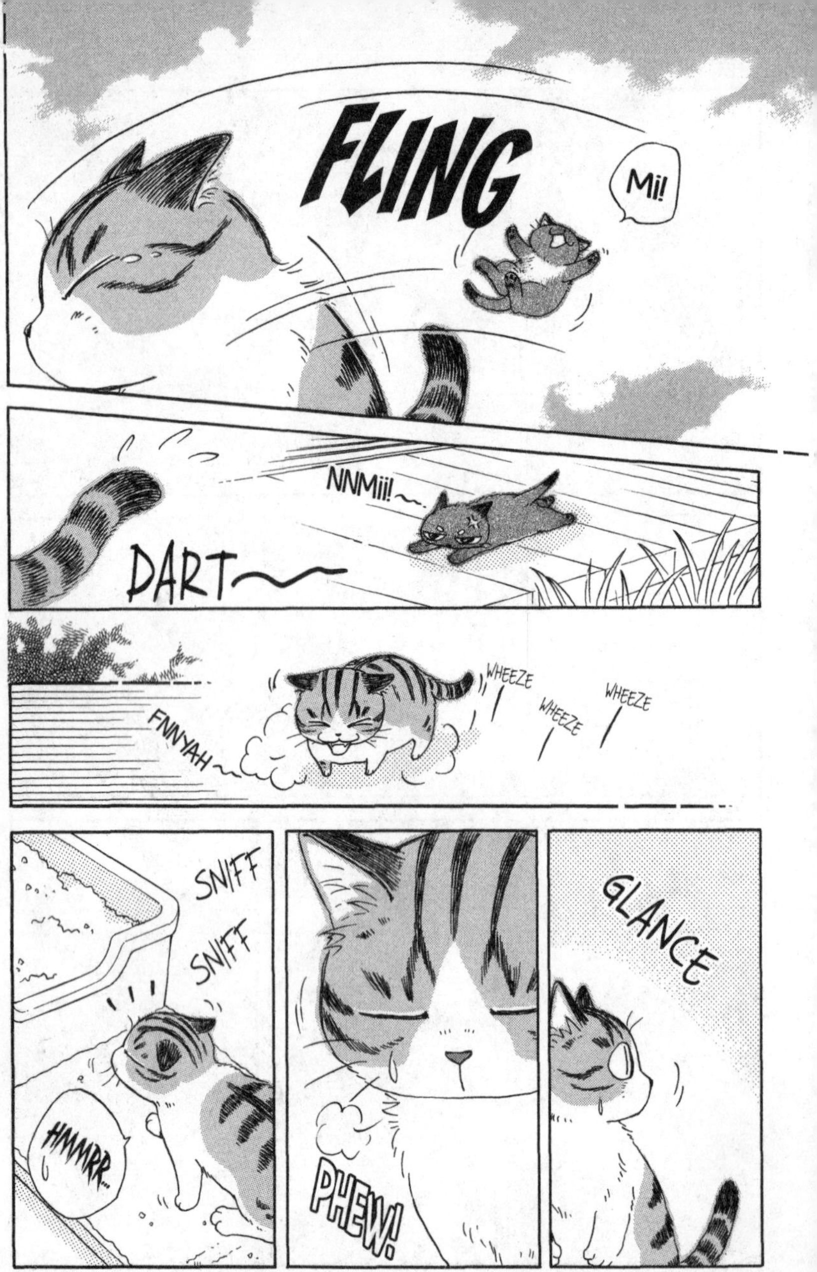
Mi!
FLING
NNMii!~
DART~
WHEEZE
WHEEZE
WHEEZE
FNNYAH~
GLANCE
PHEW!
SNIFF
SNIFF
HMMRR...

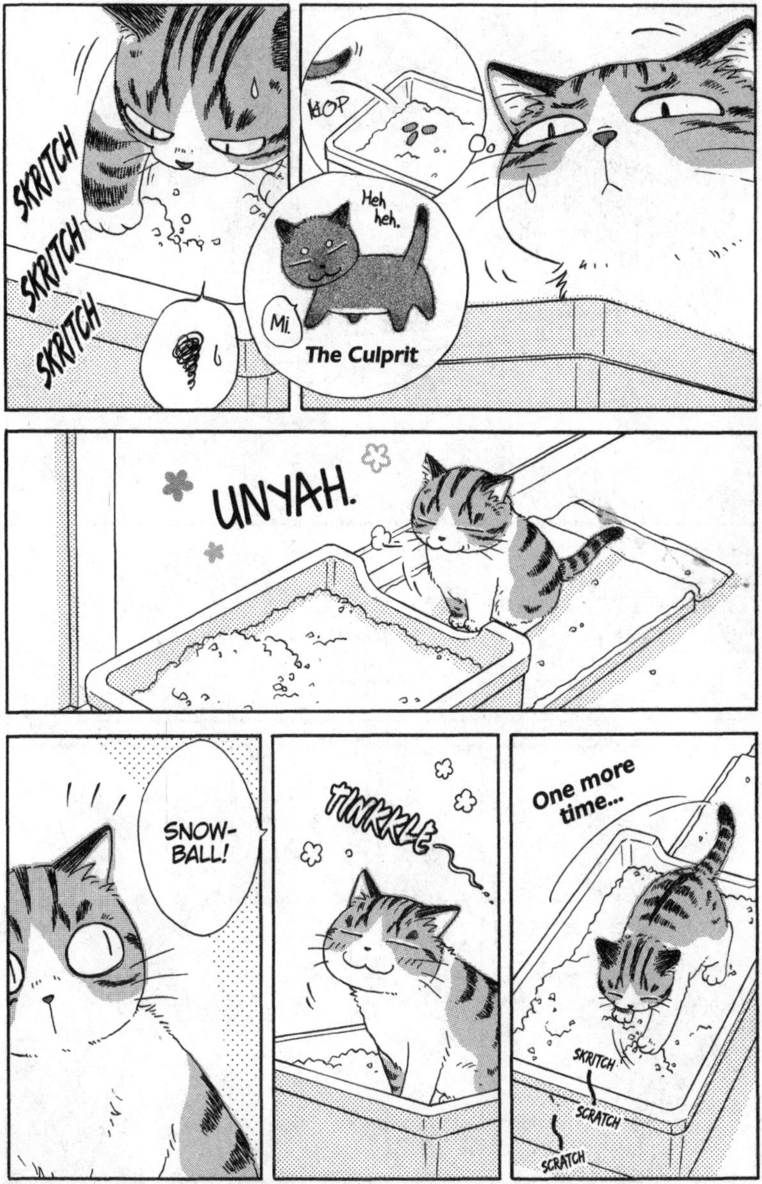
PLOP
Heh heh.
Mi.
The Culprit
SKRITCH
SKRITCH
SKRITCH
UNYAH.
One more time...
SKRITCH
SCRATCH
SCRATCH
TINKKLE
SNOW-BALL!

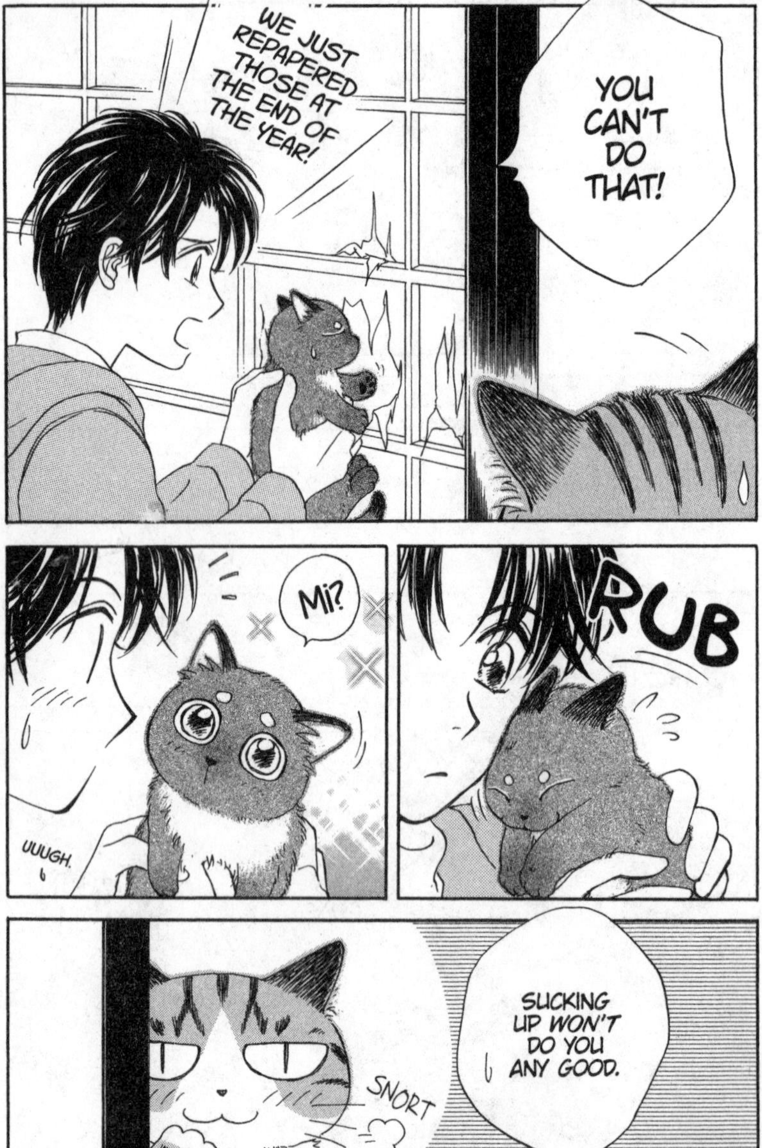
YOU CAN'T DO THAT!
WE JUST REPAPERED THOSE AT THE END OF THE YEAR!
RUB
Mi?
UUUGH.
SUCKING UP WON'T DO YOU ANY GOOD.
SNORT

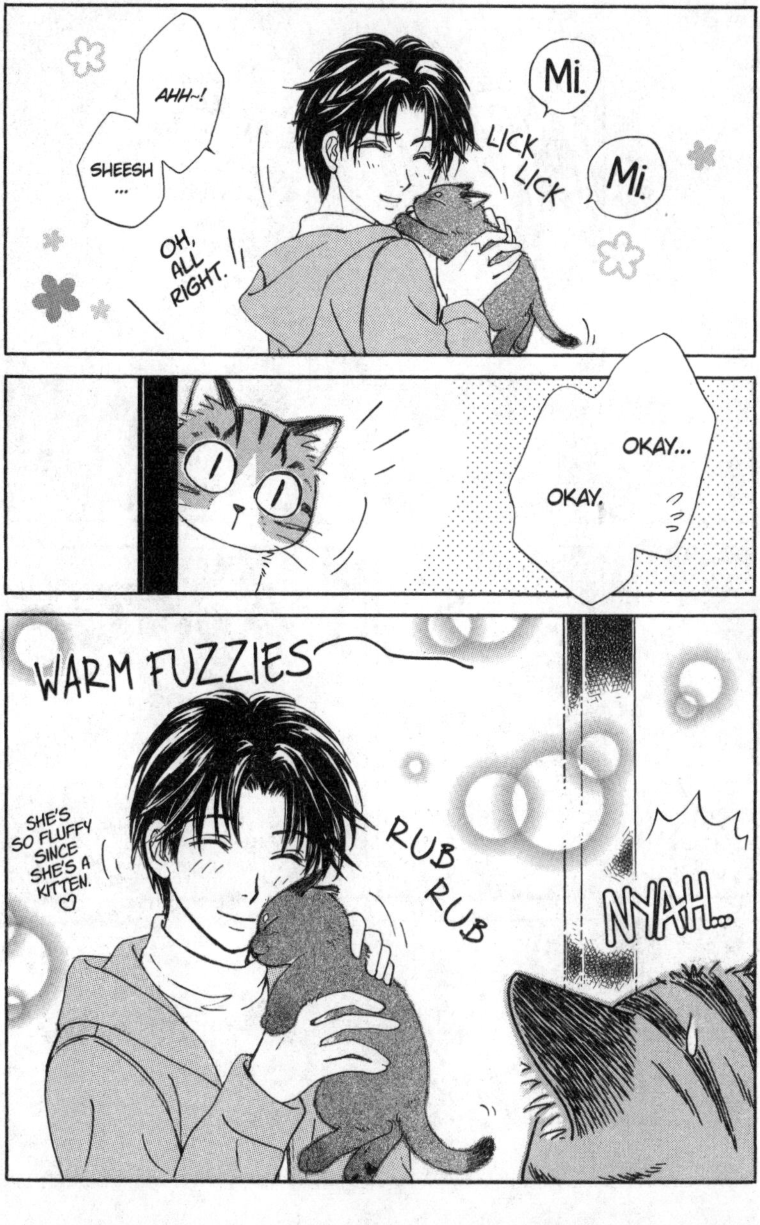
Mi.
Mi.
LICK LICK
AHH~! SHEESH ...
OH, ALL RIGHT.
OKAY...
OKAY.
WARM FUZZIES
RUB RUB
SHE'S SO FLUFFY SINCE SHE'S A KITTEN. ♡
NYAH...

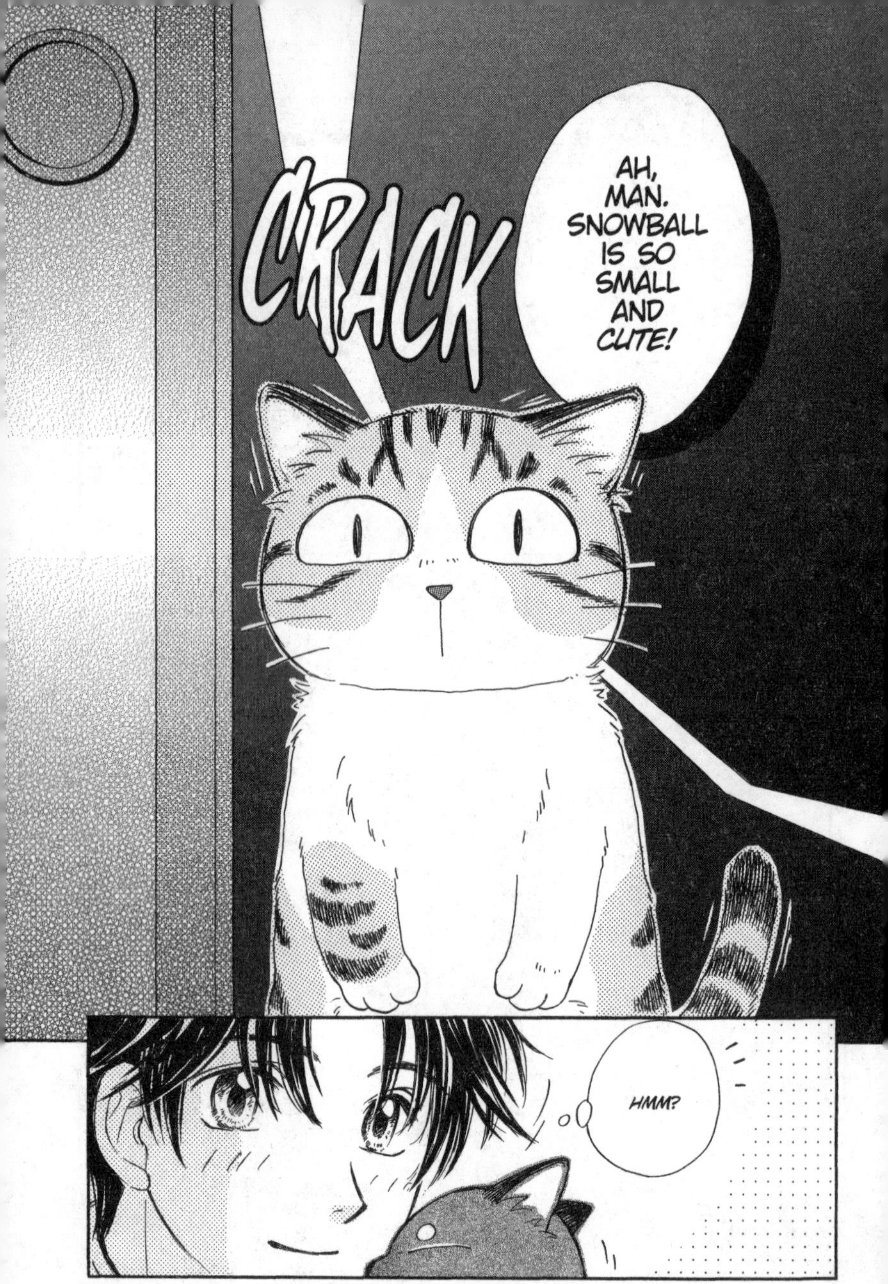
AH, MAN. SNOWBALL IS SO SMALL AND CUTE!
CRACK
HMM?

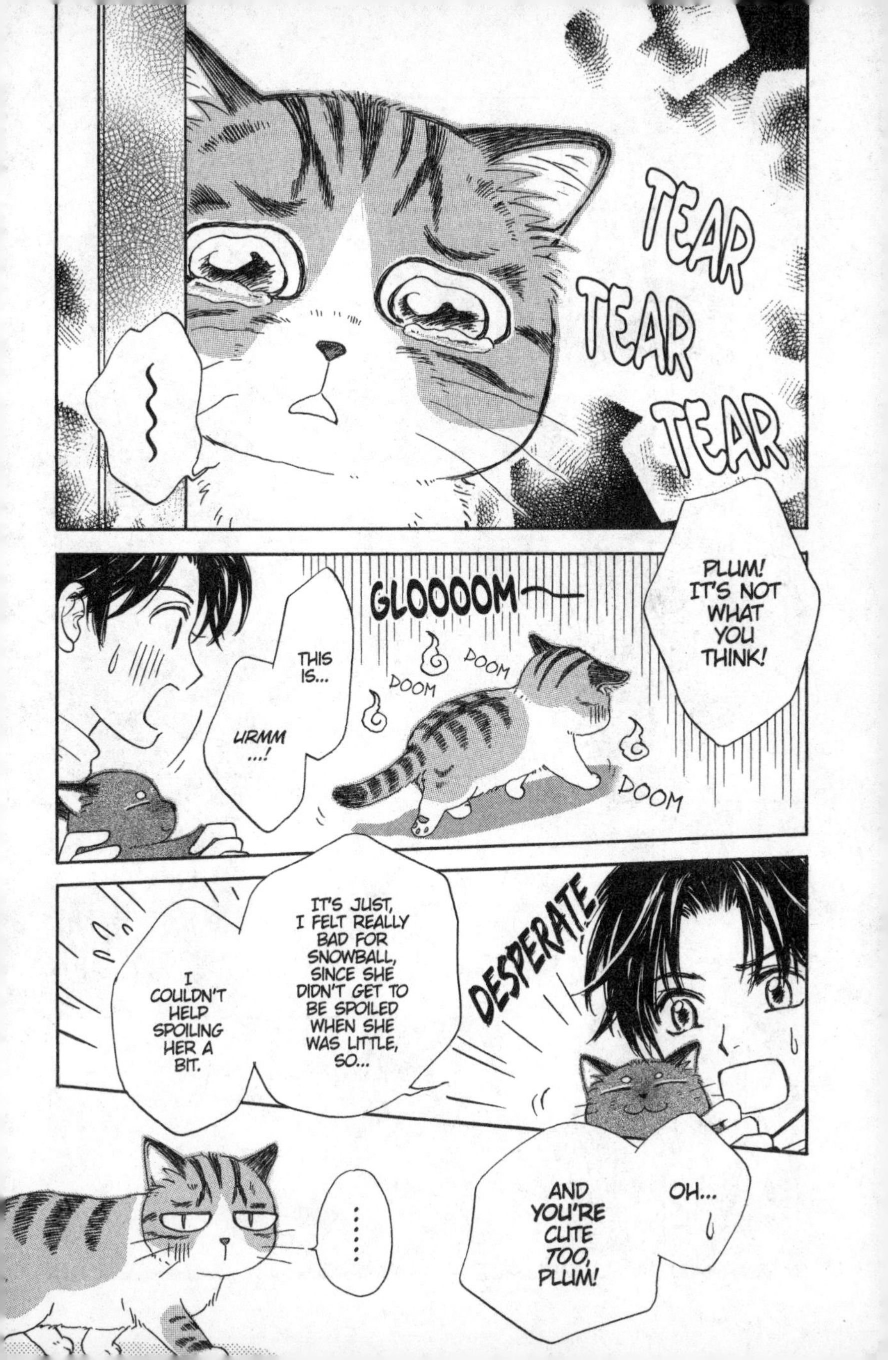
TEAR TEAR TEAR
PLUM! IT'S NOT WHAT YOU THINK!
GLOOOOM
DOOM DOOM DOOM
THIS IS...
URMM ...!
DESPERATE
IT'S JUST, I FELT REALLY BAD FOR SNOWBALL, SINCE SHE DIDN'T GET TO BE SPOILED WHEN SHE WAS LITTLE, SO...
I COULDN'T HELP SPOILING HER A BIT.
OH...
AND YOU'RE CUTE TOO, PLUM!
......

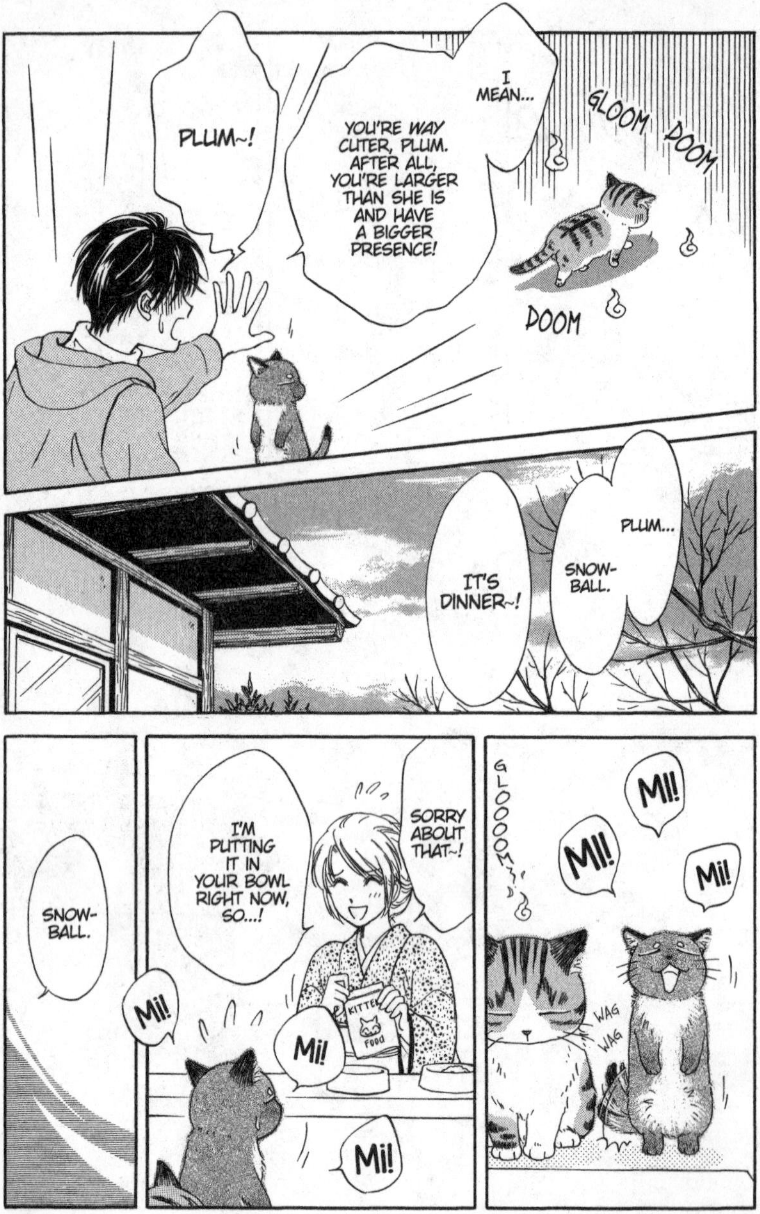
I MEAN...
GLOOM DOOM
YOU'RE WAY CUTER, PLUM. AFTER ALL, YOU'RE LARGER THAN SHE IS AND HAVE A BIGGER PRESENCE!
DOOM
PLUM~!
PLUM...
SNOW-BALL.
IT'S DINNER~!
GLOOOOOM
MI!
MI!
Mi!
WAG WAG
SORRY ABOUT THAT~!
I'M PUTTING IT IN YOUR BOWL RIGHT NOW, SO...!
Mi!
Mi!
Mi!
SNOW-BALL.

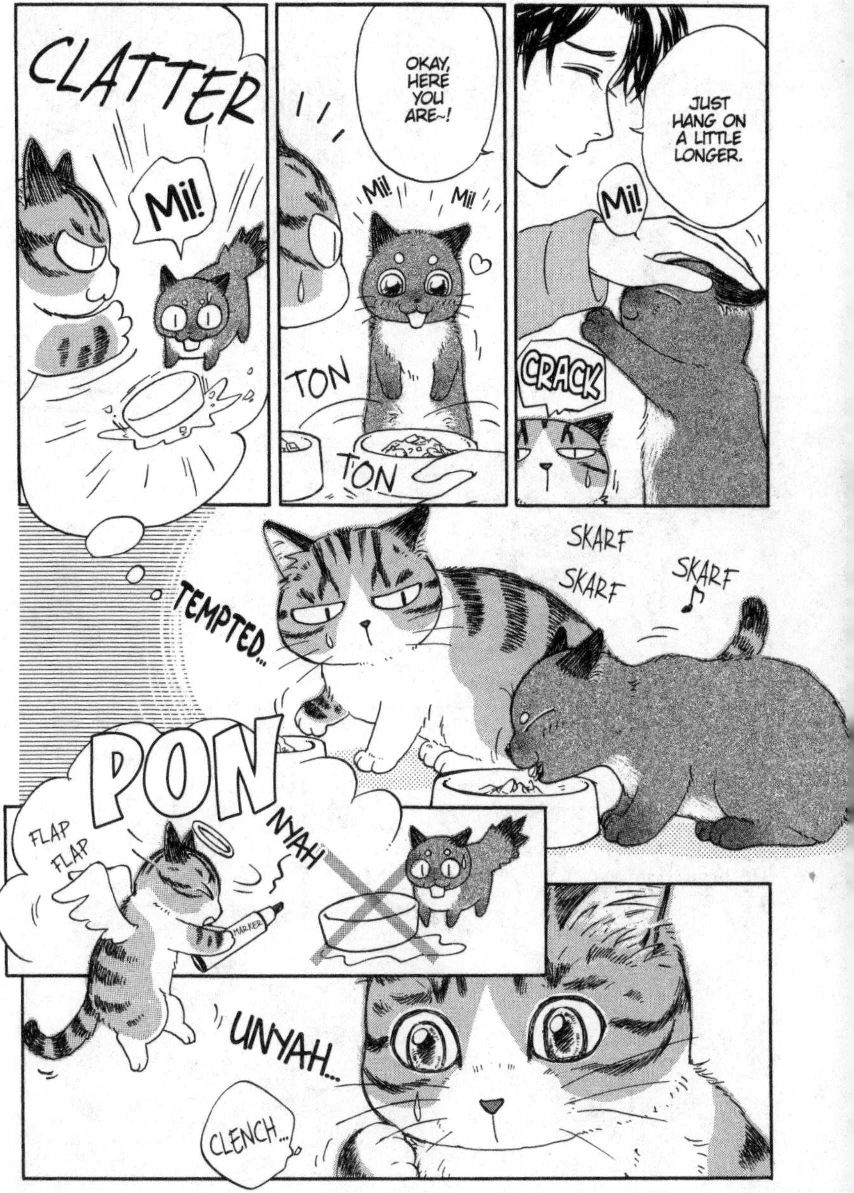
JUST HANG ON A LITTLE LONGER.
Mi!
CRACK
OKAY, HERE YOU ARE~!
Mi!
Mi!
TON
TON
CLATTER
Mi!
SKARF
SKARF
SKARF
TEMPTED...
PON
NYAH
FLAP
FLAP
MARKER
UNYAH...
CLENCH...

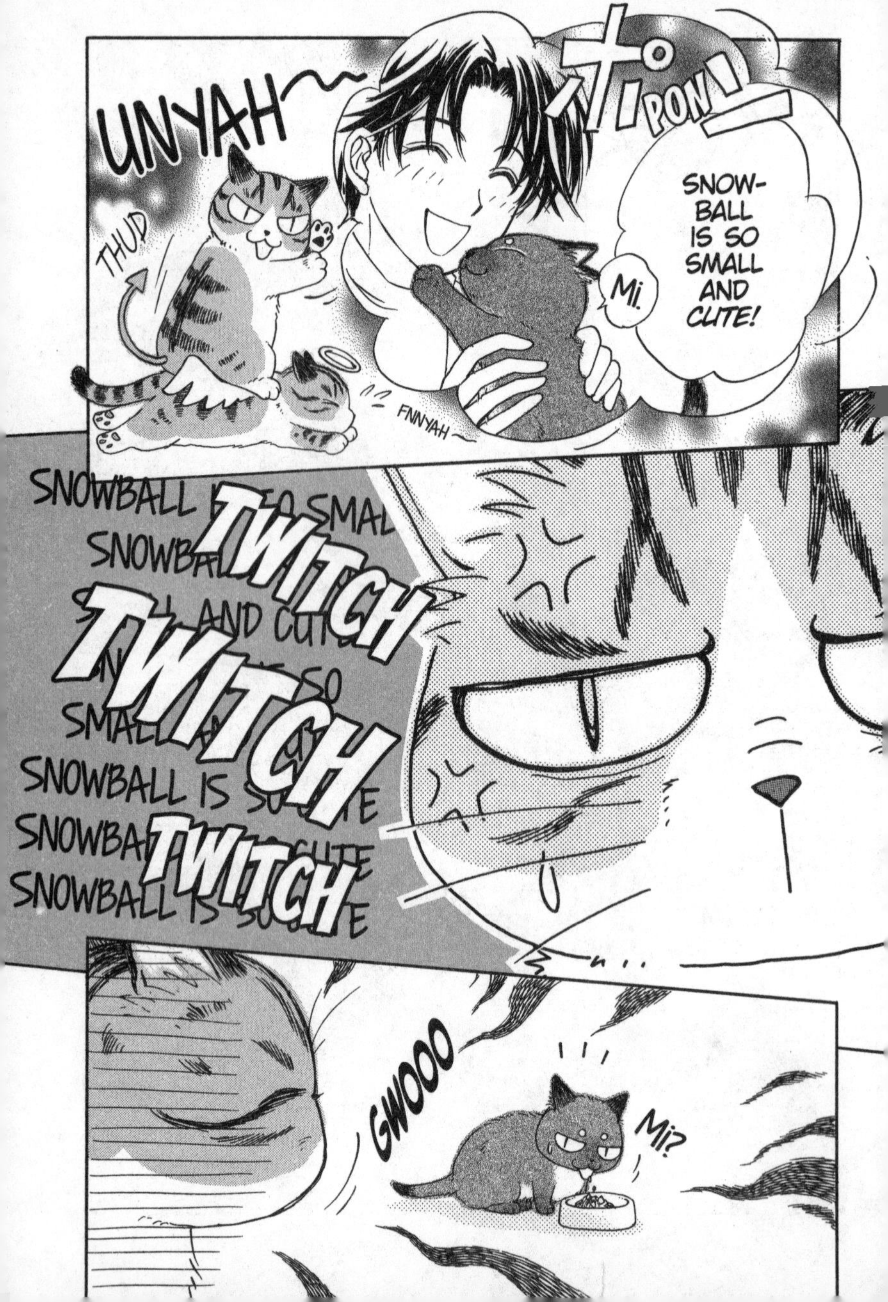
ポ PON!
SNOW-BALL IS SO SMALL AND CUTE!
Mi.
UNYAH~~
THUD
FNNYAH
TWITCH
TWITCH
TWITCH
Mi?
GWOOO

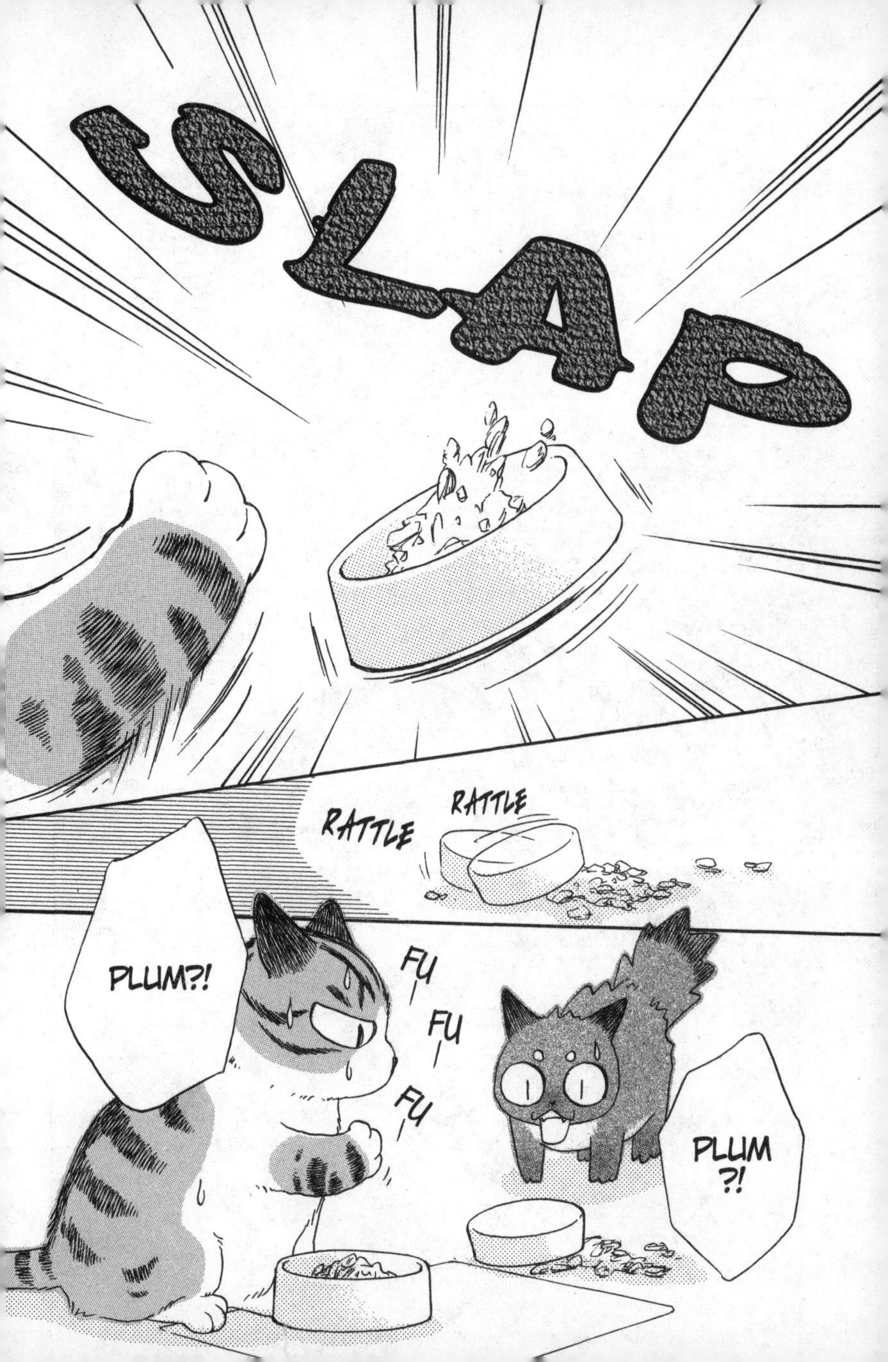
SLAP
RATTLE
RATTLE
PLUM ?!
FU
FU
FU
PLUM?!

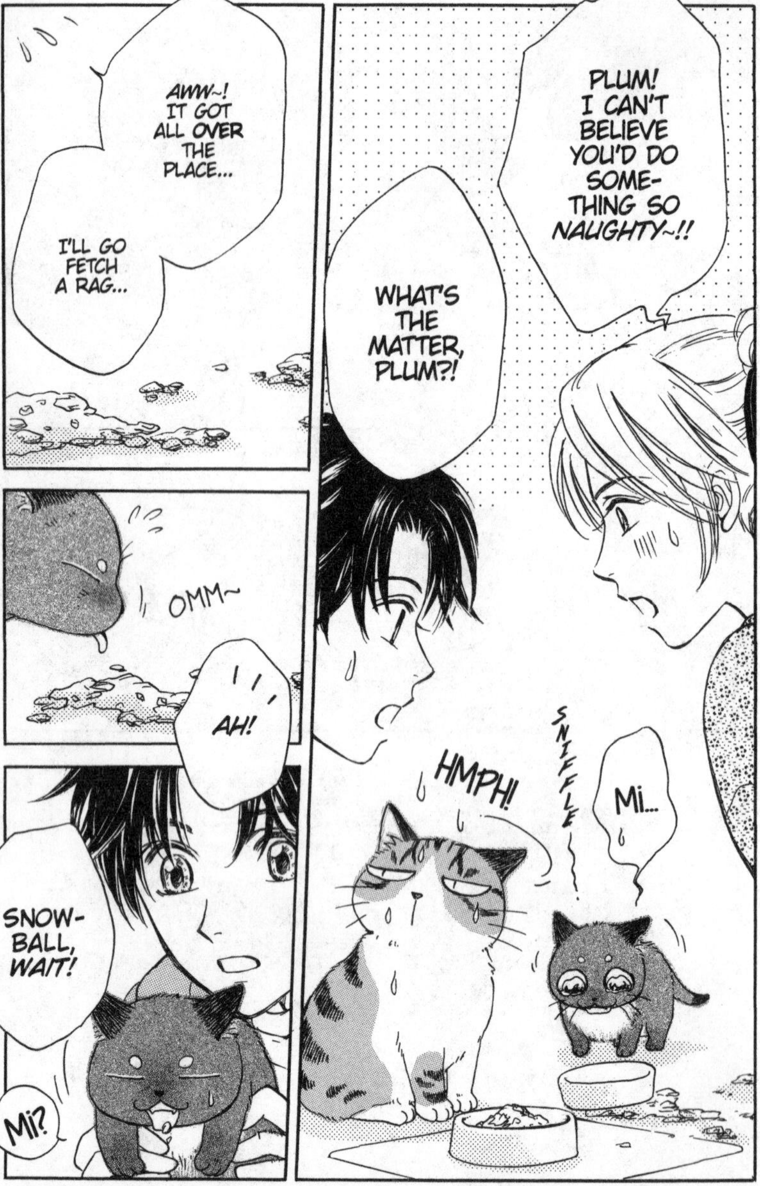
PLUM! I CAN'T BELIEVE YOU'D DO SOME-THING SO NAUGHTY~!!
WHAT'S THE MATTER, PLUM?!
SNIFFLE
Mi...
HMPH!
AWW~! IT GOT ALL OVER THE PLACE...
I'LL GO FETCH A RAG...
OMM~
AH!
SNOW-BALL, WAIT!
Mi?

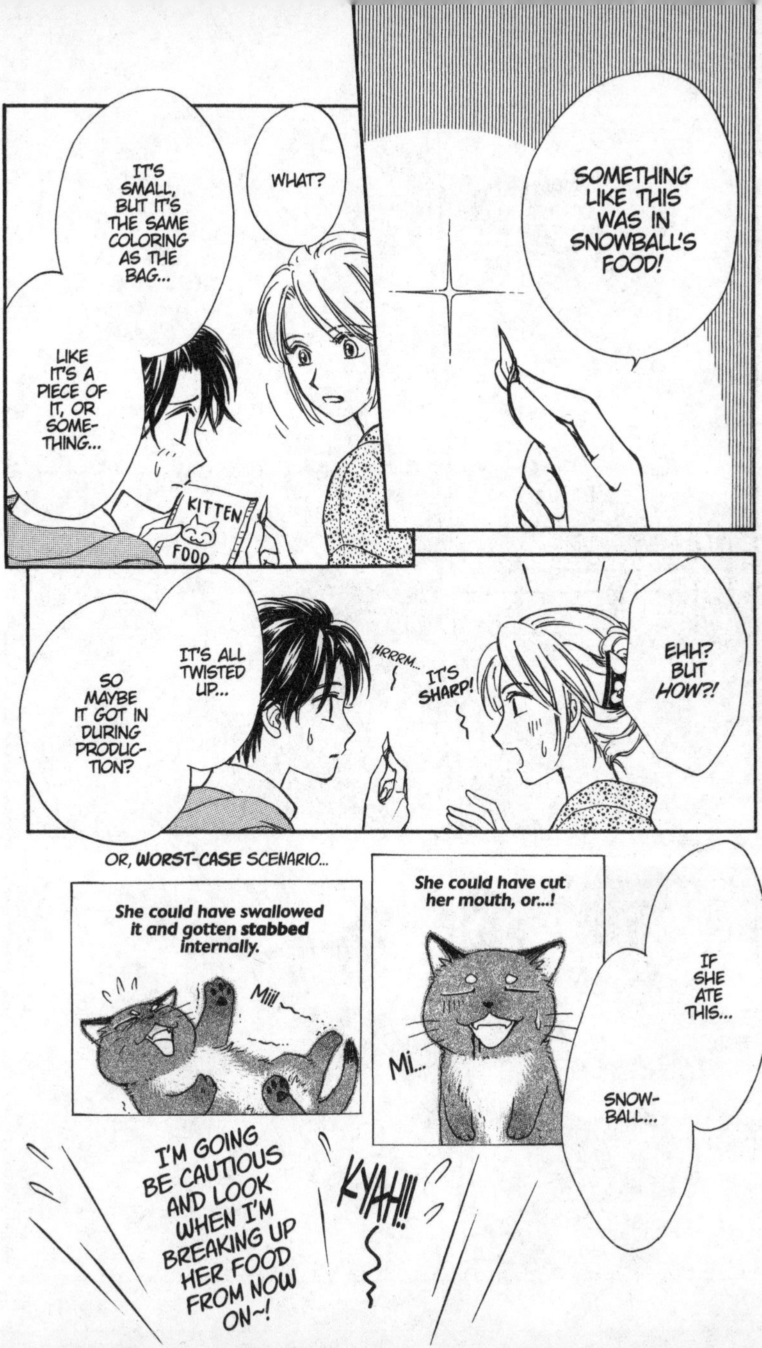
SOMETHING LIKE THIS WAS IN SNOWBALL'S FOOD!
WHAT?
IT'S SMALL, BUT IT'S THE SAME COLORING AS THE BAG...
LIKE IT'S A PIECE OF IT, OR SOME-THING...
KITTEN FOOD
EHH? BUT HOW?!
IT'S SHARP!
HRRRM...
IT'S ALL TWISTED UP...
SO MAYBE IT GOT IN DURING PRODUC-TION?
IF SHE ATE THIS...
SNOW-BALL...
She could have cut her mouth, or...!
Mi...
OR, WORST-CASE SCENARIO...
She could have swallowed it and gotten stabbed internally.
Mii!
KYAH!!
I'M GOING BE CAUTIOUS AND LOOK WHEN I'M BREAKING UP HER FOOD FROM NOW ON~!

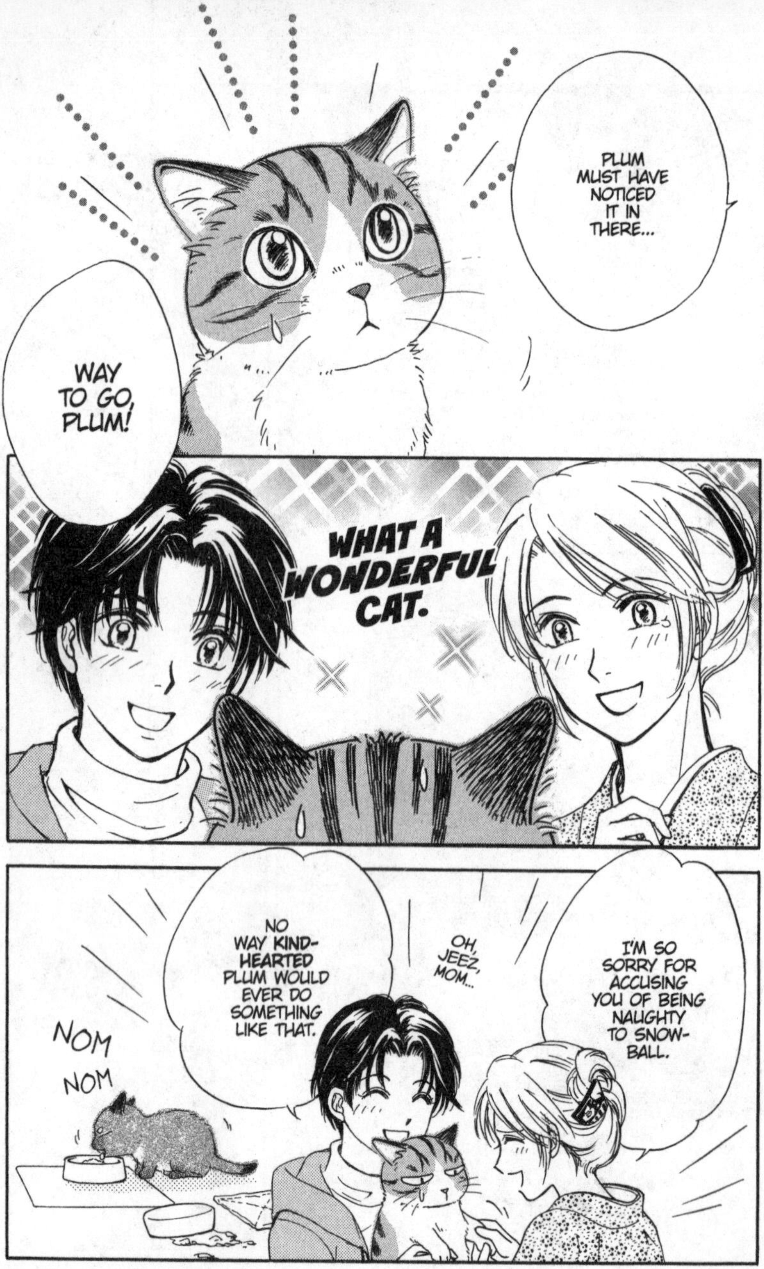
PLUM MUST HAVE NOTICED IT IN THERE...
WAY TO GO, PLUM!
WHAT A WONDERFUL CAT.
I'M SO SORRY FOR ACCUSING YOU OF BEING NAUGHTY TO SNOW-BALL.
OH, JEEZ, MOM...
NO WAY KIND-HEARTED PLUM WOULD EVER DO SOMETHING LIKE THAT.
NOM NOM

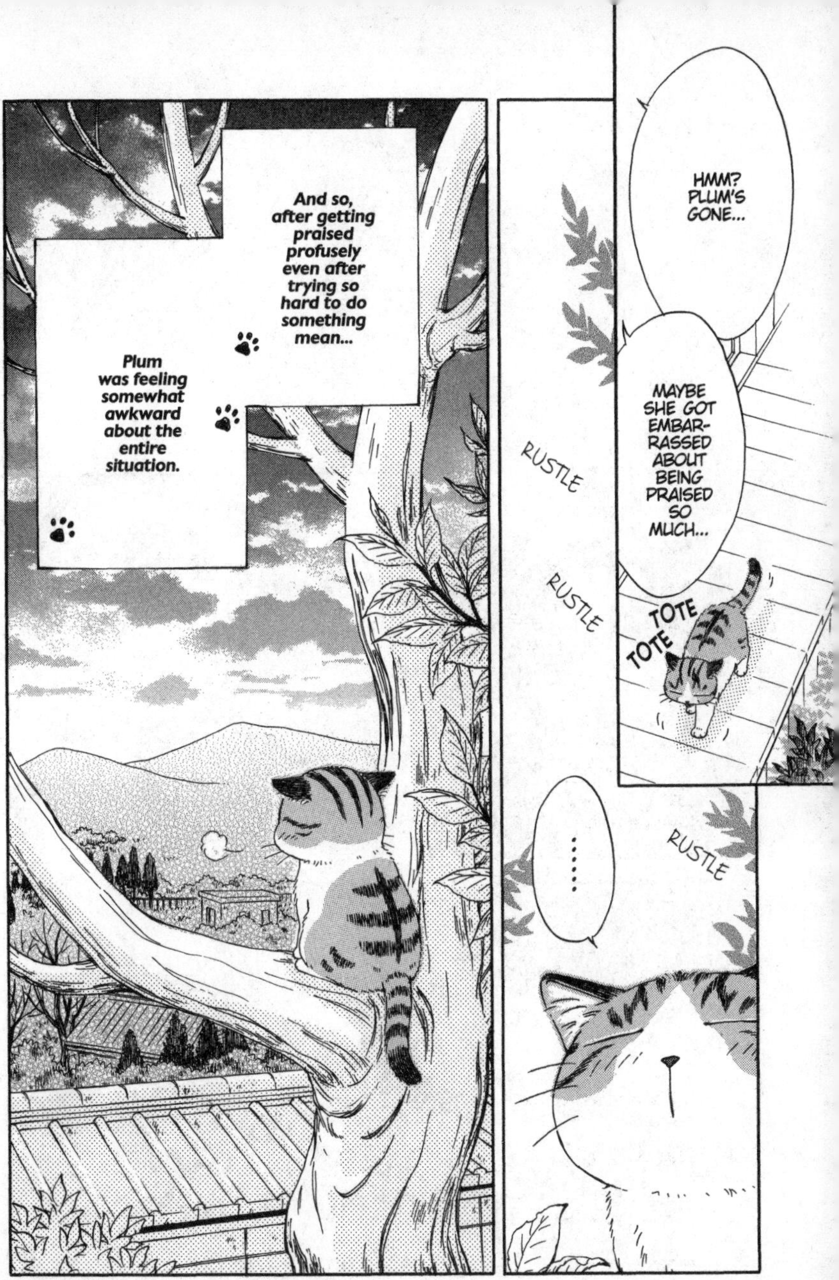
HMM? PLUM'S GONE...
MAYBE SHE GOT EMBAR-RASSED ABOUT BEING PRAISED SO MUCH...
TOTE TOTE
RUSTLE
RUSTLE
......
RUSTLE
And so, after getting praised profusely even after trying so hard to do something mean...
Plum was feeling somewhat awkward about the entire situation.

THE END

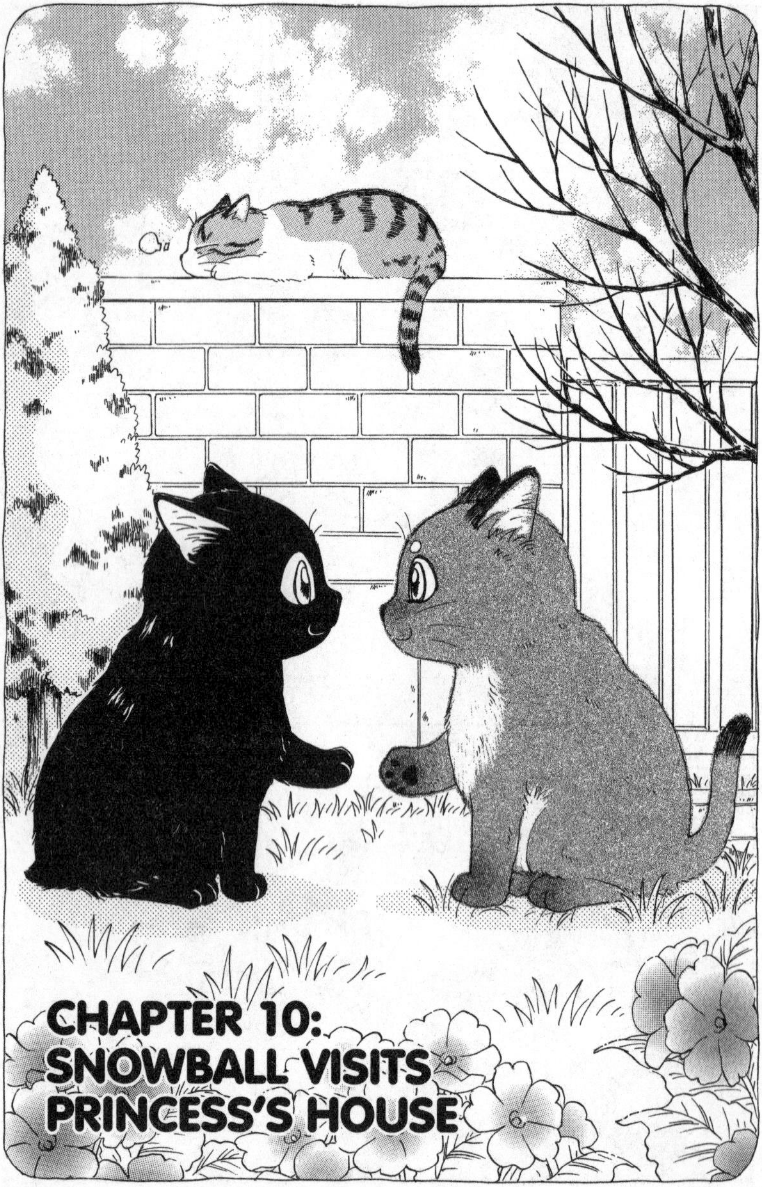
CHAPTER 10:
SNOWBALL VISITS
PRINCESS'S HOUSE

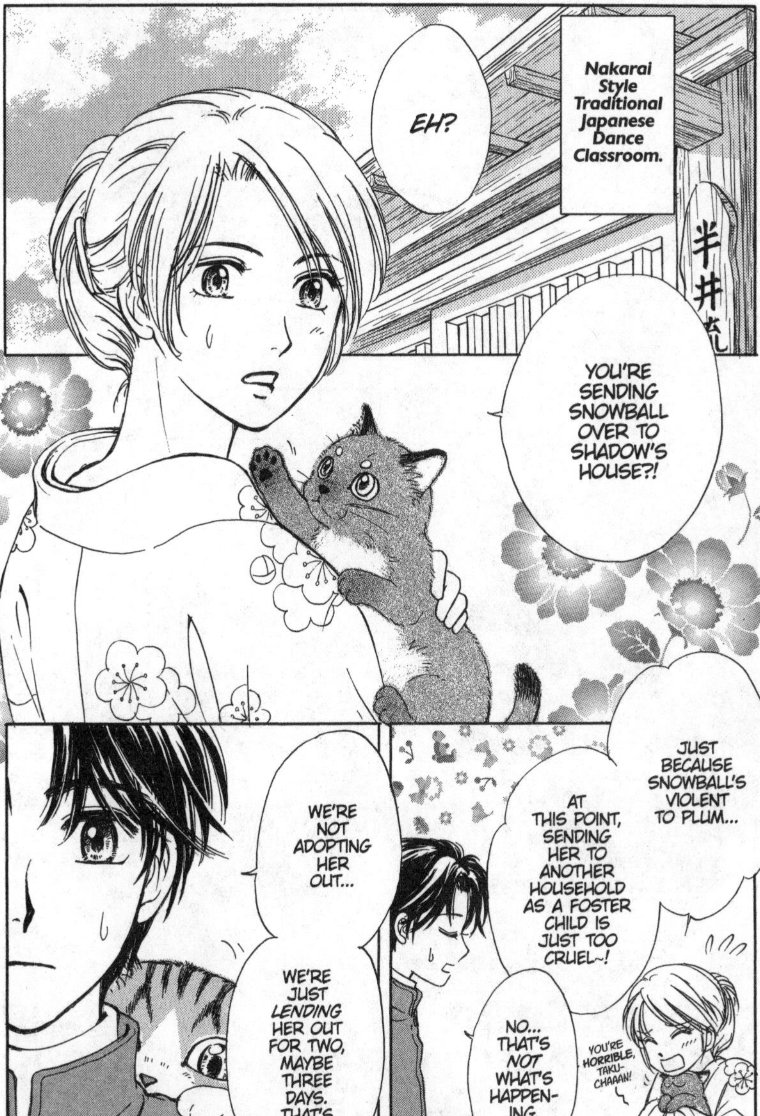

Nakarai Style Traditional Japanese Dance Classroom.
EH?
半井
YOU'RE SENDING SNOWBALL OVER TO SHADOW'S HOUSE?!
JUST BECAUSE SNOWBALL'S VIOLENT TO PLUM...
AT THIS POINT, SENDING HER TO ANOTHER HOUSEHOLD AS A FOSTER CHILD IS JUST TOO CRUEL~!
YOU'RE HORRIBLE, TAKU-CHAAAN!
NO... THAT'S *NOT* WHAT'S HAPPEN-ING.
WE'RE NOT ADOPTING HER OUT...
WE'RE JUST *LENDING* HER OUT FOR TWO, MAYBE THREE DAYS. THAT'S ALL.

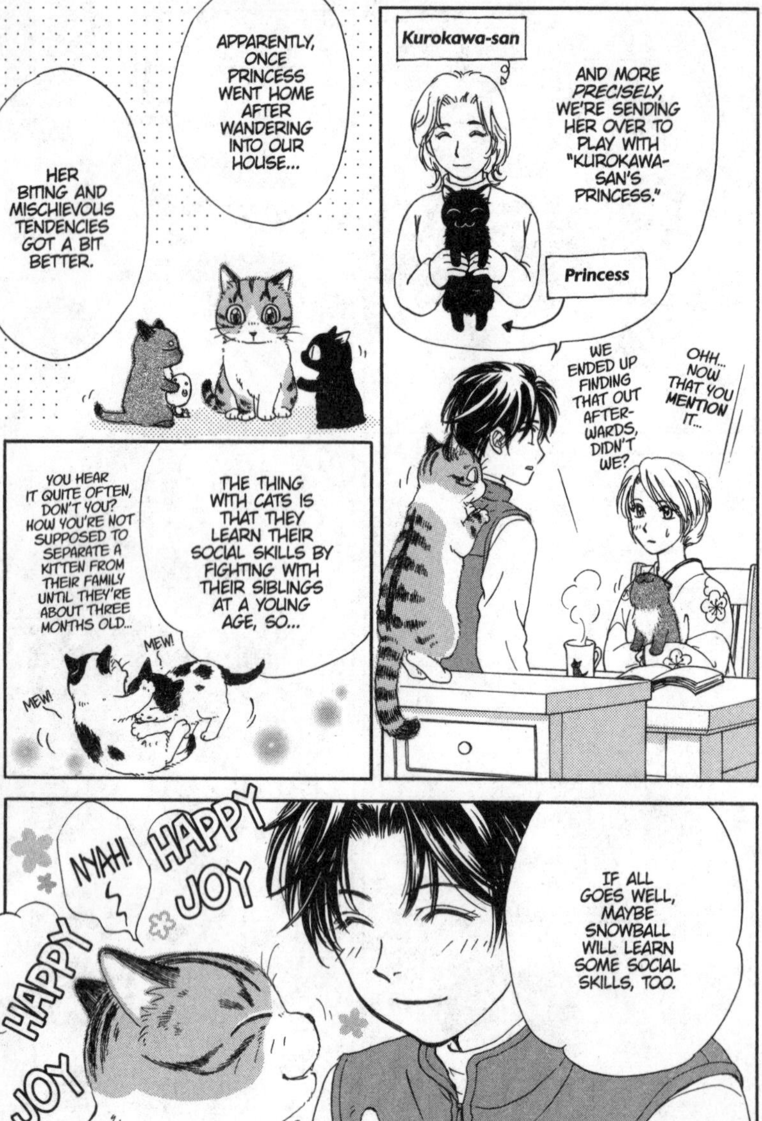
AND MORE PRECISELY, WE'RE SENDING HER OVER TO PLAY WITH "KUROKAWA-SAN'S PRINCESS."
Kurokawa-san
Princess
OHH... NOW THAT YOU MENTION IT...
WE ENDED UP FINDING THAT OUT AFTER-WARDS, DIDN'T WE?
APPARENTLY, ONCE PRINCESS WENT HOME AFTER WANDERING INTO OUR HOUSE...
HER BITING AND MISCHIEVOUS TENDENCIES GOT A BIT BETTER.
THE THING WITH CATS IS THAT THEY LEARN THEIR SOCIAL SKILLS BY FIGHTING WITH THEIR SIBLINGS AT A YOUNG AGE, SO...
YOU HEAR IT QUITE OFTEN, DON'T YOU? HOW YOU'RE NOT SUPPOSED TO SEPARATE A KITTEN FROM THEIR FAMILY UNTIL THEY'RE ABOUT THREE MONTHS OLD...
MEW!
MEW!
IF ALL GOES WELL, MAYBE SNOWBALL WILL LEARN SOME SOCIAL SKILLS, TOO.
HAPPY JOY
NYAH!
HAPPY JOY

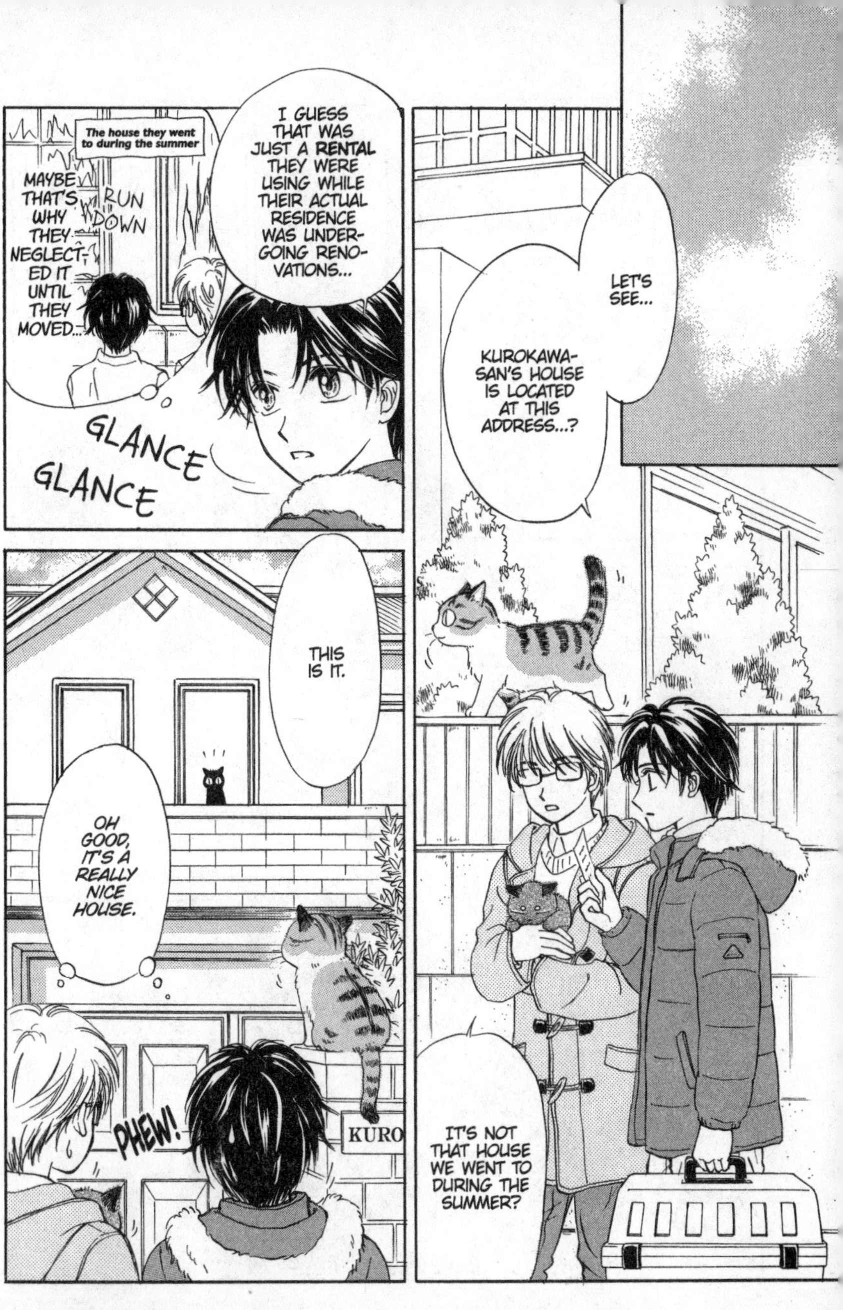
LET'S SEE...
KUROKAWA-SAN'S HOUSE IS LOCATED AT THIS ADDRESS...?
IT'S NOT THAT HOUSE WE WENT TO DURING THE SUMMER?
I GUESS THAT WAS JUST A RENTAL THEY WERE USING WHILE THEIR ACTUAL RESIDENCE WAS UNDER-GOING RENO-VATIONS...
The house they went to during the summer
RUN DOWN
MAYBE THAT'S WHY THEY NEGLECT-ED IT UNTIL THEY MOVED...
GLANCE GLANCE
THIS IS IT.
OH GOOD, IT'S A REALLY NICE HOUSE.
KURO
PHEW!

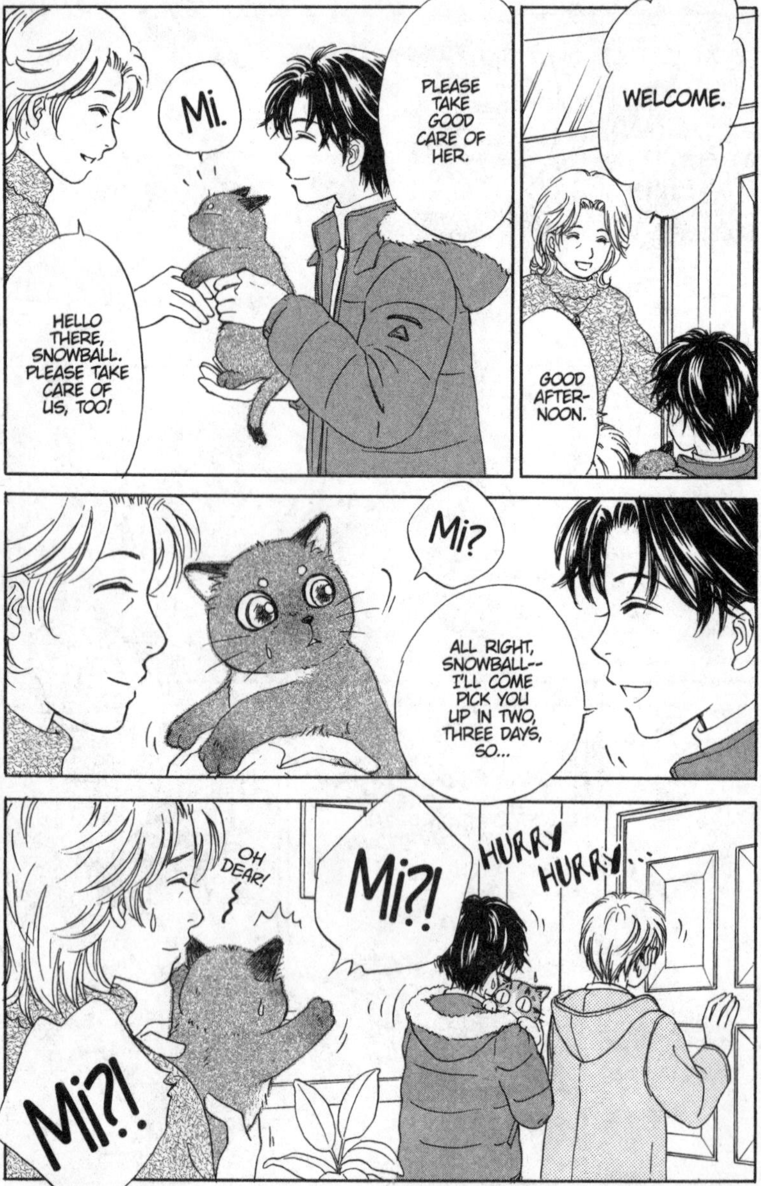
WELCOME.
GOOD AFTER-NOON.
PLEASE TAKE GOOD CARE OF HER.
Mi.
HELLO THERE, SNOWBALL. PLEASE TAKE CARE OF US, TOO!
Mi?
ALL RIGHT, SNOWBALL-- I'LL COME PICK YOU UP IN TWO, THREE DAYS, SO...
HURRY HURRY...
Mi?!
OH DEAR!
Mi?!

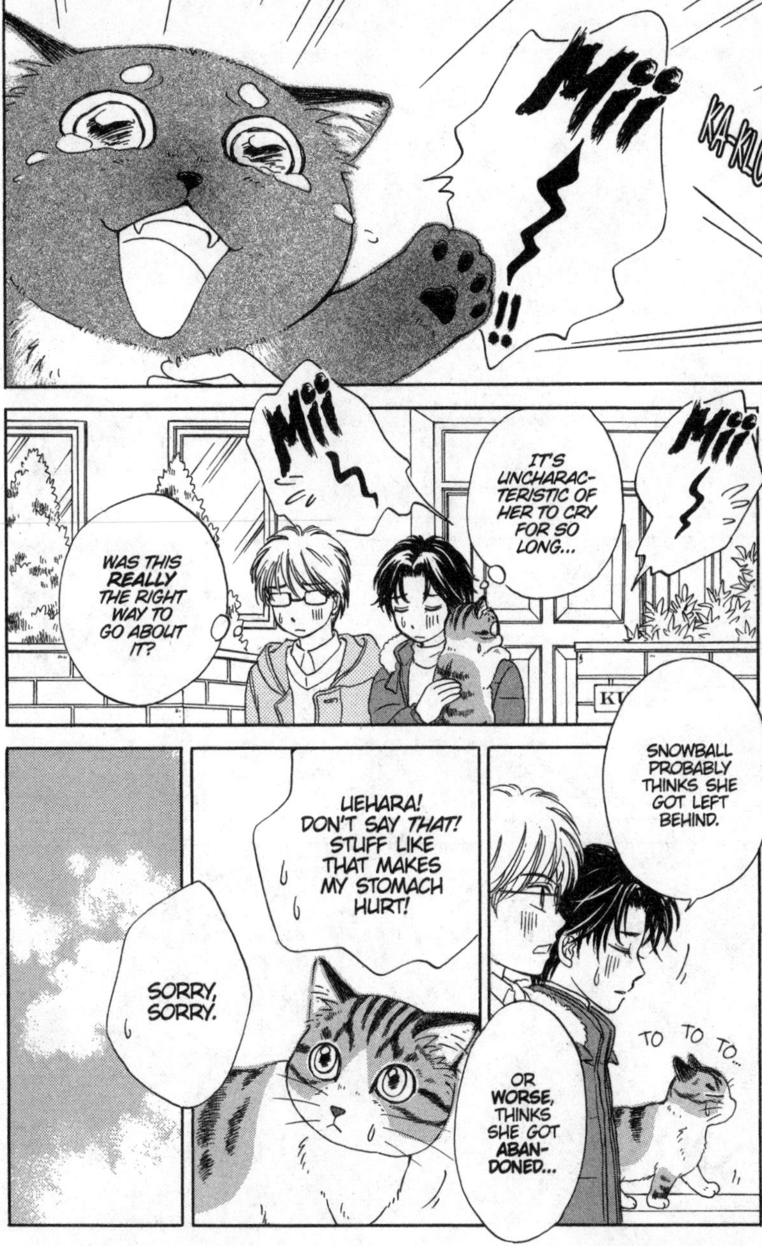
KA-KLUNK...
Mii!!
Mii
IT'S UNCHARACTERISTIC OF HER TO CRY FOR SO LONG...
Mii
WAS THIS REALLY THE RIGHT WAY TO GO ABOUT IT?
SNOWBALL PROBABLY THINKS SHE GOT LEFT BEHIND.
OR WORSE, THINKS SHE GOT ABANDONED...
TO TO TO...
UEHARA! DON'T SAY THAT! STUFF LIKE THAT MAKES MY STOMACH HURT!
SORRY, SORRY.

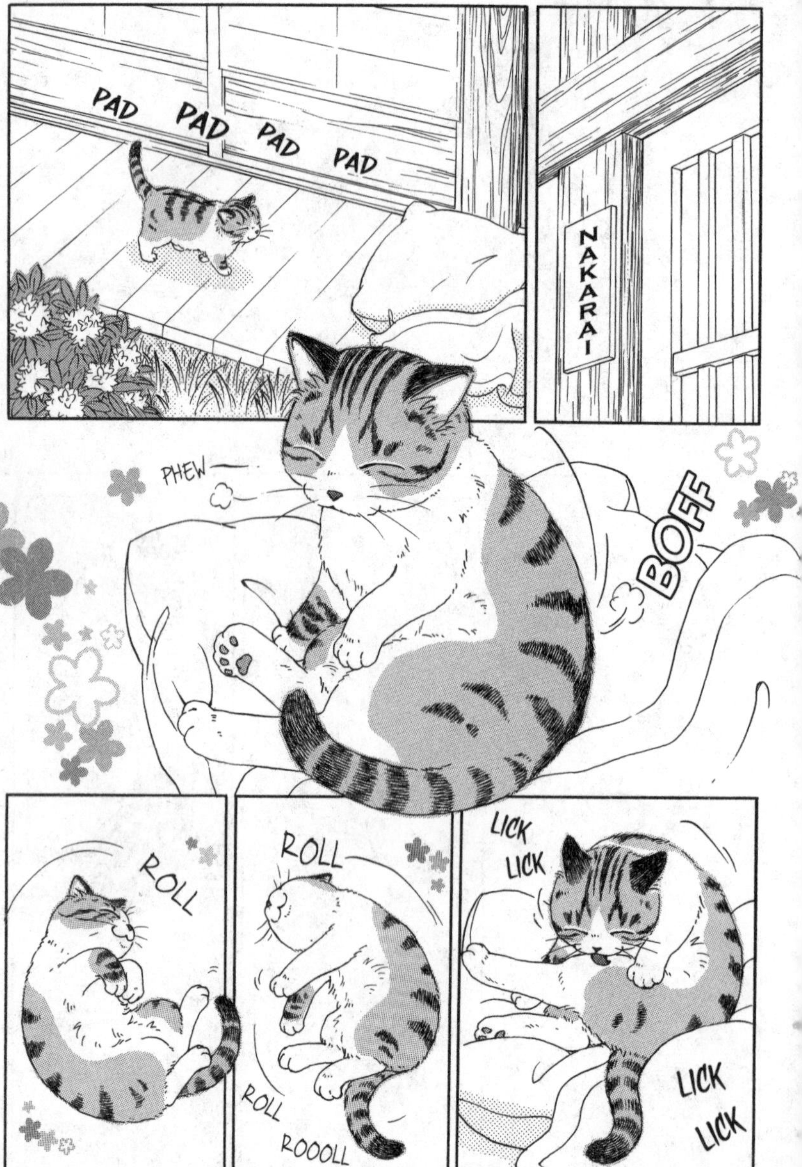
NAKARAI
PAD
PAD
PAD
PAD
BOFF
PHEW
LICK
LICK
LICK
LICK
ROLL
ROLL
ROOOLL
ROLL

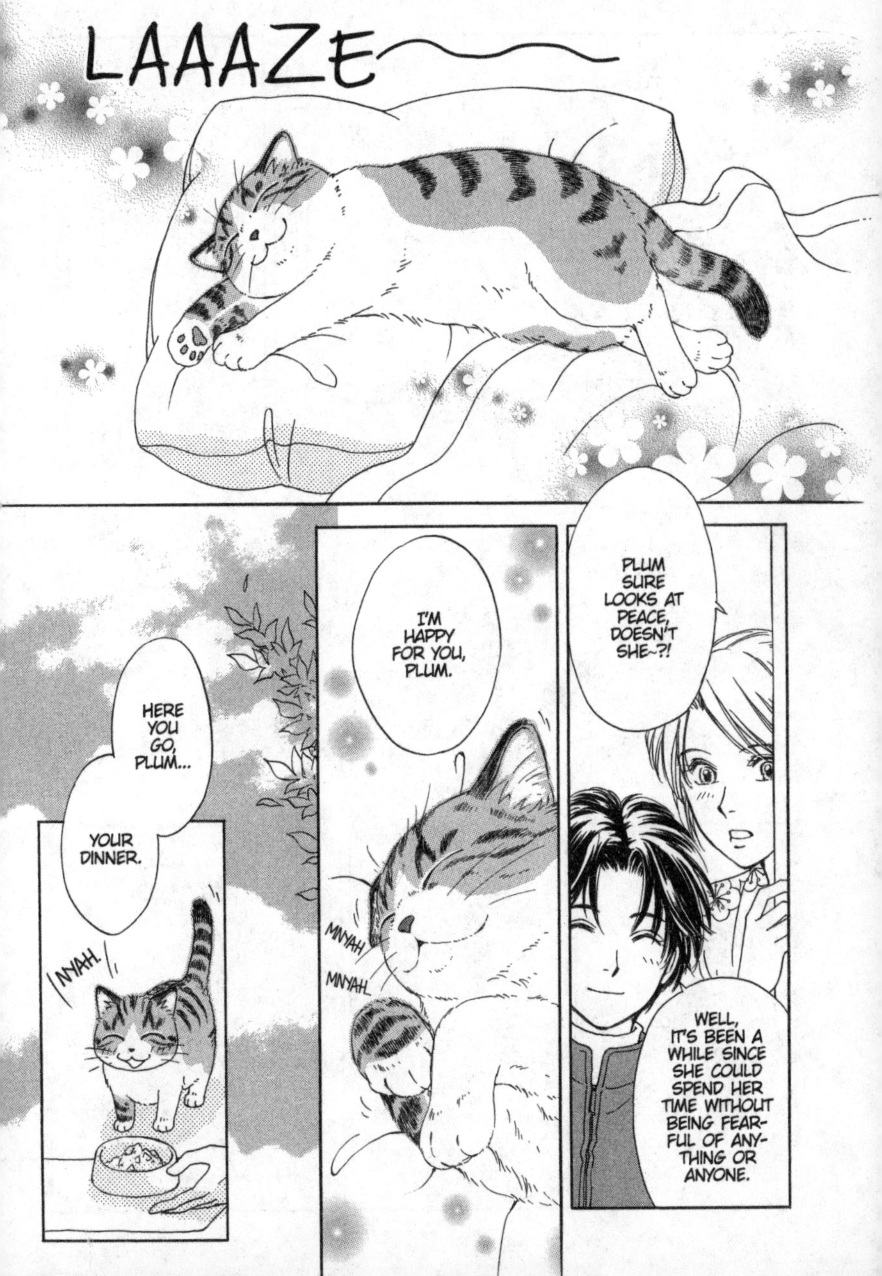
LAAAZE
PLUM SURE LOOKS AT PEACE, DOESN'T SHE~?!
WELL, IT'S BEEN A WHILE SINCE SHE COULD SPEND HER TIME WITHOUT BEING FEAR-FUL OF ANY-THING OR ANYONE.
I'M HAPPY FOR YOU, PLUM.
MNYAH
MNYAH
HERE YOU GO, PLUM...
YOUR DINNER.
NYAH.

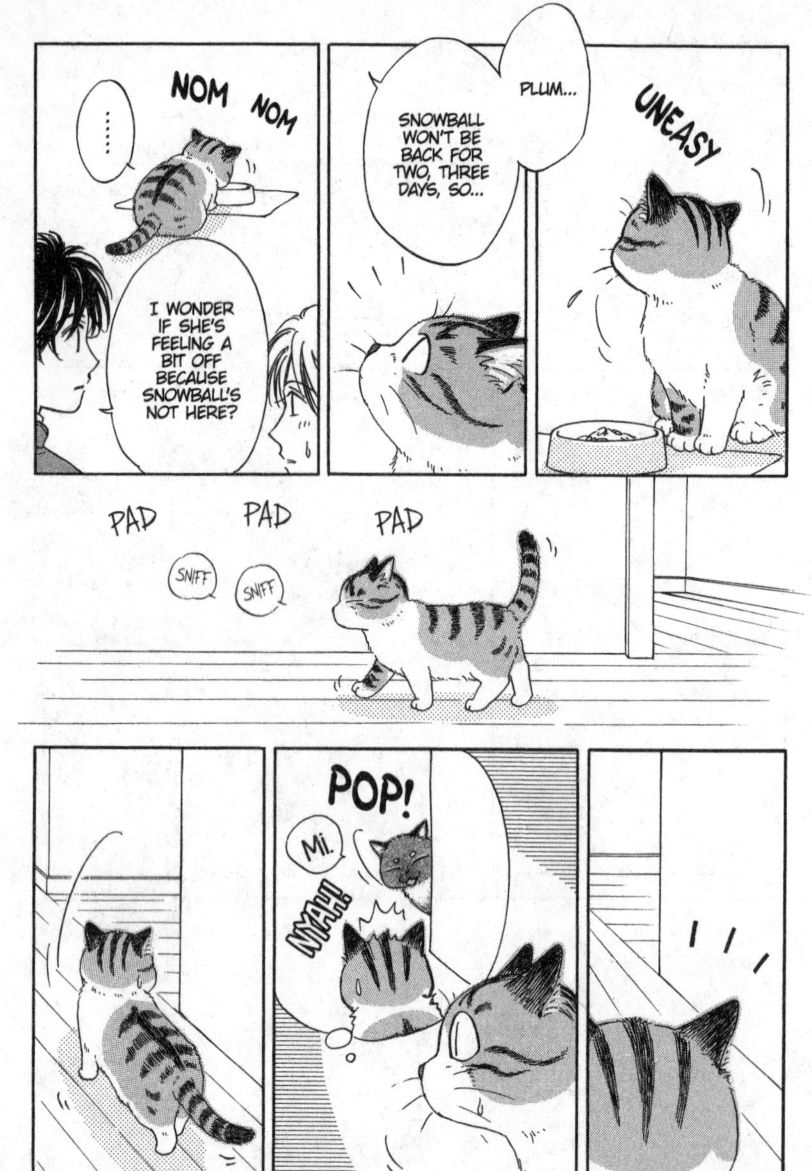
UNEASY
PLUM...
SNOWBALL WON'T BE BACK FOR TWO, THREE DAYS, SO...
NOM NOM
......
I WONDER IF SHE'S FEELING A BIT OFF BECAUSE SNOWBALL'S NOT HERE?
PAD PAD PAD
SNIFF SNIFF
POP!
Mi.
NYAH!

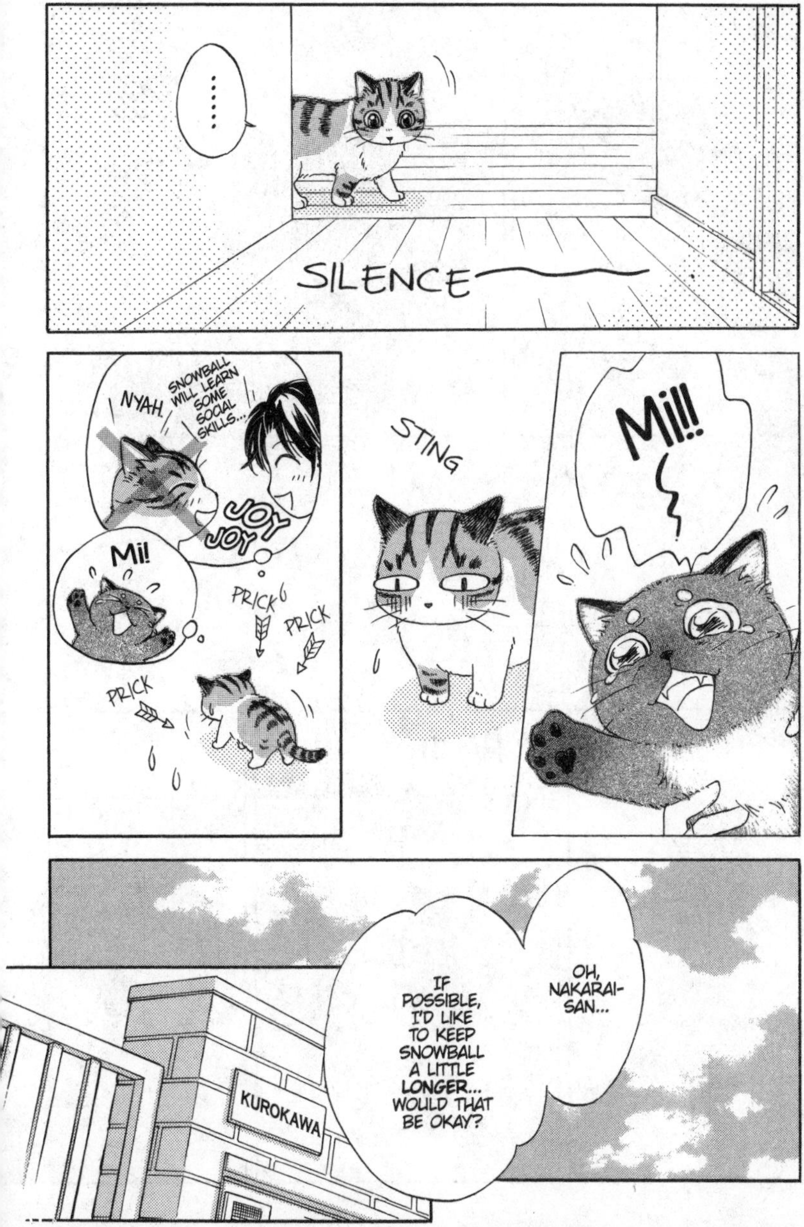
......
SILENCE
Mi!!
STING
SNOWBALL WILL LEARN SOME SOCIAL SKILLS...
NYAH
JOY JOY
Mi!
PRICK
PRICK
PRICK
OH, NAKARAI-SAN...
IF POSSIBLE, I'D LIKE TO KEEP SNOWBALL A LITTLE LONGER... WOULD THAT BE OKAY?
KUROKAWA

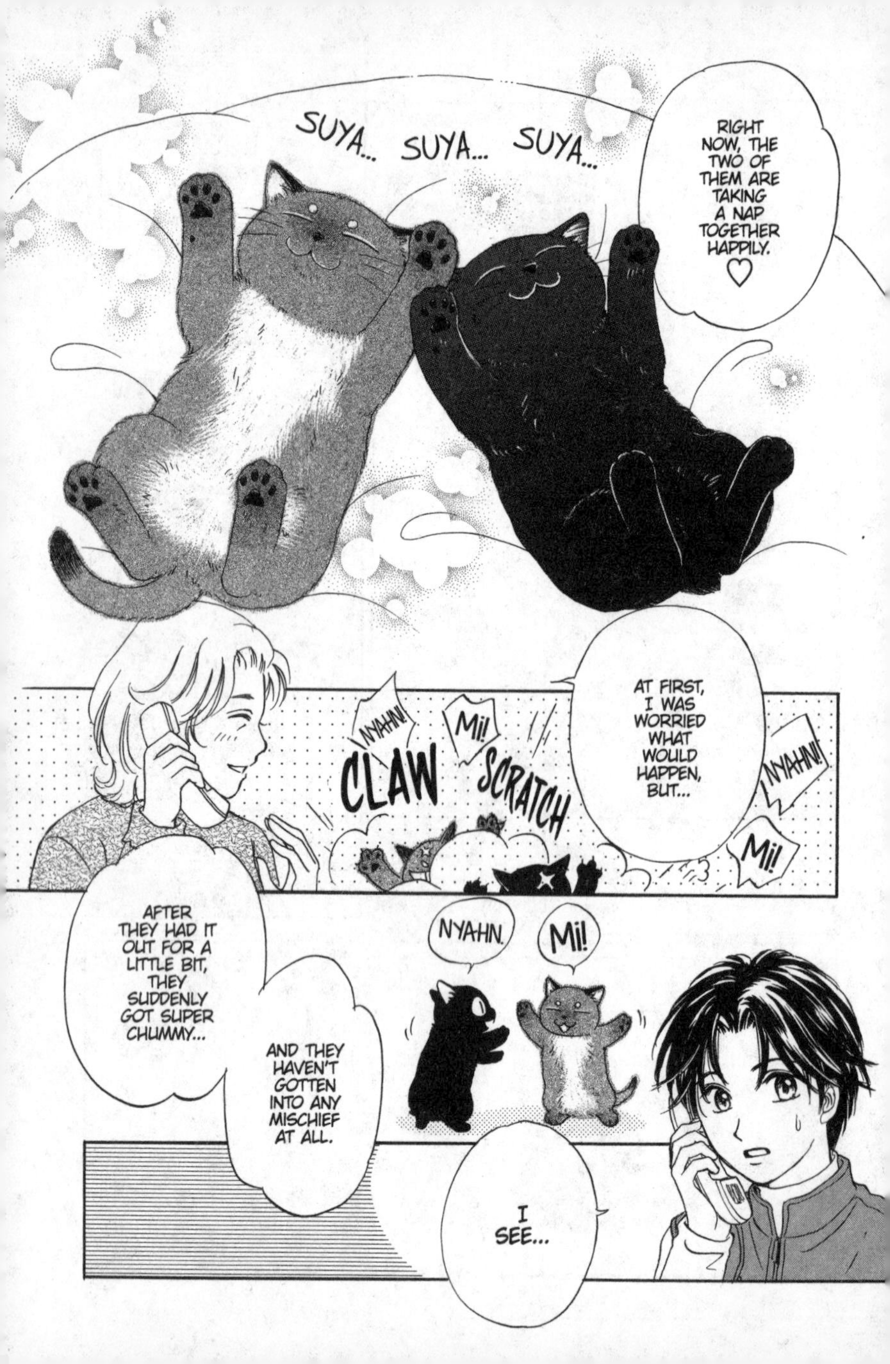

RIGHT NOW, THE TWO OF THEM ARE TAKING A NAP TOGETHER HAPPILY. ♡
SUYA... SUYA... SUYA...
AT FIRST, I WAS WORRIED WHAT WOULD HAPPEN, BUT...
NYAHN!
Mi!
SCRATCH
Mi!
CLAW
NYAHN!
Mi!
NYAHN.
AFTER THEY HAD IT OUT FOR A LITTLE BIT, THEY SUDDENLY GOT SUPER CHUMMY...
AND THEY HAVEN'T GOTTEN INTO ANY MISCHIEF AT ALL.
I SEE...

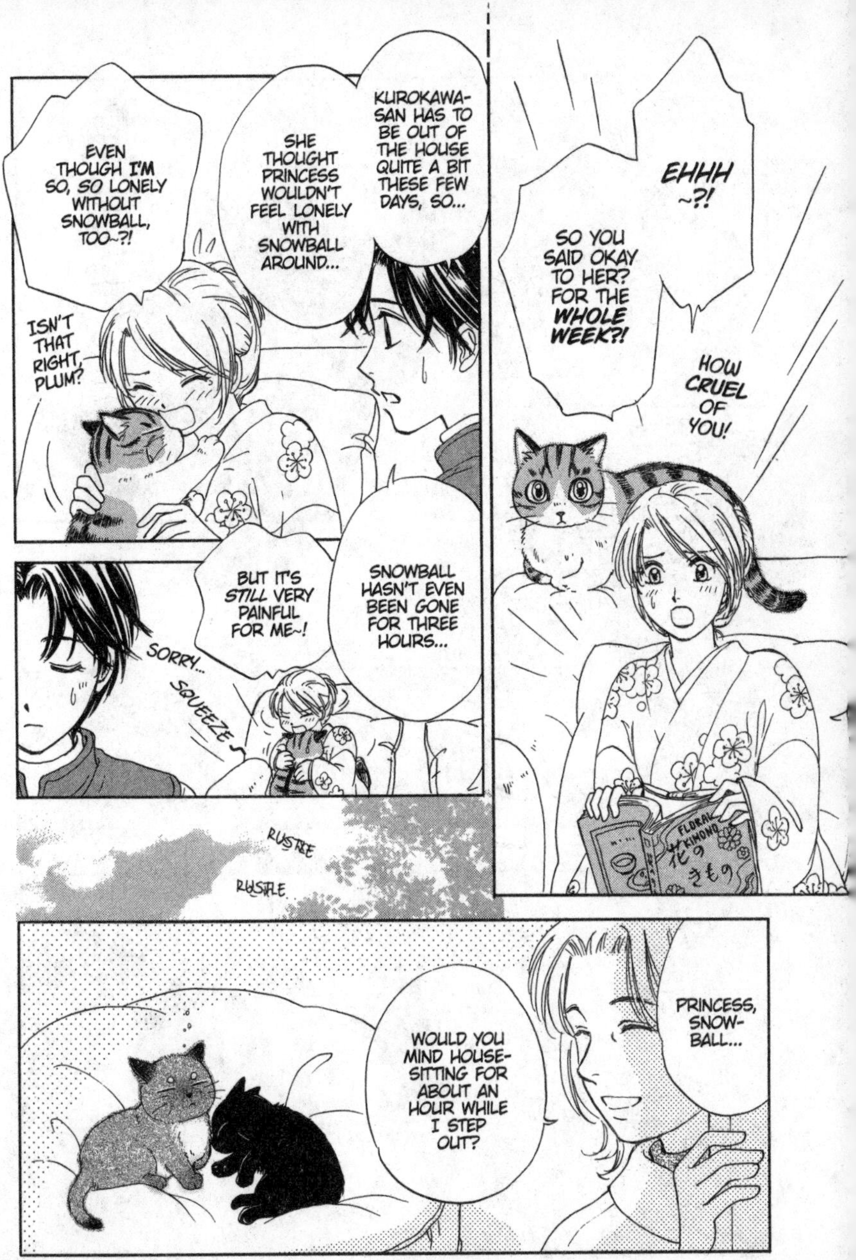
EHHH ~?!
SO YOU SAID OKAY TO HER? FOR THE *WHOLE WEEK?!*
HOW CRUEL OF YOU!
FLORAL KIMONO
花のきもの
KUROKAWA-SAN HAS TO BE OUT OF THE HOUSE QUITE A BIT THESE FEW DAYS, SO...
SHE THOUGHT PRINCESS WOULDN'T FEEL LONELY WITH SNOWBALL AROUND...
EVEN THOUGH I'M SO, SO LONELY WITHOUT SNOWBALL, TOO~?!
ISN'T THAT RIGHT, PLUM?
SNOWBALL HASN'T EVEN BEEN GONE FOR THREE HOURS...
BUT IT'S *STILL* VERY PAINFUL FOR ME~!
SQUEEZE
SORRY...
RUSTLE
RUSTLE
PRINCESS, SNOW-BALL...
WOULD YOU MIND HOUSE-SITTING FOR ABOUT AN HOUR WHILE I STEP OUT?

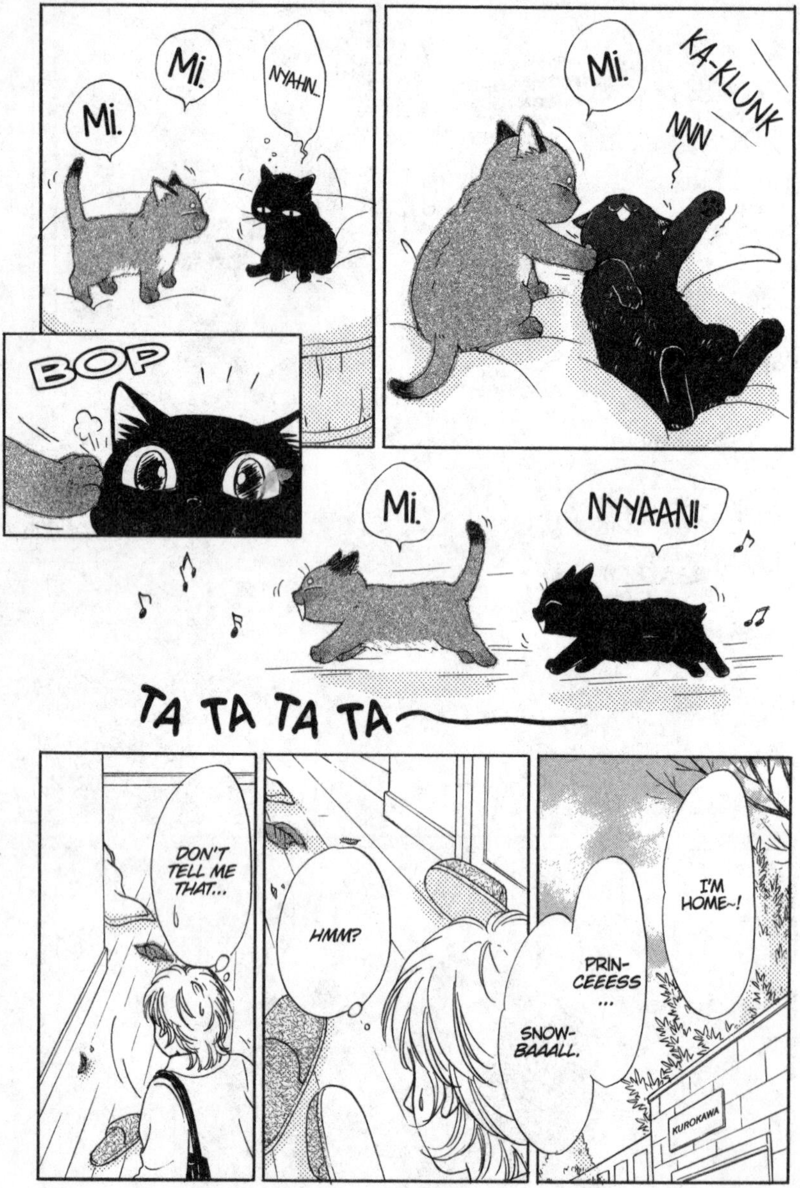
KA-KLUNK
Mi.
NNN
NYAHN...
Mi.
Mi.
BOP
NYYAAN!
Mi.
TA TA TA TA
I'M HOME~!
PRIN-CEEESS ...
SNOW-BAAALL.
KUROKAWA
HMM?
DON'T TELL ME THAT...

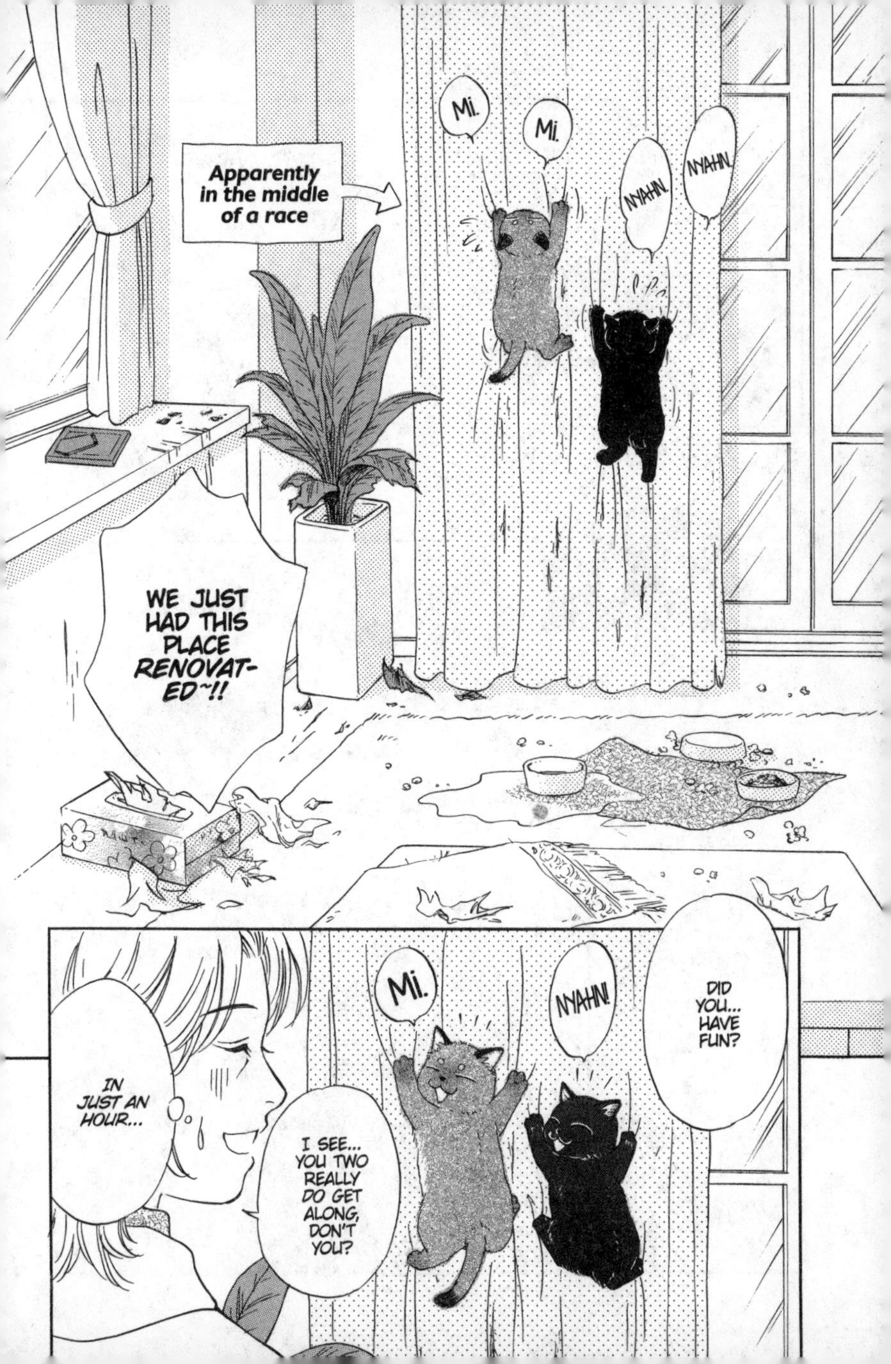
NYAHN.
NYAHN.
Mi.
Mi.
Apparently in the middle of a race
WE JUST HAD THIS PLACE RENOVATED~!!
DID YOU... HAVE FUN?
NYAHN!
Mi.
I SEE... YOU TWO REALLY DO GET ALONG, DON'T YOU?
IN JUST AN HOUR...

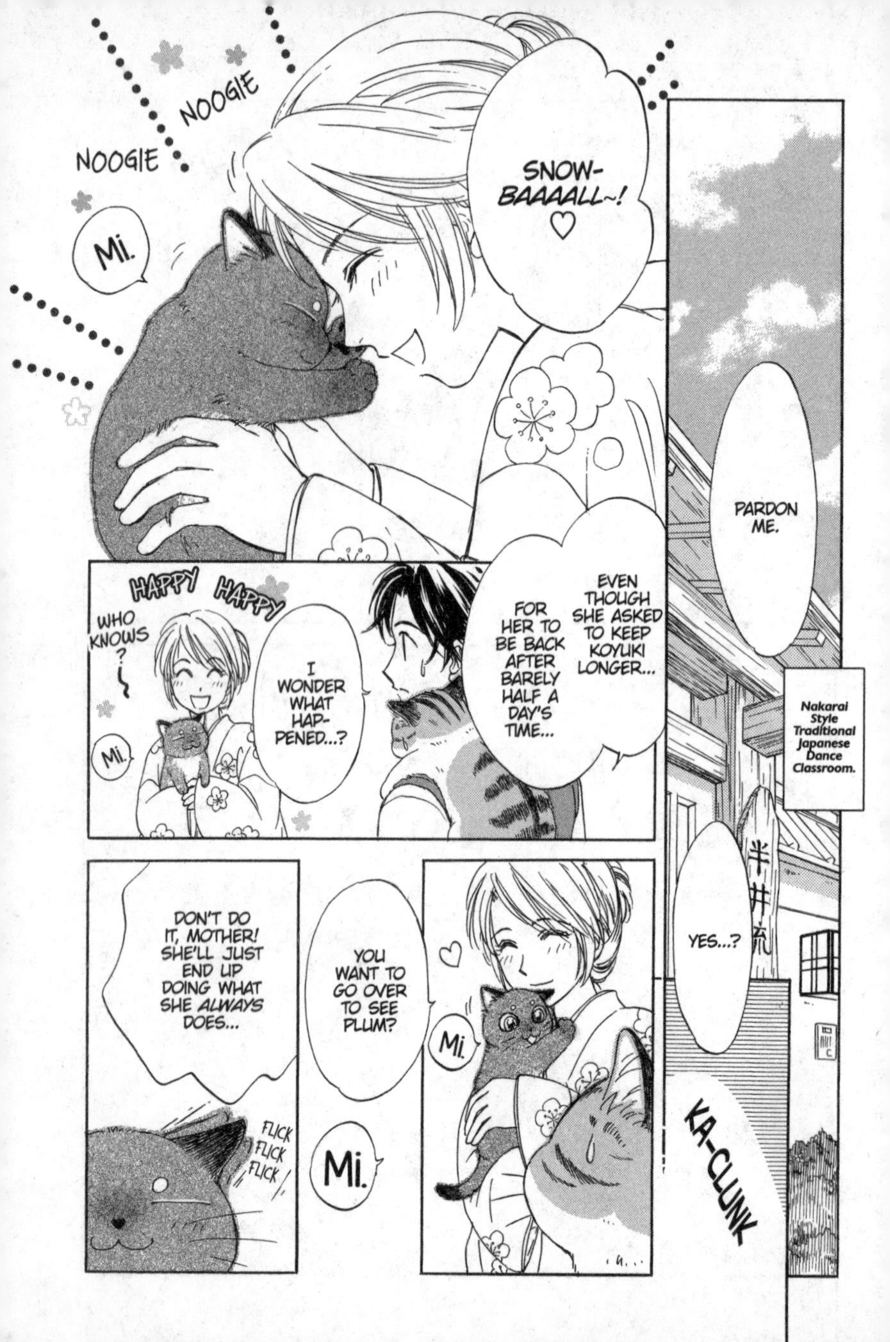
PARDON ME.
Nakarai Style Traditional Japanese Dance Classroom.
YES...?
KA-CLUNK
SNOW-BAAAALL~! ♡
NOOGIE
NOOGIE
Mi.
EVEN THOUGH SHE ASKED TO KEEP KOYUKI LONGER...
FOR HER TO BE BACK AFTER BARELY HALF A DAY'S TIME...
I WONDER WHAT HAP-PENED...?
HAPPY HAPPY
WHO KNOWS?
Mi.
♡
Mi.
YOU WANT TO GO OVER TO SEE PLUM?
Mi.
DON'T DO IT, MOTHER! SHE'LL JUST END UP DOING WHAT SHE *ALWAYS* DOES...
FLICK FLICK FLICK

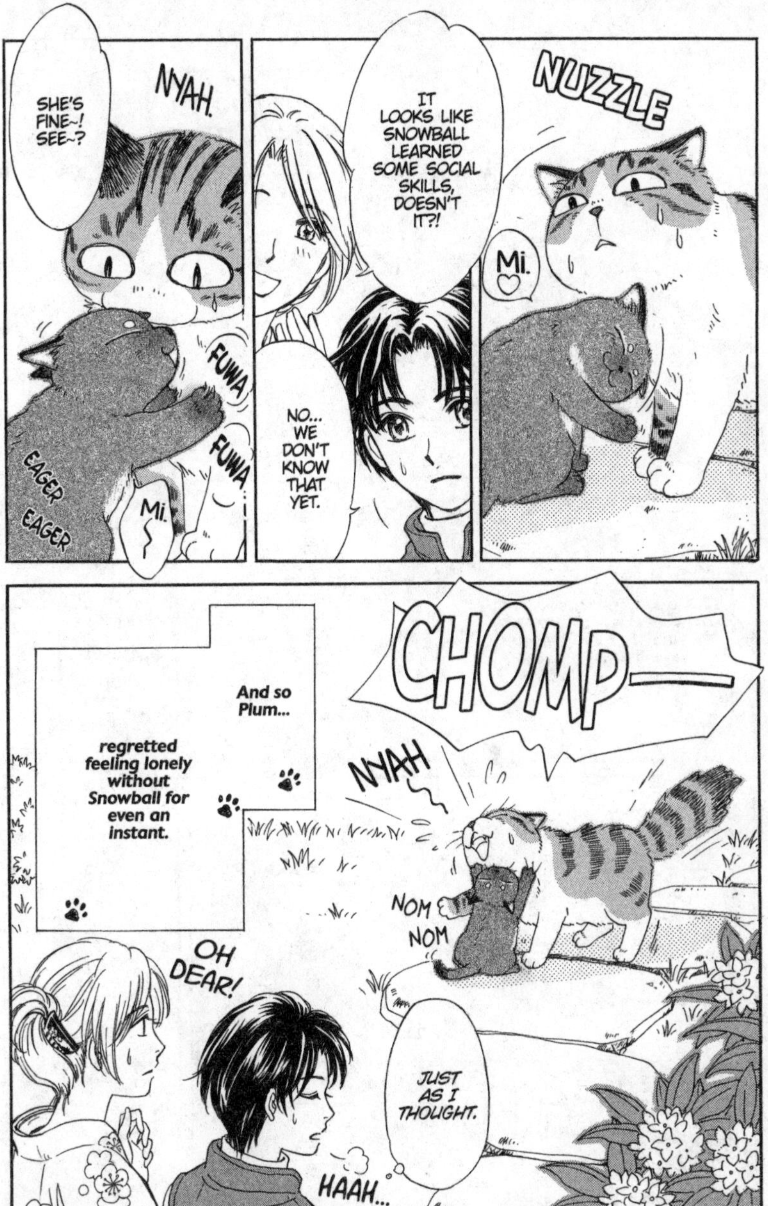
NUZZLE
Mi. ♡
IT LOOKS LIKE SNOWBALL LEARNED SOME SOCIAL SKILLS, DOESN'T IT?!
NO... WE DON'T KNOW THAT YET.
SHE'S FINE~! SEE~?
NYAH.
FUWA
FUWA
EAGER EAGER
Mi.
CHOMP—
NYAH
NOM NOM
And so Plum...
regretted feeling lonely without Snowball for even an instant.
OH DEAR!
JUST AS I THOUGHT.
HAAH...

OMAKE PAGE

Snowball's Favorite

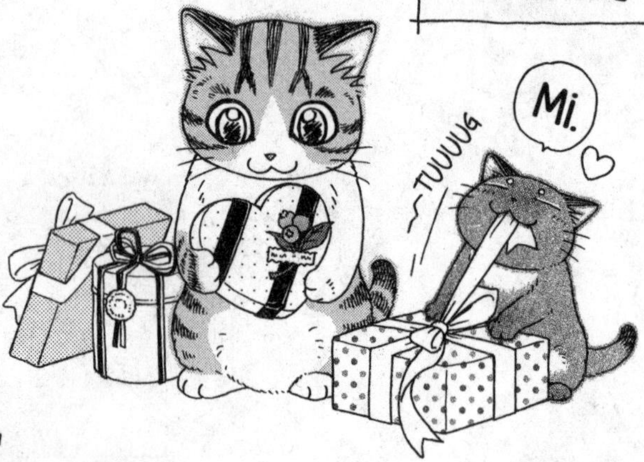

Mi.
TUUUUG

Back cover illustration of the "Chocolate" volume of *Neko Panchi* No.5

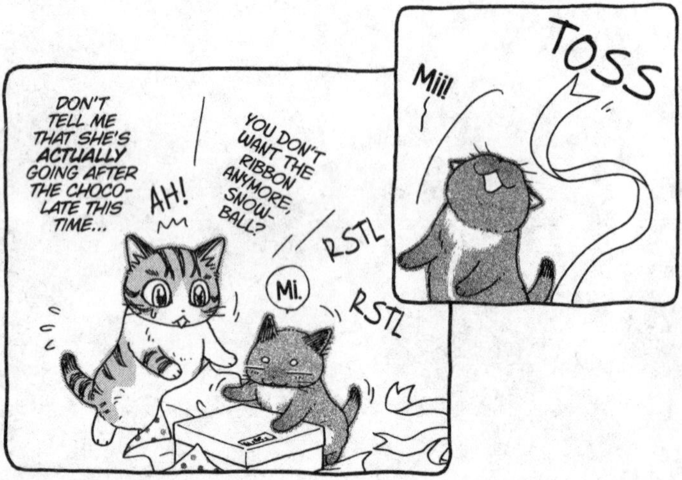

TOSS
Mii!
YOU DON'T WANT THE RIBBON ANYMORE, SNOW-BALL?
RSTL
DON'T TELL ME THAT SHE'S ACTUALLY GOING AFTER THE CHOCO-LATE THIS TIME...
AH!
Mi.
RSTL

← Continued in three pages!

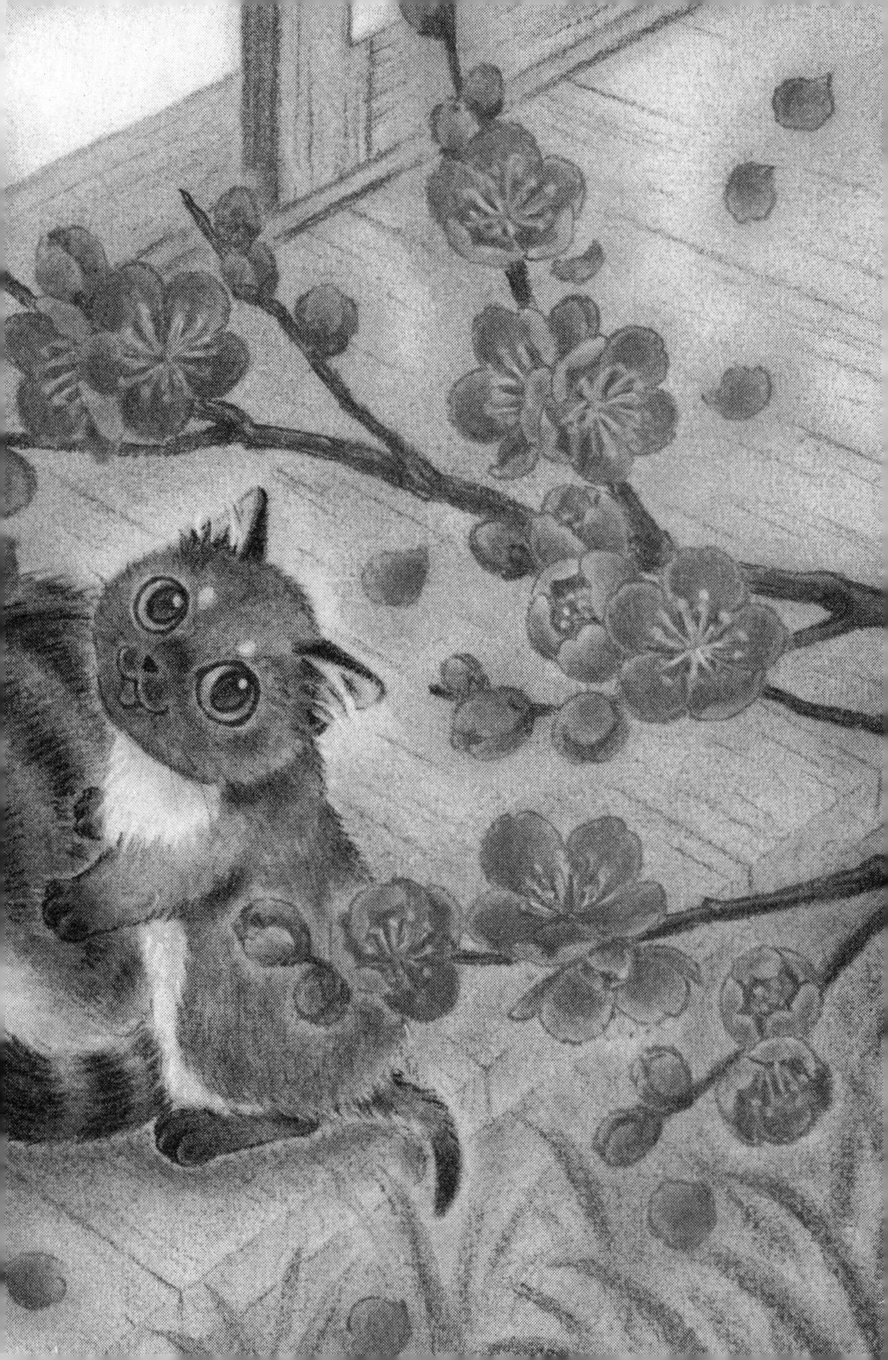

SHORT.6
GIRLS' FESTIVAL AT PRINCESS'S HOUSE

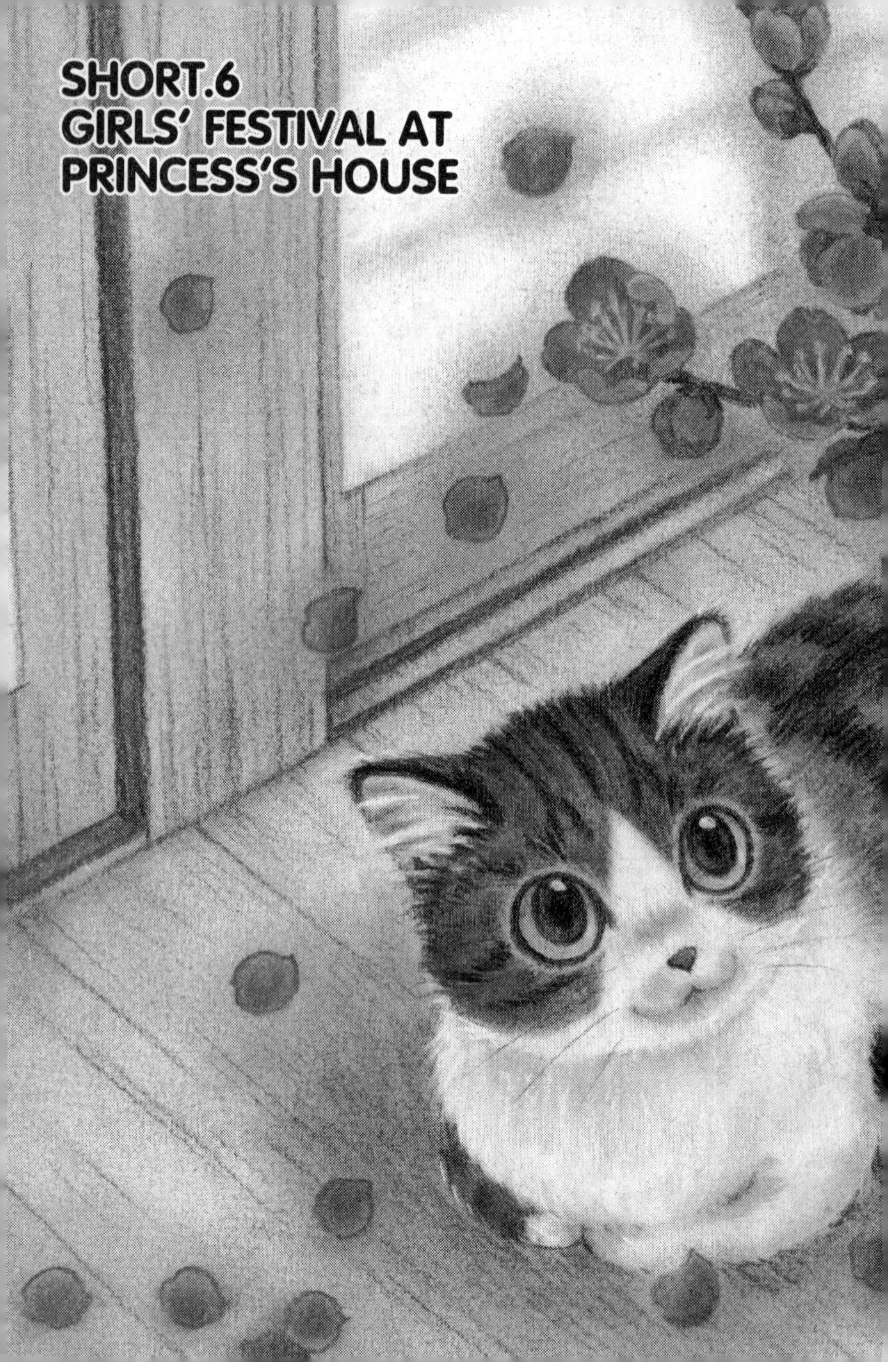

OMAKE PAGE

THE CONTINUATION!

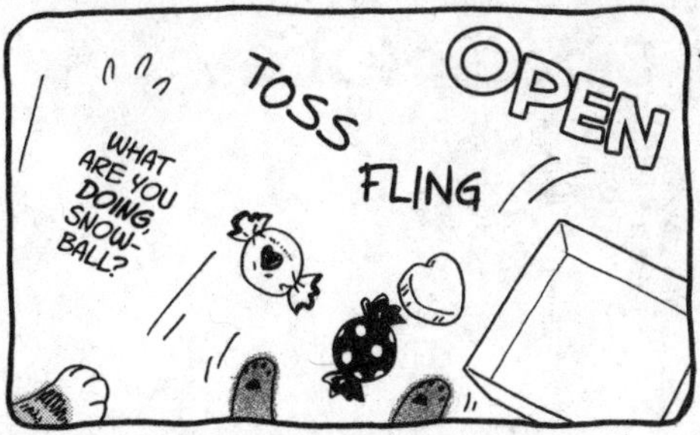
OPEN
TOSS
FLING
WHAT ARE YOU DOING, SNOW-BALL?

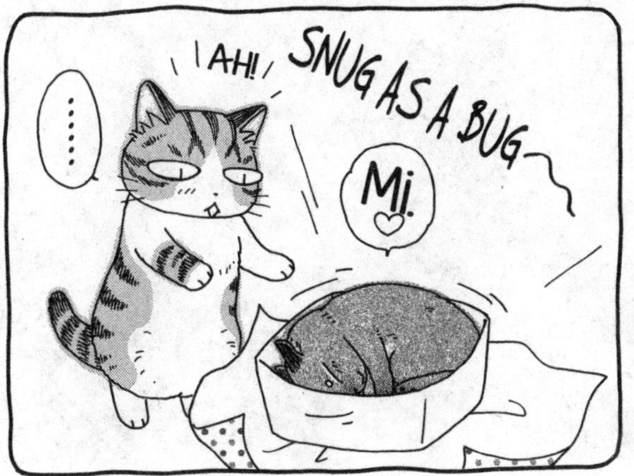
SNUG AS A BUG~
AH!
Mi.
......

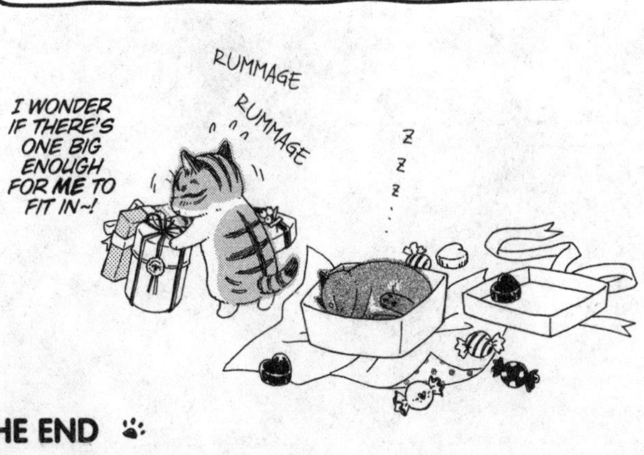
RUMMAGE
RUMMAGE
I WONDER IF THERE'S ONE BIG ENOUGH FOR ME TO FIT IN~!
Z Z Z...

THE END

SHORT.6

GIRLS' FESTIVAL AT PRINCESS'S HOUSE

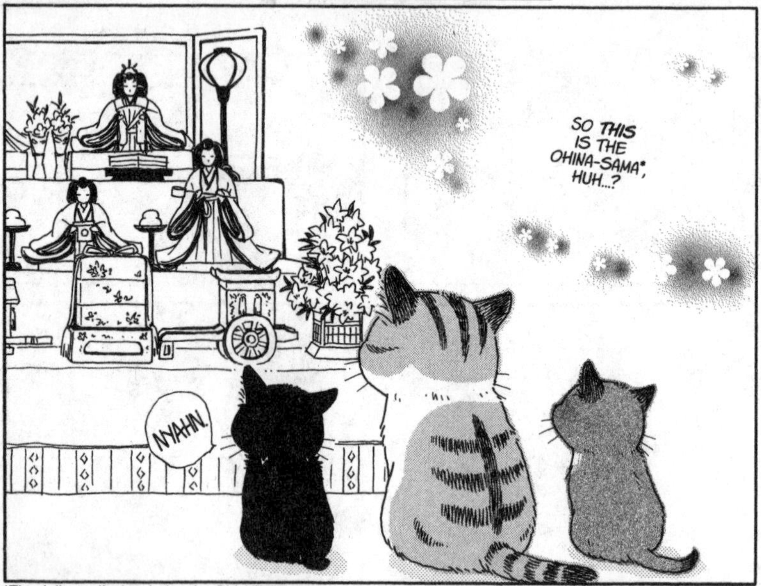
SO THIS IS THE OHINA-SAMA*, HUH...?
NYAHN.

*The dolls on display during the Girls' Fest.

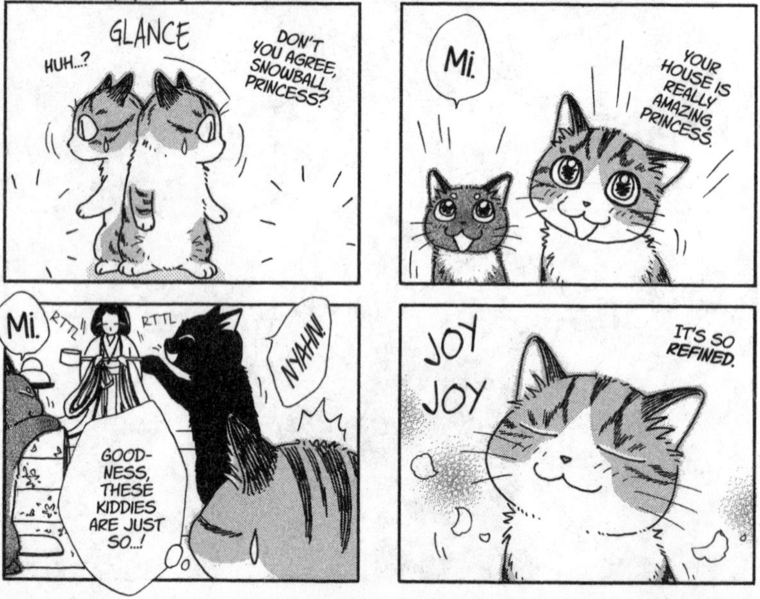
YOUR HOUSE IS REALLY AMAZING, PRINCESS.
Mi.
DON'T YOU AGREE, SNOWBALL, PRINCESS?
GLANCE
HUH...?
IT'S SO REFINED.
JOY
JOY
NYAHN!
RTTL
RTTL
Mi.
GOOD-NESS, THESE KIDDIES ARE JUST SO...!

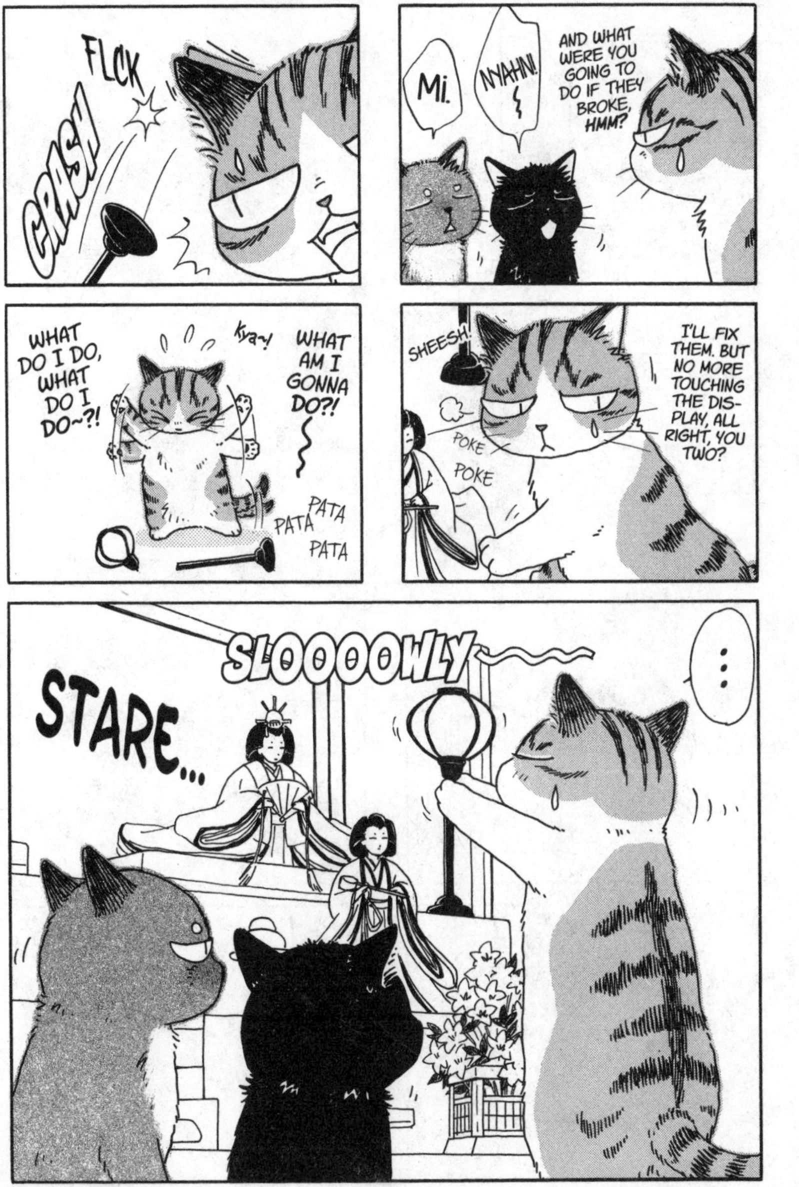
AND WHAT WERE YOU GOING TO DO IF THEY BROKE, HMM?
NYAHN!
Mi.
FLCK
CRASH
I'LL FIX THEM. BUT NO MORE TOUCHING THE DIS-PLAY, ALL RIGHT, YOU TWO?
SHEESH!
POKE
POKE
WHAT AM I GONNA DO?!
Kya~!
WHAT DO I DO, WHAT DO I DO~?!
PATA
PATA
PATA
…
SLOOOOWLY
STARE...

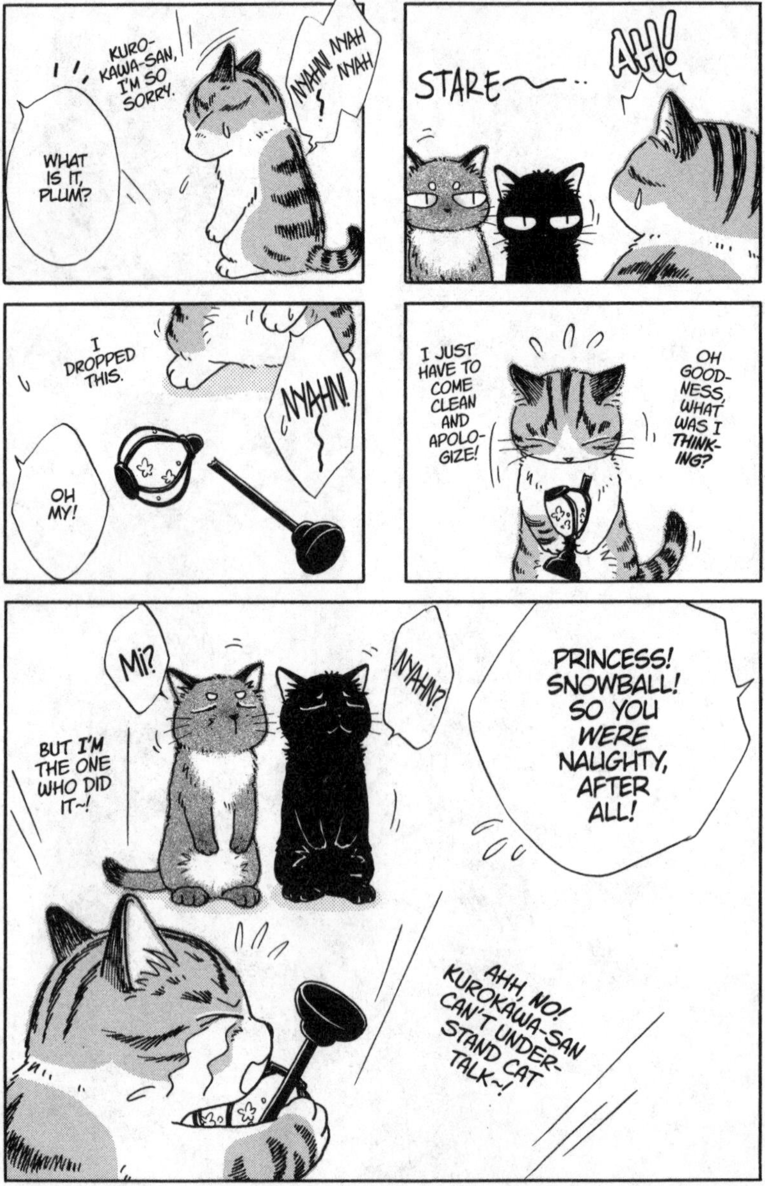
AH!
STARE~~..
NYAH NYAH
NYAHN!
KURO-KAWA-SAN, I'M SO SORRY.
WHAT IS IT, PLUM?
OH GOODNESS, WHAT WAS I THINKING?
I JUST HAVE TO COME CLEAN AND APOLOGIZE!
NYAHN!
I DROPPED THIS.
OH MY!
PRINCESS! SNOWBALL! SO YOU WERE NAUGHTY, AFTER ALL!
NYAHN?
Mi?
BUT I'M THE ONE WHO DID IT~!
AHH, NO! KUROKAWA-SAN CAN'T UNDER-STAND CAT TALK~!

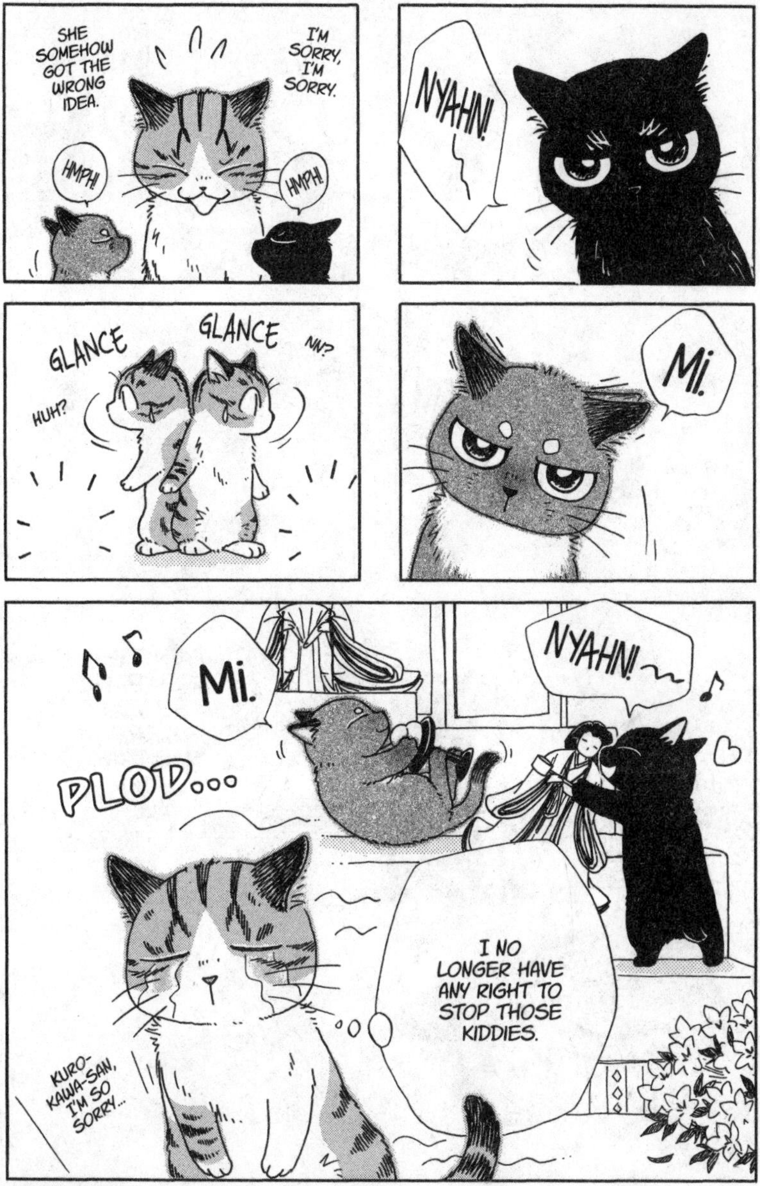
NYAHN!
I'M SORRY, I'M SORRY.
HMPH!
SHE SOMEHOW GOT THE WRONG IDEA.
HMPH!
Mi.
NN?
GLANCE
GLANCE
HUH?
NYAHN!~
Mi.
PLOD...
I NO LONGER HAVE ANY RIGHT TO STOP THOSE KIDDIES.
KURO-KAWA-SAN, I'M SO SORRY...

THE END

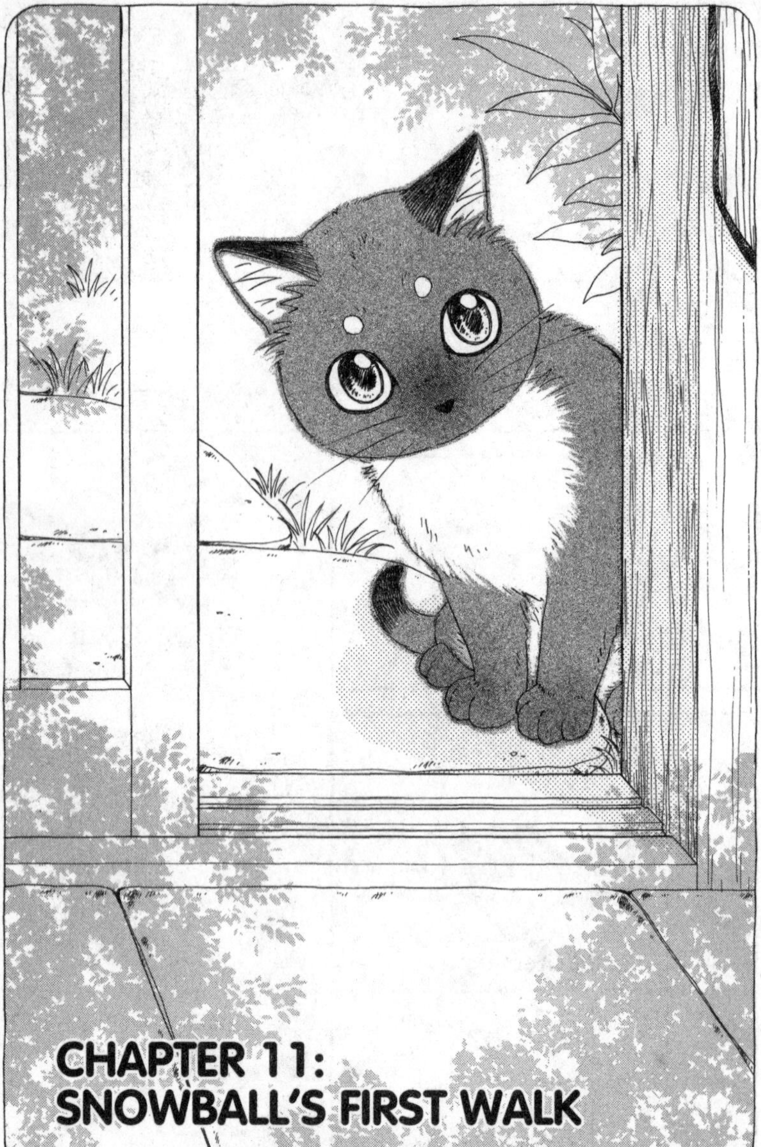
CHAPTER 11:
SNOWBALL'S FIRST WALK

SNIFF
SNIFF
SNIFF
PAD PAD
PAD PAD...
SIT
HMM?
FWUP
SNIFF
SNIFF
SNIFF...
FWUP
A Light Greeting
FWIP
SQUIRM
SQUIRM

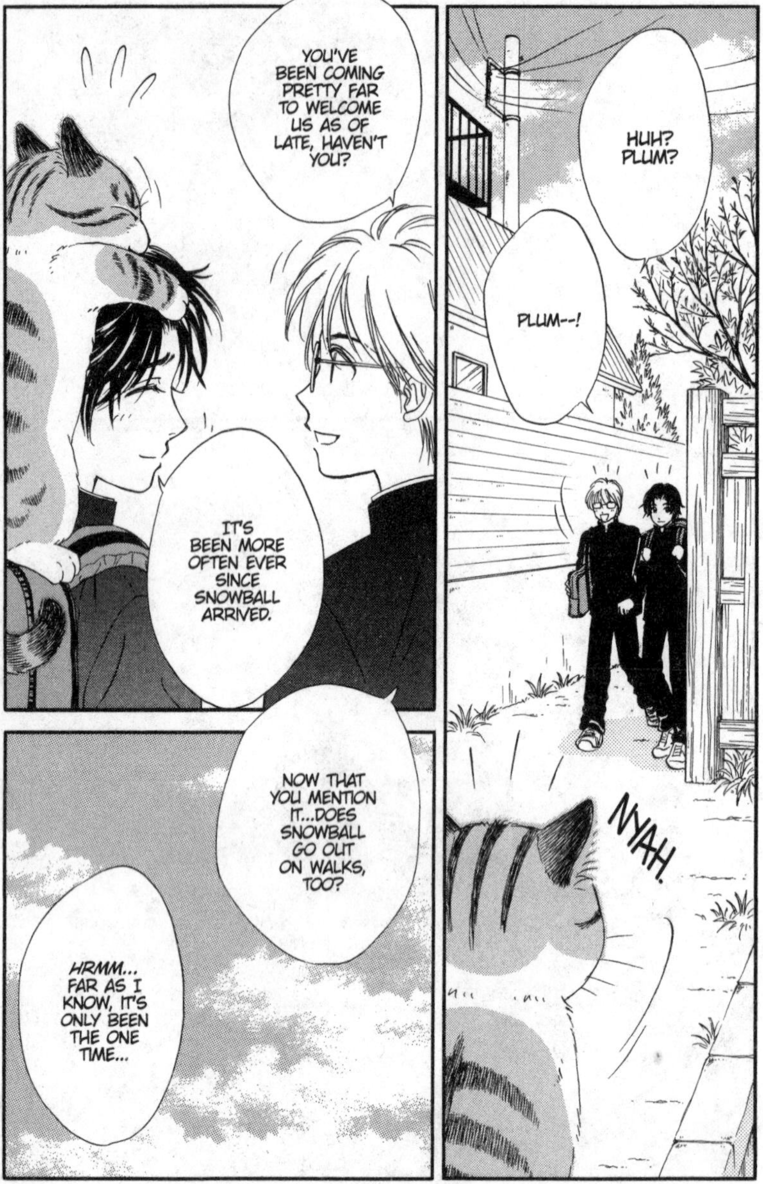
HUH? PLUM?
PLUM--!
NYAH.
YOU'VE BEEN COMING PRETTY FAR TO WELCOME US AS OF LATE, HAVEN'T YOU?
IT'S BEEN MORE OFTEN EVER SINCE SNOWBALL ARRIVED.
NOW THAT YOU MENTION IT...DOES SNOWBALL GO OUT ON WALKS, TOO?
HRMM... FAR AS I KNOW, IT'S ONLY BEEN THE ONE TIME...

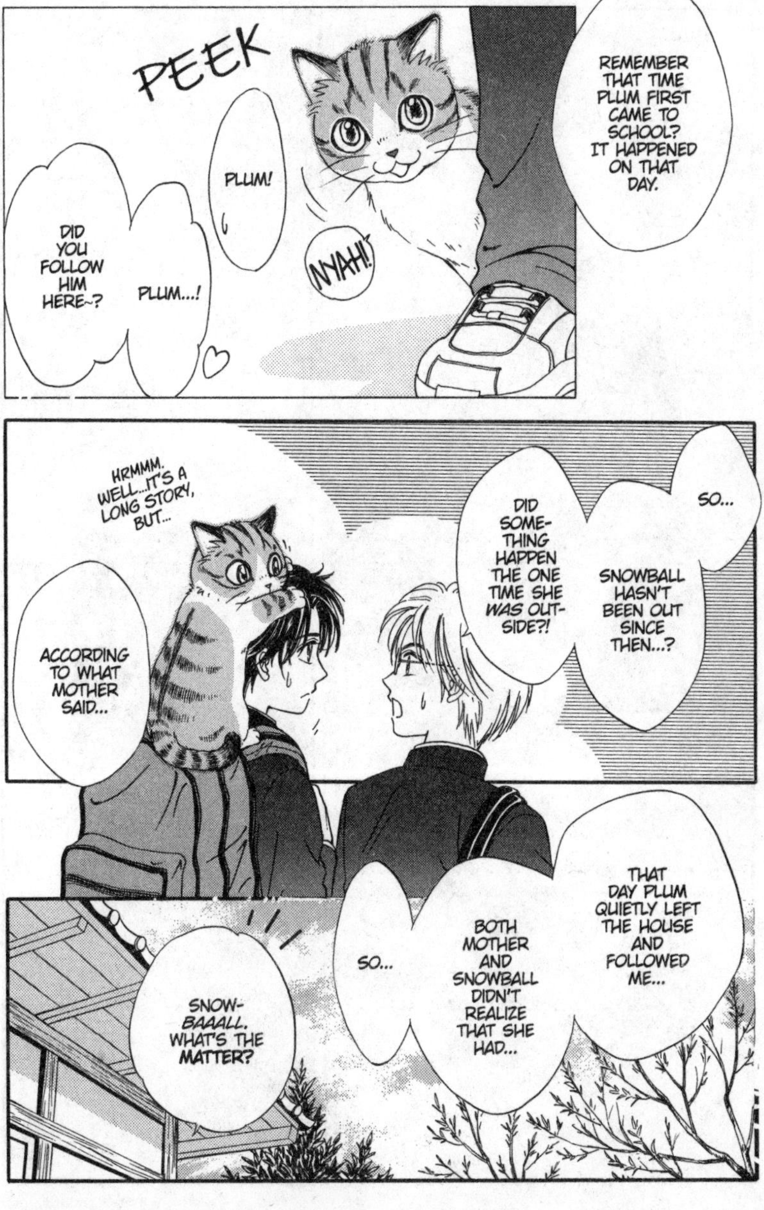
REMEMBER THAT TIME PLUM FIRST CAME TO SCHOOL? IT HAPPENED ON THAT DAY.
PEEK
NYAH!
PLUM!
PLUM...!
DID YOU FOLLOW HIM HERE~?
SO...
SNOWBALL HASN'T BEEN OUT SINCE THEN...?
DID SOME-THING HAPPEN THE ONE TIME SHE *WAS* OUT-SIDE?!
HRMMM. WELL...IT'S A LONG STORY, BUT...
ACCORDING TO WHAT MOTHER SAID...
THAT DAY PLUM QUIETLY LEFT THE HOUSE AND FOLLOWED ME...
BOTH MOTHER AND SNOWBALL DIDN'T REALIZE THAT SHE HAD...
SO...
SNOW-*BAAALL*. WHAT'S THE MATTER?

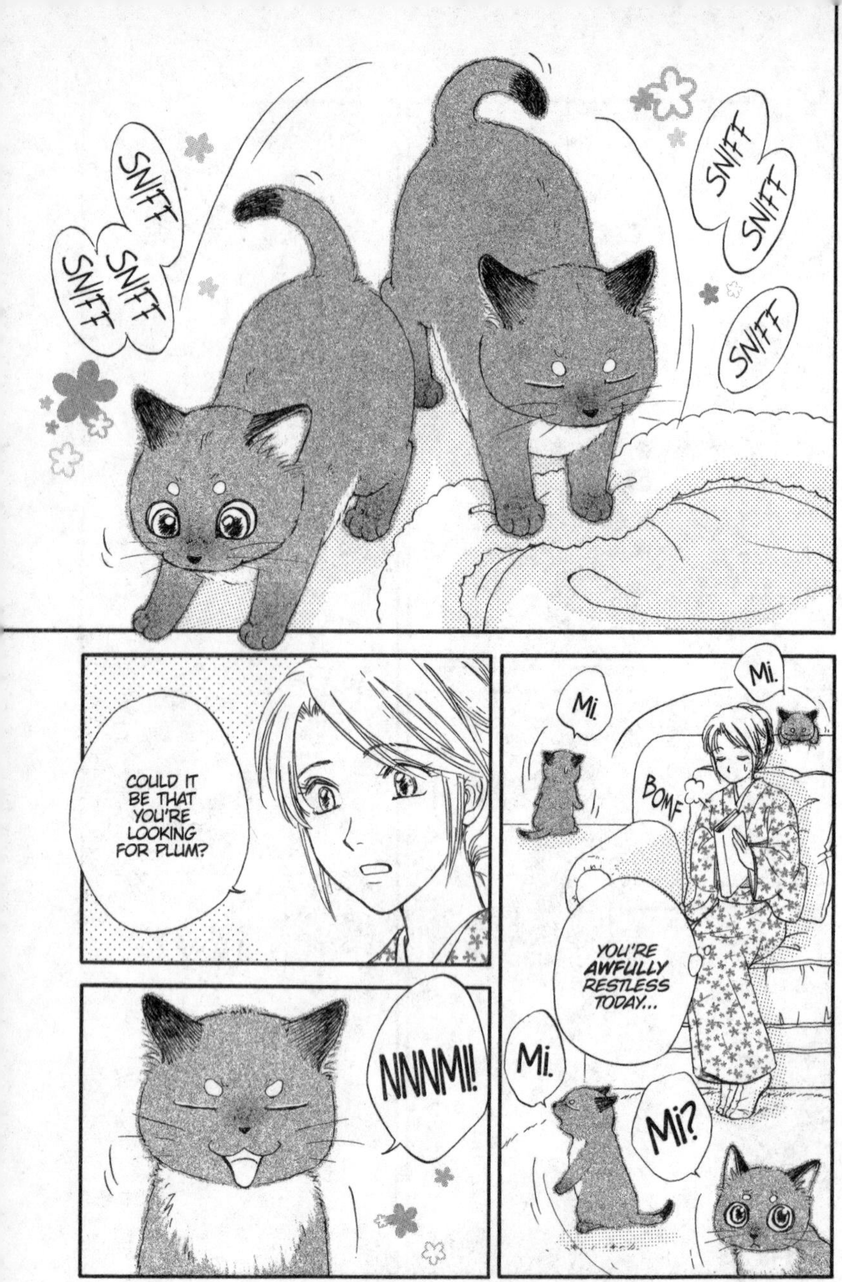
SNIFF SNIFF
SNIFF
SNIFF SNIFF SNIFF
Mi.
Mi.
BOMF
YOU'RE AWFULLY RESTLESS TODAY...
Mi.
Mi?
COULD IT BE THAT YOU'RE LOOKING FOR PLUM?
NNNMI!

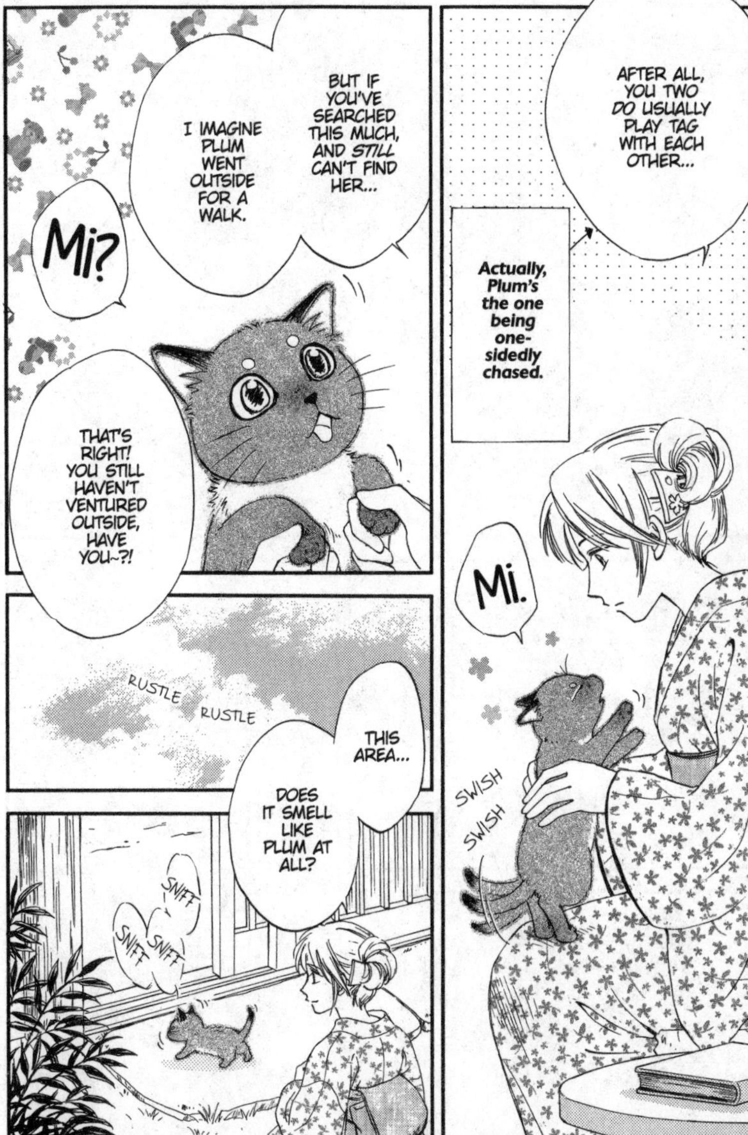
AFTER ALL, YOU TWO DO USUALLY PLAY TAG WITH EACH OTHER...
Actually, Plum's the one being one-sidedly chased.
Mi.
SWISH
SWISH
BUT IF YOU'VE SEARCHED THIS MUCH, AND STILL CAN'T FIND HER...
I IMAGINE PLUM WENT OUTSIDE FOR A WALK.
Mi?
THAT'S RIGHT! YOU STILL HAVEN'T VENTURED OUTSIDE, HAVE YOU~?!
THIS AREA...
RUSTLE
RUSTLE
DOES IT SMELL LIKE PLUM AT ALL?
SNIFF
SNIFF
SNIFF

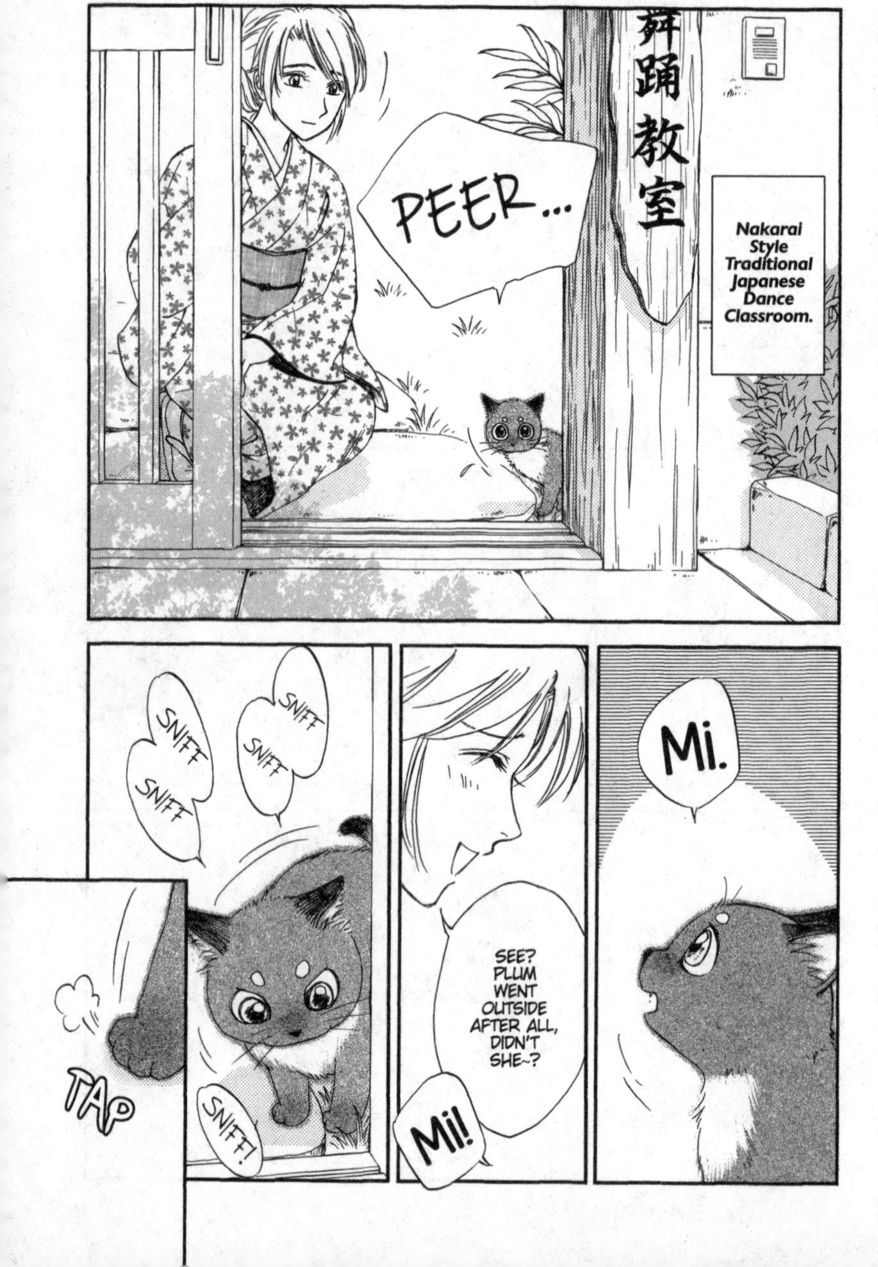
舞踊教室
Nakarai Style Traditional Japanese Dance Classroom.
PEER...
Mi.
SEE? PLUM WENT OUTSIDE AFTER ALL, DIDN'T SHE~?
Mi!
SNIFF SNIFF
SNIFF SNIFF
SNIFF!
TAP

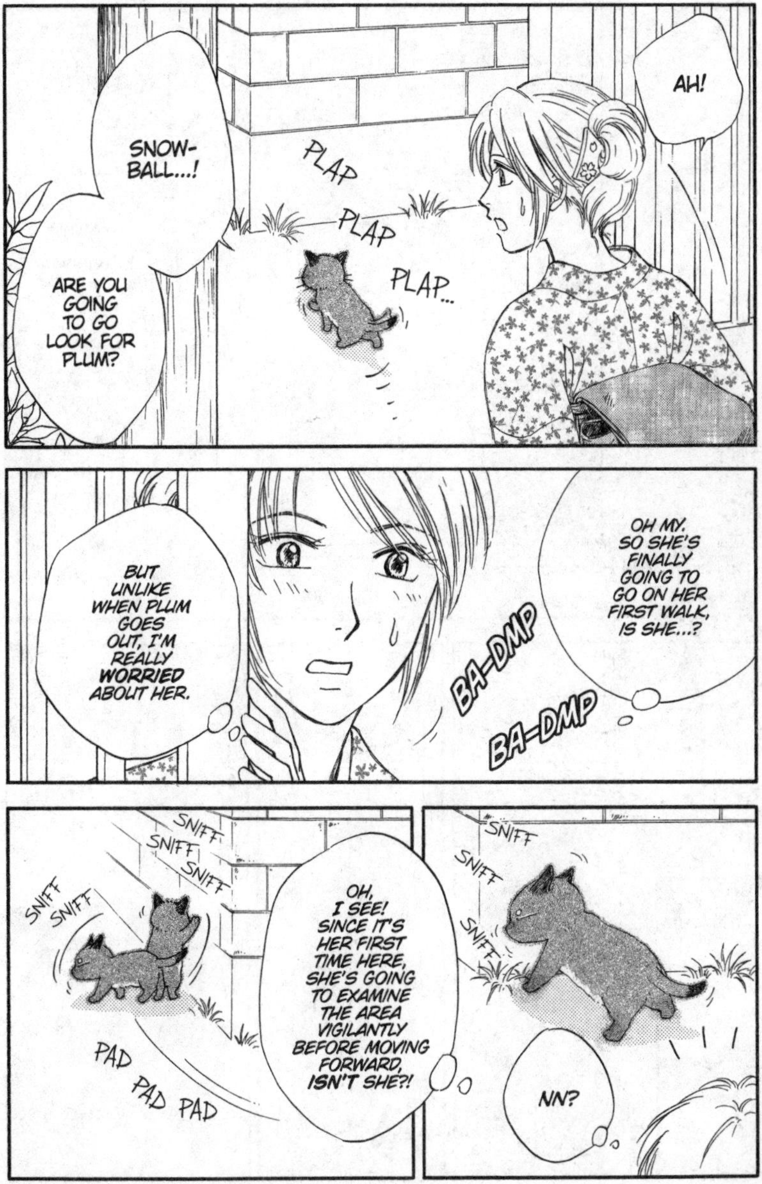
AH!
PLAP
PLAP
PLAP...
SNOW-BALL...!
ARE YOU GOING TO GO LOOK FOR PLUM?
OH MY. SO SHE'S FINALLY GOING TO GO ON HER FIRST WALK, IS SHE...?
BA-DMP
BA-DMP
BUT UNLIKE WHEN PLUM GOES OUT, I'M REALLY **WORRIED** ABOUT HER.
SNIFF
SNIFF
SNIFF
NN?
OH, I SEE! SINCE IT'S HER FIRST TIME HERE, SHE'S GOING TO EXAMINE THE AREA VIGILANTLY BEFORE MOVING FORWARD, **ISN'T SHE?!**
SNIFF
SNIFF
SNIFF
SNIFF
SNIFF
PAD
PAD PAD

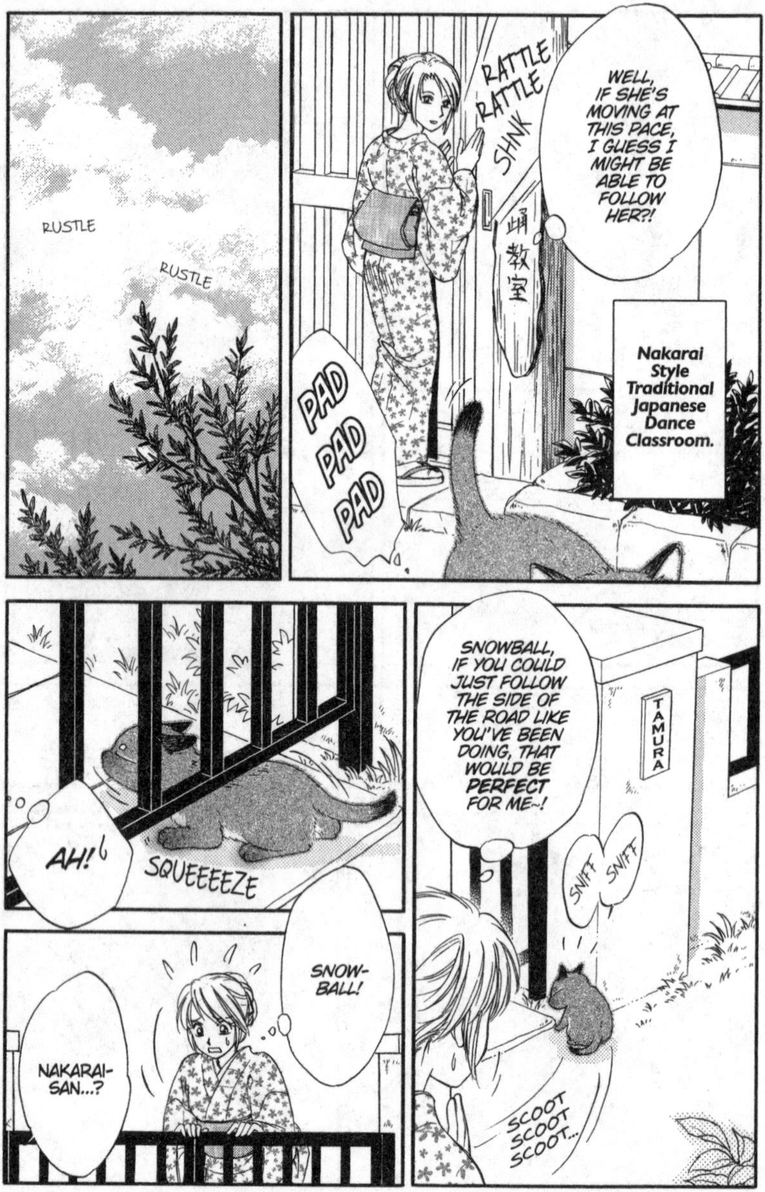
WELL, IF SHE'S MOVING AT THIS PACE, I GUESS I MIGHT BE ABLE TO FOLLOW HER?!
RATTLE RATTLE
SHNK
Nakarai Style Traditional Japanese Dance Classroom.
PAD PAD PAD
RUSTLE
RUSTLE
SNOWBALL, IF YOU COULD JUST FOLLOW THE SIDE OF THE ROAD LIKE YOU'VE BEEN DOING, THAT WOULD BE PERFECT FOR ME~!
TAMURA
SNIFF SNIFF
SCOOT SCOOT SCOOT...
AH!
SQUEEEEZE
SNOW-BALL!
NAKARAI-SAN...?

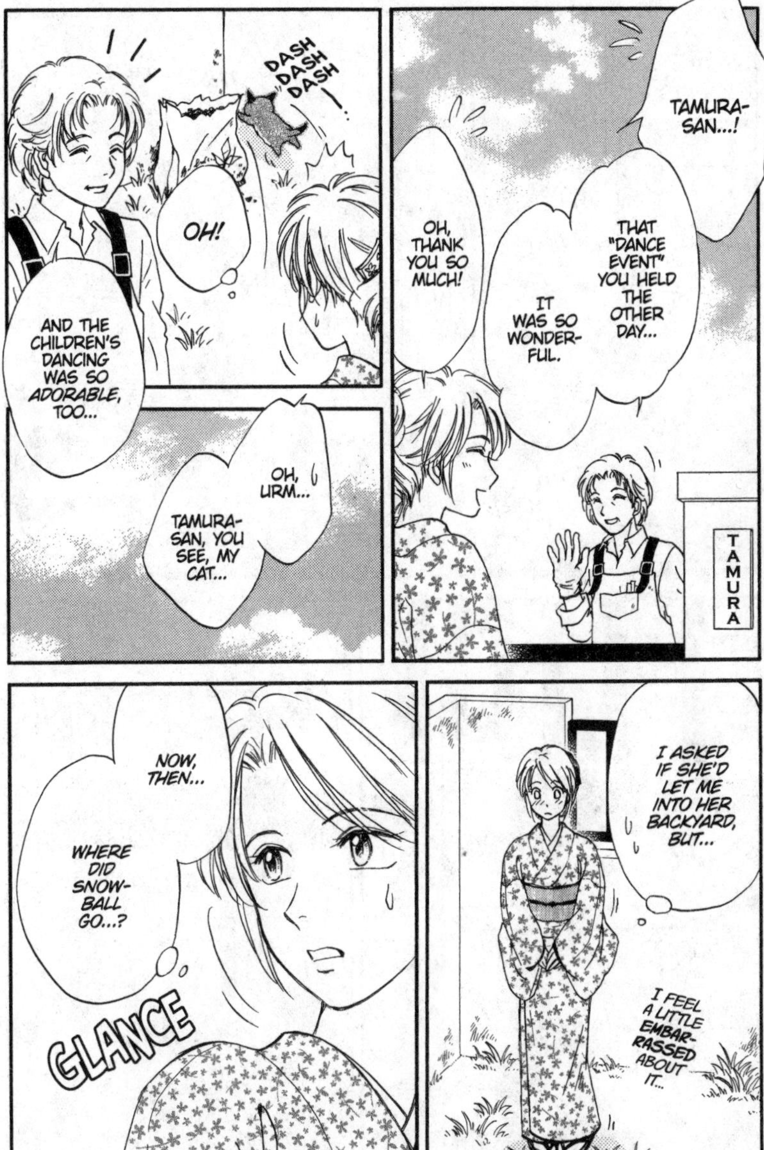
TAMURA-SAN...!
THAT "DANCE EVENT" YOU HELD THE OTHER DAY...
IT WAS SO WONDERFUL.
OH, THANK YOU SO MUCH!
TAMURA
DASH DASH DASH
OH!
AND THE CHILDREN'S DANCING WAS SO ADORABLE, TOO...
OH, URM...
TAMURA-SAN, YOU SEE, MY CAT...
I ASKED IF SHE'D LET ME INTO HER BACKYARD, BUT...
I FEEL A LITTLE EMBARRASSED ABOUT IT...
NOW, THEN...
WHERE DID SNOWBALL GO...?
GLANCE

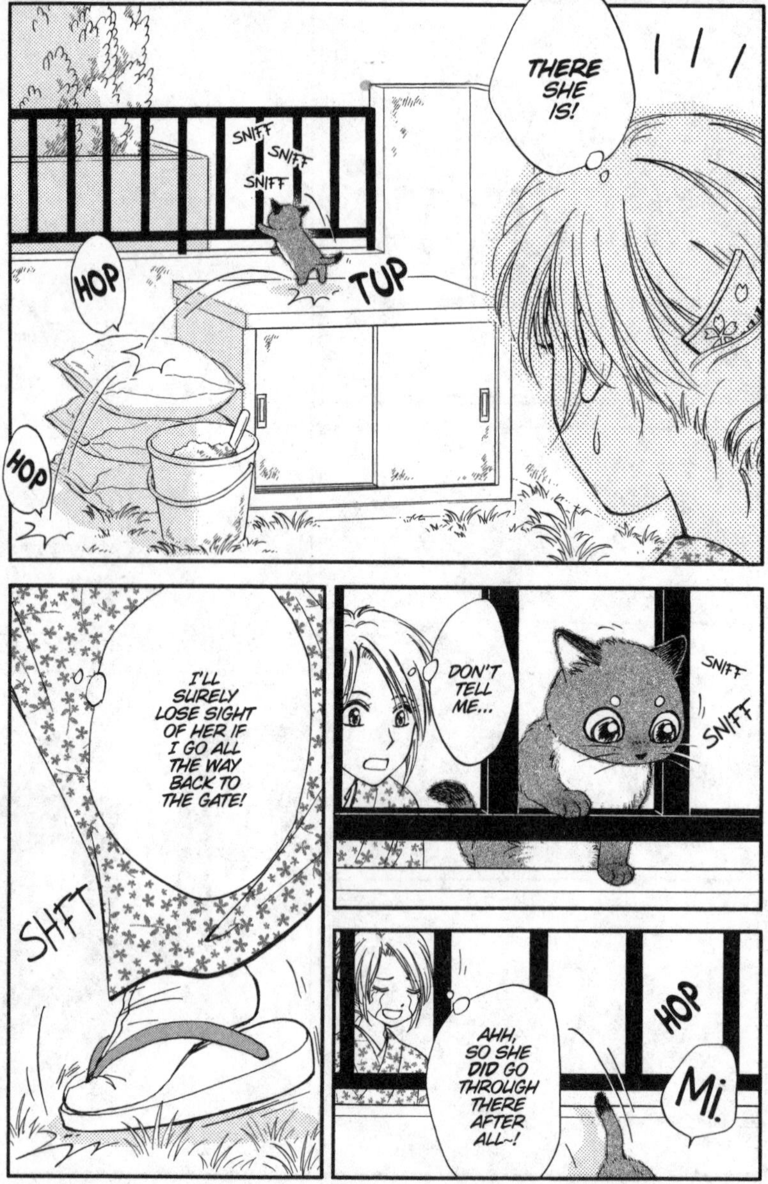
THERE SHE IS!
SNIFF
SNIFF
SNIFF
TUP
HOP
HOP
SNIFF
SNIFF
DON'T TELL ME...
HOP
Mi.
AHH, SO SHE DID GO THROUGH THERE AFTER ALL~!
I'LL SURELY LOSE SIGHT OF HER IF I GO ALL THE WAY BACK TO THE GATE!
SHFT

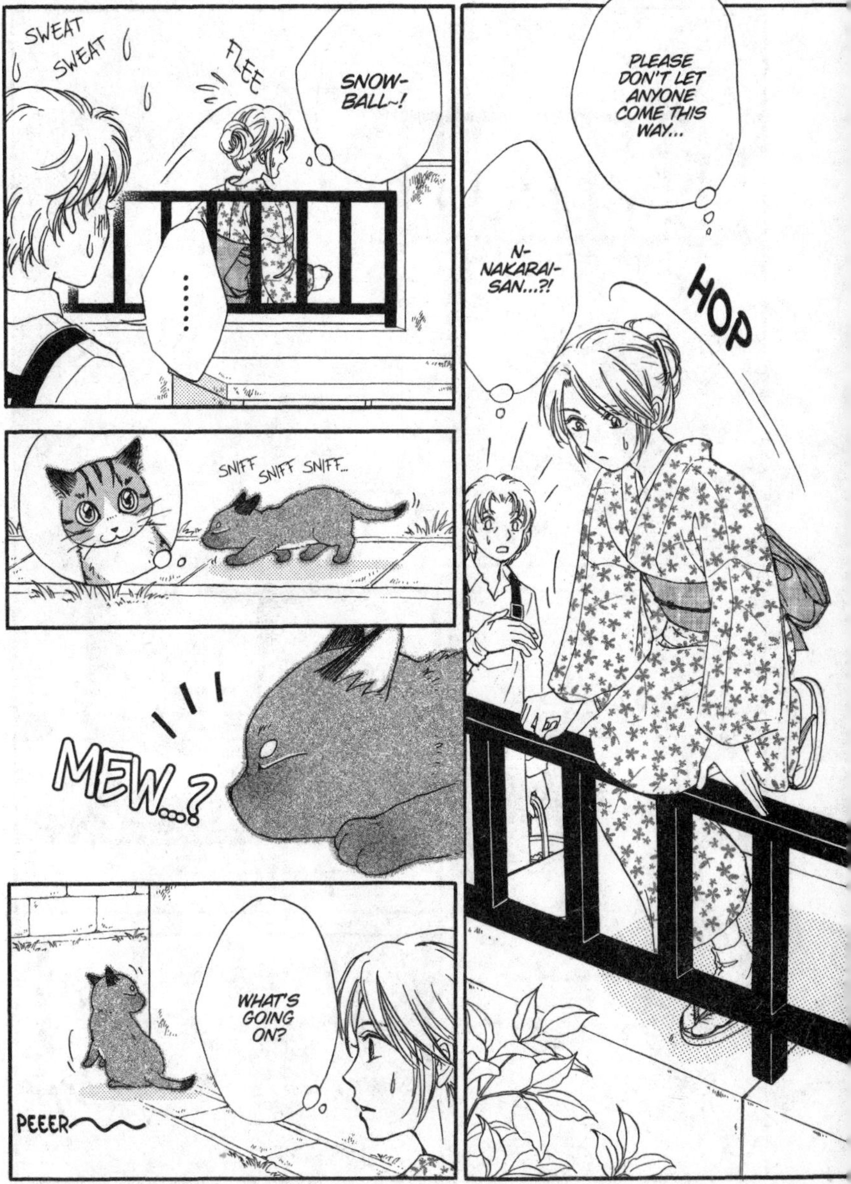
PLEASE DON'T LET ANYONE COME THIS WAY...
HOP
N-NAKARAI-SAN...?!
SNOW-BALL~!
FLEE
SWEAT SWEAT
......
SNIFF SNIFF SNIFF...
MEW...?
WHAT'S GOING ON?
PEEER~~

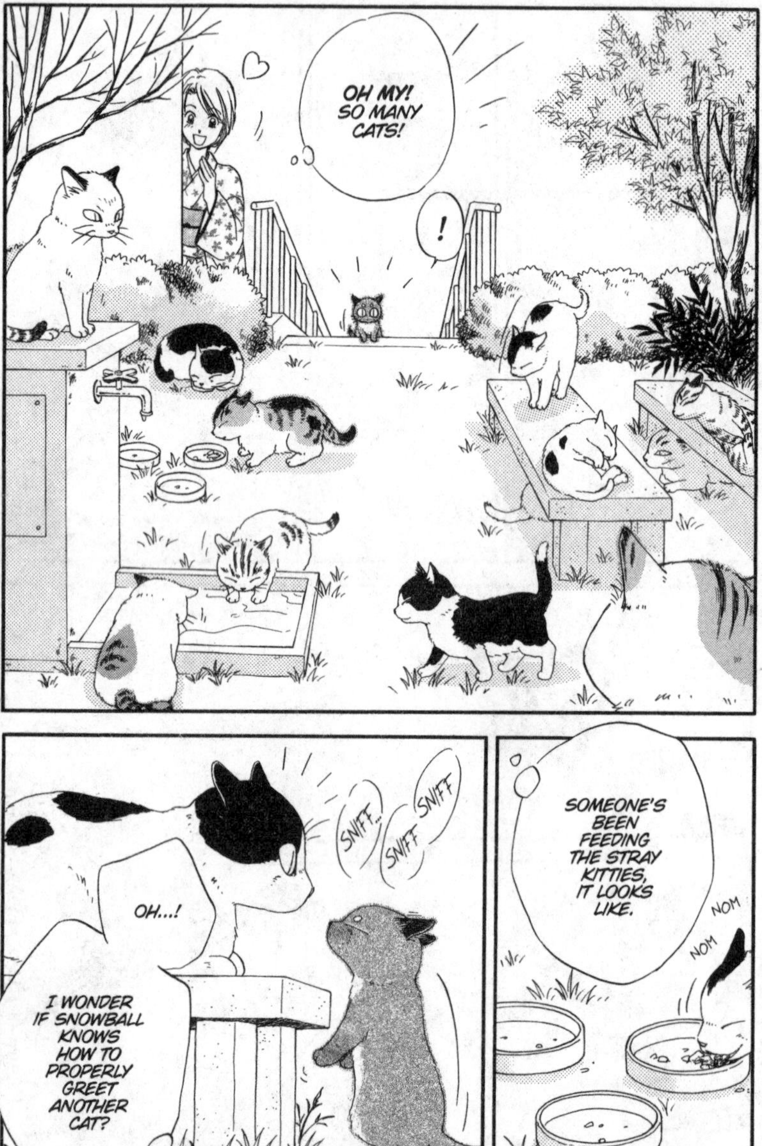
OH MY! SO MANY CATS!
!
SOMEONE'S BEEN FEEDING THE STRAY KITTIES, IT LOOKS LIKE.
NOM
NOM
SNIFF...
SNIFF
SNIFF
OH...!
I WONDER IF SNOWBALL KNOWS HOW TO PROPERLY GREET ANOTHER CAT?

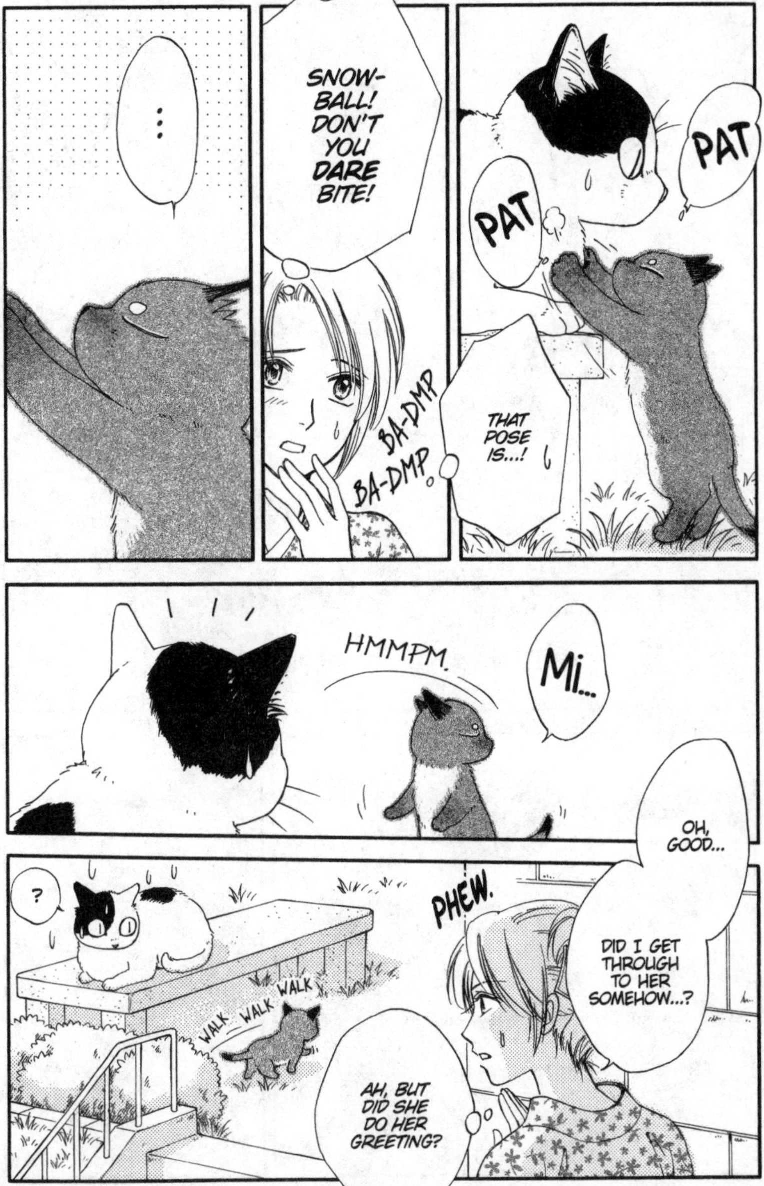
PAT
PAT
THAT POSE IS...!
SNOW-BALL! DON'T YOU DARE BITE!
BA-DMP
BA-DMP
...
Mi...
HMMPM.
OH, GOOD...
DID I GET THROUGH TO HER SOMEHOW...?
PHEW.
AH, BUT DID SHE DO HER GREETING?
WALK
WALK
WALK
?

EH ?!
PAT
HOP
PAT
NYAH!
PAT
PAT
PAT
NYAH?!
PAT
WHAT ARE YOU DOING, SNOWBALL? IS THAT SUPPOSED TO BE A GREETING?!
FLUTTER
FLUTTER
FUU...

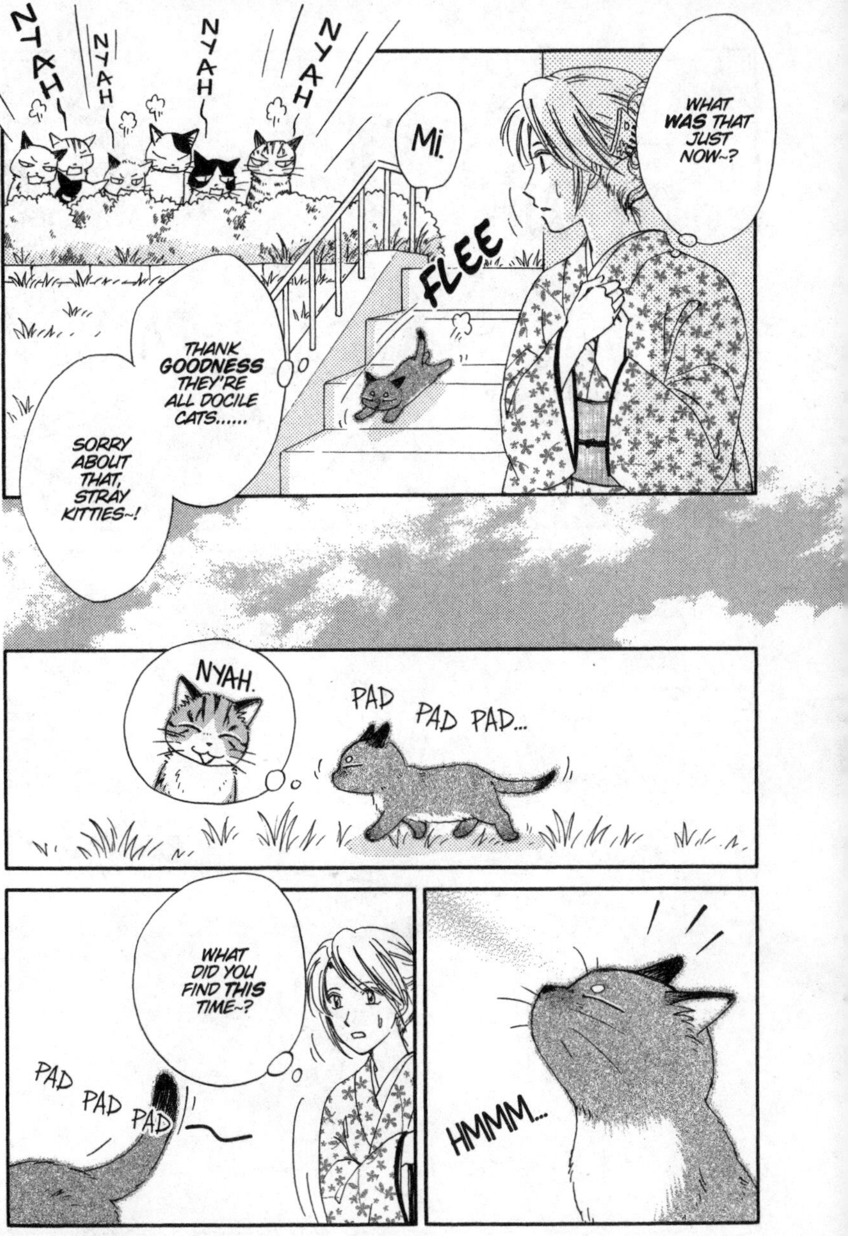

WHAT WAS THAT JUST NOW~?
NYAH~
Mi.
NYAH~
NYAH~
NYAH~
FLEE
THANK GOODNESS THEY'RE ALL DOCILE CATS......
SORRY ABOUT THAT, STRAY KITTIES~!
NYAH.
PAD PAD PAD...
HMMM...
WHAT DID YOU FIND THIS TIME~?
PAD PAD PAD

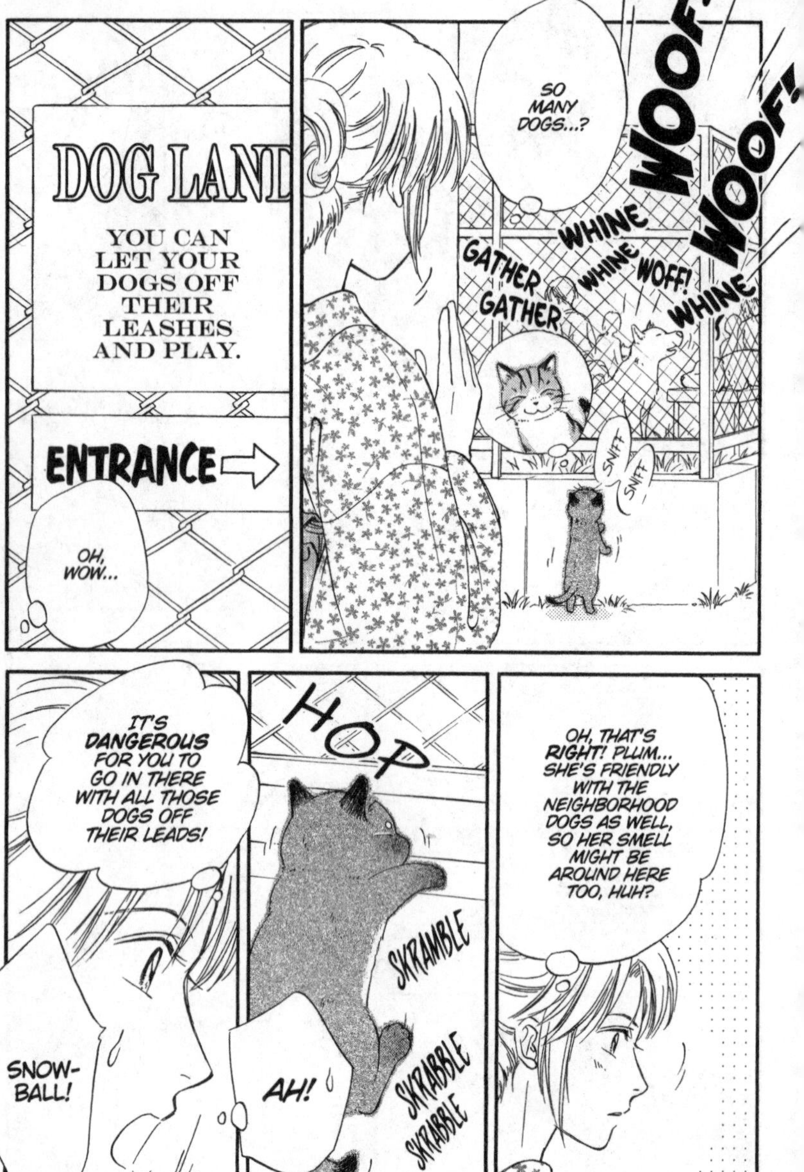
WOOF!
WOOF!
SO MANY DOGS...?
WHINE
WHINE
WOFF!
WHINE
GATHER GATHER
SNIFF
SNIFF
DOG LAND
YOU CAN LET YOUR DOGS OFF THEIR LEASHES AND PLAY.
ENTRANCE
OH, WOW...
OH, THAT'S RIGHT! PLUM... SHE'S FRIENDLY WITH THE NEIGHBORHOOD DOGS AS WELL, SO HER SMELL MIGHT BE AROUND HERE TOO, HUH?
HOP
SKRAMBLE
SKRABBLE
SKRABBLE
AH!
IT'S DANGEROUS FOR YOU TO GO IN THERE WITH ALL THOSE DOGS OFF THEIR LEADS!
SNOW-BALL!

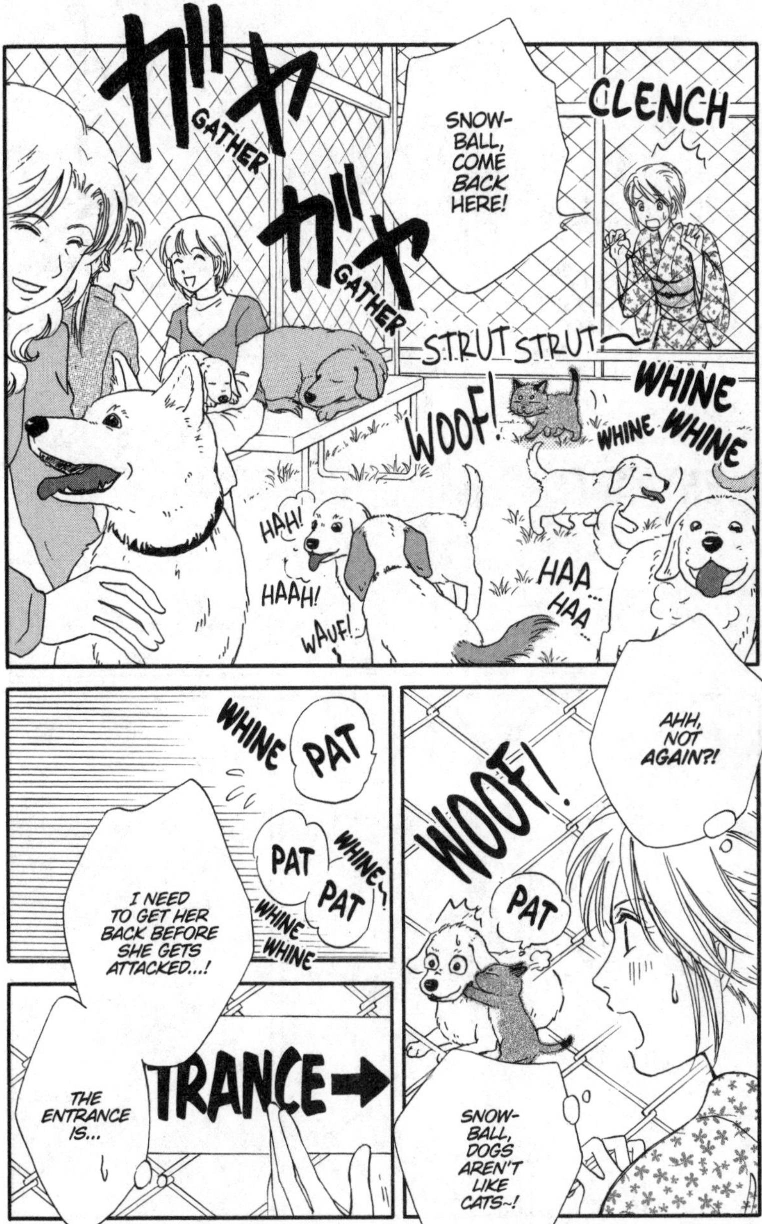
CLENCH
SNOW-BALL, COME BACK HERE!
ガヤ
GATHER
ガヤ
GATHER
STRUT STRUT
WHINE WHINE WHINE
WOOF!
HAH!
HAAH!
WAUF!
HAA... HAA...
AHH, NOT AGAIN?!
WOOF!
PAT
SNOW-BALL, DOGS AREN'T LIKE CATS~!
WHINE
PAT
PAT
WHINE~
PAT
WHINE WHINE
I NEED TO GET HER BACK BEFORE SHE GETS ATTACKED...!
TRANCE
THE ENTRANCE IS...

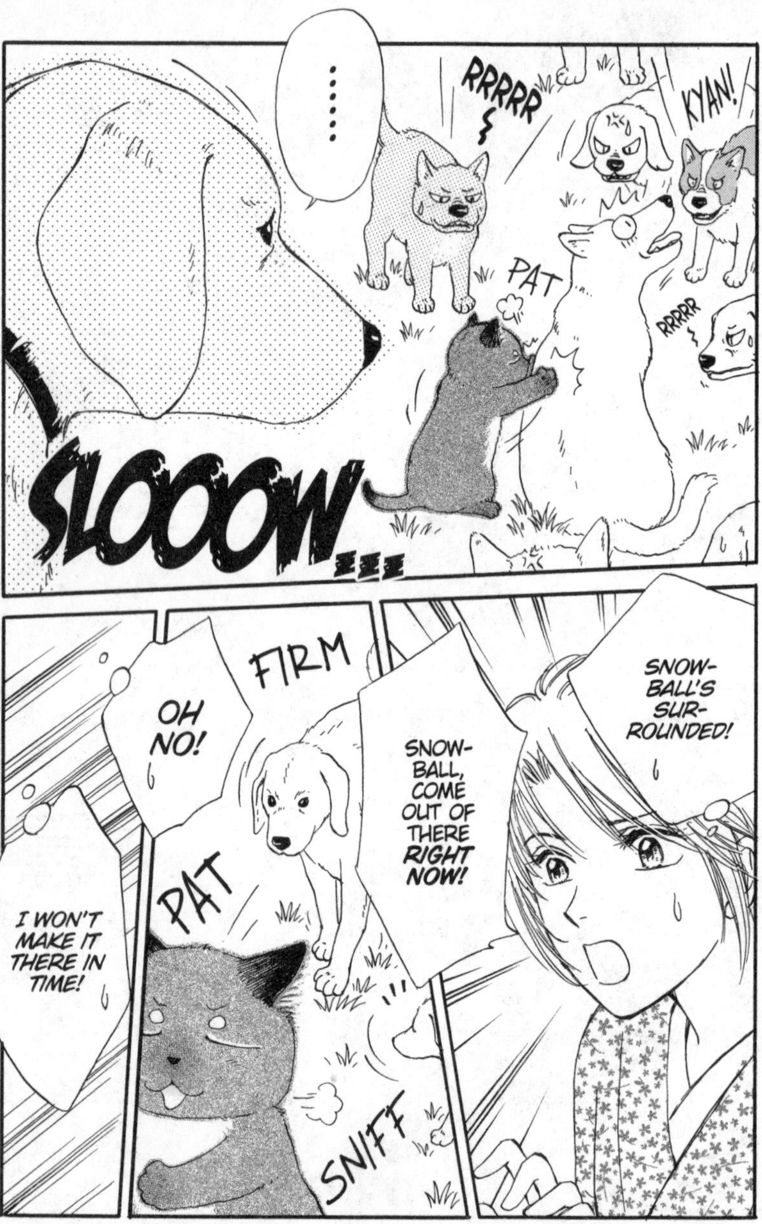
KYAN!
RRRRRR
......
PAT
RRRRR
SLOOOW
SNOW-BALL'S SUR-ROUNDED!
SNOW-BALL, COME OUT OF THERE RIGHT NOW!
FIRM
PAT
SNIFF
OH NO!
I WON'T MAKE IT THERE IN TIME!

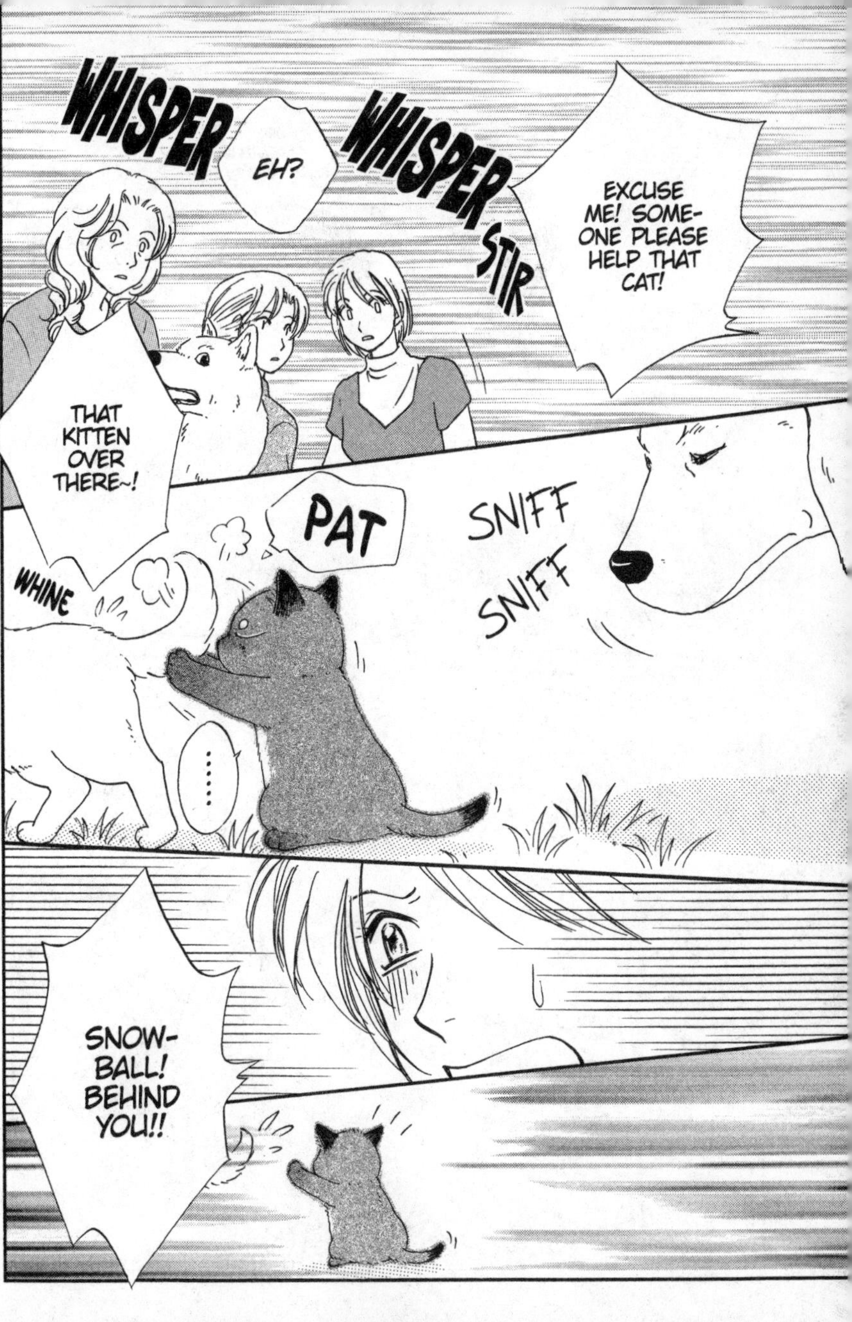
EXCUSE ME! SOME-ONE PLEASE HELP THAT CAT!
WHISPER
STIR
EH?
WHISPER
THAT KITTEN OVER THERE~!
SNIFF
SNIFF
PAT
WHINE
......
SNOW-BALL! BEHIND YOU!!

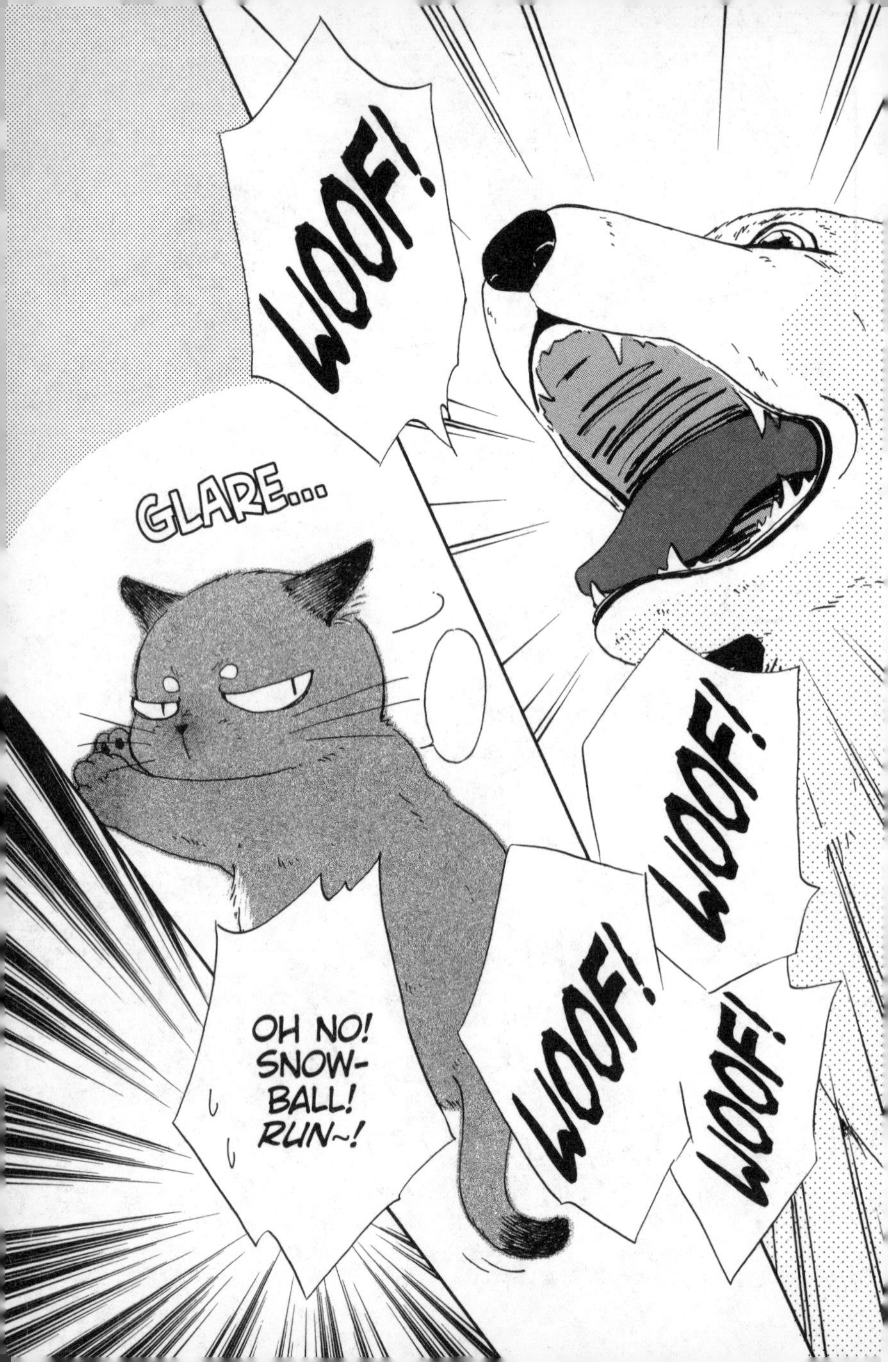
WOOF!
GLARE...
WOOF!
WOOF!
WOOF!
OH NO! SNOW-BALL! RUN~!

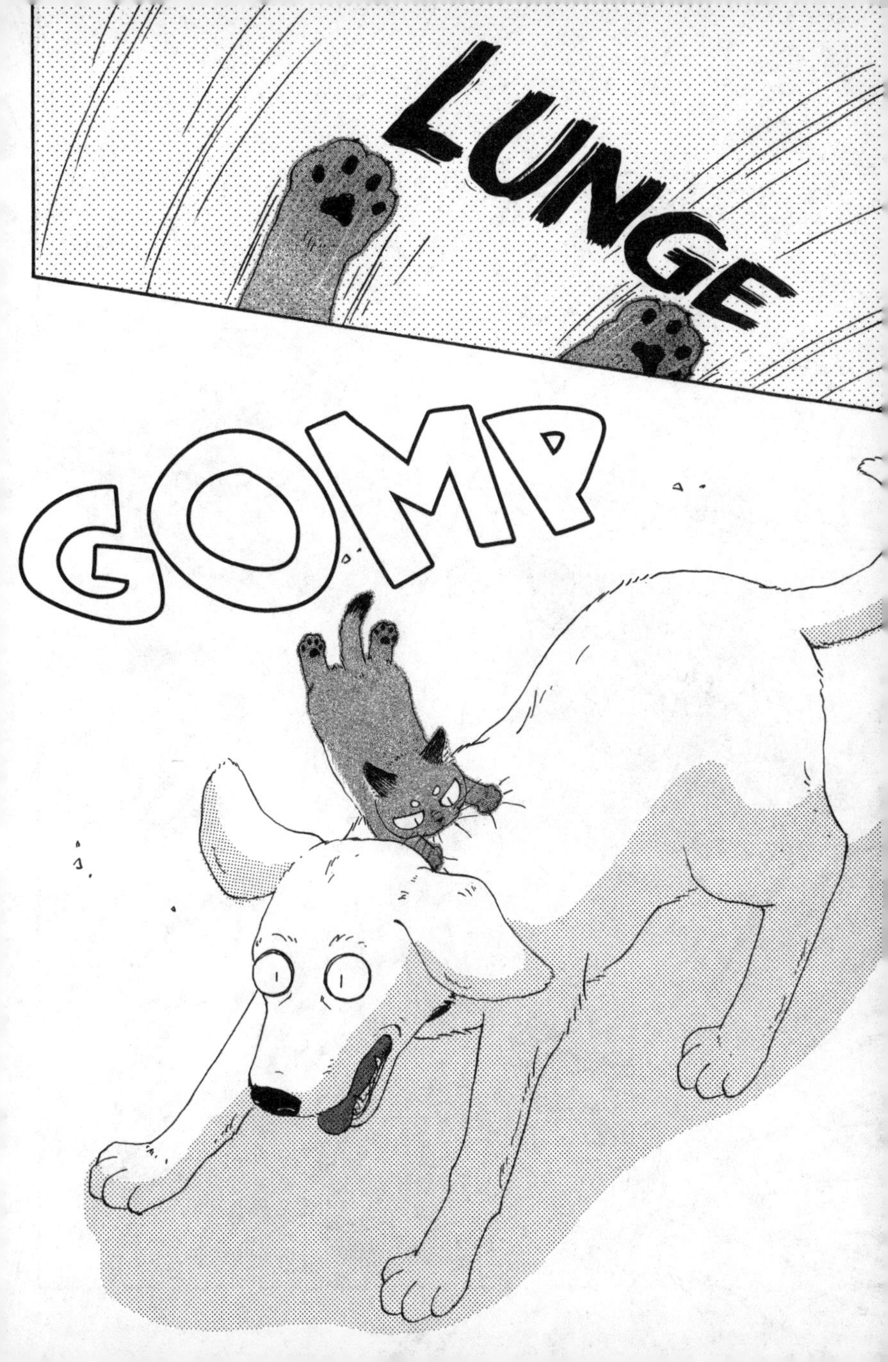
LUNGE
GOMP

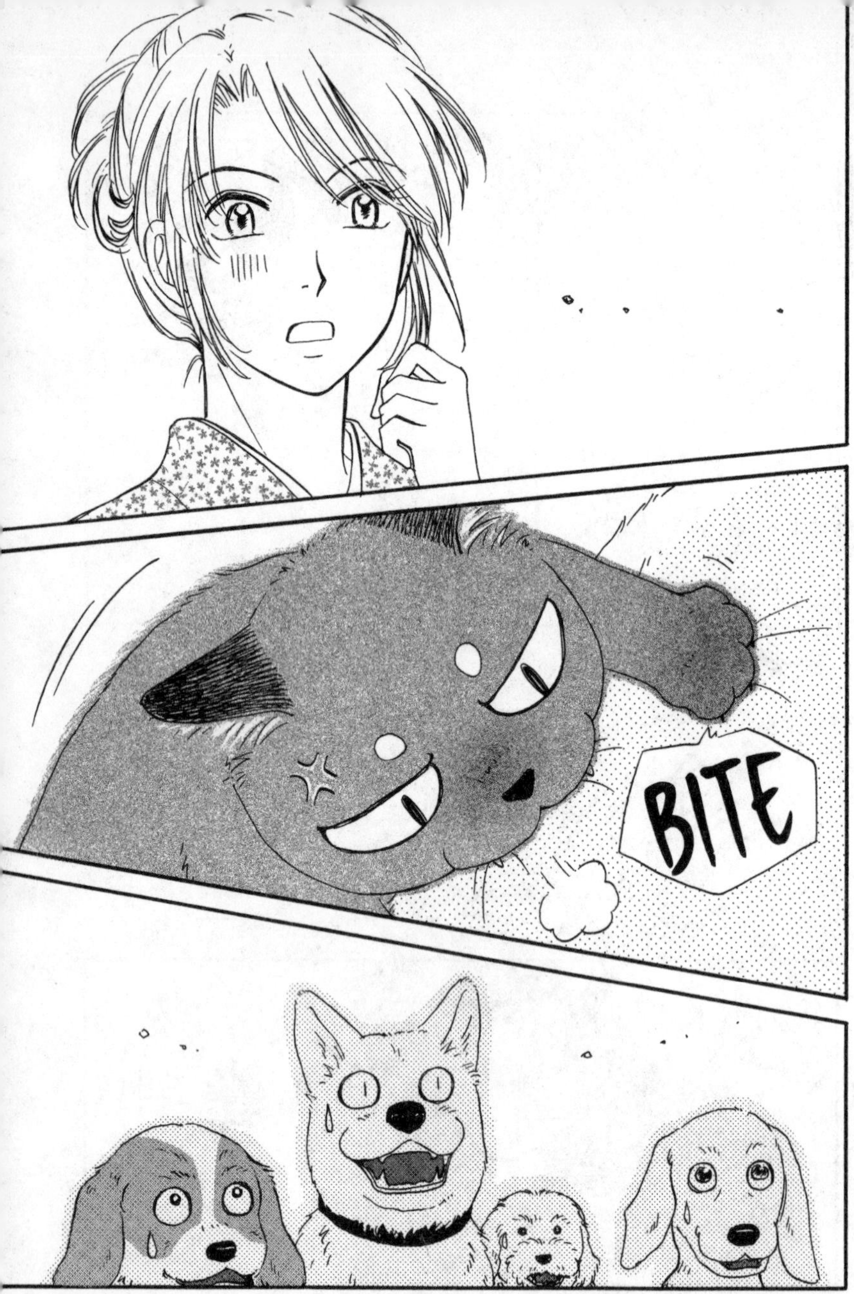
BITE

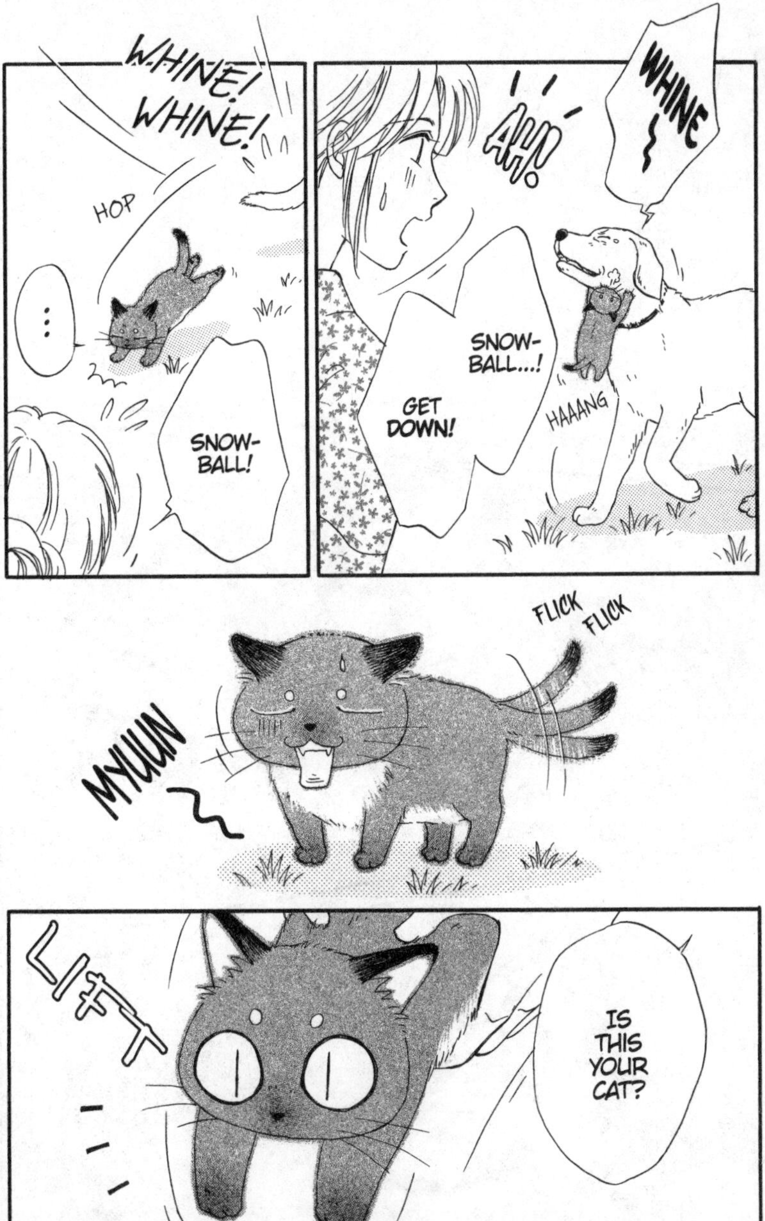
WHINE ~
AH!?
SNOW-BALL...!
HAAANG
GET DOWN!
WHINE! WHINE!
HOP
...
SNOW-BALL!
FLICK FLICK
MYUUN
IS THIS YOUR CAT?
LIFT

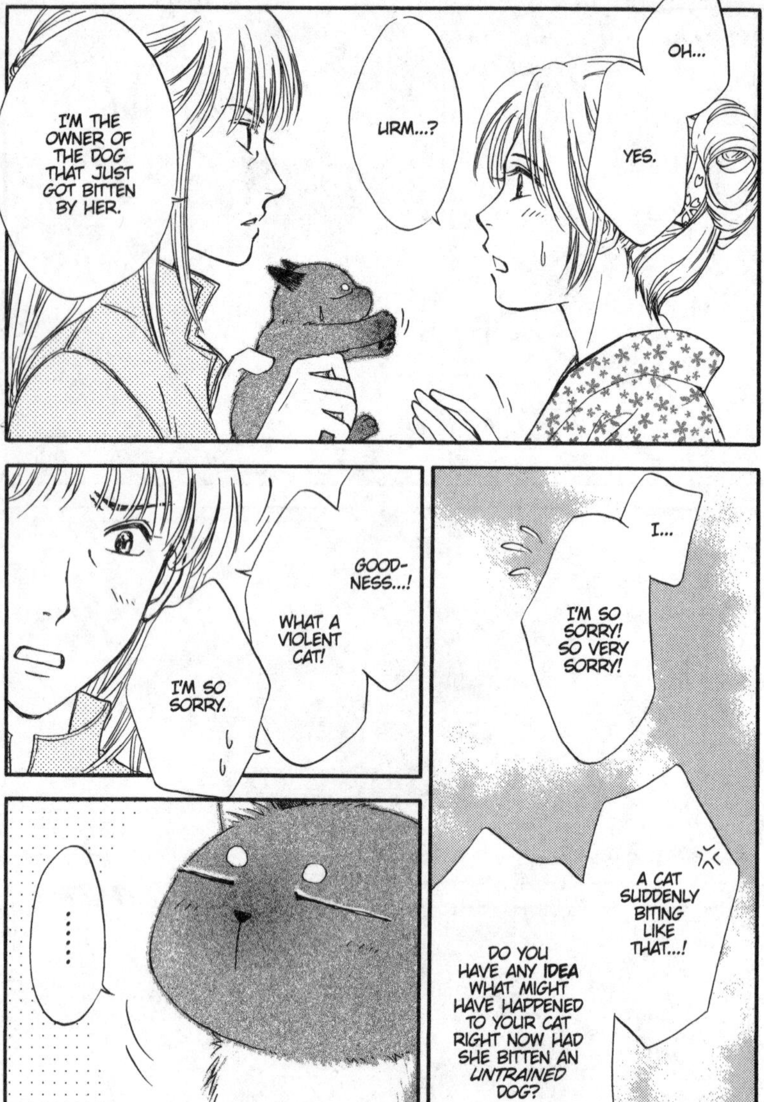
OH...
YES.
URM...?
I'M THE OWNER OF THE DOG THAT JUST GOT BITTEN BY HER.
I...
I'M SO SORRY! SO VERY SORRY!
A CAT SUDDENLY BITING LIKE THAT...!
DO YOU HAVE ANY IDEA WHAT MIGHT HAVE HAPPENED TO YOUR CAT RIGHT NOW HAD SHE BITTEN AN *UNTRAINED* DOG?
GOOD-NESS...!
WHAT A VIOLENT CAT!
I'M SO SORRY.
......

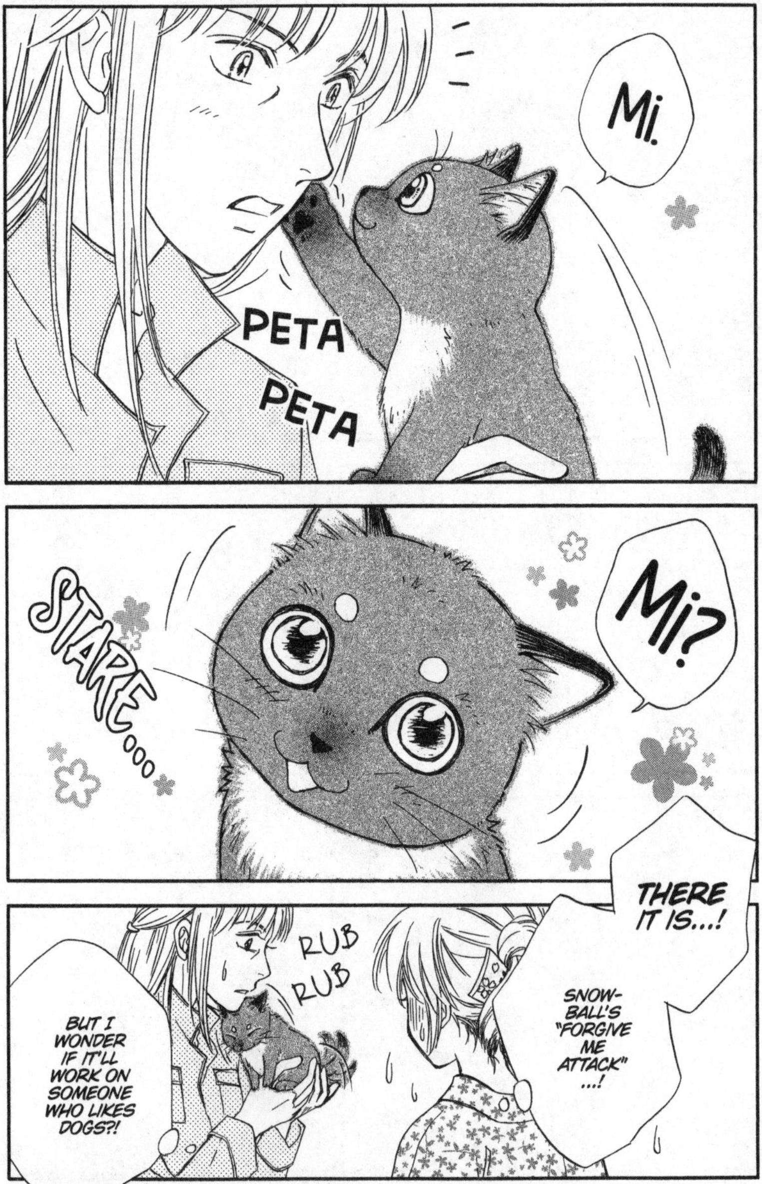
Mi.
PETA PETA
Mi?
STARE...
THERE IT IS...!
SNOW-BALL'S "FORGIVE ME ATTACK"...!
RUB RUB
BUT I WONDER IF IT'LL WORK ON SOMEONE WHO LIKES DOGS?!

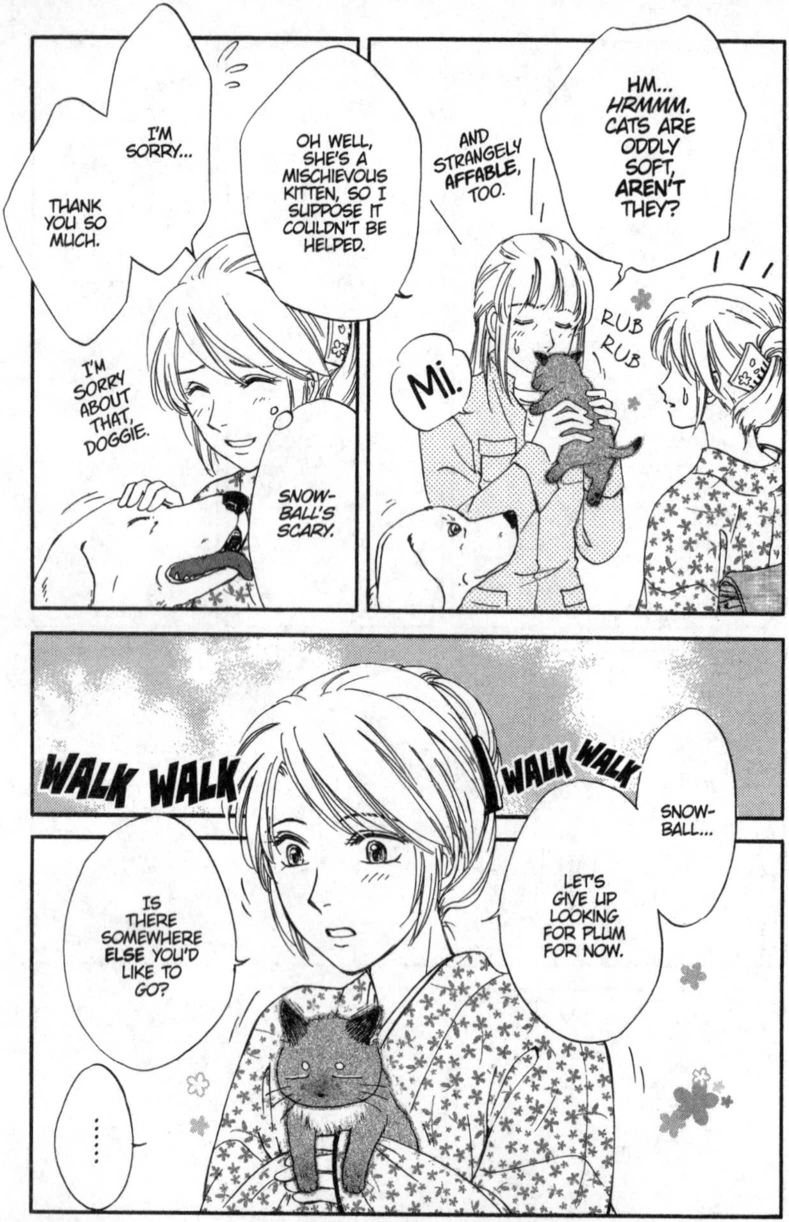
HM... HRMMM. CATS ARE ODDLY SOFT, AREN'T THEY?
AND STRANGELY AFFABLE, TOO.
RUB RUB
Mi.
OH WELL, SHE'S A MISCHIEVOUS KITTEN, SO I SUPPOSE IT COULDN'T BE HELPED.
I'M SORRY... THANK YOU SO MUCH.
I'M SORRY ABOUT THAT, DOGGIE.
SNOW-BALL'S SCARY.
WALK WALK
WALK WALK
SNOW-BALL... LET'S GIVE UP LOOKING FOR PLUM FOR NOW.
IS THERE SOMEWHERE ELSE YOU'D LIKE TO GO?
......

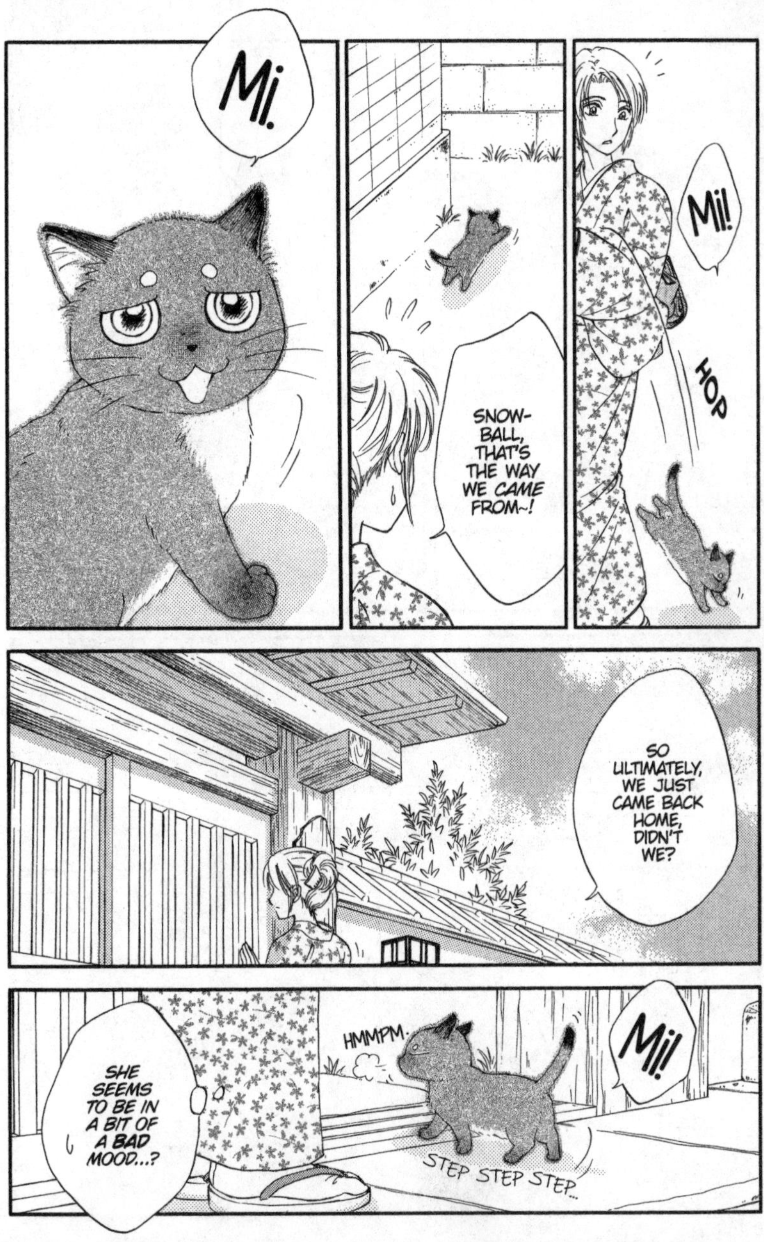
Mi!
HOP
SNOW-BALL, THAT'S THE WAY WE CAME FROM~!
Mi.
SO ULTIMATELY, WE JUST CAME BACK HOME, DIDN'T WE?
Mi!
HMMPM.
STEP STEP STEP...
SHE SEEMS TO BE IN A BIT OF A BAD MOOD...?

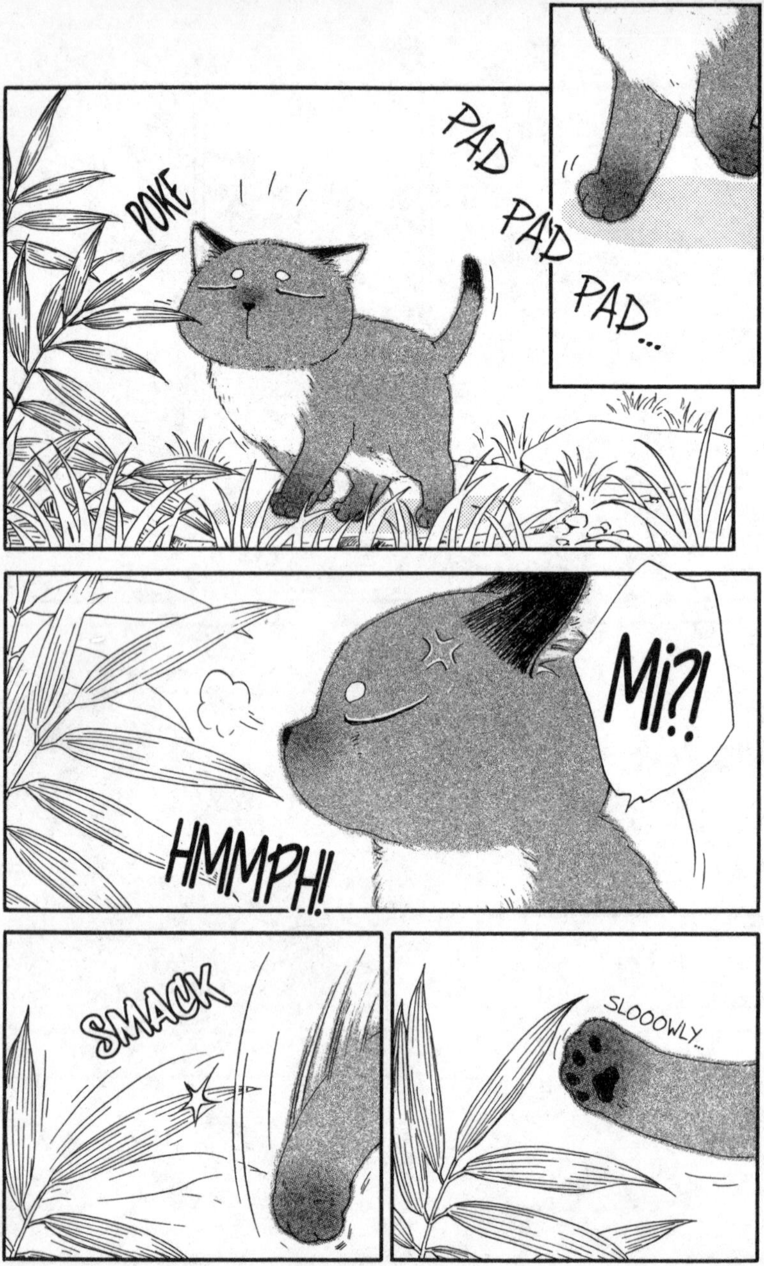
PAD
PAD
PAD...
POKE
Mi?!
HMMPH!
SLOOOWLY...
SMACK

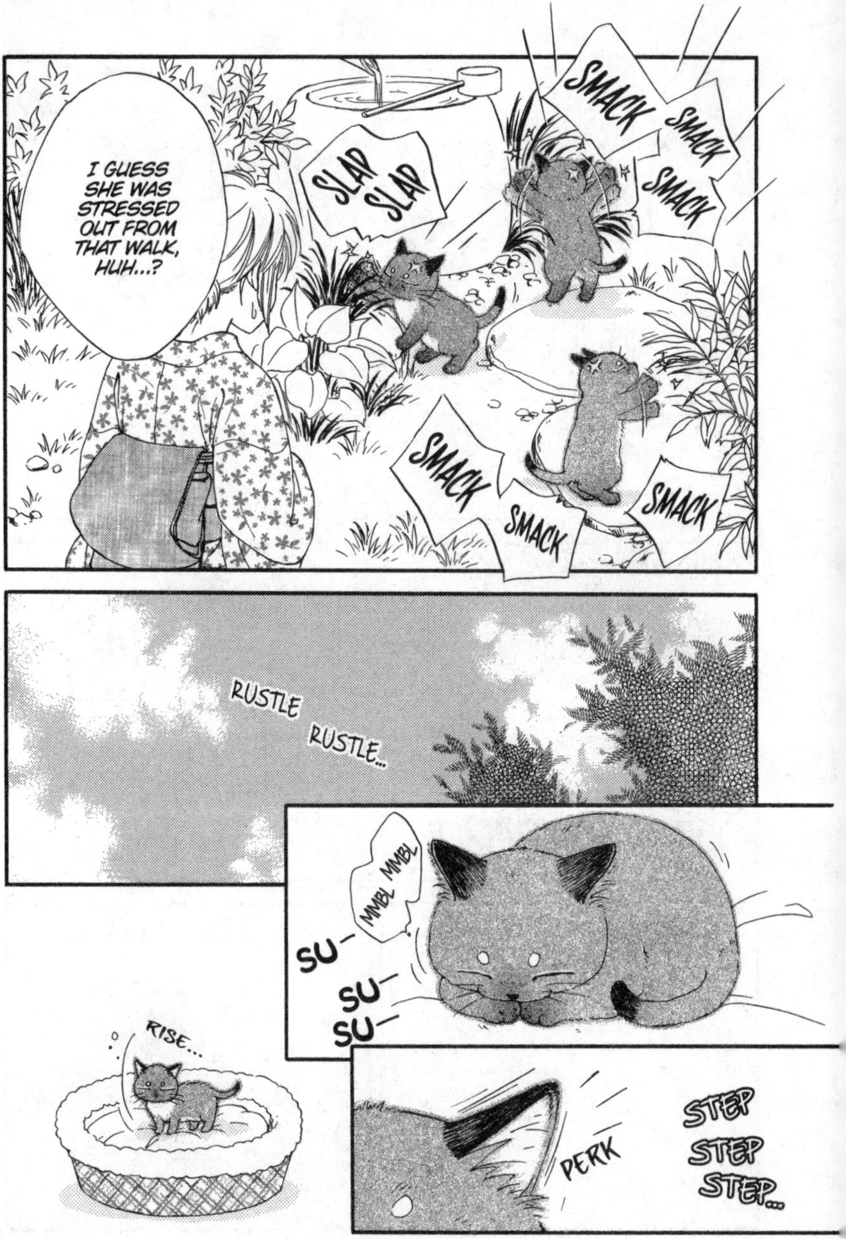
SMACK
SMACK
SMACK
SLAP SLAP
I GUESS SHE WAS STRESSED OUT FROM THAT WALK, HUH...?
SMACK
SMACK
SMACK
RUSTLE
RUSTLE...
MMBL MMBL
SU—
SU—
SU—
RISE...
STEP
STEP
STEP...
PERK

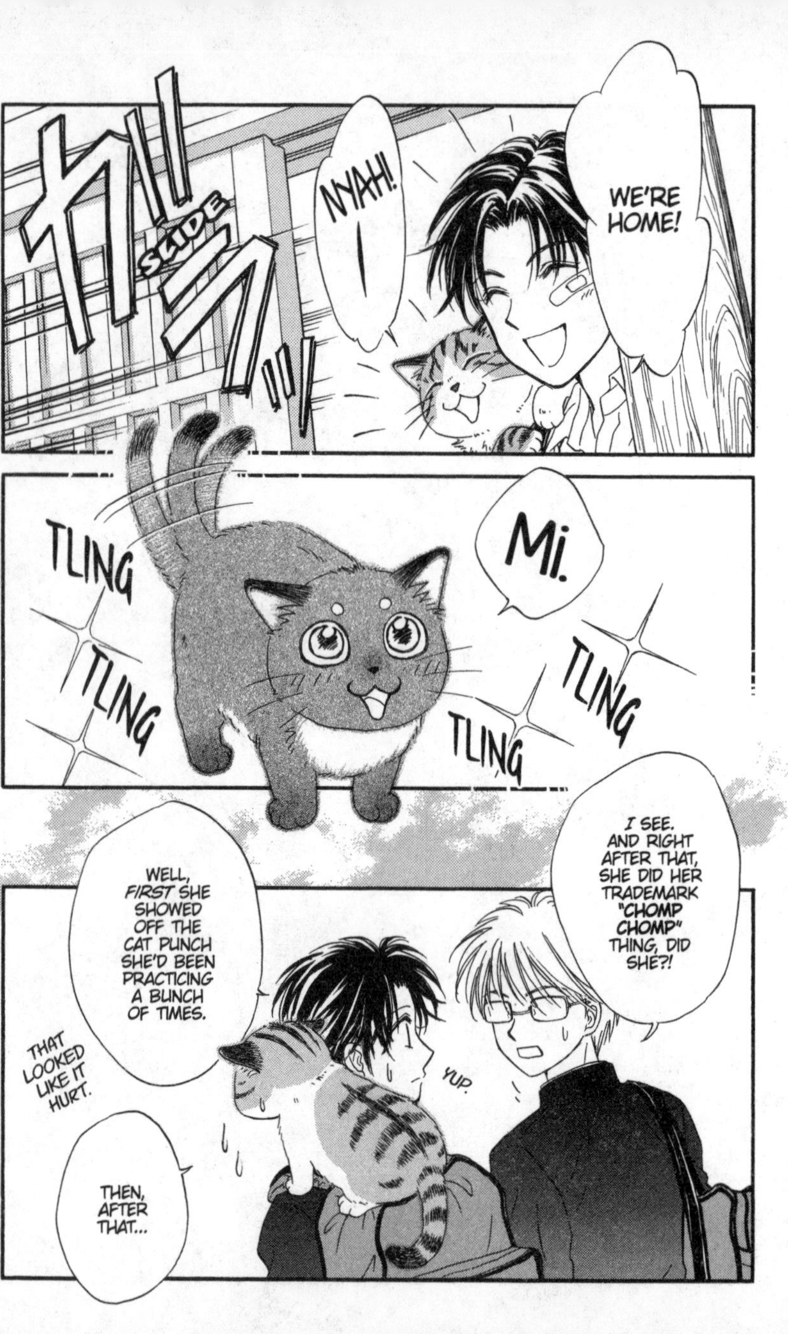
WE'RE HOME!
NYAH!
SLIDE
Mi.
TLING
TLING
TLING
TLING
I SEE. AND RIGHT AFTER THAT, SHE DID HER TRADEMARK "CHOMP CHOMP" THING, DID SHE?!
WELL, *FIRST* SHE SHOWED OFF THE CAT PUNCH SHE'D BEEN PRACTICING A BUNCH OF TIMES.
YUP.
THAT LOOKED LIKE IT HURT.
THEN, AFTER THAT...

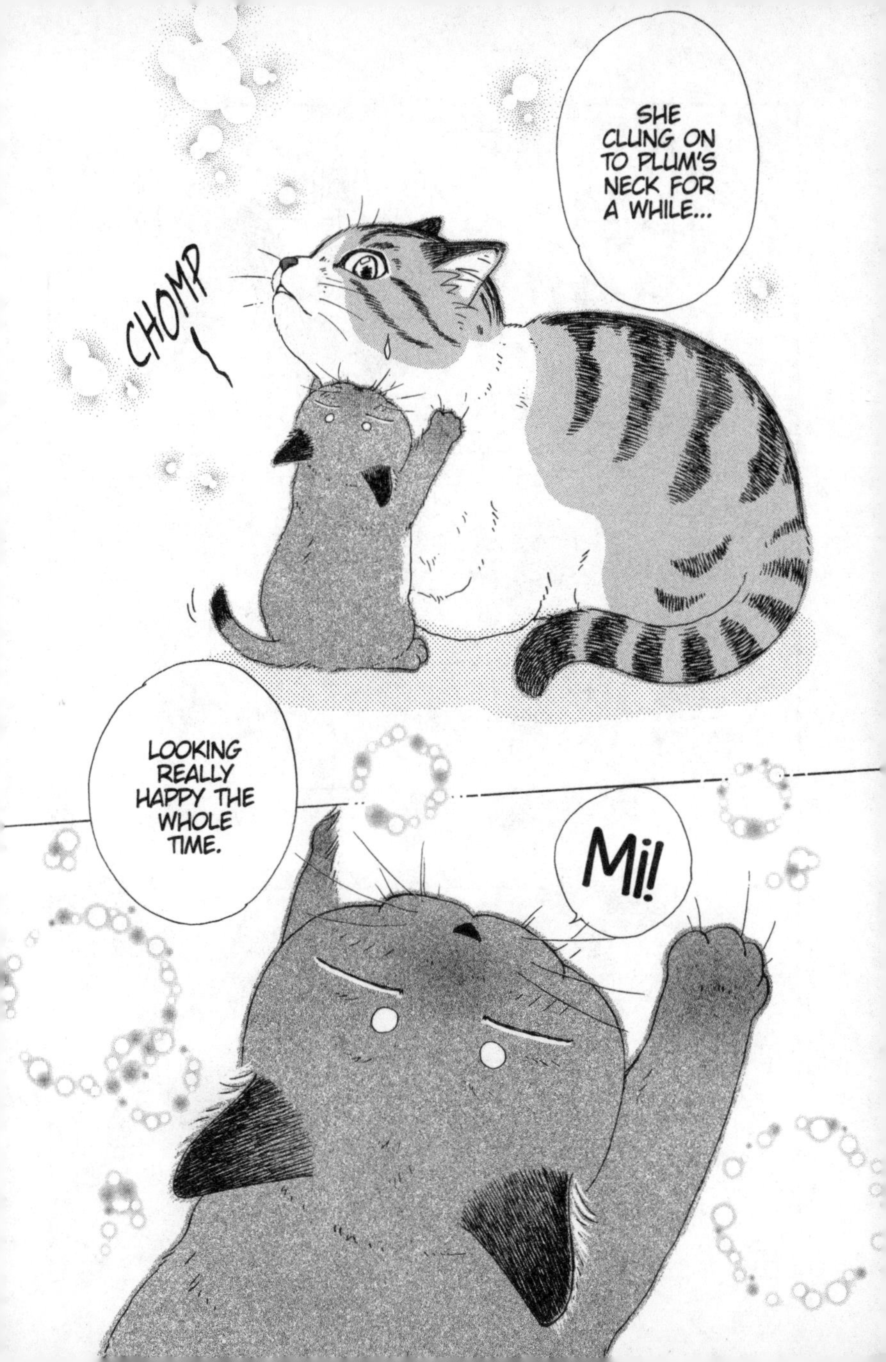
SHE CLUNG ON TO PLUM'S NECK FOR A WHILE...
CHOMP
LOOKING REALLY HAPPY THE WHOLE TIME.
Mi!

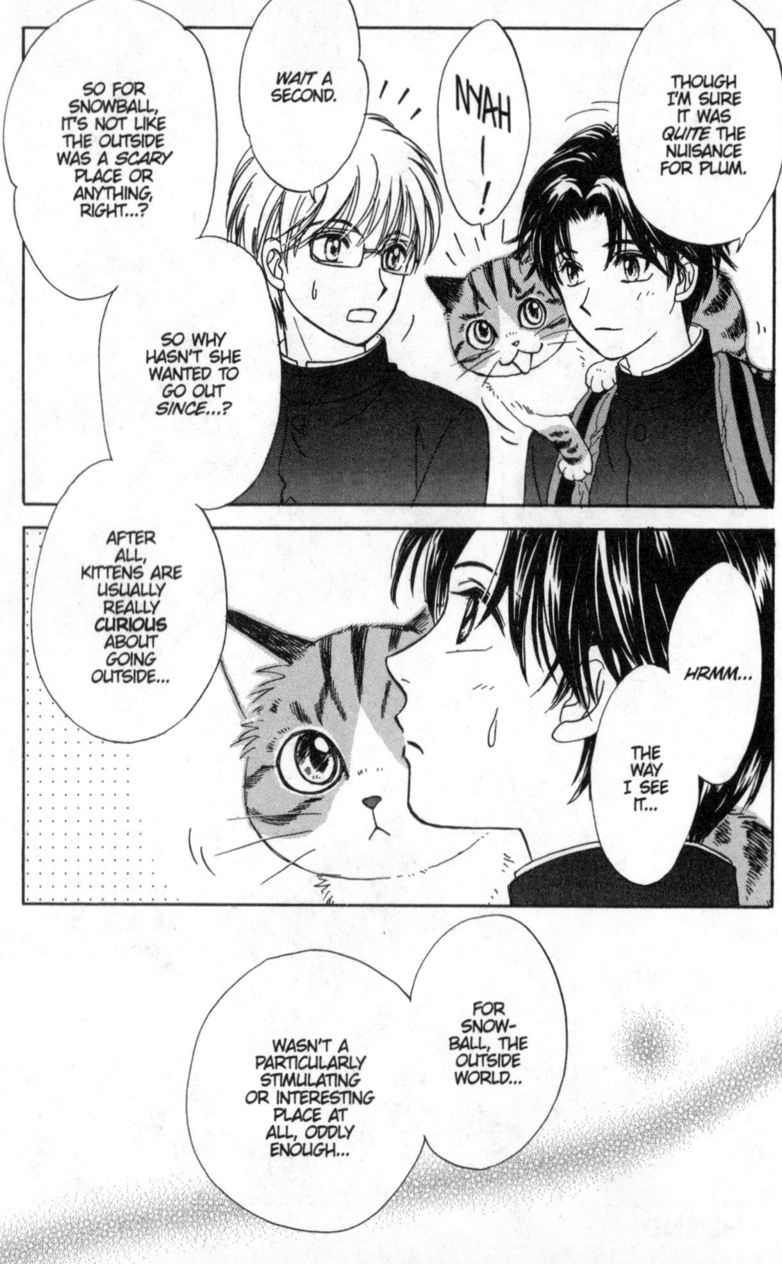
THOUGH I'M SURE IT WAS *QUITE* THE NUISANCE FOR PLUM.
NYAH!!
WAIT A SECOND.
SO FOR SNOWBALL, IT'S NOT LIKE THE OUTSIDE WAS A *SCARY* PLACE OR ANYTHING, RIGHT...?
SO WHY HASN'T SHE WANTED TO GO OUT *SINCE*...?
AFTER ALL, KITTENS ARE USUALLY REALLY **CURIOUS** ABOUT GOING OUTSIDE...
HRMM...
THE WAY I SEE IT...
FOR SNOW-BALL, THE OUTSIDE WORLD...
WASN'T A PARTICULARLY STIMULATING OR INTERESTING PLACE AT ALL, ODDLY ENOUGH...

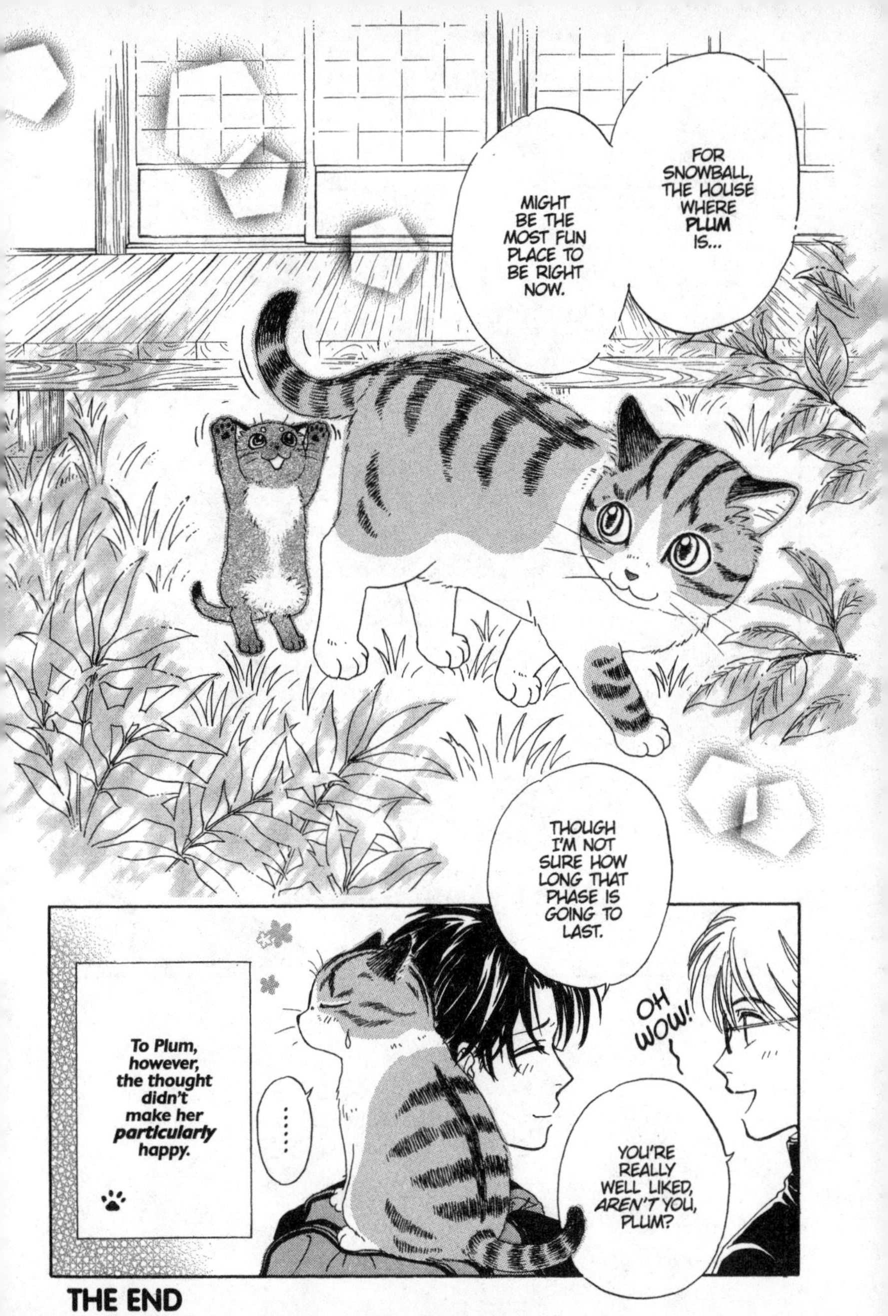
FOR SNOWBALL, THE HOUSE WHERE **PLUM** IS...
MIGHT BE THE MOST FUN PLACE TO BE RIGHT NOW.
THOUGH I'M NOT SURE HOW LONG THAT PHASE IS GOING TO LAST.
OH WOW!!
YOU'RE REALLY WELL LIKED, *AREN'T* YOU, PLUM?
......
To Plum, however, the thought didn't make her ***particularly*** happy.

THE END

OMAKE PAGE

HOW TO PROPERLY USE A TUB

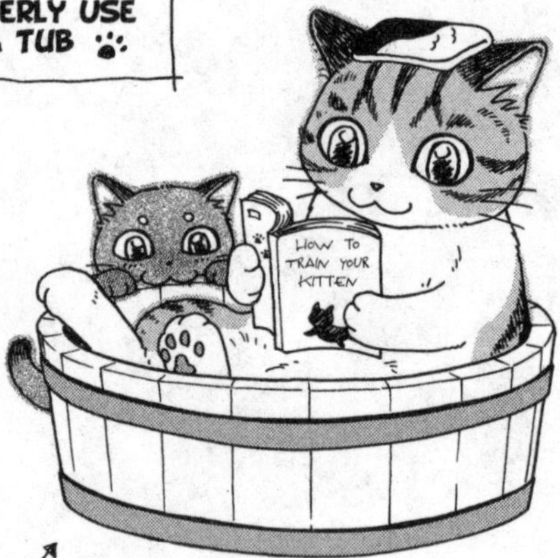
HOW TO TRAIN YOUR KITTEN

Back cover illustration from the "Very First Autumn" volume of *Neko Panchi*

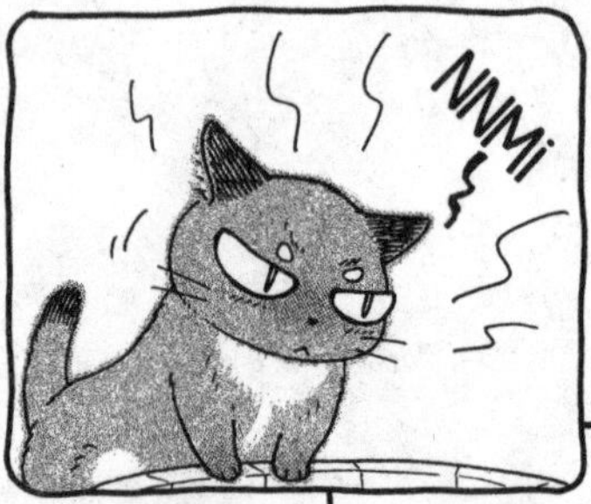
NNMi

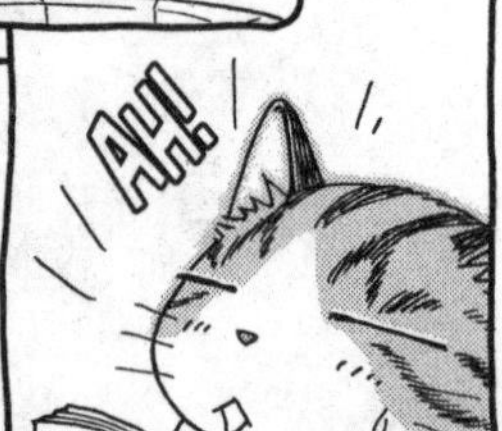
AH!?

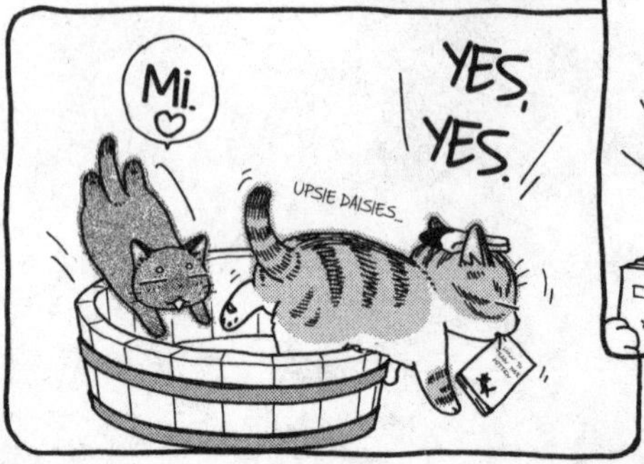
YES, YES.
Mi.
UPSIE DAISIES...

← *Continued in three pages!*

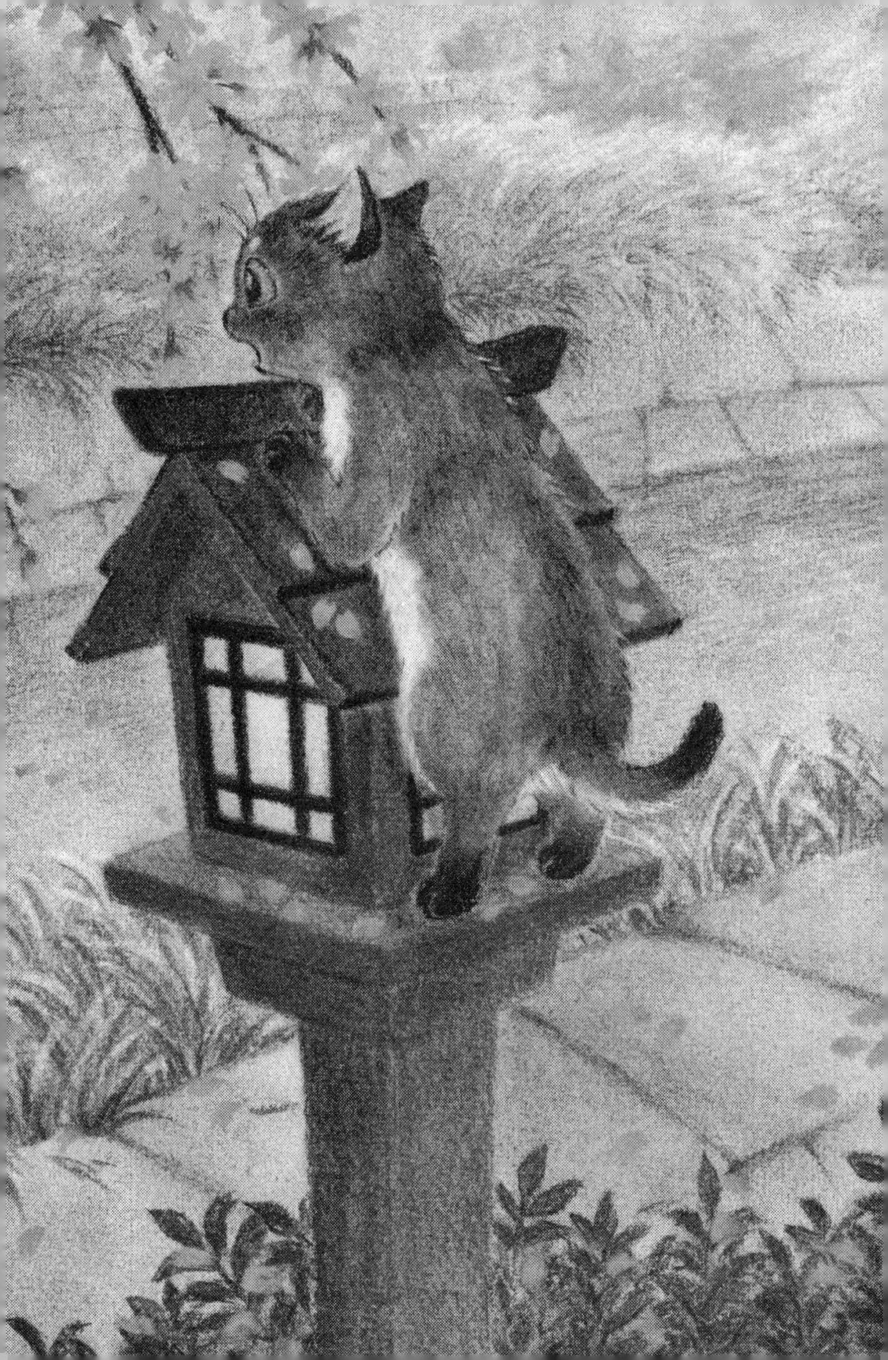

SHORT.7
A THINKING SNOWBALL

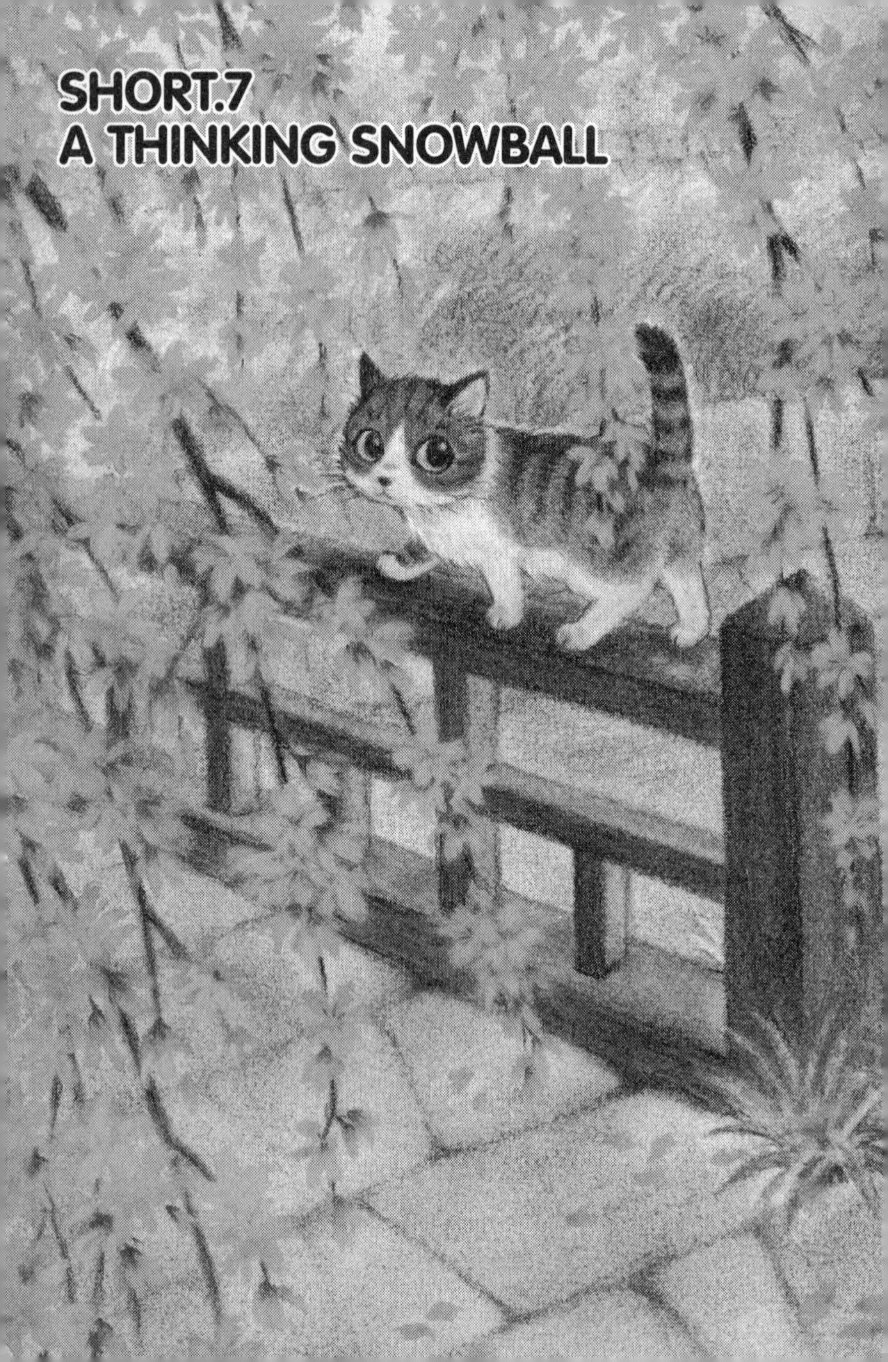

OMAKE PAGE

The continuation! ←

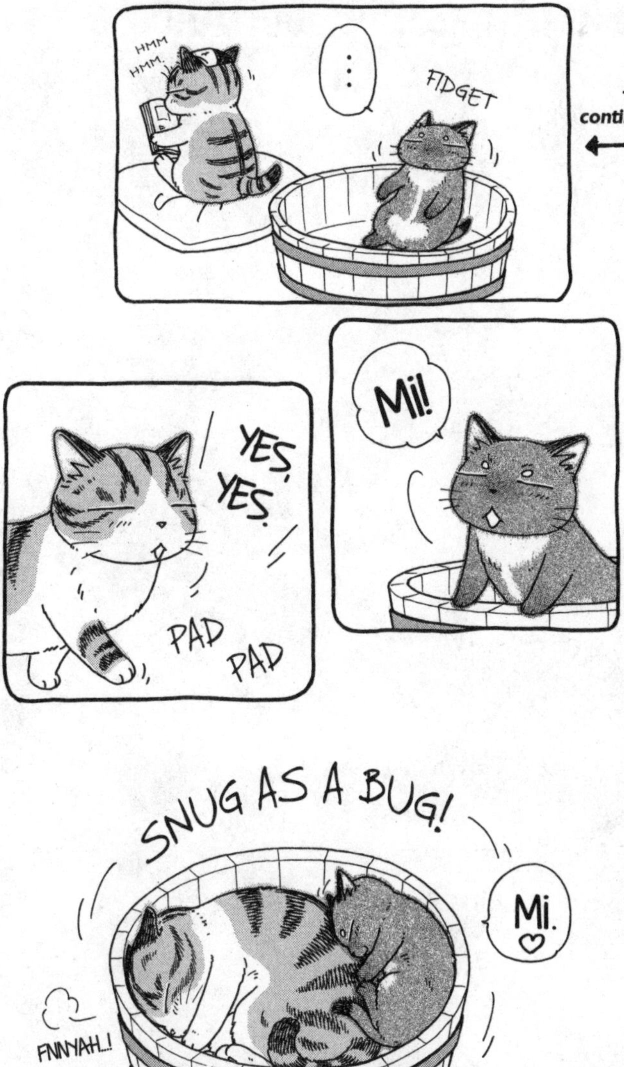
HMM HMM.
...
FIDGET
Mi!
YES, YES.
PAD PAD
SNUG AS A BUG!
Mi. ♡
FNNYAH..!

THE END

SHORT.7

A THINKING SNOWBALL

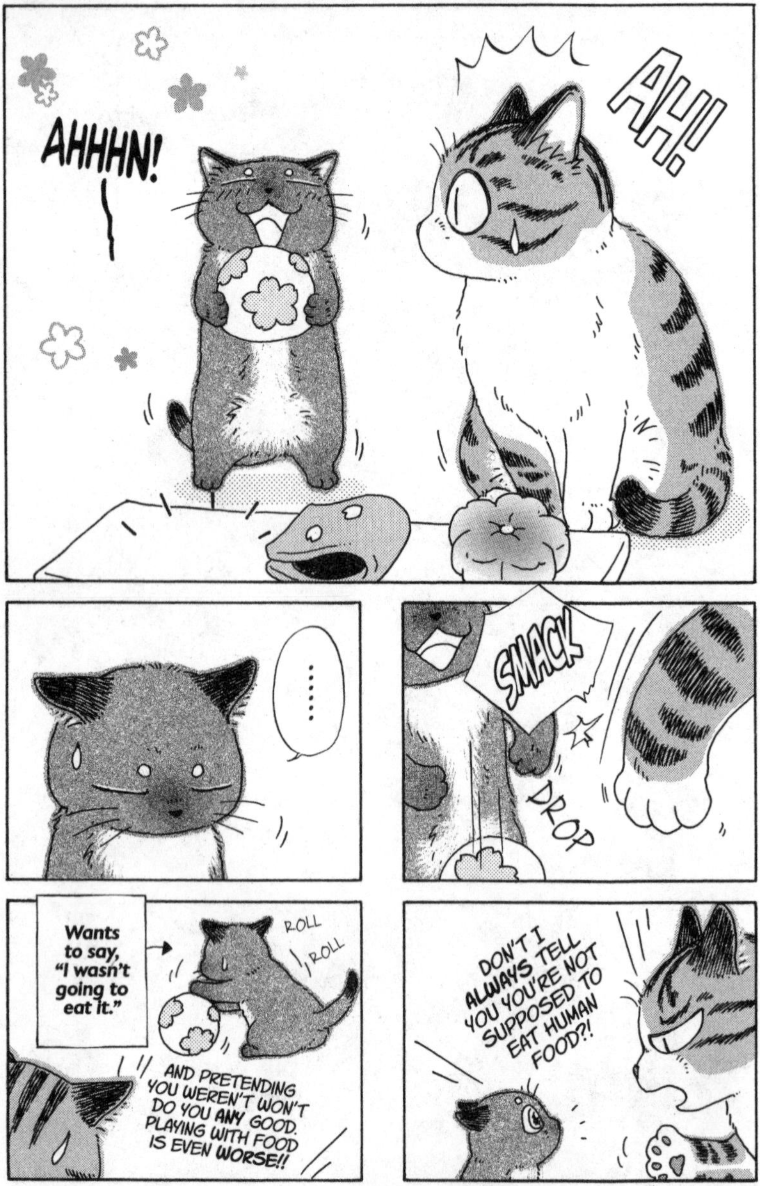
AH!
AHHHN!
SMACK
DROP
......
DON'T I ALWAYS TELL YOU YOU'RE NOT SUPPOSED TO EAT HUMAN FOOD?!
Wants to say, "I wasn't going to eat it."
ROLL
ROLL
AND PRETENDING YOU WEREN'T WON'T DO YOU ANY GOOD. PLAYING WITH FOOD IS EVEN WORSE!!

THE SHAVED EYEBROW CAT SNOWBALL

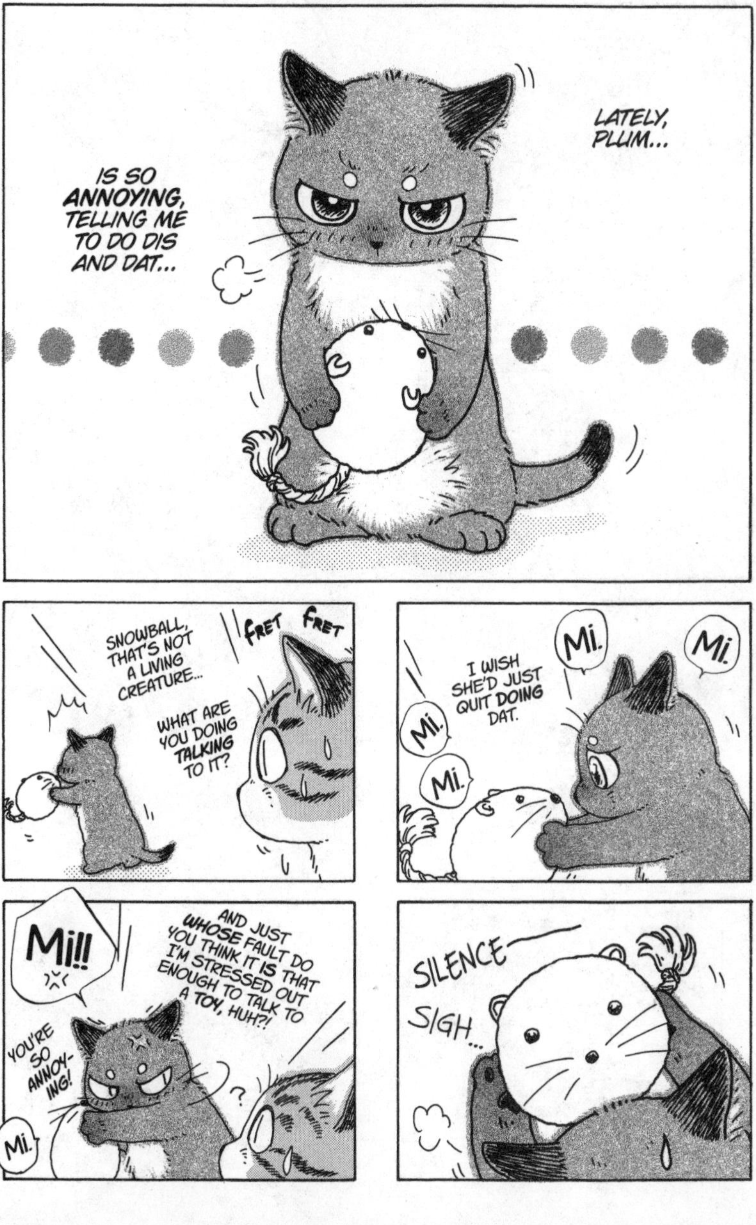
LATELY, PLUM...
IS SO ANNOYING, TELLING ME TO DO DIS AND DAT...
Mi.
Mi.
I WISH SHE'D JUST QUIT DOING DAT.
Mi.
Mi.
FRET FRET
SNOWBALL, THAT'S NOT A LIVING CREATURE...
WHAT ARE YOU DOING TALKING TO IT?
SILENCE
SIGH...
AND JUST WHOSE FAULT DO YOU THINK IT IS THAT I'M STRESSED OUT ENOUGH TO TALK TO A TOY, HUH?!
Mi!!
YOU'RE SO ANNOY-ING!
Mi.

SNOWBALL'S DAILY ROUTINE

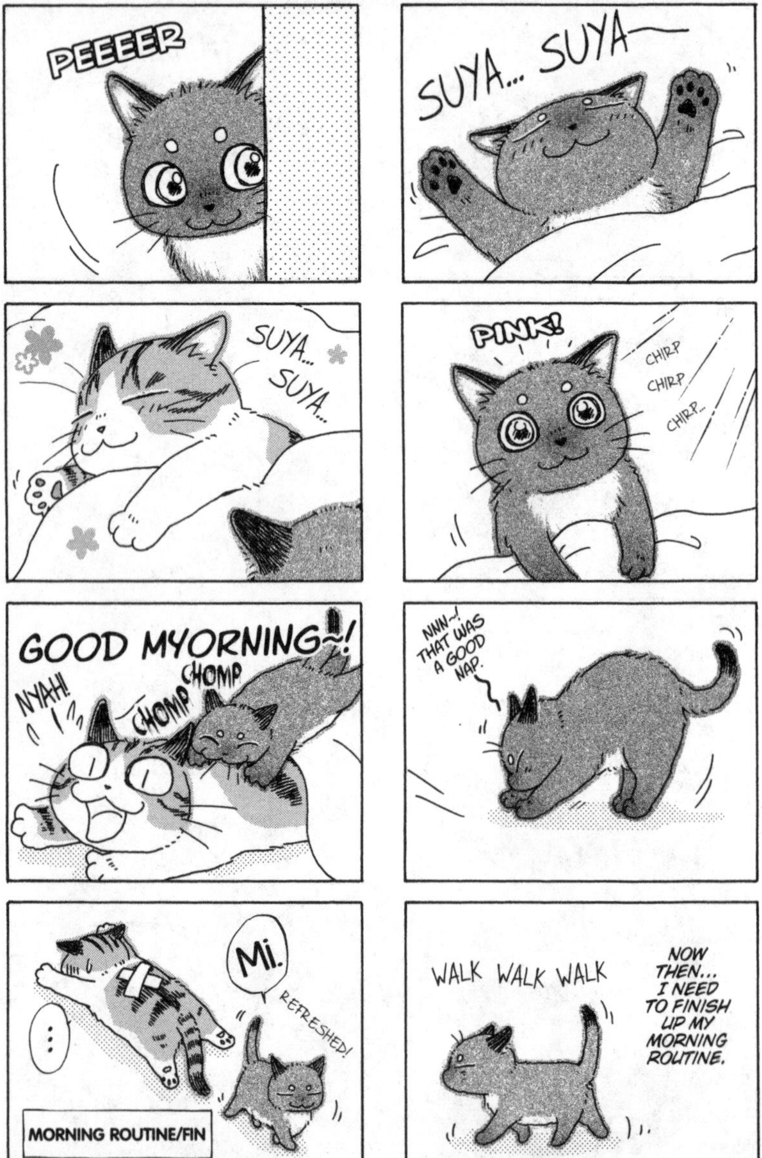
SUYA... SUYA~
PEEEER
CHIRP
CHIRP
CHIRP...
PINK!
SUYA... SUYA...
NNN~! THAT WAS A GOOD NAP.
GOOD MYORNING~!
CHOMP CHOMP
NYAH!
NOW THEN... I NEED TO FINISH UP MY MORNING ROUTINE.
WALK WALK WALK
Mi.
REFRESHED!
...
MORNING ROUTINE/FIN

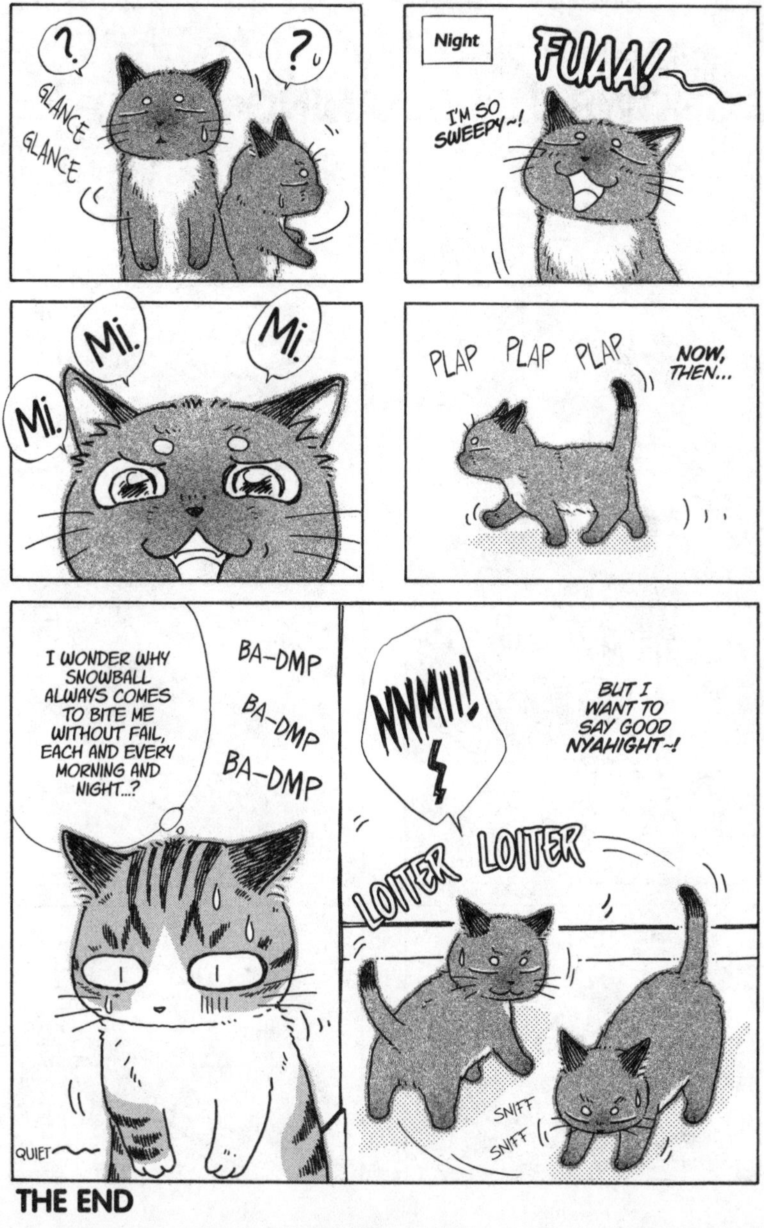
Night
FUAA!
I'M SO SWEEPY~!
?
?
GLANCE GLANCE
NOW, THEN...
PLAP PLAP PLAP
Mi.
Mi.
Mi.
NNMII!
BUT I WANT TO SAY GOOD NYAHIGHT~!
LOITER LOITER
SNIFF SNIFF
I WONDER WHY SNOWBALL ALWAYS COMES TO BITE ME WITHOUT FAIL, EACH AND EVERY MORNING AND NIGHT...?
BA-DMP
BA-DMP
BA-DMP
QUIET

THE END

CHAPTER 12: SNOWBALL'S LEARNING ABILITY

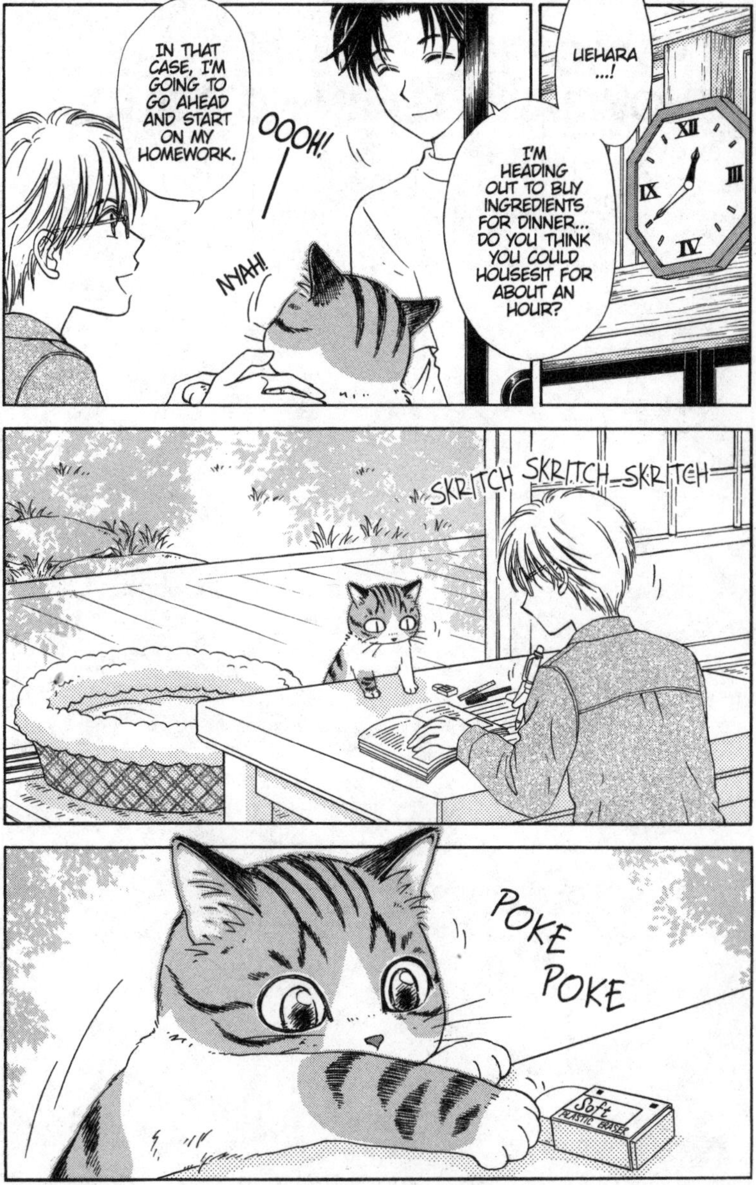
UEHARA ...!
I'M HEADING OUT TO BUY INGREDIENTS FOR DINNER... DO YOU THINK YOU COULD HOUSESIT FOR ABOUT AN HOUR?
IN THAT CASE, I'M GOING TO GO AHEAD AND START ON MY HOMEWORK.
OOOH!
NYAH!
SKRITCH SKRITCH SKRITCH
POKE POKE
Soft
PLASTIC ERASER

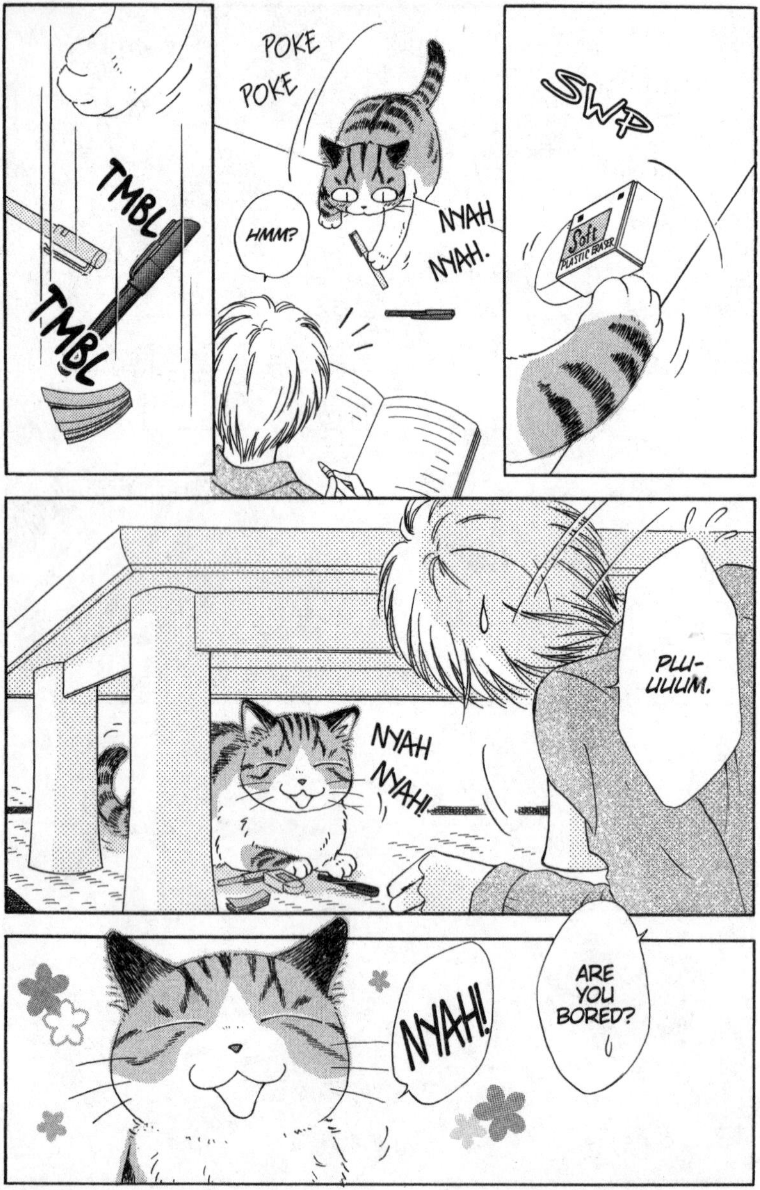
SWP
Soft
PLASTIC ERASER
POKE
POKE
NYAH
NYAH.
HMM?
TMBL
TMBL
PLUU-UULUM.
NYAH
NYAH!
ARE YOU BORED?
NYAH!

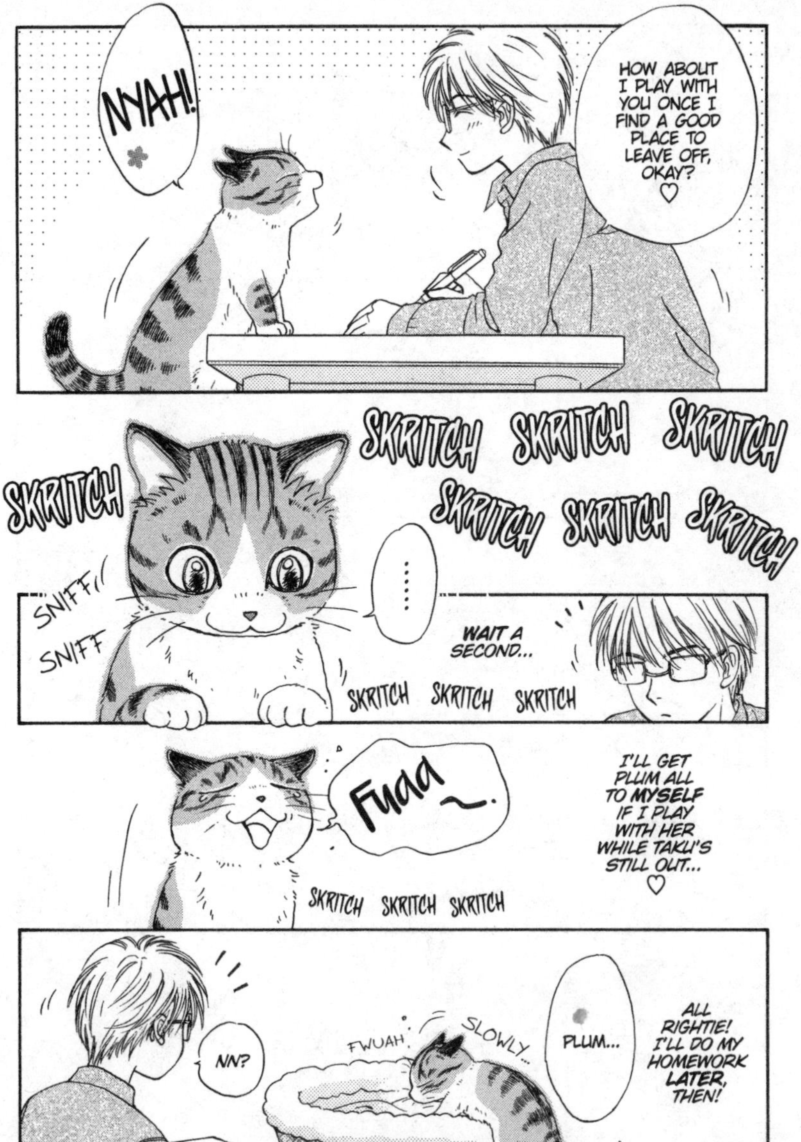
HOW ABOUT I PLAY WITH YOU ONCE I FIND A GOOD PLACE TO LEAVE OFF, OKAY? ♡
NYAH!
SKRITCH SKRITCH SKRITCH
SKRITCH SKRITCH SKRITCH
SKRITCH
WAIT A SECOND...
SKRITCH SKRITCH SKRITCH
......
SNIFF SNIFF
I'LL GET PLUM ALL TO MYSELF IF I PLAY WITH HER WHILE TAKU'S STILL OUT... ♡
Fuaa~.
SKRITCH SKRITCH SKRITCH
ALL RIGHTIE! I'LL DO MY HOMEWORK LATER, THEN!
PLUM...
SLOWLY...
FWUAH
NN?

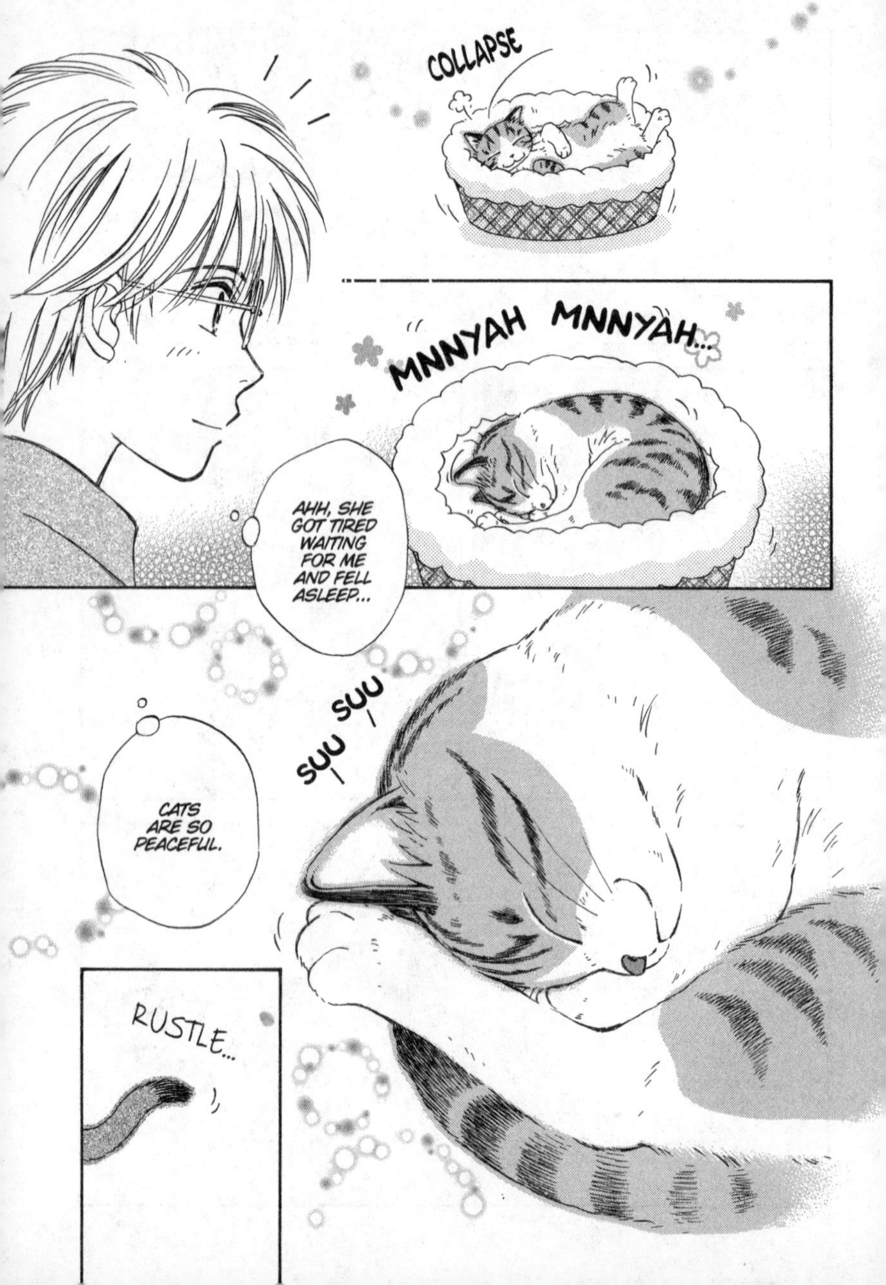
COLLAPSE
MNNYAH MNNYAH...
AHH, SHE GOT TIRED WAITING FOR ME AND FELL ASLEEP...
SUU SUU
CATS ARE SO PEACEFUL.
RUSTLE...

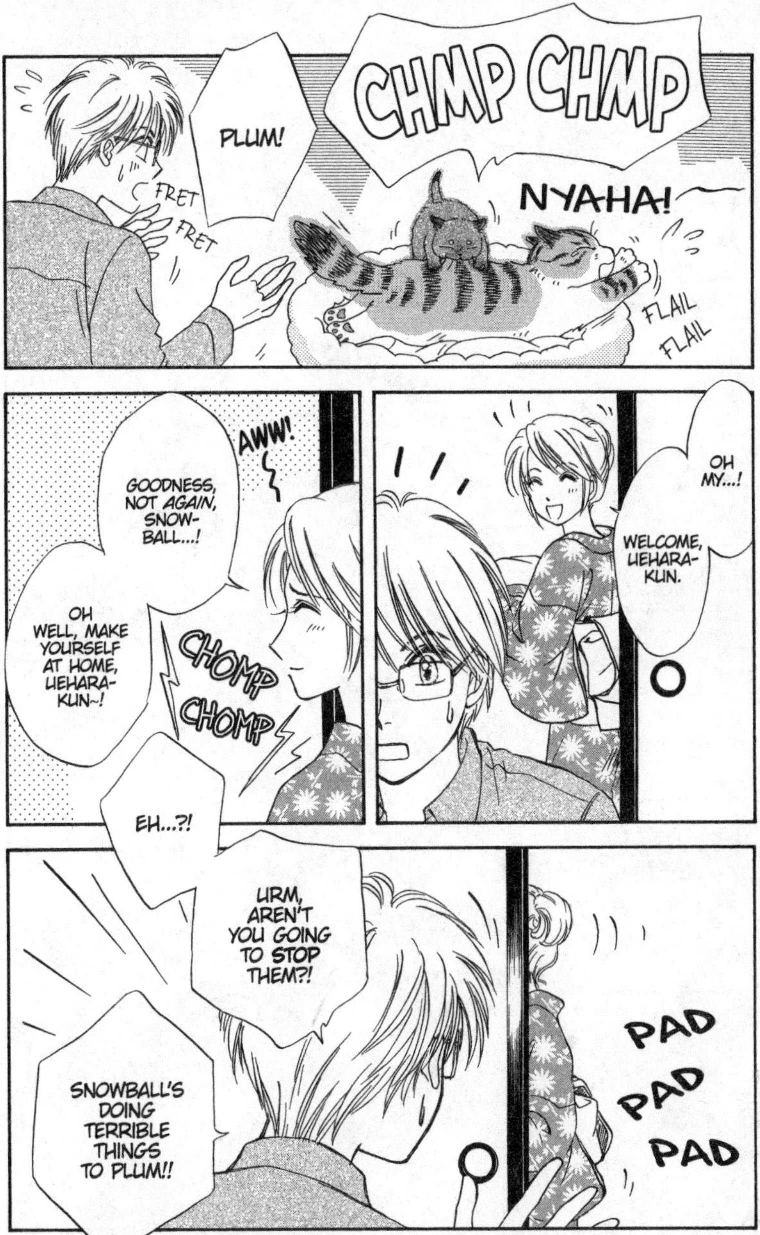

CHMP CHMP
PLUM!
NYAHA!
FRET FRET
FLAIL FLAIL
OH MY...!
WELCOME, UEHARA-KUN.
AWW!
GOODNESS, NOT AGAIN, SNOW-BALL...!
OH WELL, MAKE YOURSELF AT HOME, UEHARA-KUN~!
CHOMP CHOMP
EH...?!
PAD PAD PAD
URM, AREN'T YOU GOING TO STOP THEM?!
SNOWBALL'S DOING TERRIBLE THINGS TO PLUM!!

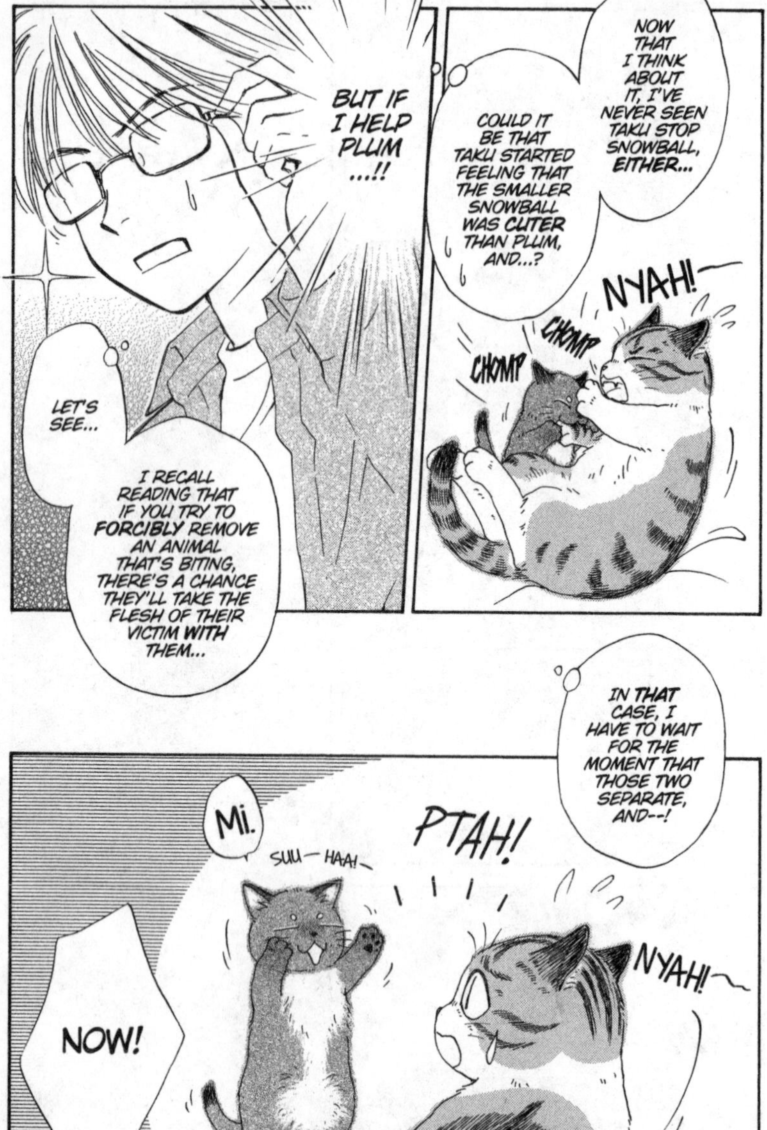
NOW THAT I THINK ABOUT IT, I'VE NEVER SEEN TAKU STOP SNOWBALL, EITHER...
COULD IT BE THAT TAKU STARTED FEELING THAT THE SMALLER SNOWBALL WAS CUTER THAN PLUM, AND...?
NYAH!
CHOMP
CHOMP
BUT IF I HELP PLUM ...!!
LET'S SEE...
I RECALL READING THAT IF YOU TRY TO FORCIBLY REMOVE AN ANIMAL THAT'S BITING, THERE'S A CHANCE THEY'LL TAKE THE FLESH OF THEIR VICTIM WITH THEM...
IN THAT CASE, I HAVE TO WAIT FOR THE MOMENT THAT THOSE TWO SEPARATE, AND--!
NYAH!
PTAH!
SUU-HAA!
Mi.
NOW!

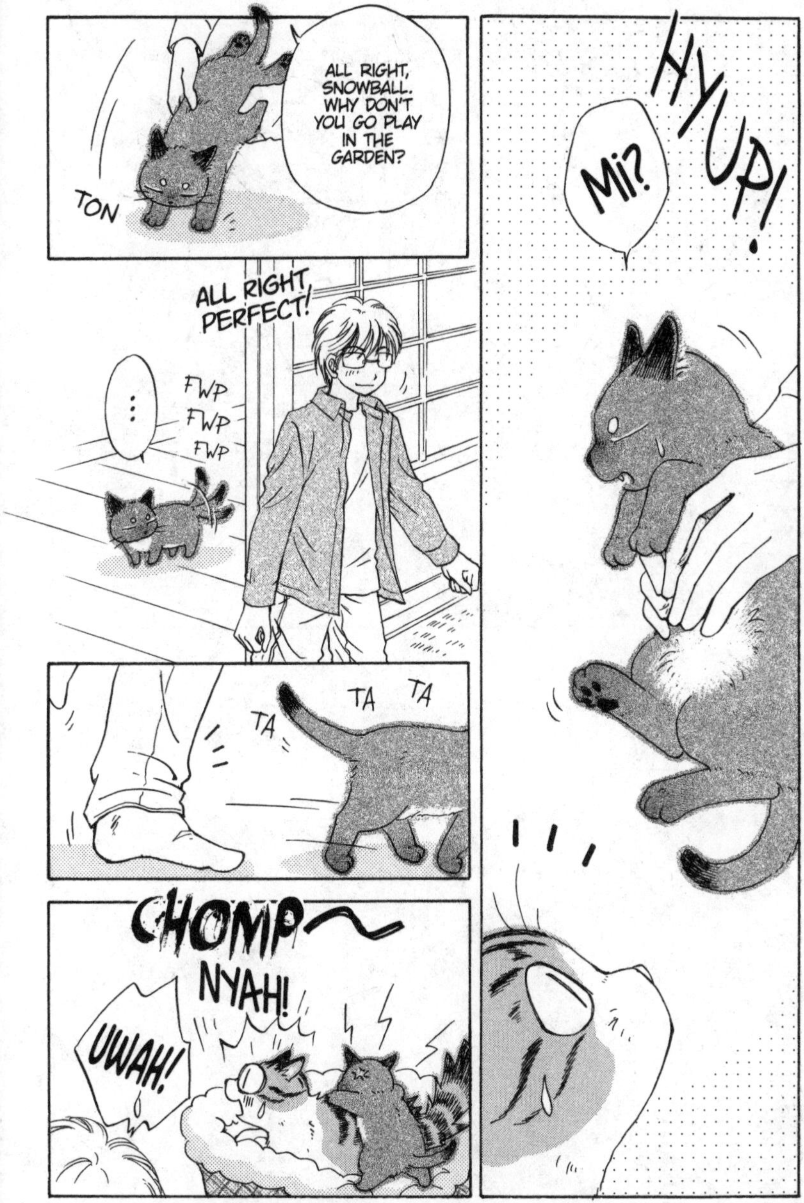
HYUP!
Mi?
ALL RIGHT, SNOWBALL. WHY DON'T YOU GO PLAY IN THE GARDEN?
TON
ALL RIGHT, PERFECT!
...
FWP
FWP
FWP
TA
TA
TA
CHOMP~
NYAH!
UWAH!

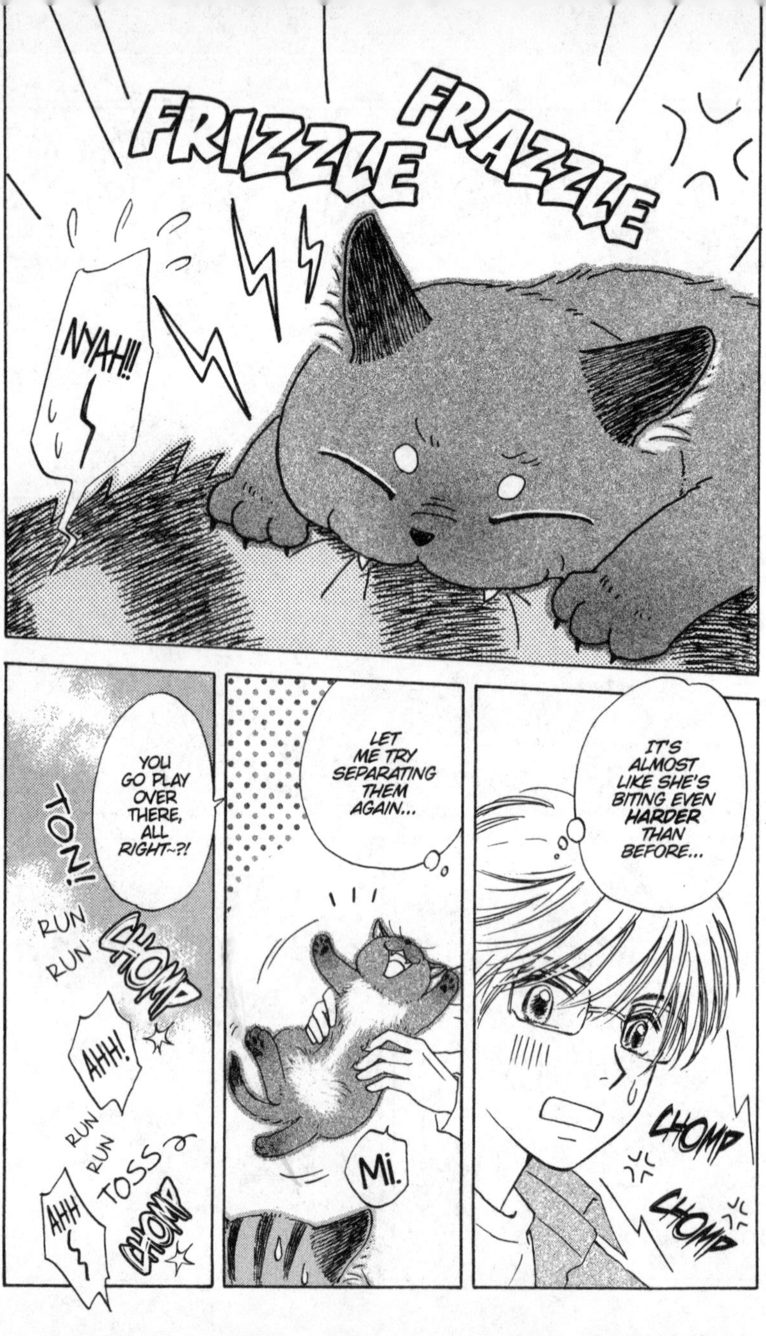
FRIZZLE FRAZZLE
NYAH!!
IT'S ALMOST LIKE SHE'S BITING EVEN HARDER THAN BEFORE...
CHOMP
CHOMP
LET ME TRY SEPARATING THEM AGAIN...
Mi.
YOU GO PLAY OVER THERE, ALL RIGHT~?!
TON!
RUN RUN
CHOMP
AHH!
RUN RUN
TOSS
CHOMP
AHH

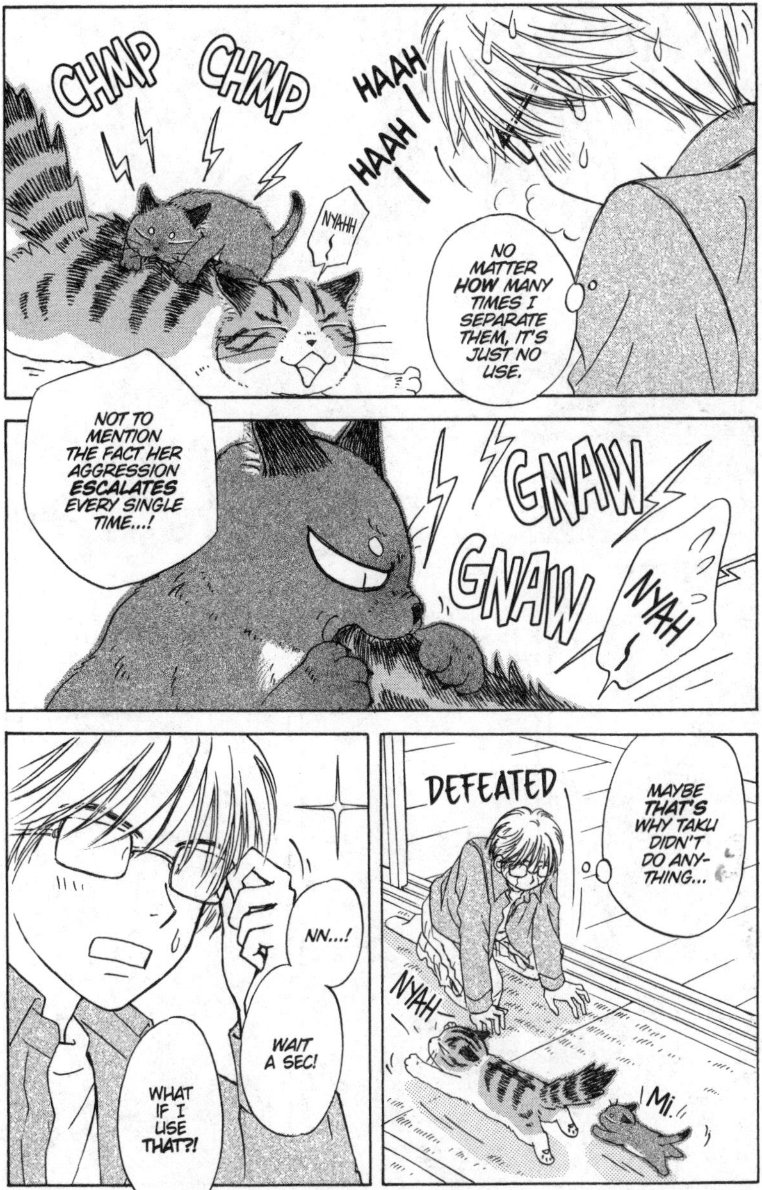
HAAH HAAH
NO MATTER HOW MANY TIMES I SEPARATE THEM, IT'S JUST NO USE.
NYAHH
CHMP CHMP
GNAW GNAW
NYAH
NOT TO MENTION THE FACT HER AGGRESSION ESCALATES EVERY SINGLE TIME...!
MAYBE THAT'S WHY TAKU DIDN'T DO ANYTHING...
DEFEATED
NYAH
Mi.
NN...!
WAIT A SEC!
WHAT IF I USE THAT?!

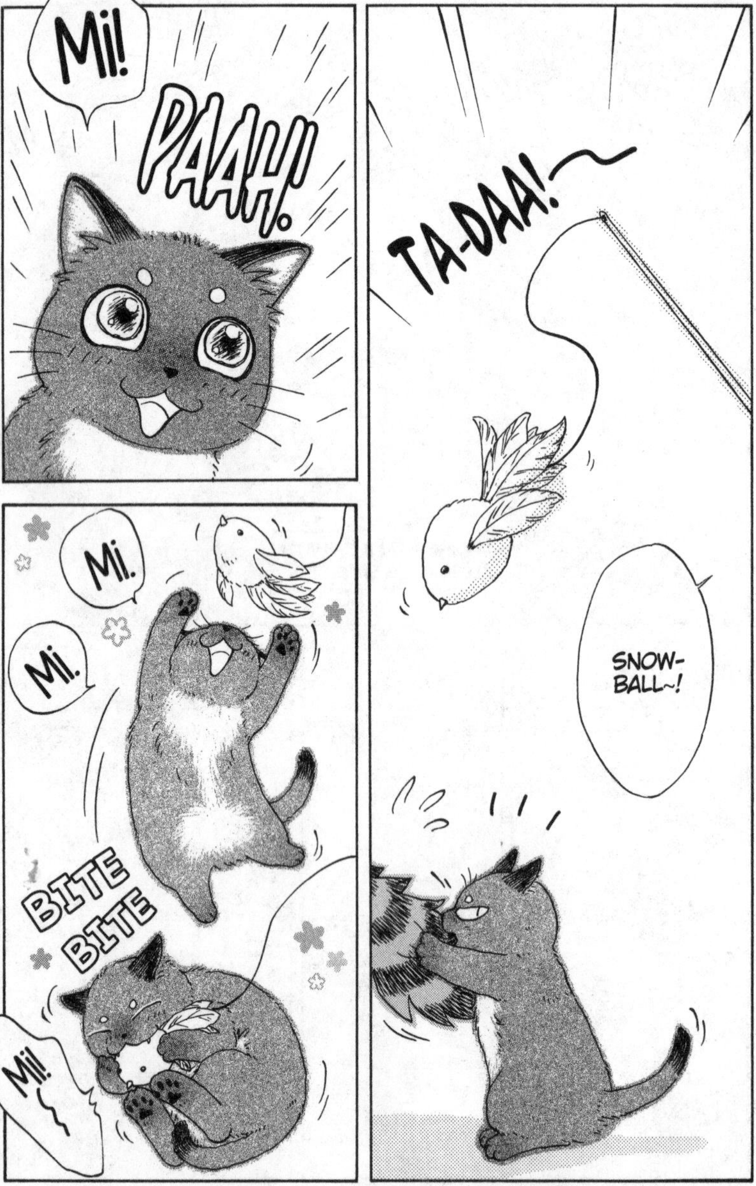
TA-DAA!~
SNOW-BALL~!
Mi!
PAAH!
Mi.
Mi.
BITE BITE
Mi!~

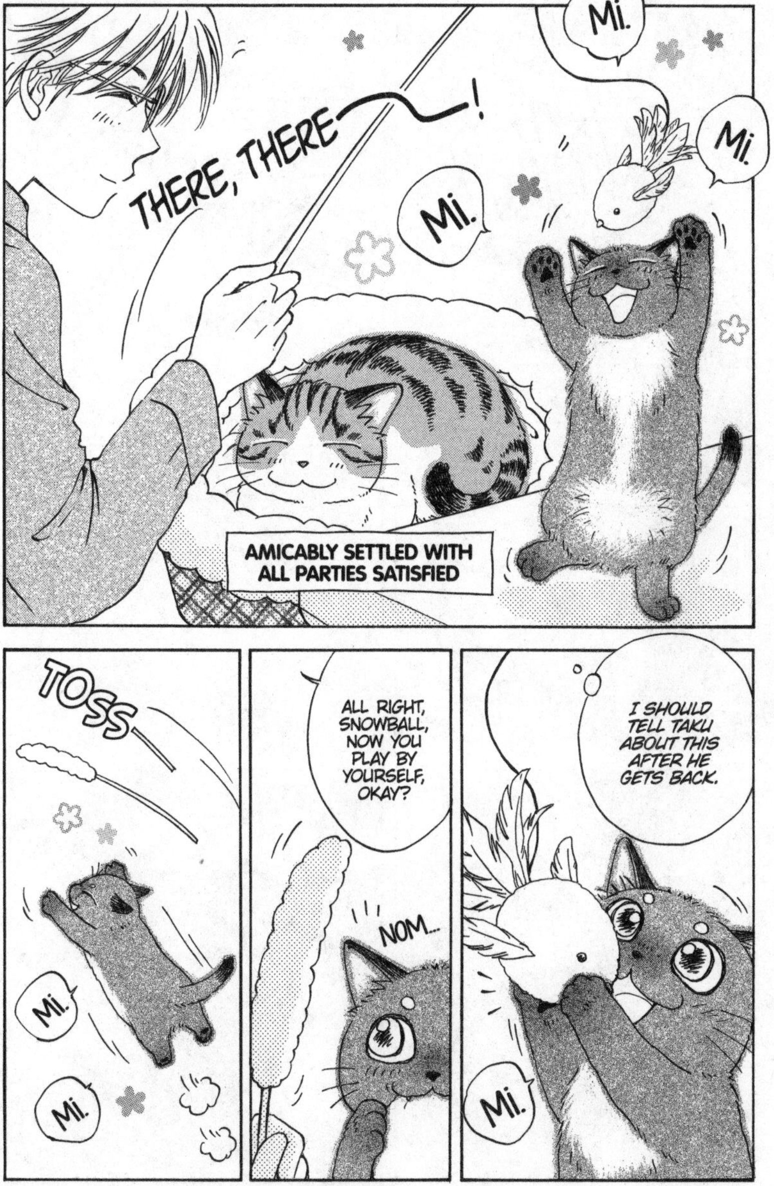
Mi.
Mi.
THERE, THERE~!
Mi.
AMICABLY SETTLED WITH ALL PARTIES SATISFIED
I SHOULD TELL TAKU ABOUT THIS AFTER HE GETS BACK.
Mi.
ALL RIGHT, SNOWBALL, NOW YOU PLAY BY YOURSELF, OKAY?
NOM...
TOSS
Mi.
Mi.

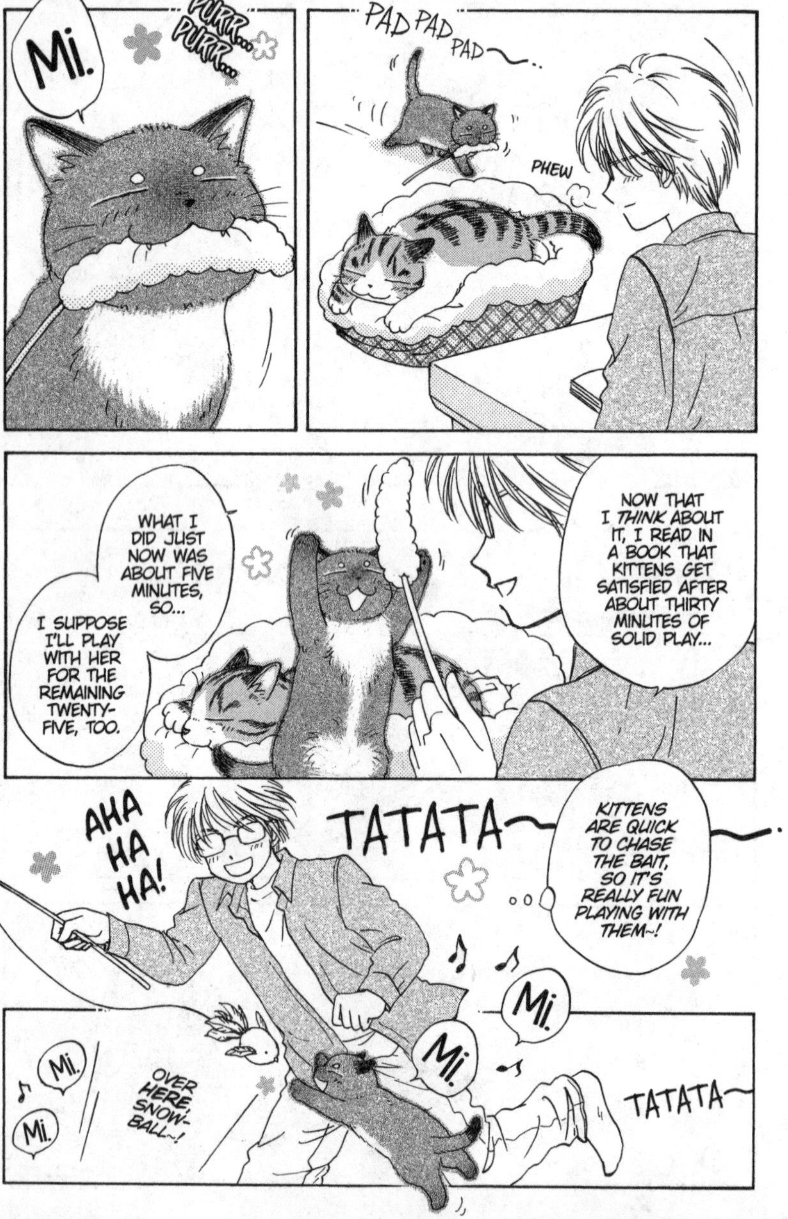
PAD PAD PAD~..
PHEW
PURRR... PURRR...
Mi.
NOW THAT I *THINK* ABOUT IT, I READ IN A BOOK THAT KITTENS GET SATISFIED AFTER ABOUT THIRTY MINUTES OF SOLID PLAY...
WHAT I DID JUST NOW WAS ABOUT FIVE MINUTES, SO...
I SUPPOSE I'LL PLAY WITH HER FOR THE REMAINING TWENTY-FIVE, TOO.
KITTENS ARE QUICK TO CHASE THE BAIT, SO IT'S REALLY FUN PLAYING WITH THEM~!
TATATA~~.
AHA HA HA!
Mi.
Mi.
TATATA~
OVER HERE, SNOWBALL~!
Mi.
Mi.

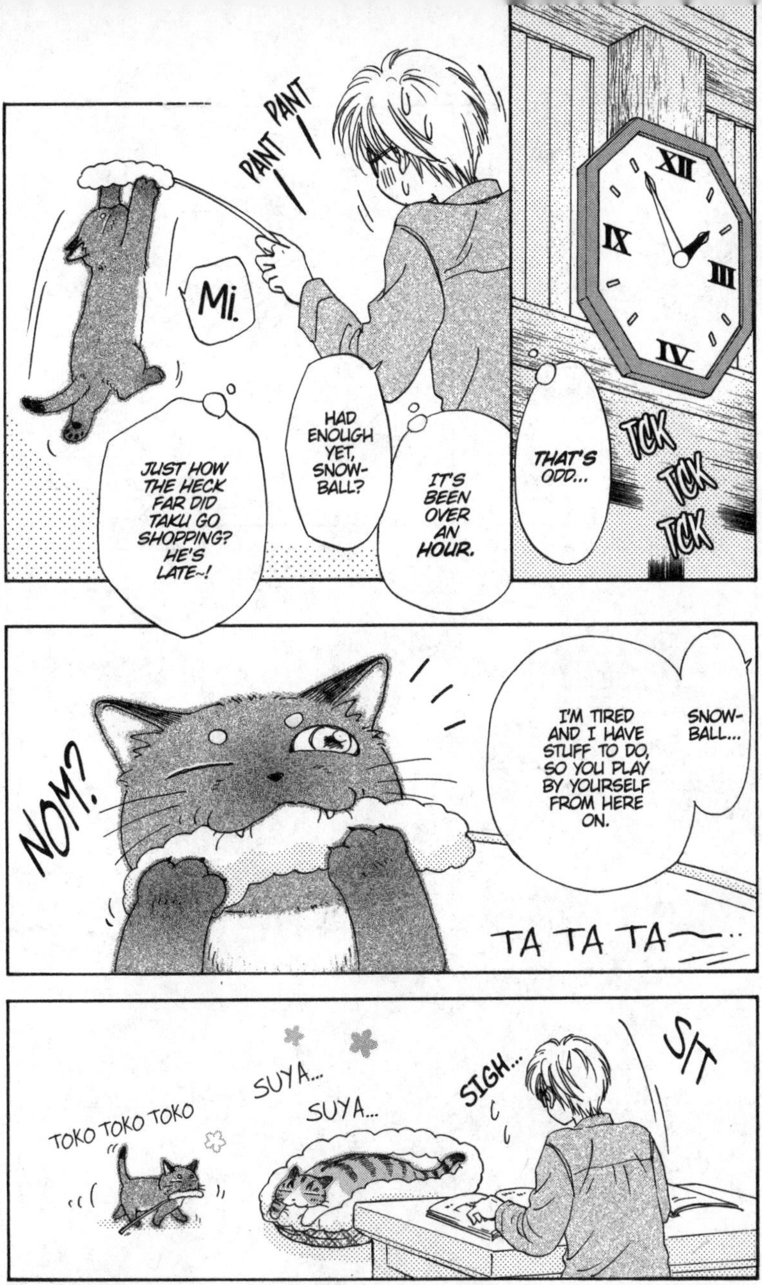
TCK TCK TCK
THAT'S ODD...
IT'S BEEN OVER AN HOUR.
PANT PANT
HAD ENOUGH YET, SNOW-BALL?
Mi.
JUST HOW THE HECK FAR DID TAKU GO SHOPPING? HE'S LATE~!
SNOW-BALL...
I'M TIRED AND I HAVE STUFF TO DO, SO YOU PLAY BY YOURSELF FROM HERE ON.
TA TA TA~...
NOM?
SIT
SIGH...
SUYA... SUYA...
TOKO TOKO TOKO

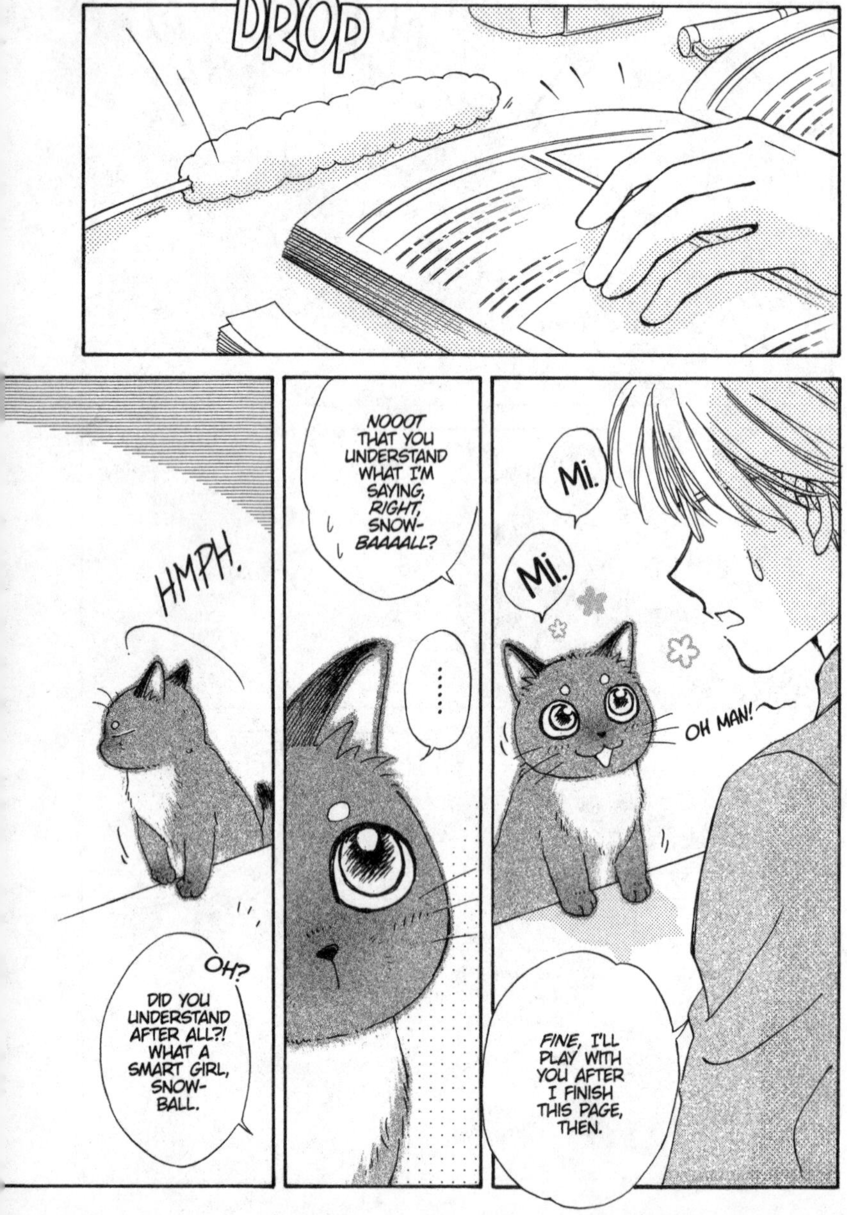
DROP
Mi.
Mi.
OH MAN!
FINE, I'LL PLAY WITH YOU AFTER I FINISH THIS PAGE, THEN.
NOOOT THAT YOU UNDERSTAND WHAT I'M SAYING, RIGHT, SNOW-BAAAALL?
......
HMPH.
OH?
DID YOU UNDERSTAND AFTER ALL?! WHAT A SMART GIRL, SNOW-BALL.

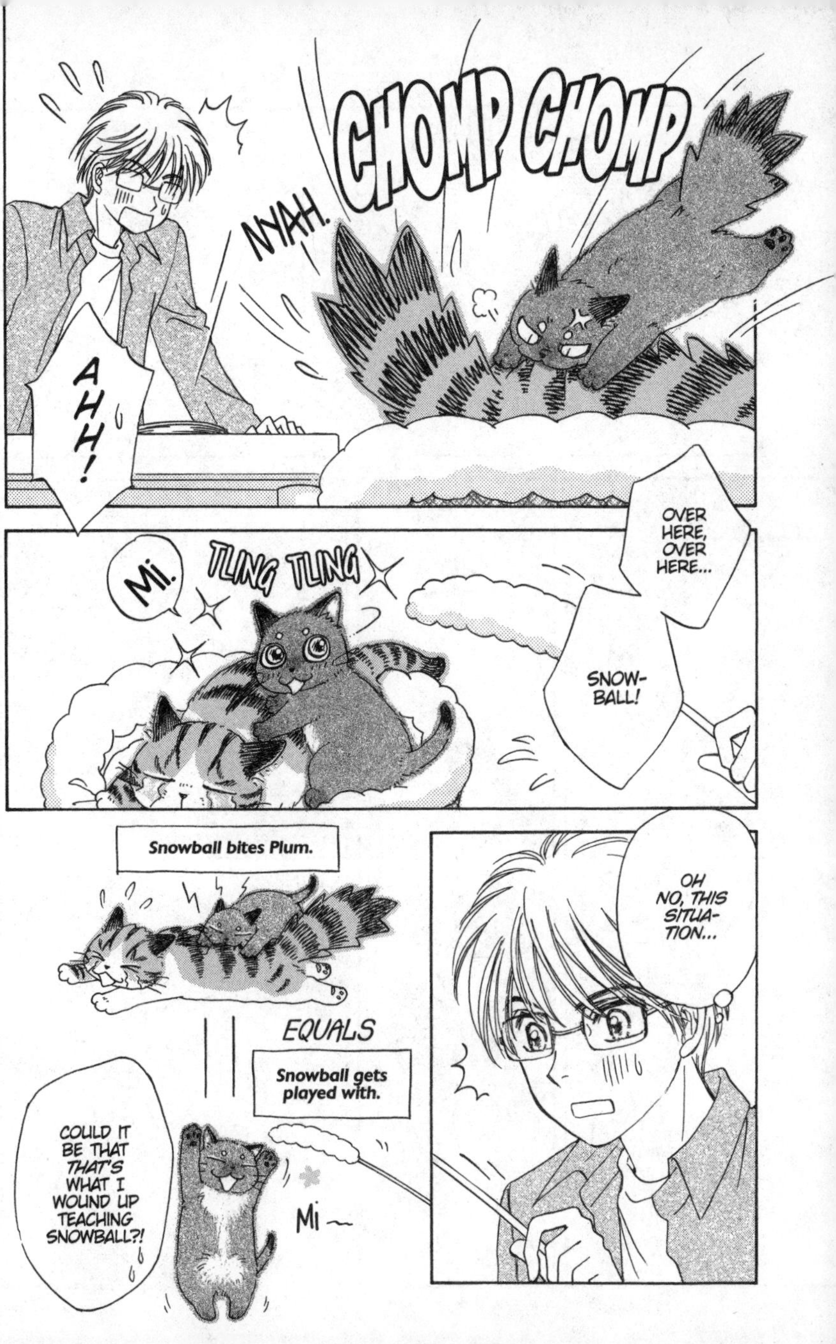
CHOMP CHOMP
NYAH.
AHH!
OVER HERE, OVER HERE...
SNOWBALL!
TLING TLING
Mi.
OH NO, THIS SITUATION...
Snowball bites Plum.
EQUALS
Snowball gets played with.
COULD IT BE THAT *THAT'S* WHAT I WOUND UP TEACHING SNOWBALL?!
Mi~

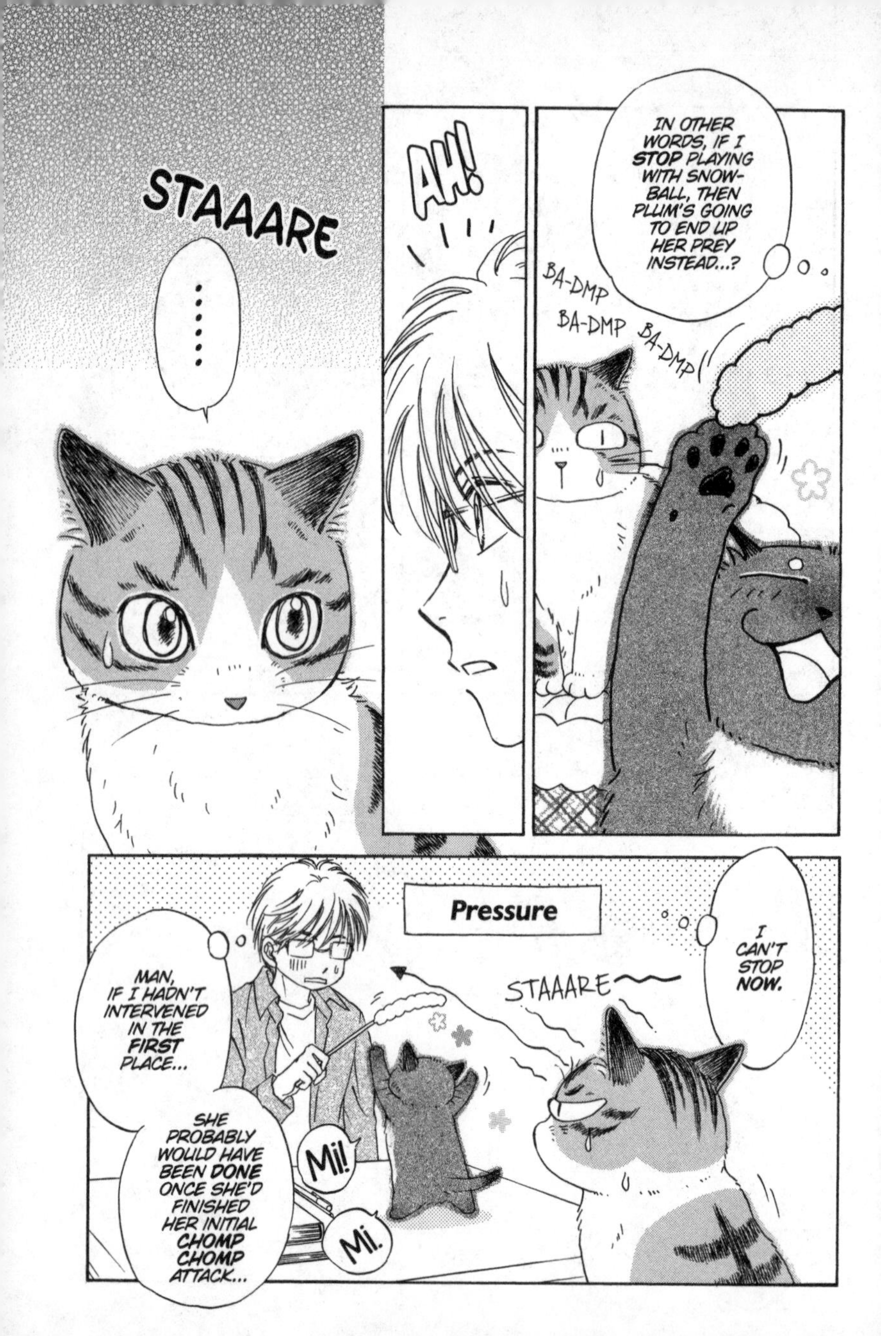
IN OTHER WORDS, IF I STOP PLAYING WITH SNOW-BALL, THEN PLUM'S GOING TO END UP HER PREY INSTEAD...?
BA-DMP
BA-DMP
BA-DMP
AH!
STAARE
......
I CAN'T STOP NOW.
Pressure
STAARE~~
MAN, IF I HADN'T INTERVENED IN THE FIRST PLACE...
Mi!
SHE PROBABLY WOULD HAVE BEEN DONE ONCE SHE'D FINISHED HER INITIAL CHOMP CHOMP ATTACK...
Mi.

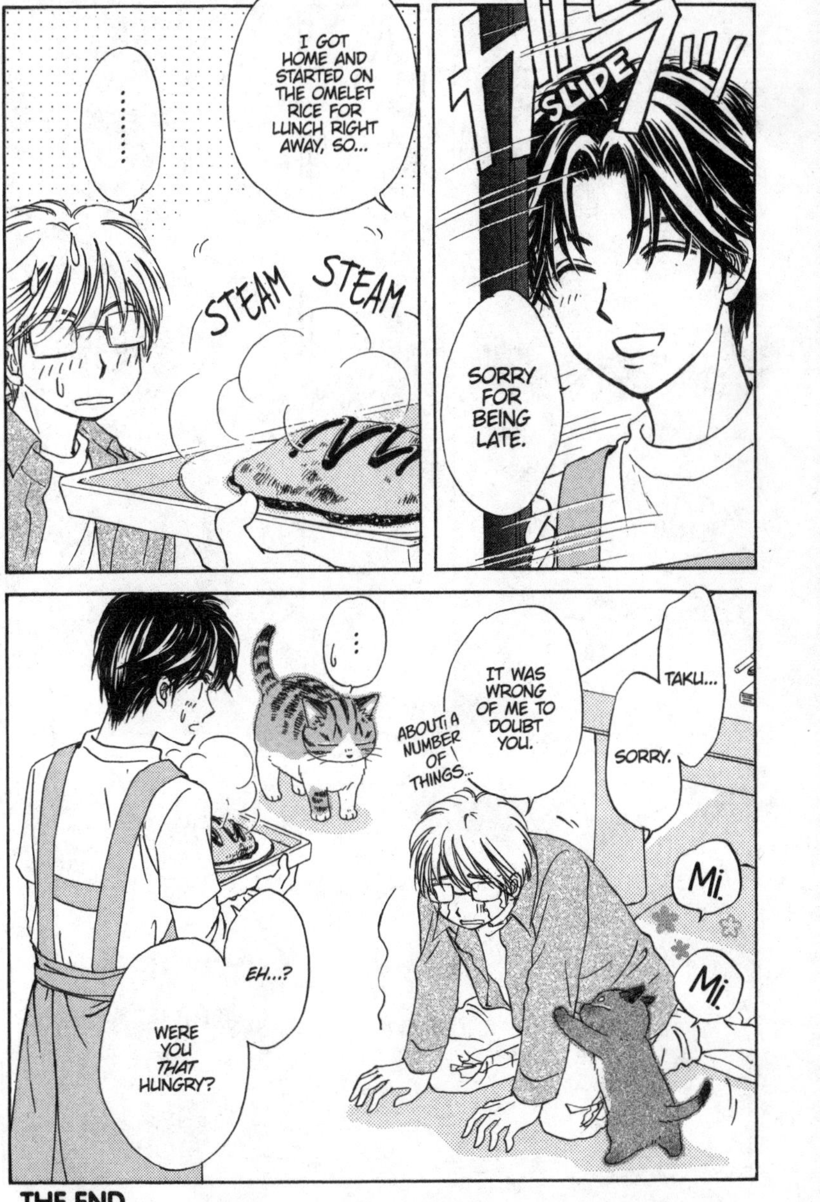
SLIDE
SORRY FOR BEING LATE.
I GOT HOME AND STARTED ON THE OMELET RICE FOR LUNCH RIGHT AWAY, SO...
......
STEAM STEAM
TAKU...
SORRY.
Mi.
Mi.
IT WAS WRONG OF ME TO DOUBT YOU.
ABOUT A NUMBER OF THINGS...
...
EH...?
WERE YOU *THAT* HUNGRY?

THE END

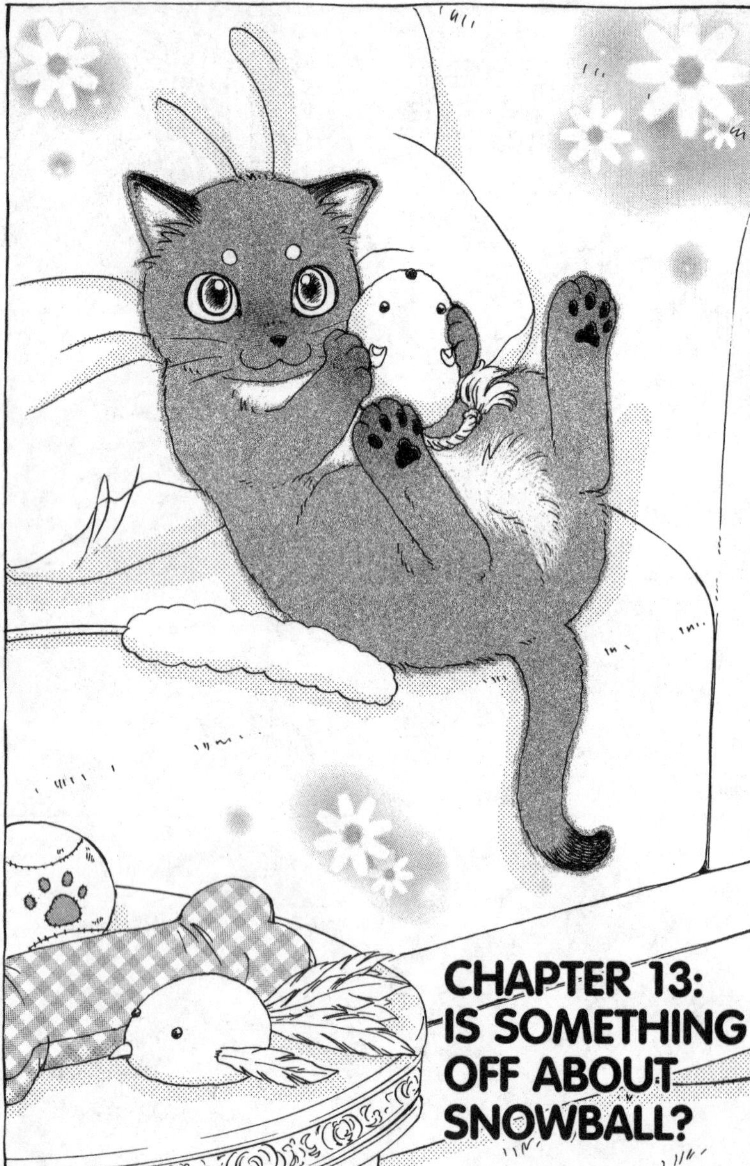
CHAPTER 13:
IS SOMETHING OFF ABOUT SNOWBALL?

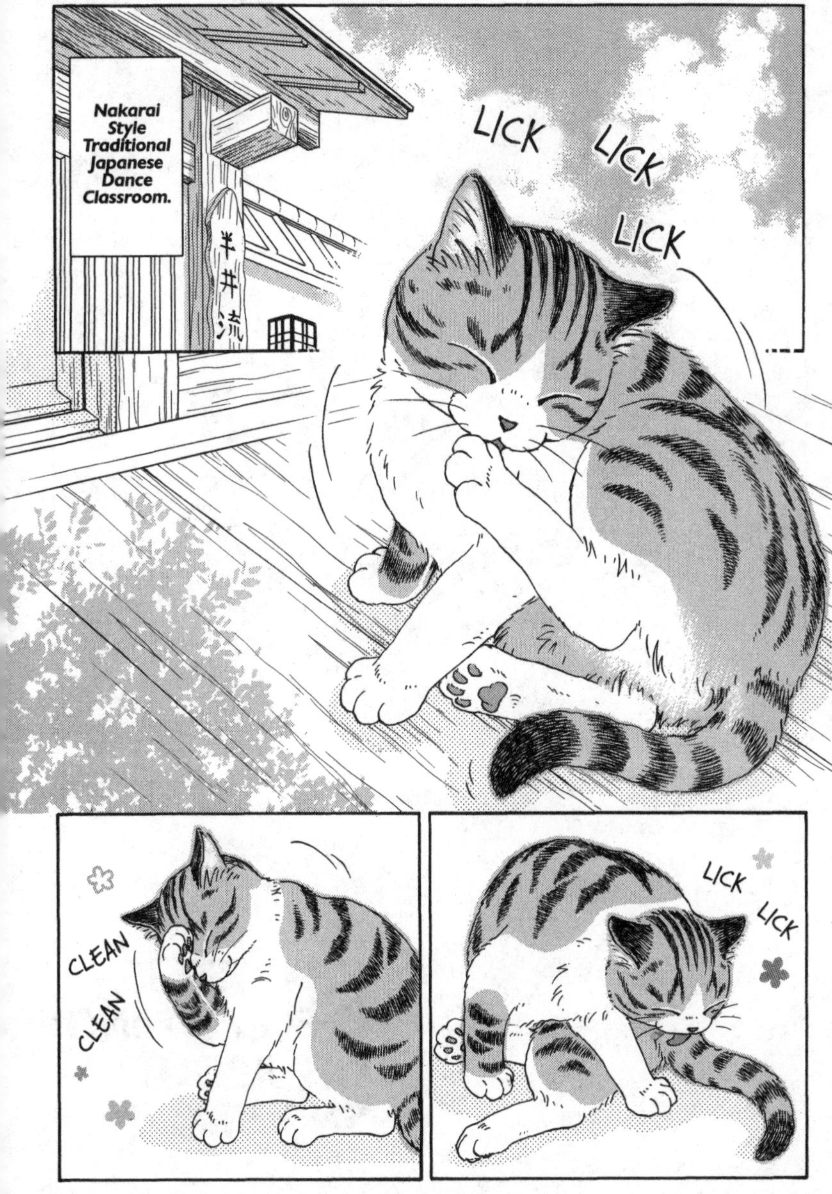
Nakarai Style Traditional Japanese Dance Classroom.
半井流
LICK
LICK
LICK
LICK
LICK
CLEAN
CLEAN

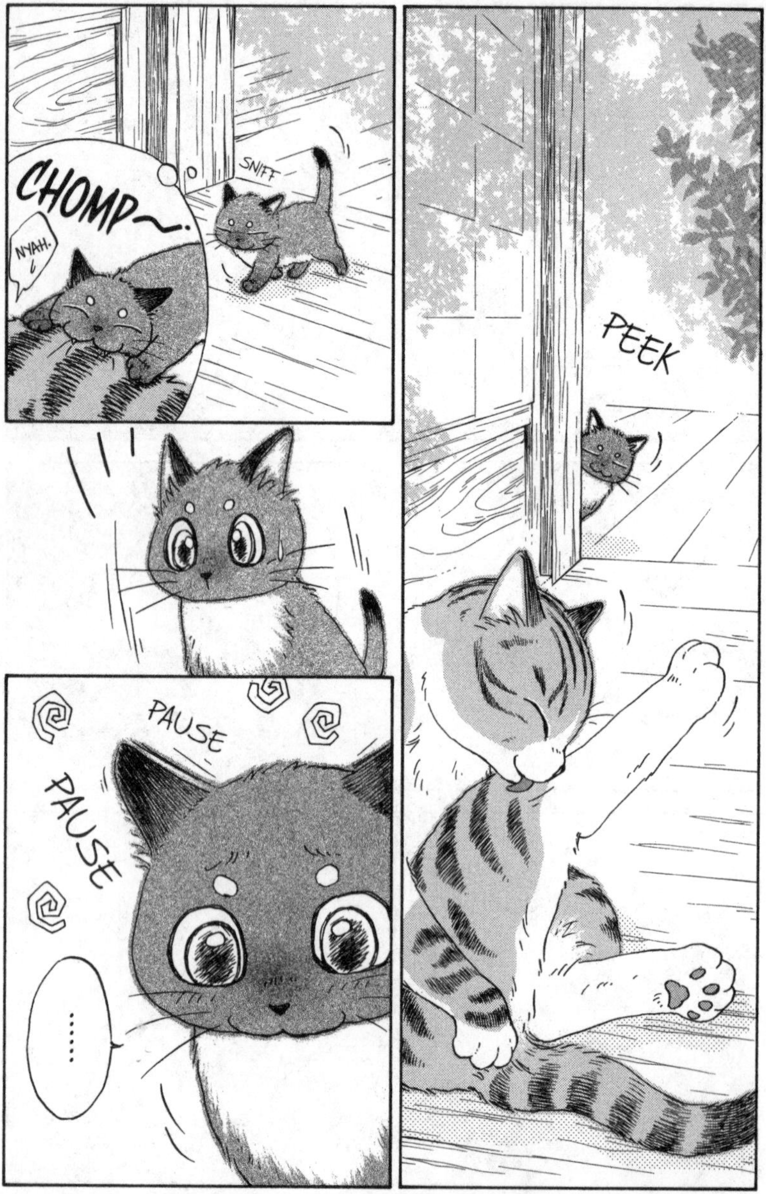
PEEK
SNIFF
CHOMP~.
NYAH.
PAUSE
PAUSE
......

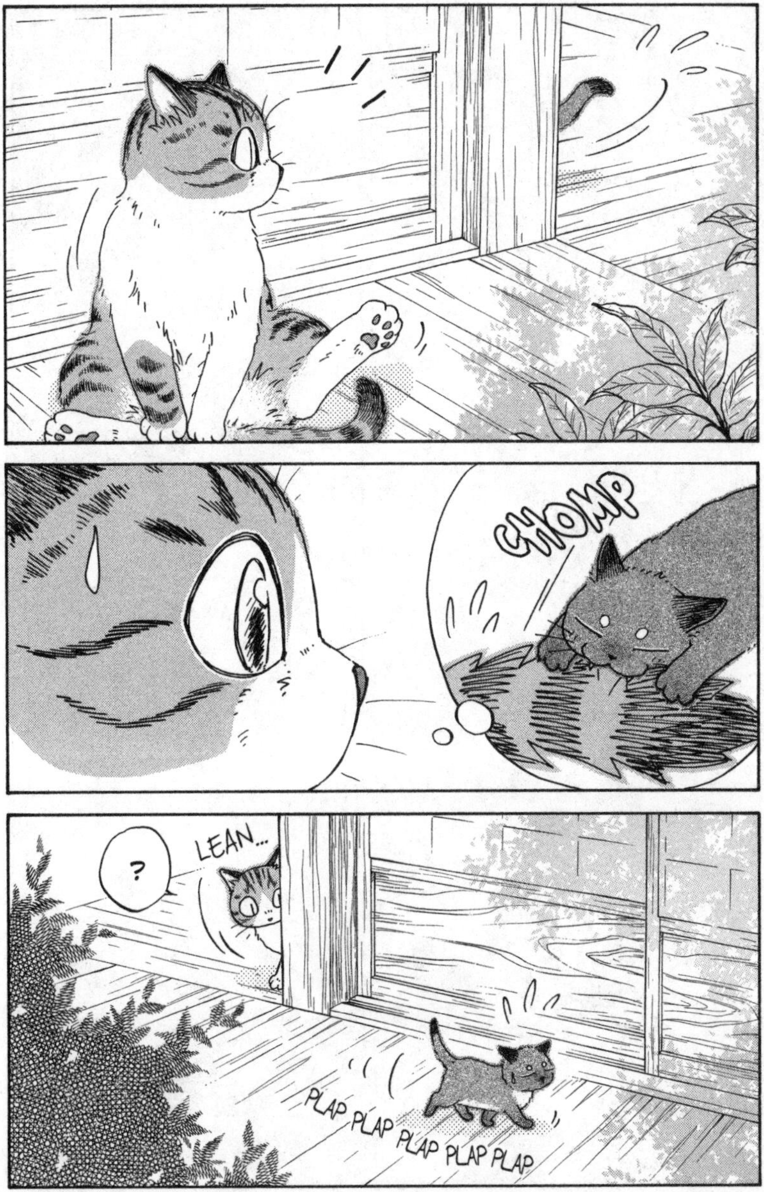
CHOMP
?
LEAN...
PLAP PLAP PLAP PLAP PLAP

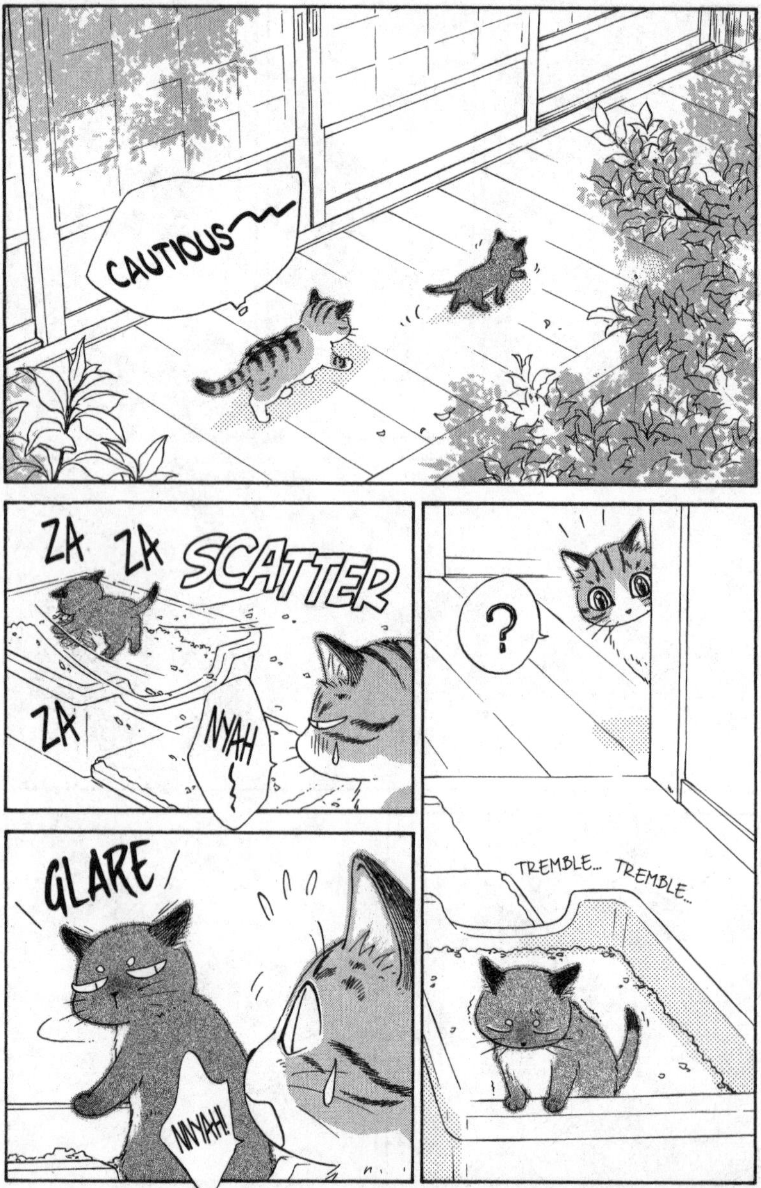
CAUTIOUS~
?
TREMBLE... TREMBLE...
SCATTER
ZA ZA
NYAH
ZA
GLARE
NNYAH!

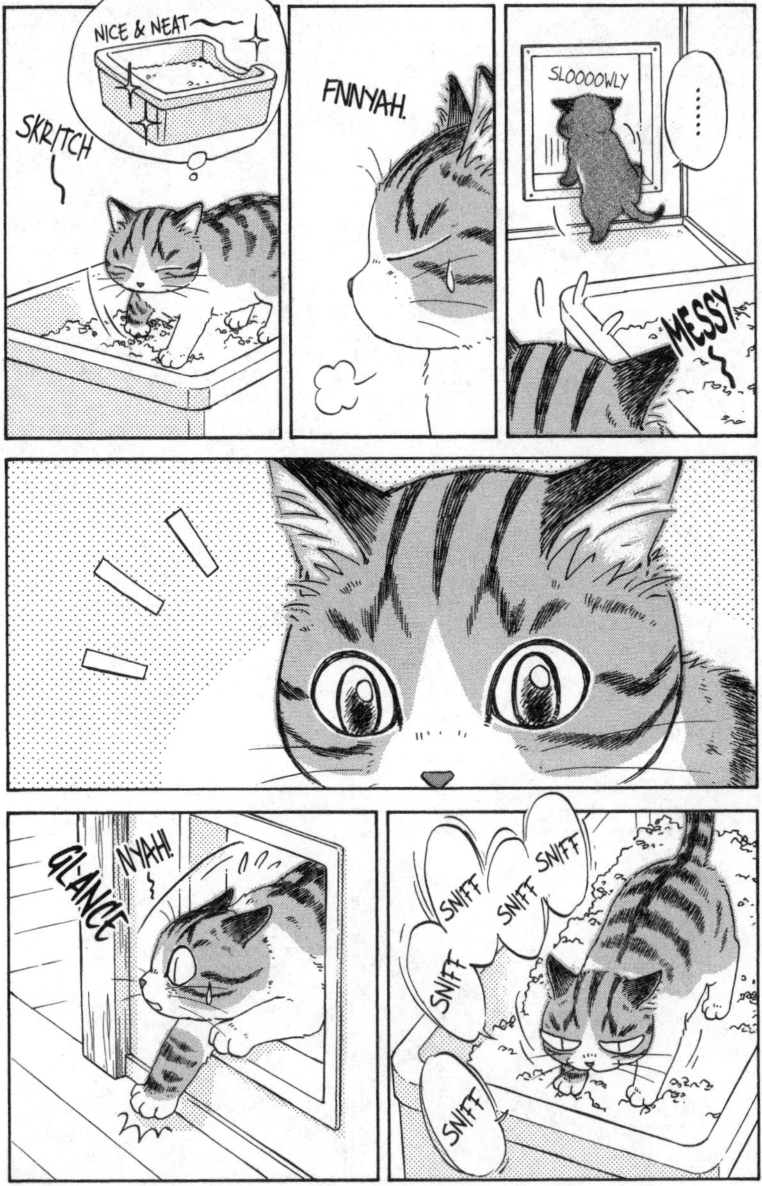
SLOOOOWLY
......
MESSY
FNNYAH.
NICE & NEAT
SKRITCH
SNIFF
SNIFF
SNIFF
SNIFF
SNIFF
SNIFF
NYAH!
GLANCE

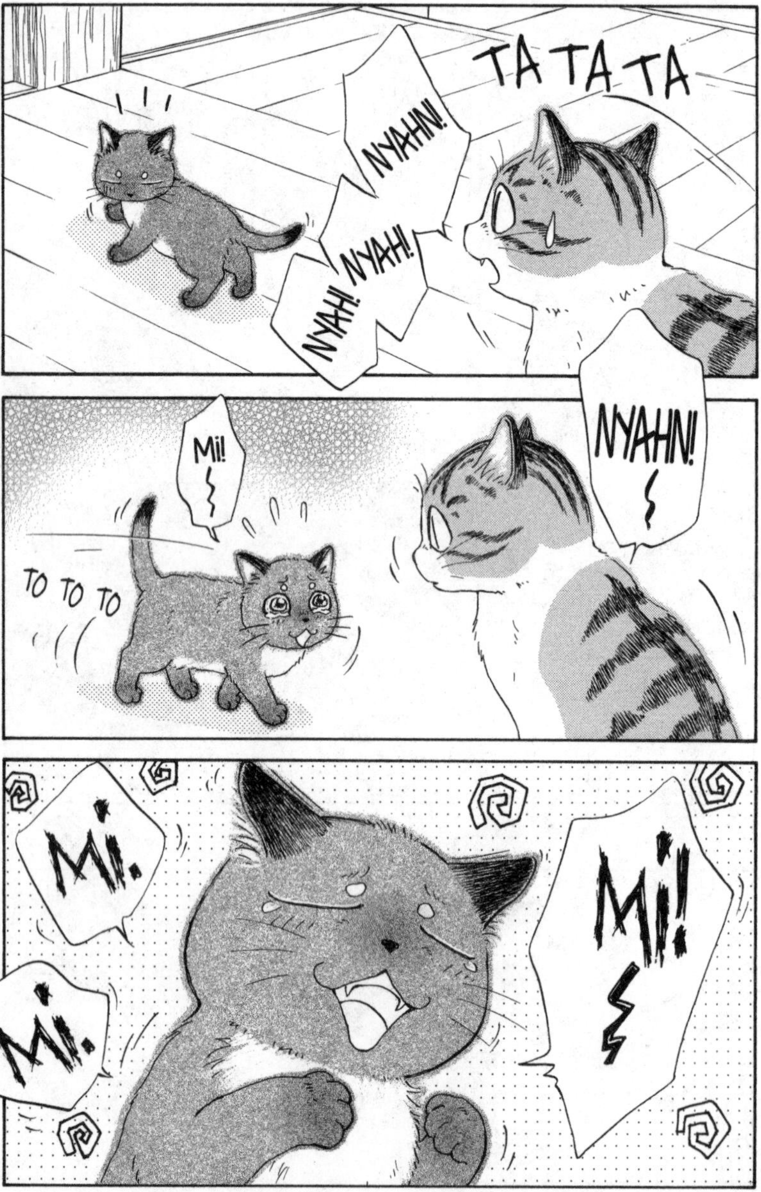
TA TA TA
NYAHN!
NYAH!
NYAH!
NYAHN!
Mi!
TO TO TO
Mi!
Mi.
Mi.

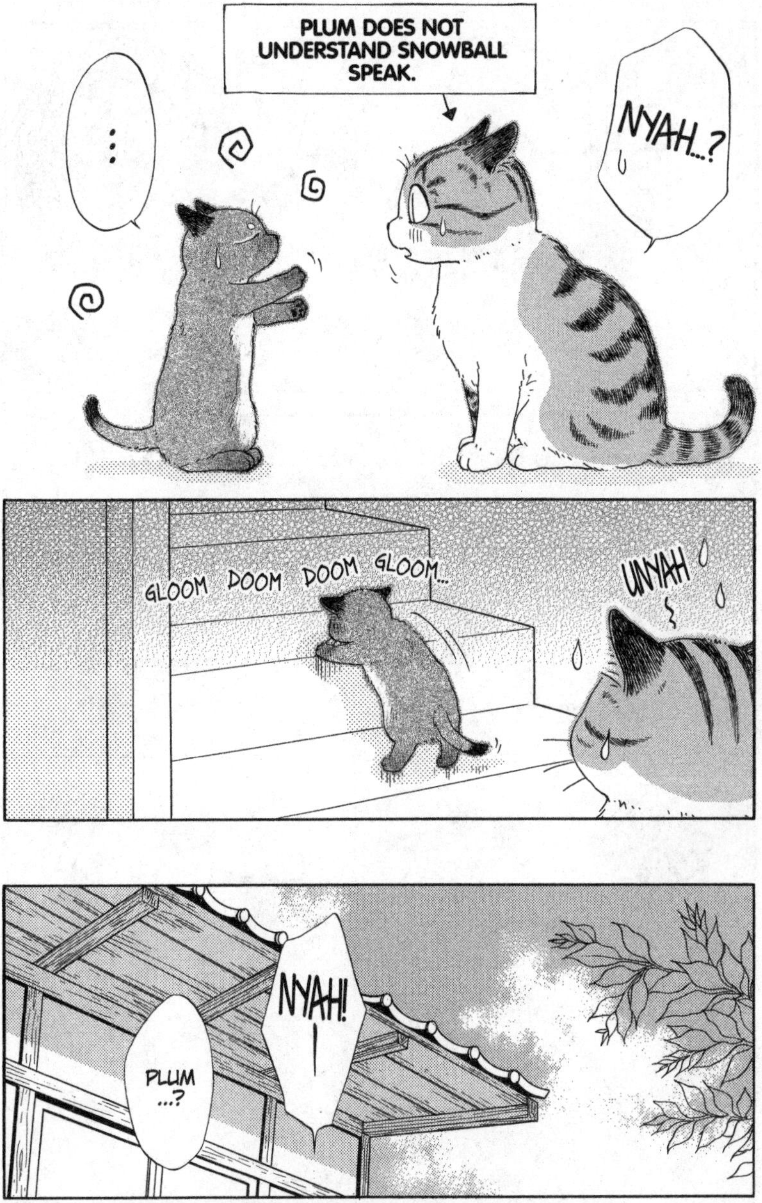
NYAH...?
PLUM DOES NOT UNDERSTAND SNOWBALL SPEAK.
...
UNYAH
GLOOM DOOM DOOM GLOOM...
NYAH!!
PLUM ...?

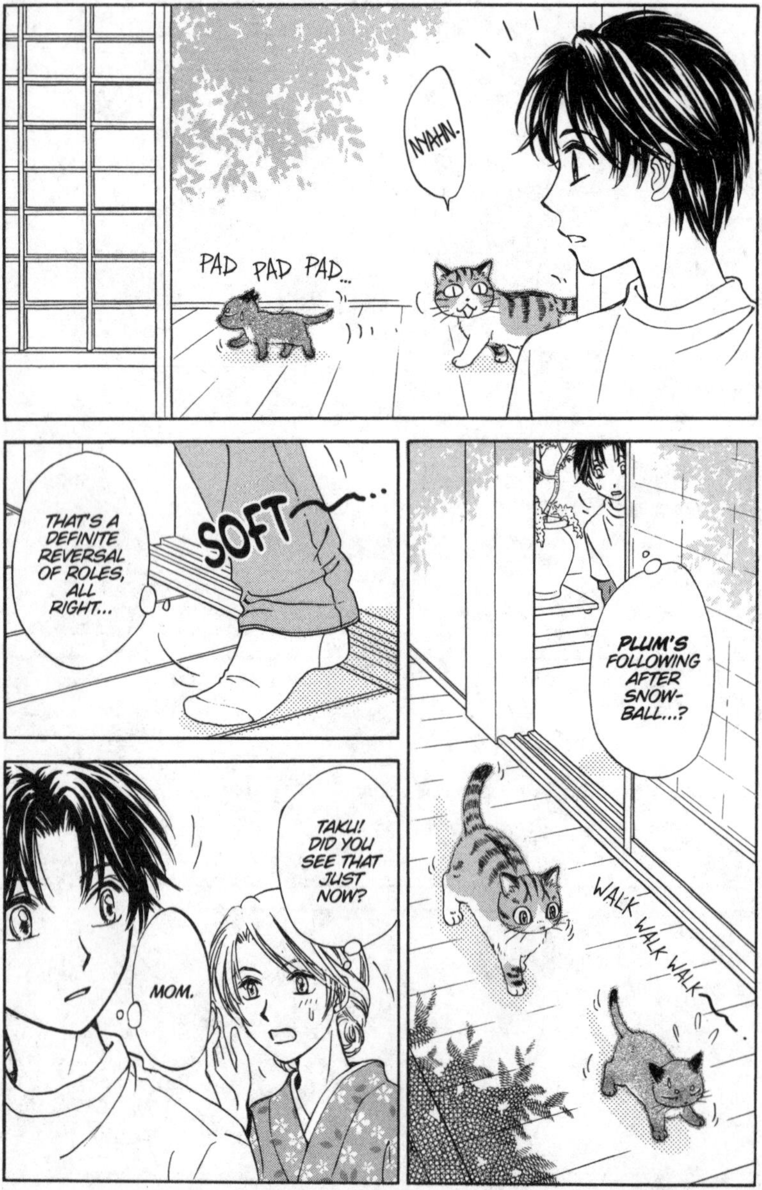
NYAHN.
PAD PAD PAD...
PLUM'S FOLLOWING AFTER SNOW-BALL...?
WALK WALK WALK~.
SOFT~...
THAT'S A DEFINITE REVERSAL OF ROLES, ALL RIGHT...
TAKU! DID YOU SEE THAT JUST NOW?
MOM.

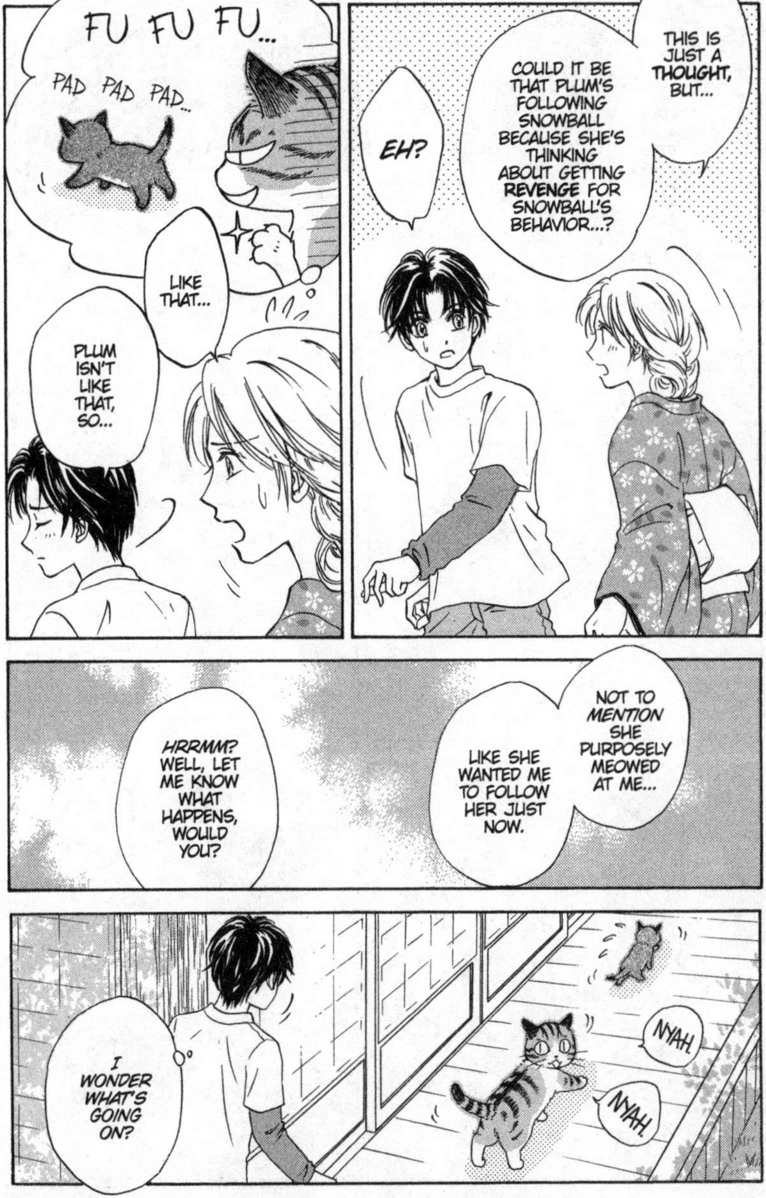
THIS IS JUST A THOUGHT, BUT...
COULD IT BE THAT PLUM'S FOLLOWING SNOWBALL BECAUSE SHE'S THINKING ABOUT GETTING REVENGE FOR SNOWBALL'S BEHAVIOR...?
EH?
FU FU FU...
PAD PAD PAD...
LIKE THAT...
PLUM ISN'T LIKE THAT, SO...
NOT TO MENTION SHE PURPOSELY MEOWED AT ME...
LIKE SHE WANTED ME TO FOLLOW HER JUST NOW.
HRRMM? WELL, LET ME KNOW WHAT HAPPENS, WOULD YOU?
NYAH.
NYAH.
I WONDER WHAT'S GOING ON?

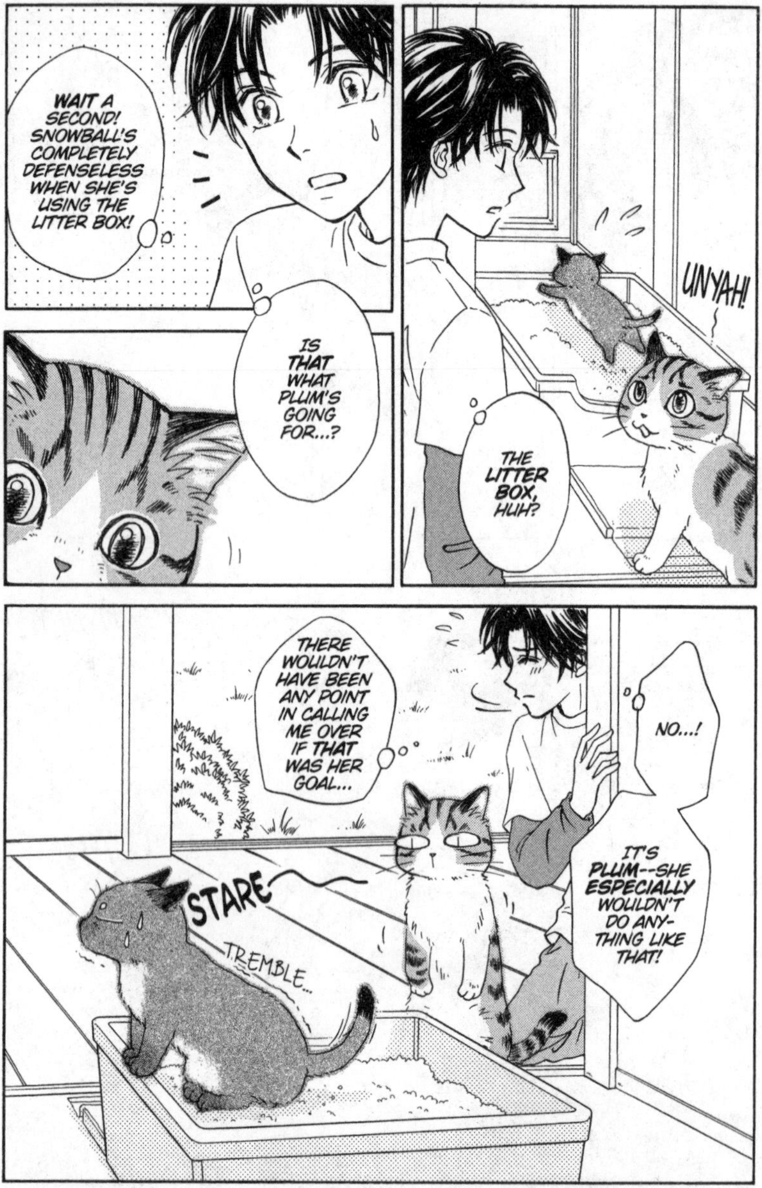
UNYAH!
THE LITTER BOX, HUH?
WAIT A SECOND! SNOWBALL'S COMPLETELY DEFENSELESS WHEN SHE'S USING THE LITTER BOX!
IS THAT WHAT PLUM'S GOING FOR...?
NO...!
THERE WOULDN'T HAVE BEEN ANY POINT IN CALLING ME OVER IF THAT WAS HER GOAL...
IT'S PLUM--SHE ESPECIALLY WOULDN'T DO ANY-THING LIKE THAT!
STARE
TREMBLE...

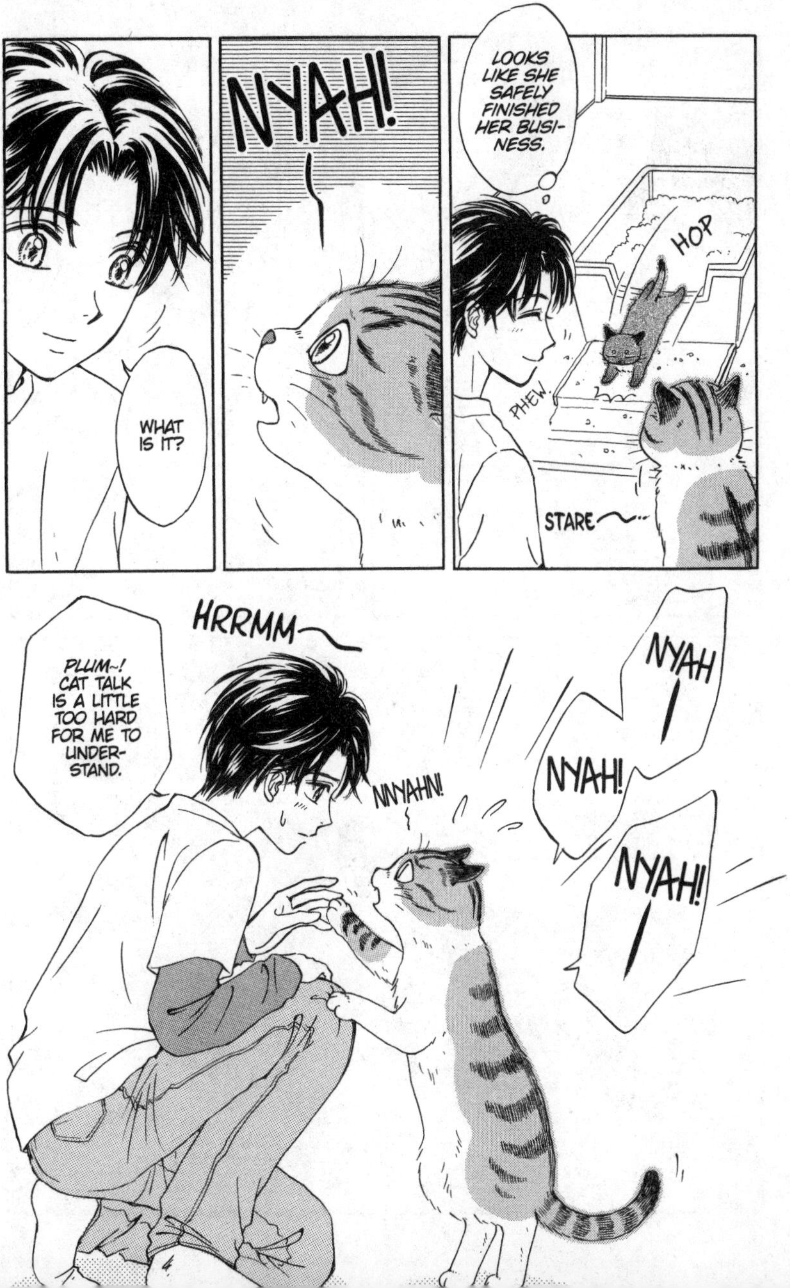
LOOKS LIKE SHE SAFELY FINISHED HER BUSI-NESS.
HOP
PHEW.
STARE~
NYAH!
WHAT IS IT?
NYAH!
NYAH!
NYAH!
HRRMM~
NNYAHN!
PLUM~! CAT TALK IS A LITTLE TOO HARD FOR ME TO UNDER-STAND.

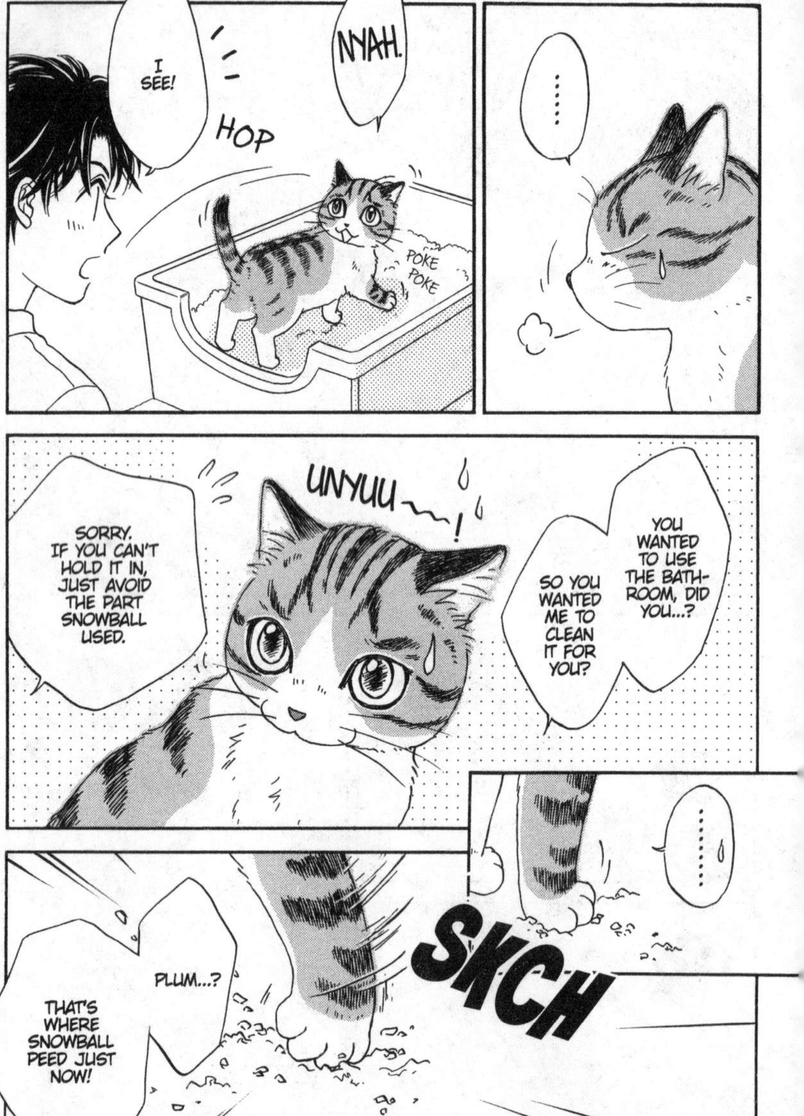
......
NYAH.
I SEE!
HOP
POKE POKE
YOU WANTED TO USE THE BATH-ROOM, DID YOU...?
SO YOU WANTED ME TO CLEAN IT FOR YOU?
UNYUU~!
SORRY. IF YOU CAN'T HOLD IT IN, JUST AVOID THE PART SNOWBALL USED.
......
SKCH
PLUM...?
THAT'S WHERE SNOWBALL PEED JUST NOW!

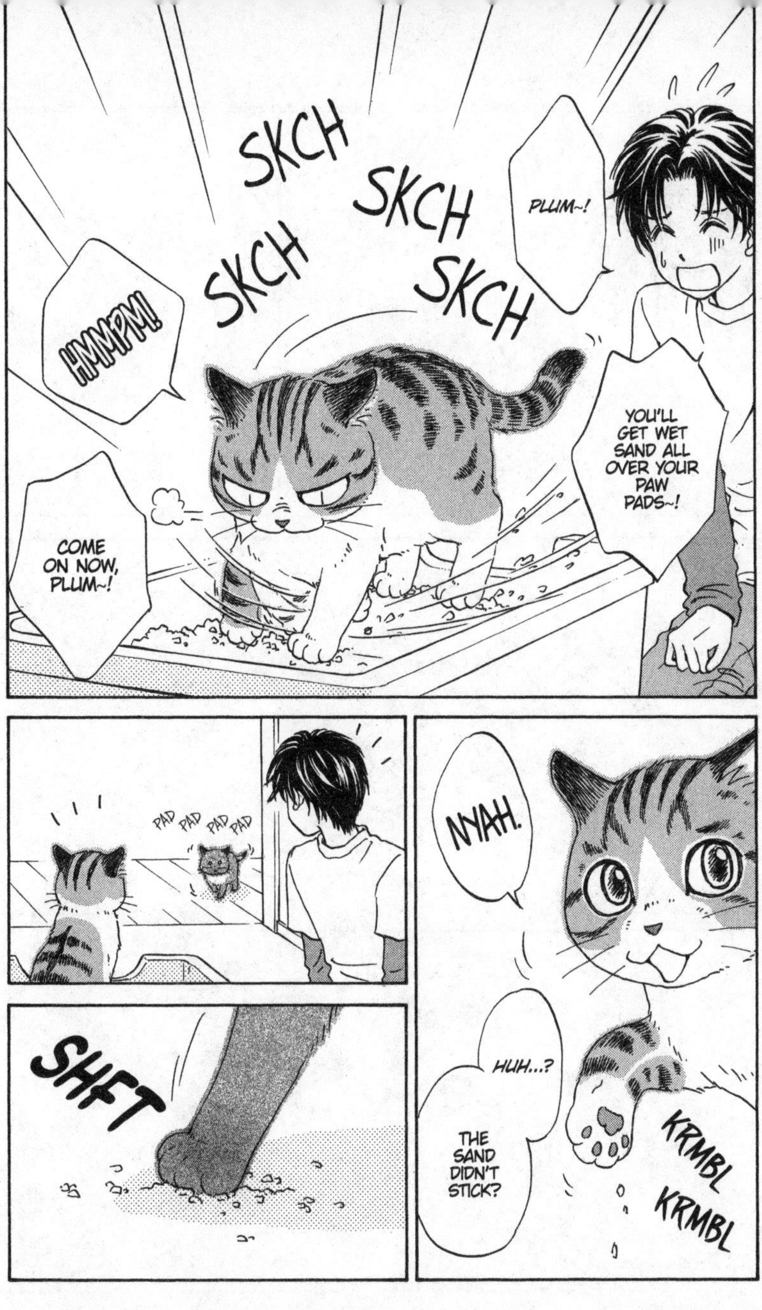
PLUM~!
YOU'LL GET WET SAND ALL OVER YOUR PAW PADS~!
SKCH SKCH SKCH SKCH
HMMPM!
COME ON NOW, PLUM~!
NYAH.
HUH...?
THE SAND DIDN'T STICK?
KRMBL KRMBL
PAD PAD PAD PAD
SHFT

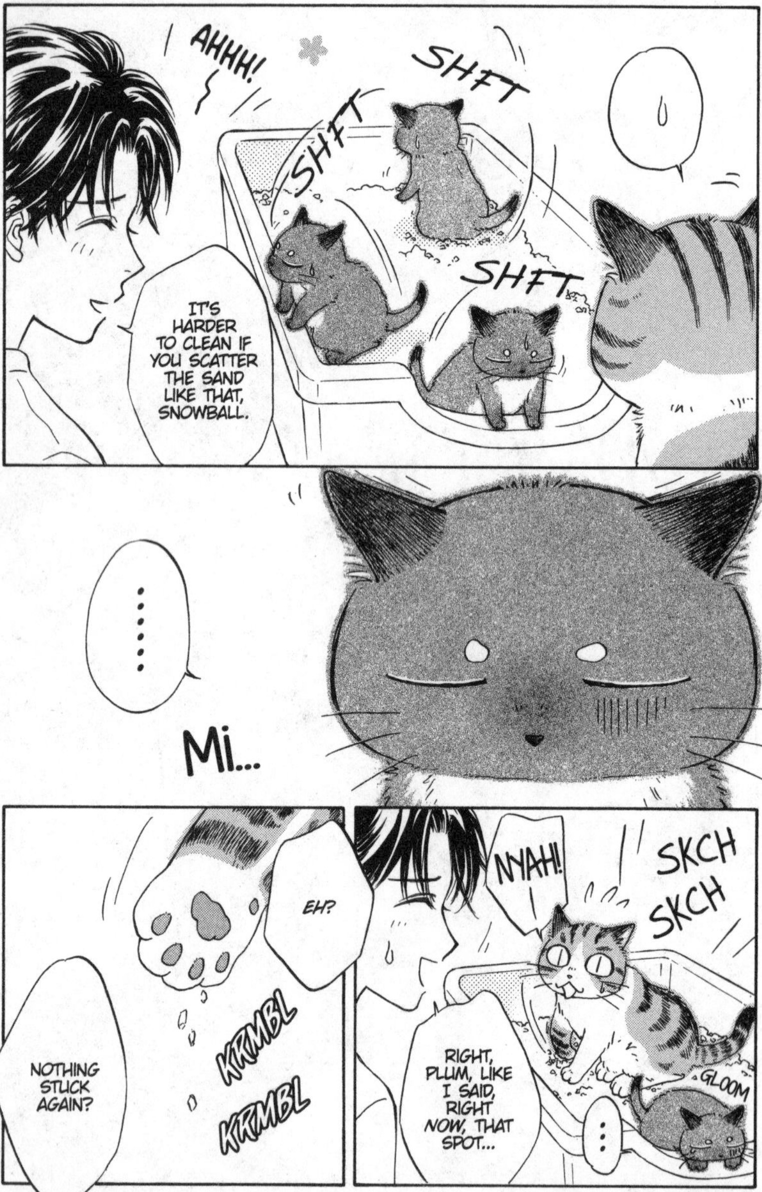
SHFT
SHFT
AHHH!
SHFT
IT'S HARDER TO CLEAN IF YOU SCATTER THE SAND LIKE THAT, SNOWBALL.
......
Mi...
SKCH SKCH
NYAH!
RIGHT, PLUM, LIKE I SAID, RIGHT NOW, THAT SPOT...
GLOOM
...
EH?
KRMBL KRMBL
NOTHING STUCK AGAIN?

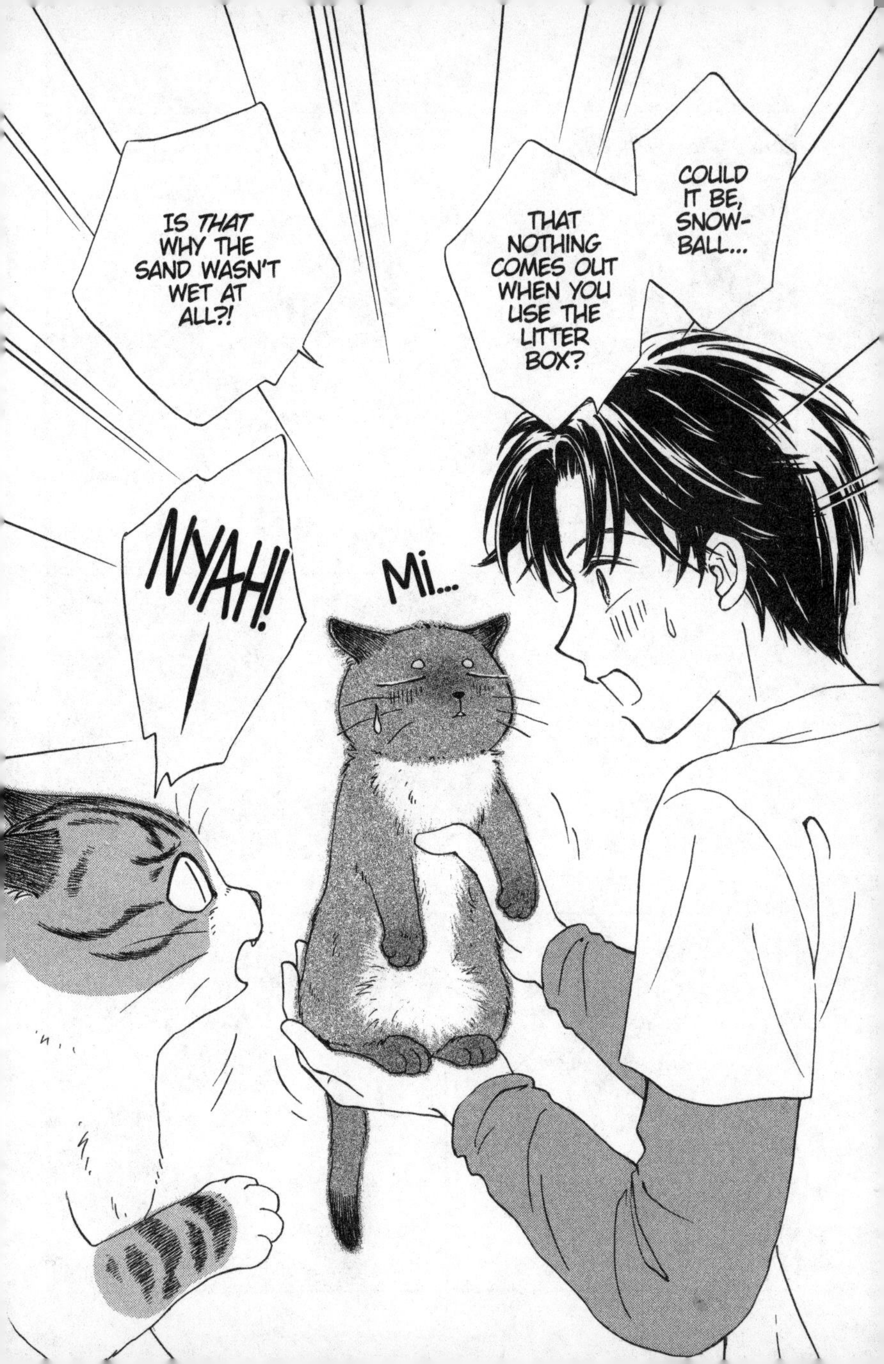
COULD IT BE, SNOWBALL...
THAT NOTHING COMES OUT WHEN YOU USE THE LITTER BOX?
IS *THAT* WHY THE SAND WASN'T WET AT ALL?!
Mi...
NYAH!

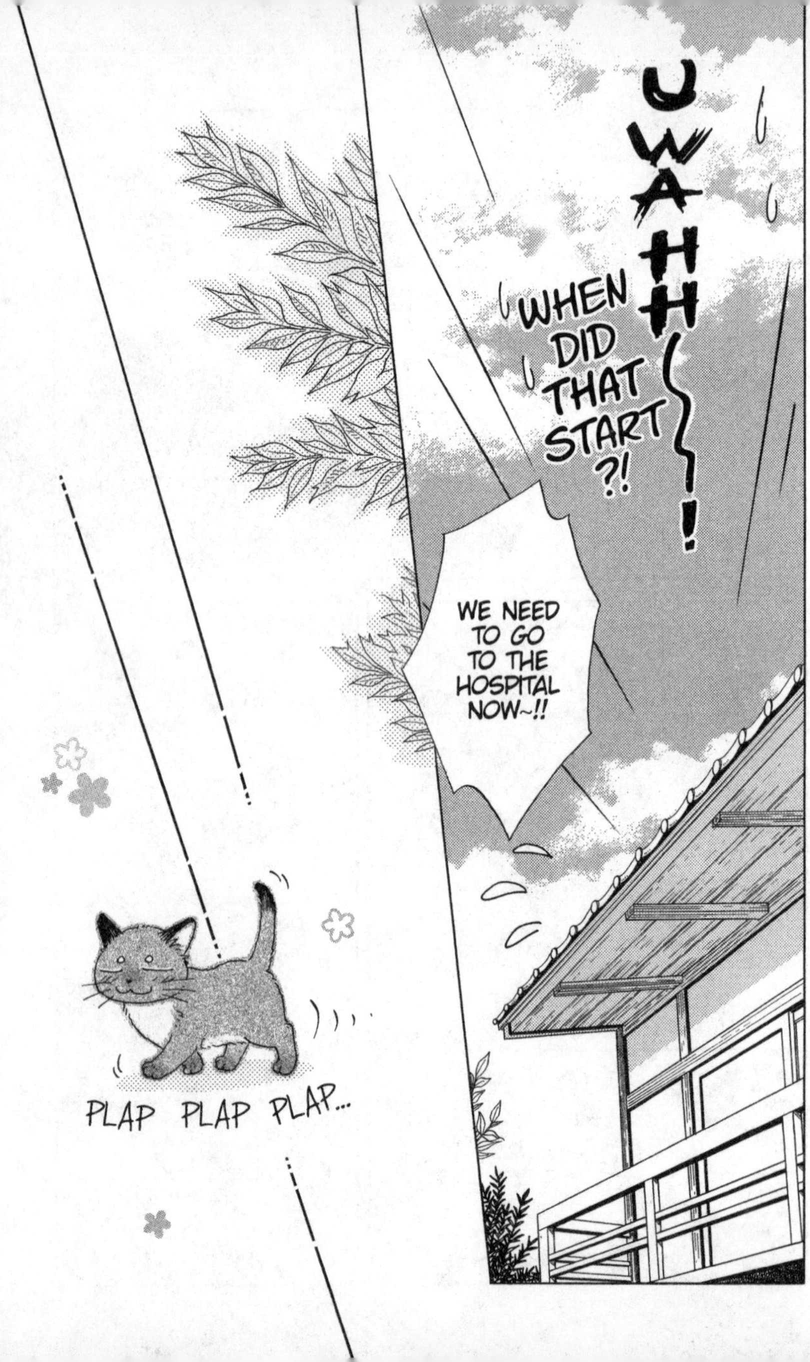
UWAHH~!
WHEN DID THAT START?!
WE NEED TO GO TO THE HOSPITAL NOW~!!
PLAP PLAP PLAP...

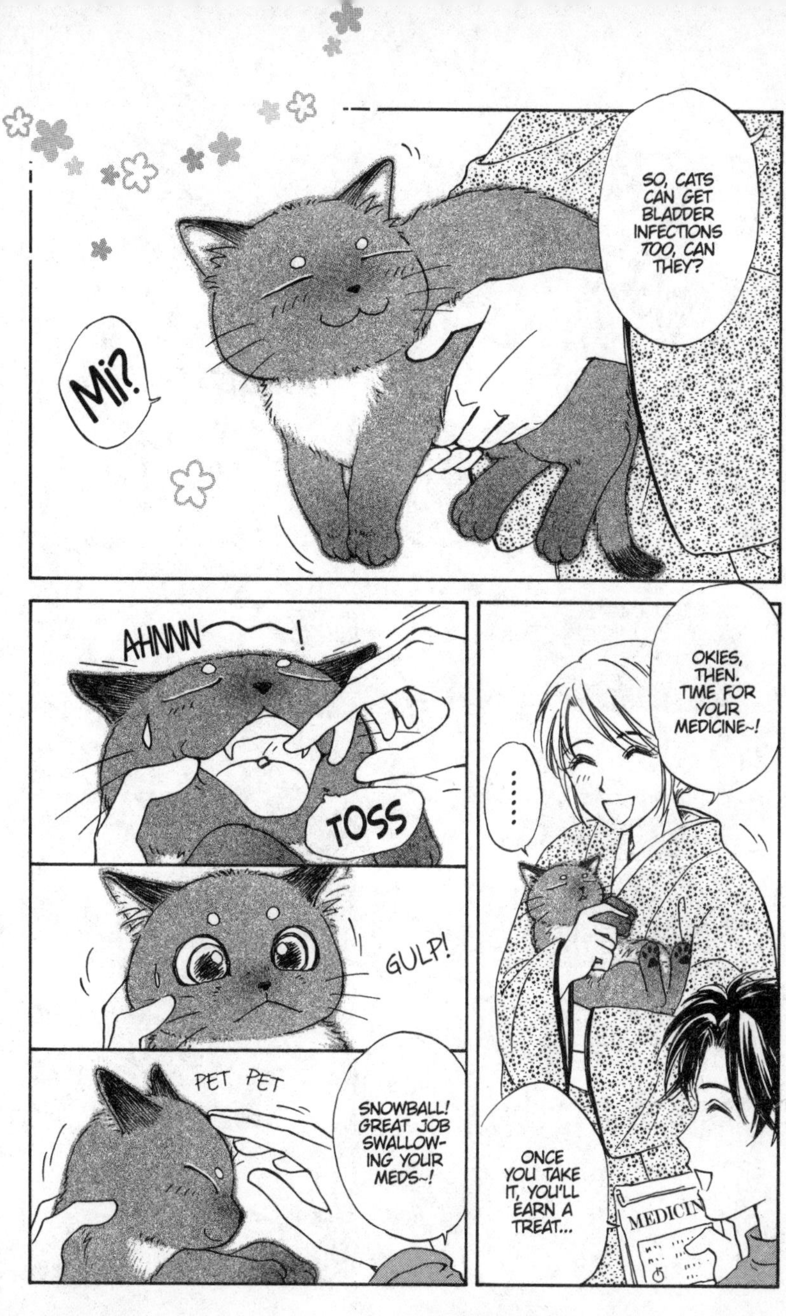
SO, CATS CAN GET BLADDER INFECTIONS *TOO*, CAN THEY?
Mi?
OKIES, THEN. TIME FOR YOUR MEDICINE~!
......
ONCE YOU TAKE IT, YOU'LL EARN A TREAT...
MEDICIN
AHNNN~~~!
TOSS
GULP!
PET PET
SNOWBALL! GREAT JOB SWALLOWING YOUR MEDS~!

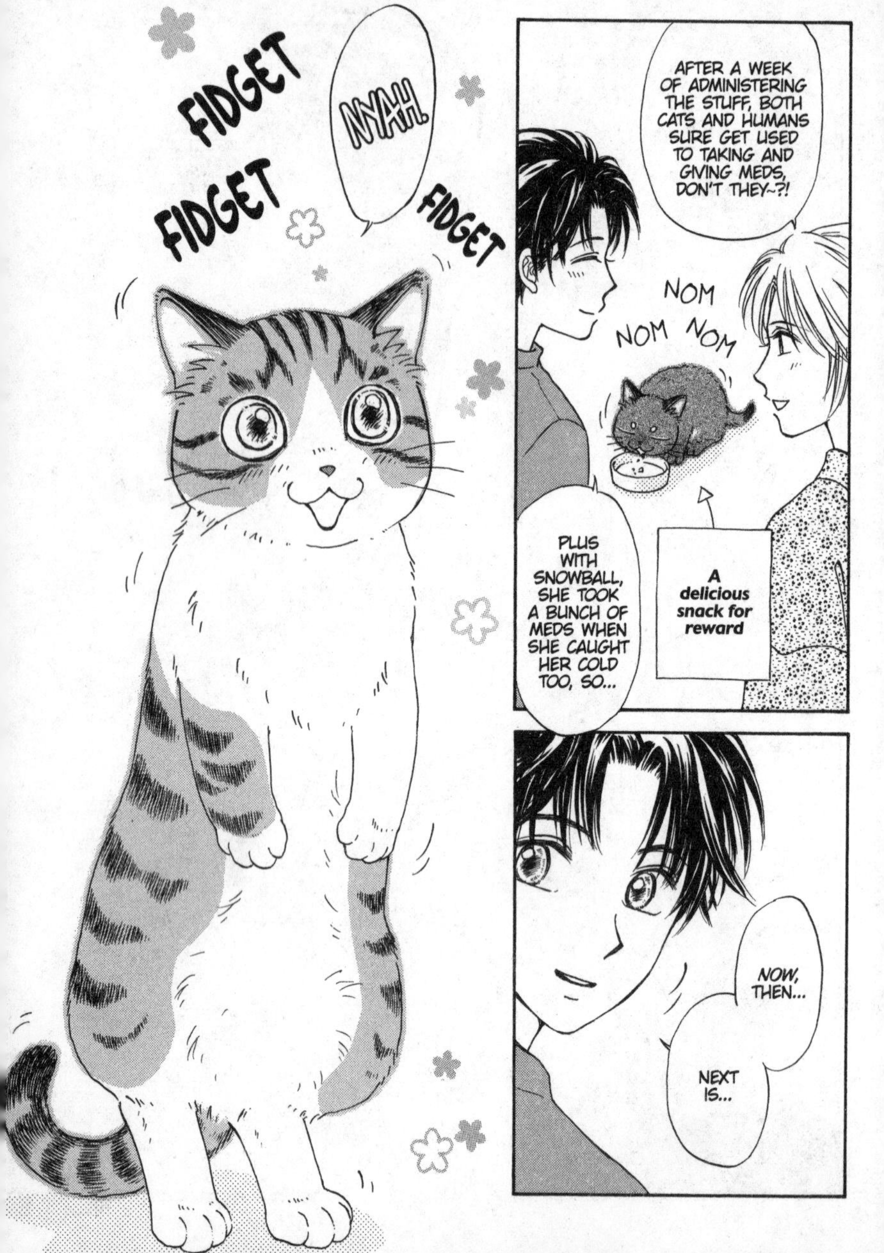
AFTER A WEEK OF ADMINISTERING THE STUFF, BOTH CATS AND HUMANS SURE GET USED TO TAKING AND GIVING MEDS, DON'T THEY~?!
NOM NOM NOM
A delicious snack for reward
PLUS WITH SNOWBALL, SHE TOOK A BUNCH OF MEDS WHEN SHE CAUGHT HER COLD TOO, SO...
NOW, THEN...
NEXT IS...
NYAH
FIDGET FIDGET
FIDGET

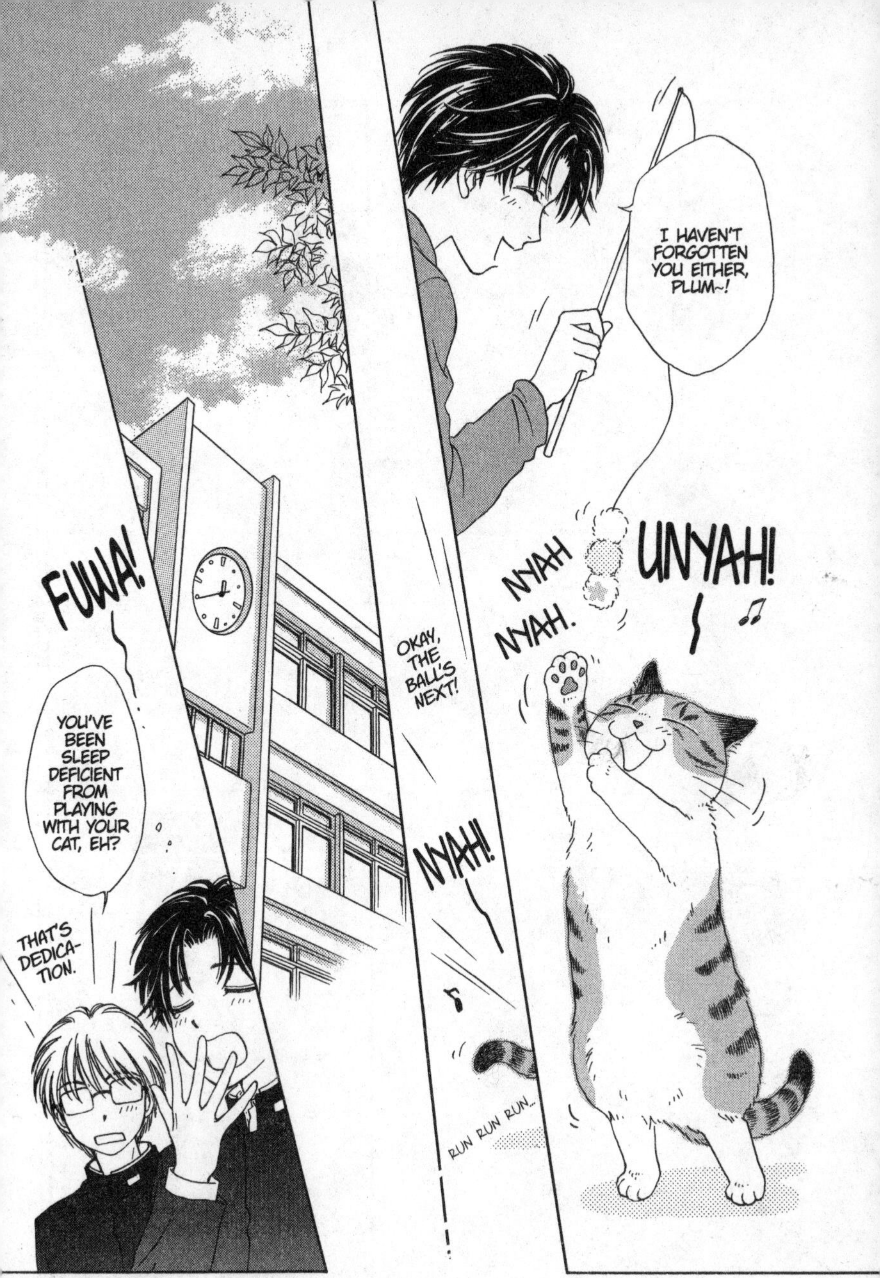
I HAVEN'T FORGOTTEN YOU EITHER, PLUM~!
UNYAH!
NYAH NYAH.
OKAY, THE BALL'S NEXT!
NYAH!
RUN RUN RUN...
FUWA!
YOU'VE BEEN SLEEP DEFICIENT FROM PLAYING WITH YOUR CAT, EH?
THAT'S DEDICA-TION.

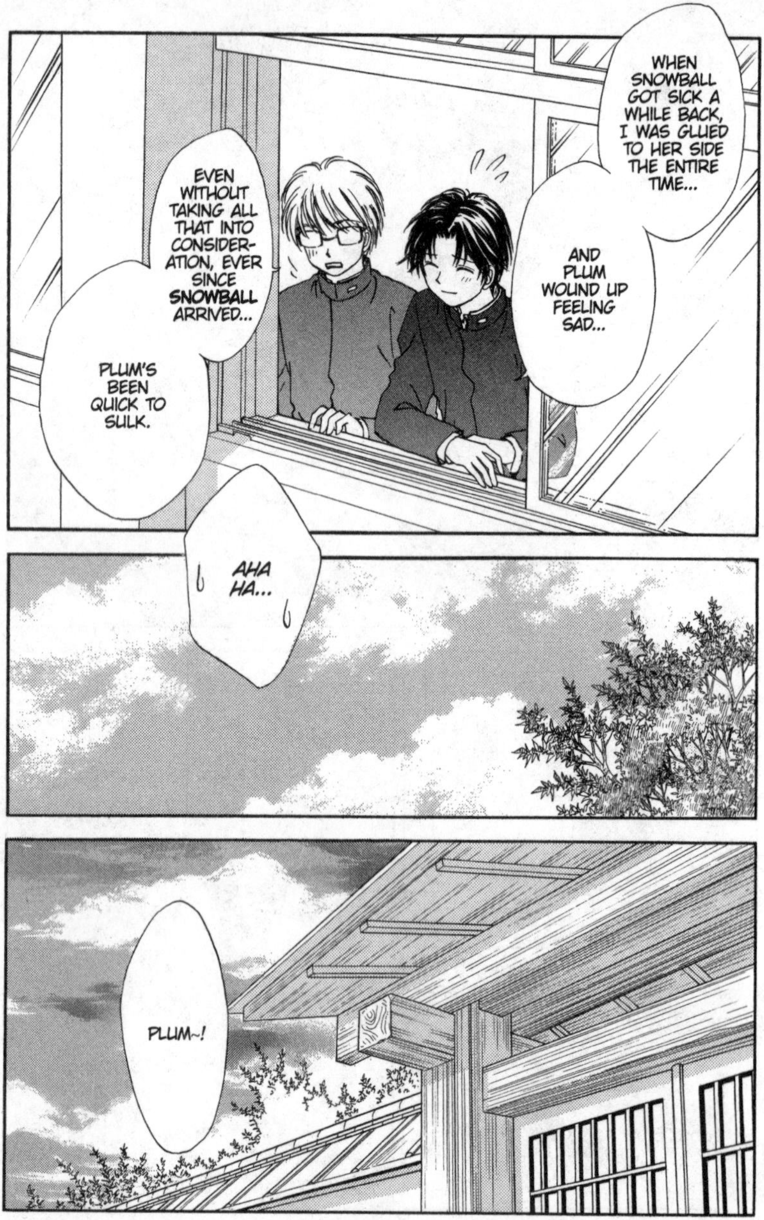
WHEN SNOWBALL GOT SICK A WHILE BACK, I WAS GLUED TO HER SIDE THE ENTIRE TIME...
AND PLUM WOUND UP FEELING SAD...
EVEN WITHOUT TAKING ALL THAT INTO CONSIDERATION, EVER SINCE SNOWBALL ARRIVED...
PLUM'S BEEN QUICK TO SULK.
AHA HA...
PLUM~!

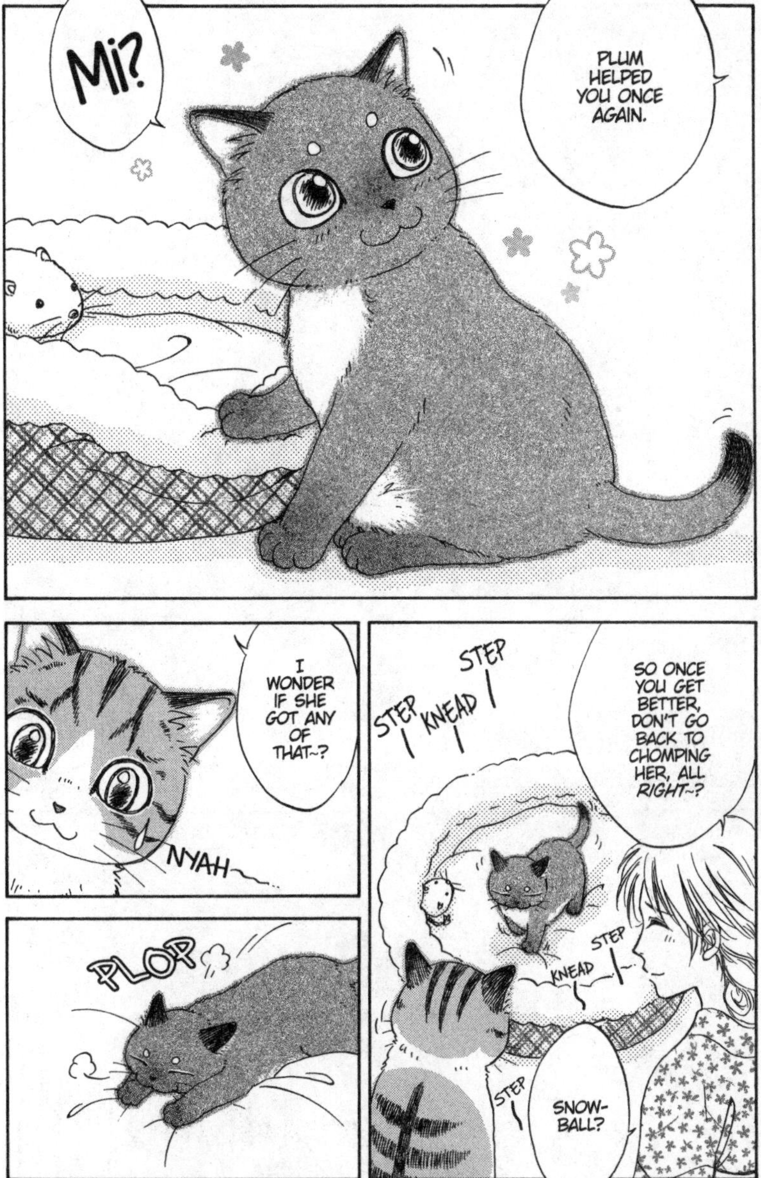
PLUM HELPED YOU ONCE AGAIN.
Mi?
STEP
KNEAD
STEP
SO ONCE YOU GET BETTER, DON'T GO BACK TO CHOMPING HER, ALL *RIGHT*~?
STEP
KNEAD
STEP
SNOW-BALL?
I WONDER IF SHE GOT ANY OF THAT~?
NYAH
PLOP

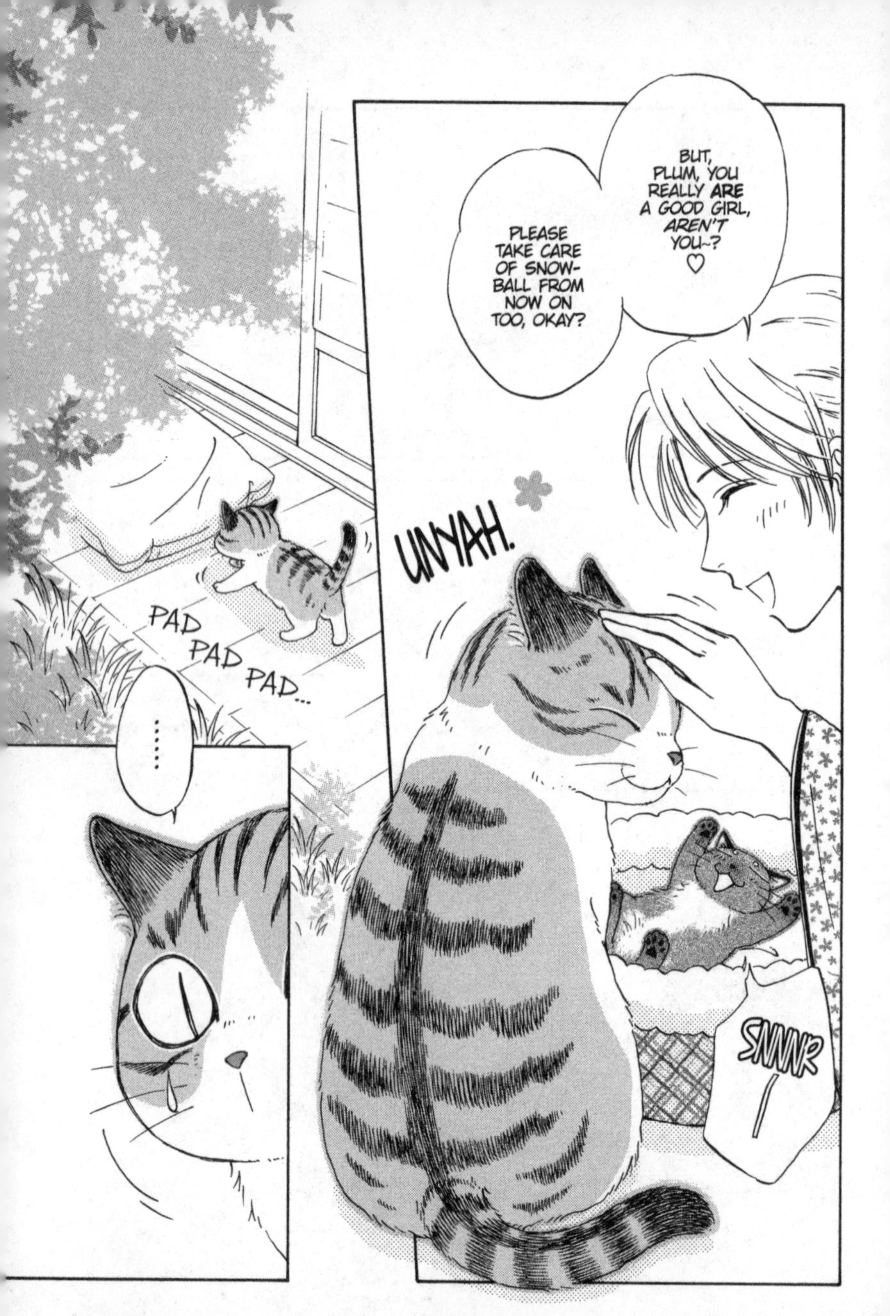
BUT, PLUM, YOU REALLY ARE A GOOD GIRL, AREN'T YOU~? ♡
PLEASE TAKE CARE OF SNOW-BALL FROM NOW ON TOO, OKAY?
UNYAH.
SNNNR
PAD PAD PAD...
......

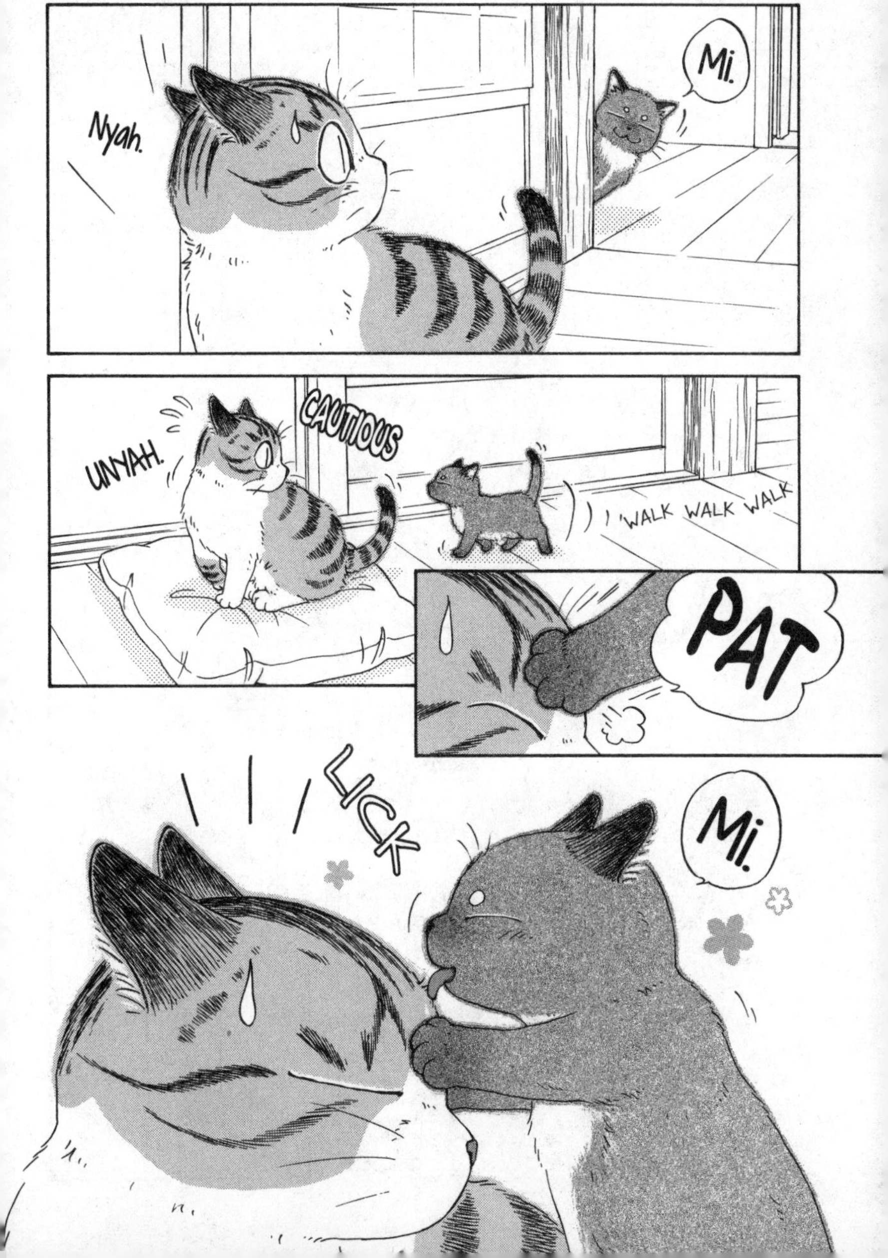
Mi.
Nyah.
WALK WALK WALK
CAUTIOUS
UNYAH.
PAT
Mi.
LICK

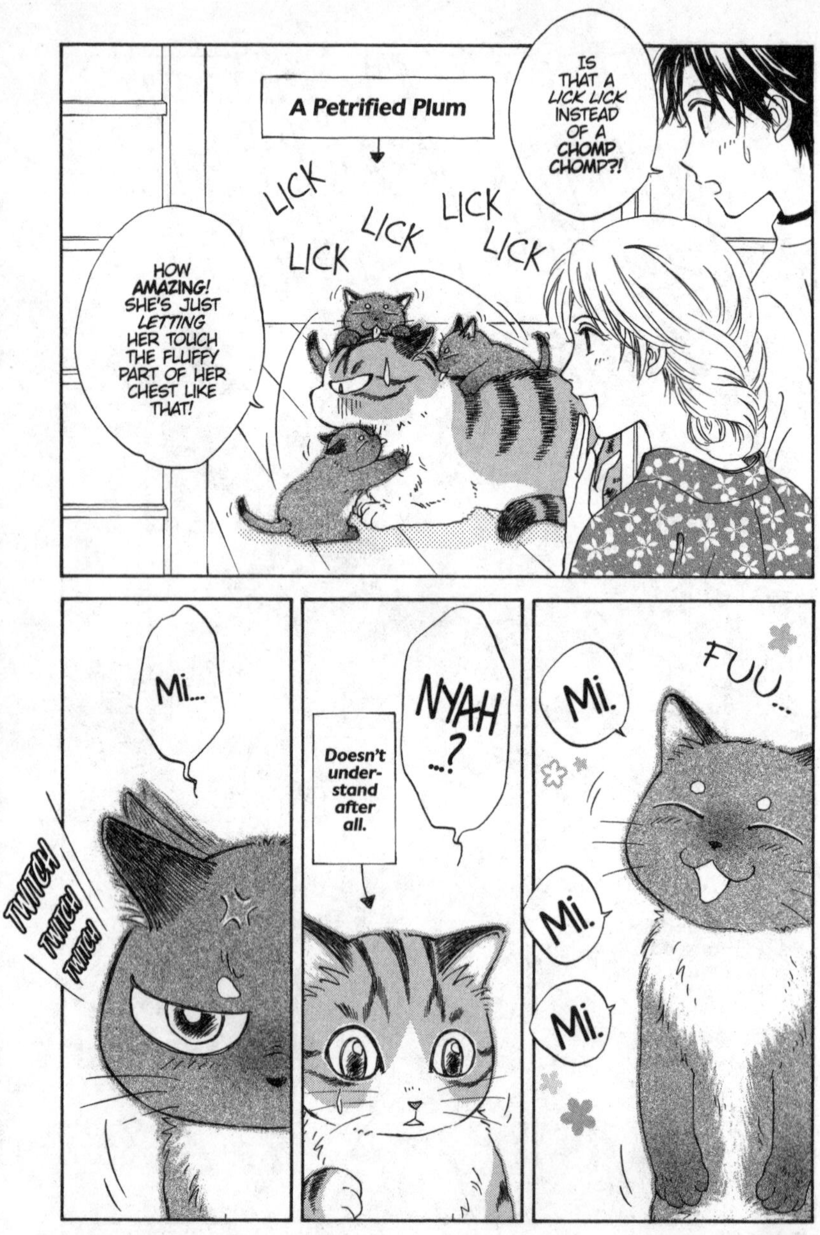
IS THAT A LICK LICK INSTEAD OF A CHOMP CHOMP?!
A Petrified Plum
LICK
LICK
LICK
LICK
LICK
HOW AMAZING! SHE'S JUST LETTING HER TOUCH THE FLUFFY PART OF HER CHEST LIKE THAT!
FUU...
Mi.
Mi.
Mi.
NYAH ...?
Doesn't under-stand after all.
Mi...
TWITCH TWITCH TWITCH

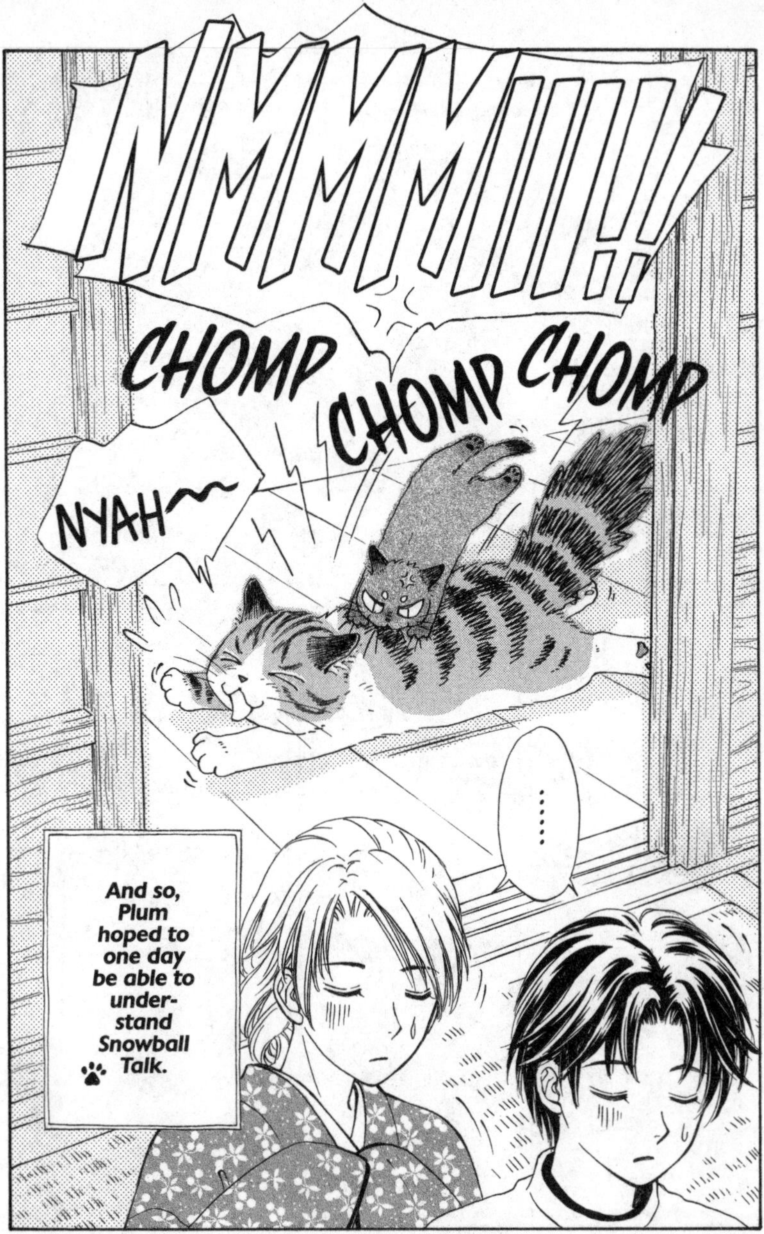
NMMMIII!!
CHOMP CHOMP CHOMP
NYAH~~
......
And so, Plum hoped to one day be able to under-stand Snowball Talk.

THE END

OMAKE PAGE

VARIOUS SPRING TIMES

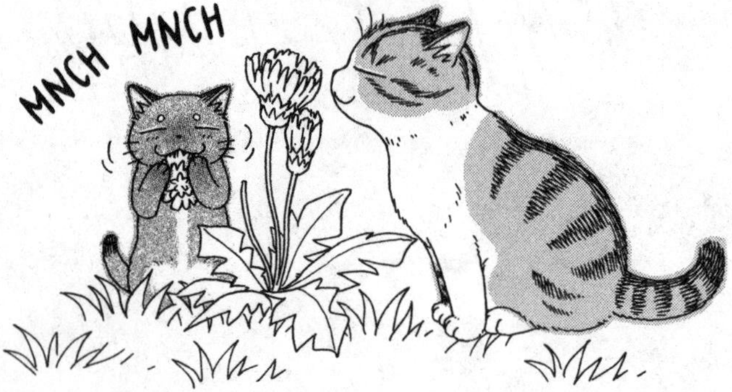
MNCH MNCH

Back cover illustration from the "Dried Bonito" volume of *Neko Panchi* No. 8.

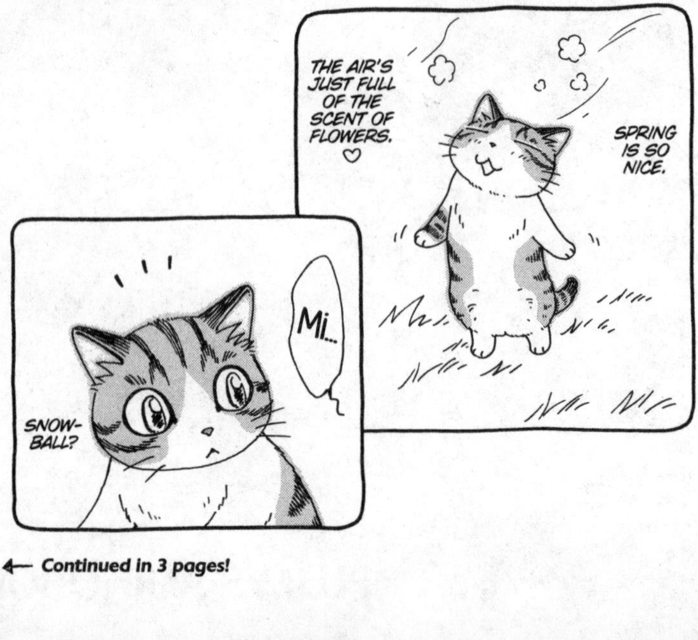
SPRING IS SO NICE.
THE AIR'S JUST FULL OF THE SCENT OF FLOWERS. ♡
Mi...
SNOW-BALL?

← Continued in 3 pages!

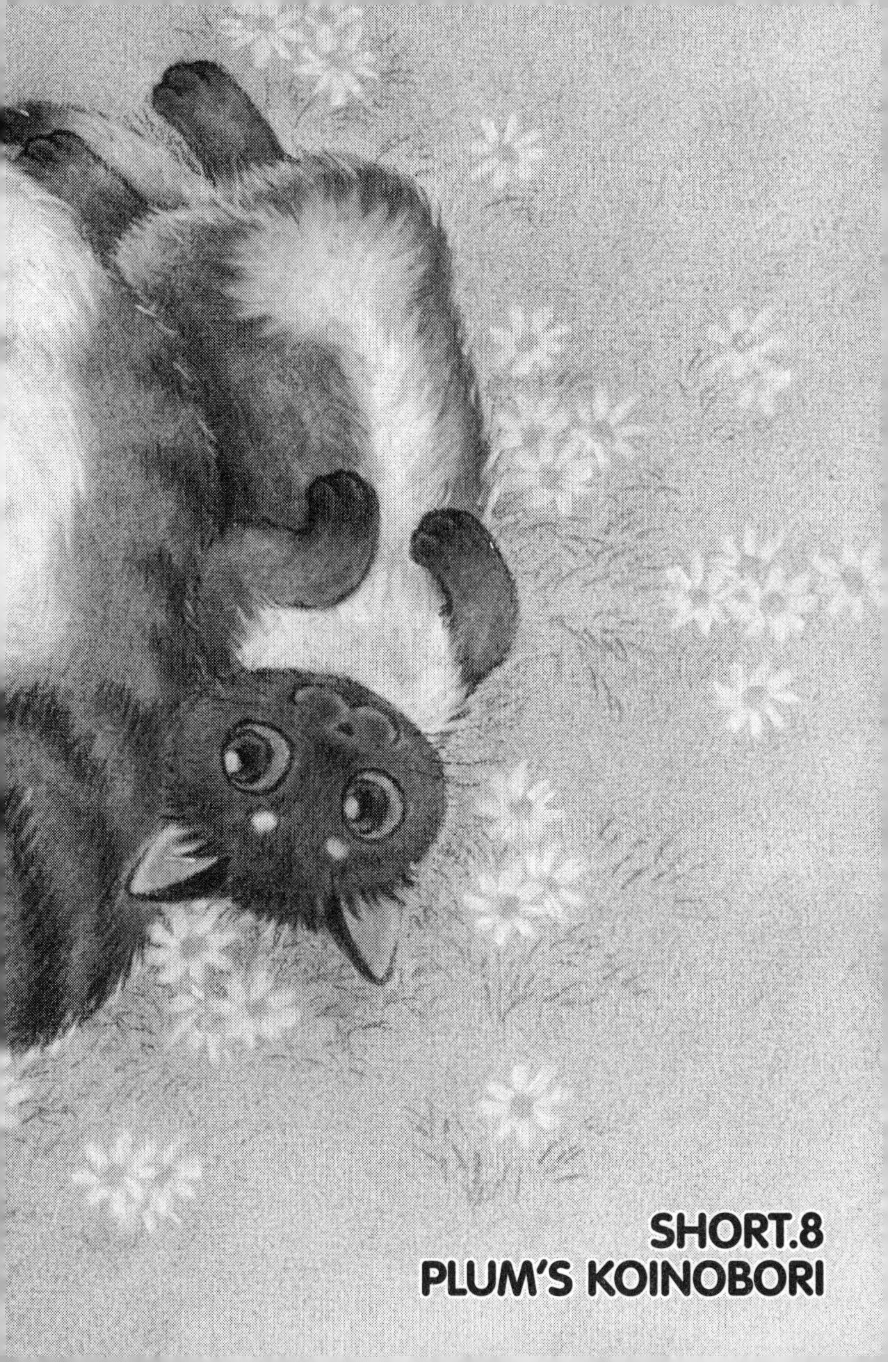

SHORT.8
PLUM'S KOINOBORI

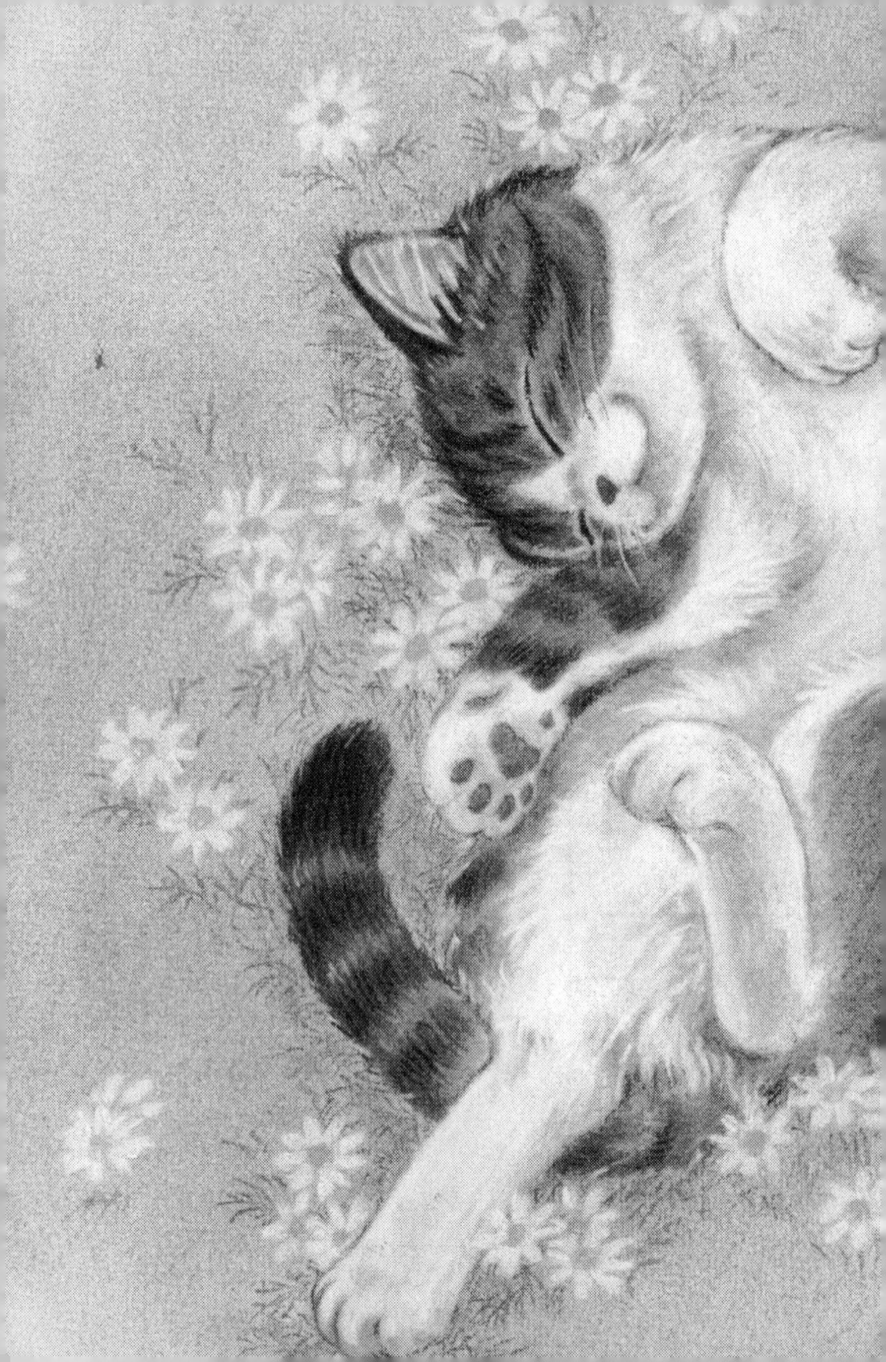

OMAKE PAGE

THE CONTINUATION!

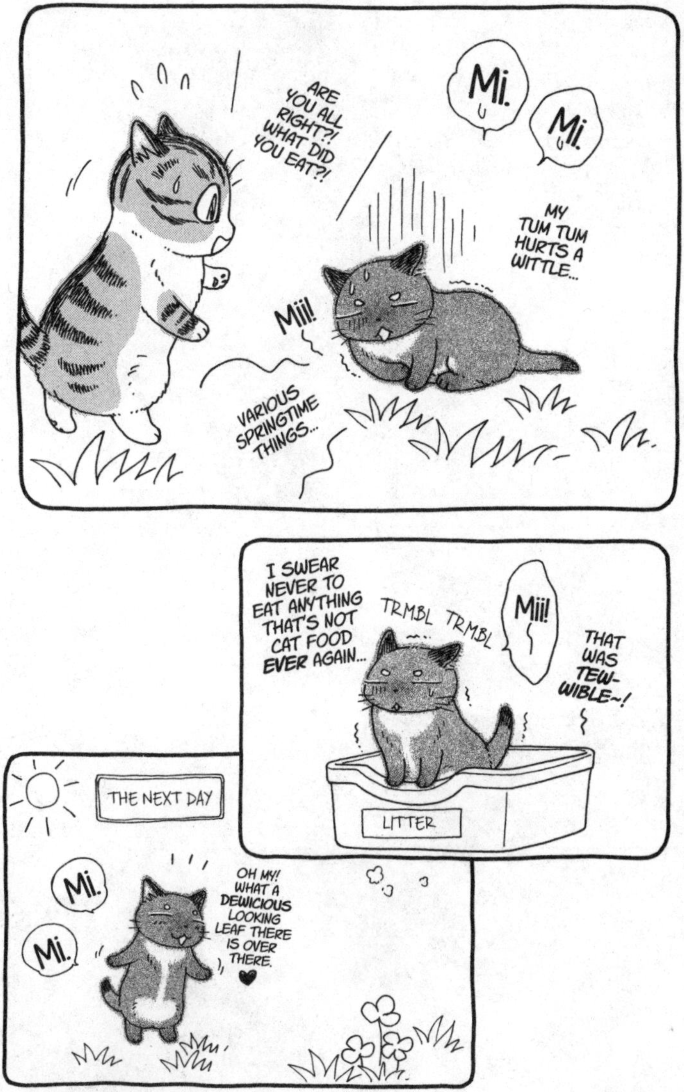
Mi.
Mi.
MY TUM TUM HURTS A WITTLE...
ARE YOU ALL RIGHT?! WHAT DID YOU EAT?!
Mii!
VARIOUS SPRINGTIME THINGS...
THAT WAS TEW-WIBLE~!
Mii!
TRMBL TRMBL
I SWEAR NEVER TO EAT ANYTHING THAT'S NOT CAT FOOD EVER AGAIN...
LITTER
THE NEXT DAY
OH MY! WHAT A DEWICIOUS LOOKING LEAF THERE IS OVER THERE. ❤
Mi.
Mi.

THE END

SHORT.8 PLUM'S KOINOBORI

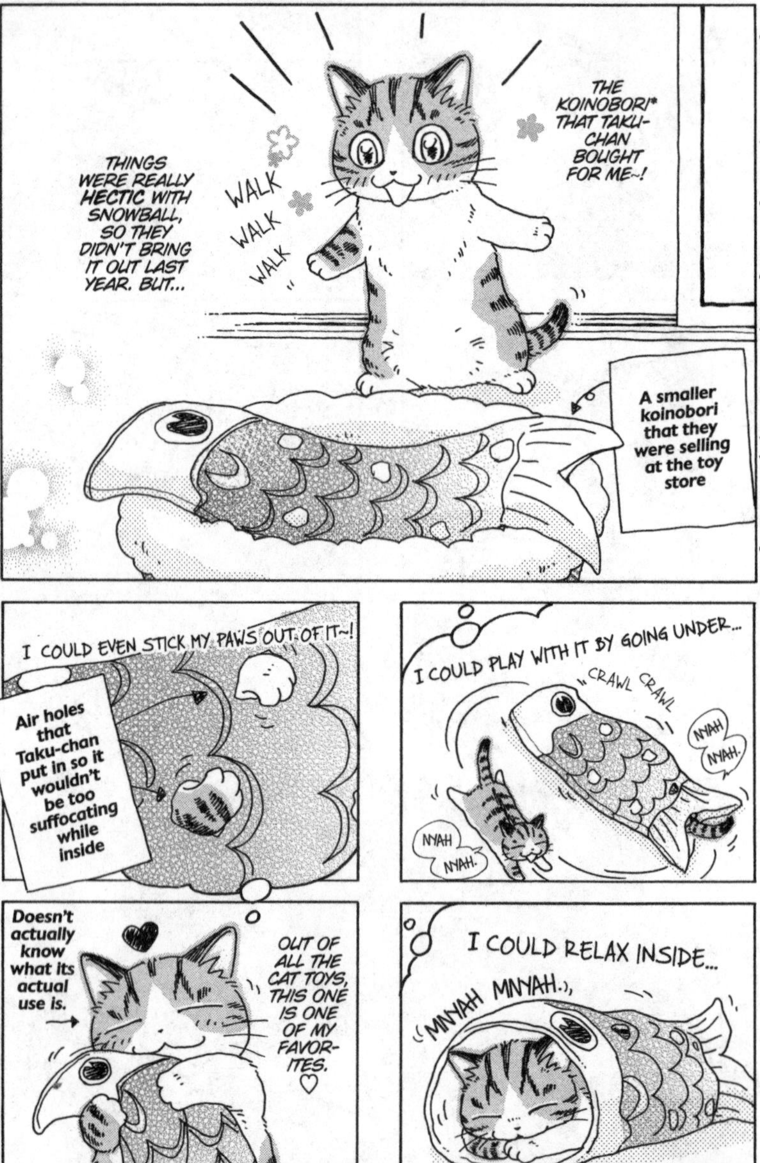
THE KOINOBORI* THAT TAKU-CHAN BOUGHT FOR ME~!
THINGS WERE REALLY HECTIC WITH SNOWBALL, SO THEY DIDN'T BRING IT OUT LAST YEAR. BUT...
WALK
WALK
WALK
A smaller koinobori that they were selling at the toy store
I COULD PLAY WITH IT BY GOING UNDER...
CRAWL CRAWL
NYAH NYAH.
NYAH NYAH.
I COULD EVEN STICK MY PAWS OUT OF IT~!
Air holes that Taku-chan put in so it wouldn't be too suffocating while inside
I COULD RELAX INSIDE...
MNYAH MNYAH.
OUT OF ALL THE CAT TOYS, THIS ONE IS ONE OF MY FAVOR-ITES. ♡
Doesn't actually know what its actual use is.

*Colorful carp streamers used to celebrate Children's Day (formerly Boys' Day), which takes place on May 5th--though the koinobori (ascending or climbing koi fish) are often on display for much longer than that.

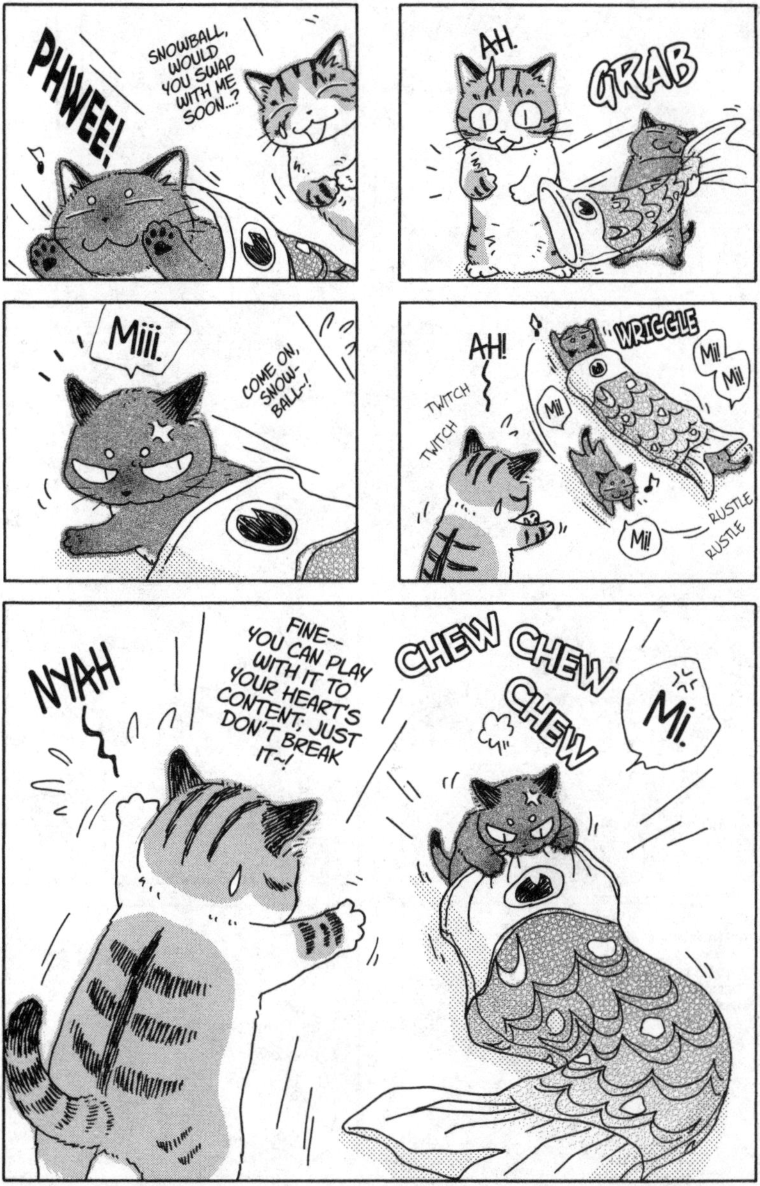
GRAB
AH.
SNOWBALL, WOULD YOU SWAP WITH ME SOON...?
PHWEE!
WRIGGLE
Mi! Mi!
AH!
Mi!
TWITCH
TWITCH
Mi!
RUSTLE
RUSTLE
COME ON, SNOW-BALL~!
Miii.
Mi.
CHEW CHEW
CHEW
FINE-- YOU CAN PLAY WITH IT TO YOUR HEART'S CONTENT; JUST DON'T BREAK IT~!
NYAH

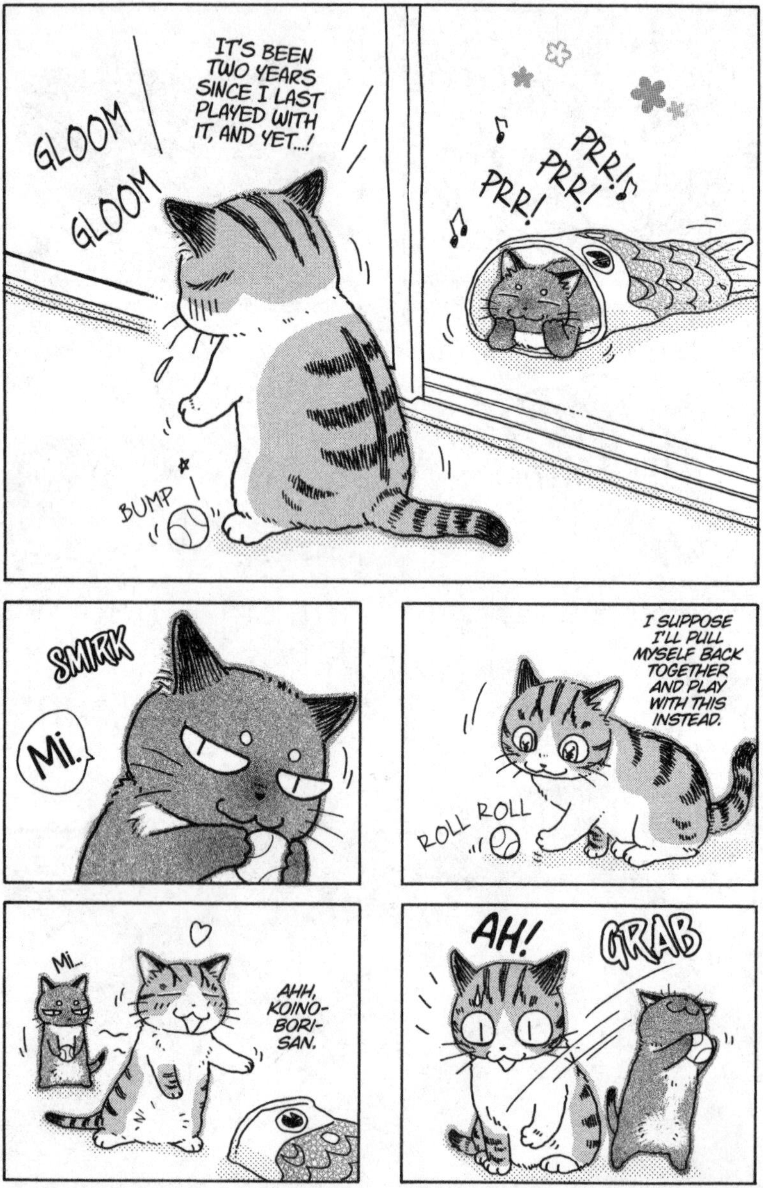
PRR! PRR! PRR!
IT'S BEEN TWO YEARS SINCE I LAST PLAYED WITH IT, AND YET...!
GLOOM GLOOM
BUMP
I SUPPOSE I'LL PULL MYSELF BACK TOGETHER AND PLAY WITH THIS INSTEAD.
ROLL ROLL
SMIRK
Mi.
GRAB
AH!
AHH, KOINOBORI-SAN.
Mi.

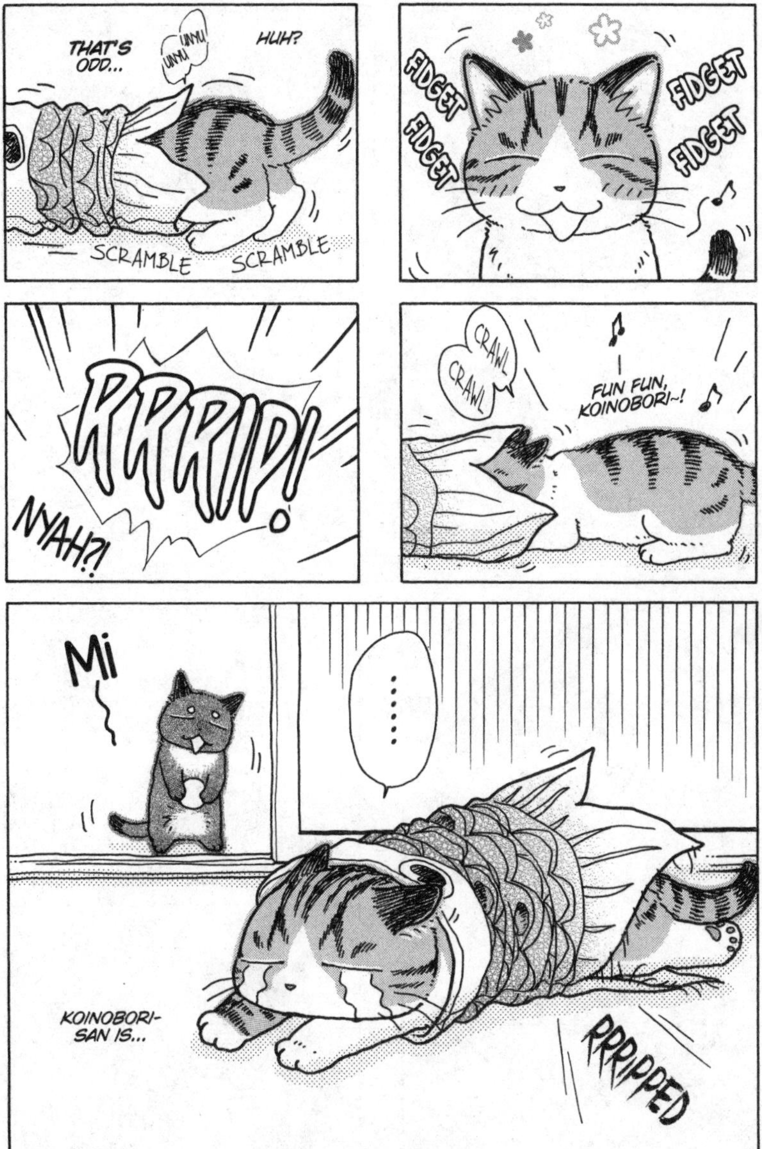
FIDGET FIDGET
FIDGET FIDGET
HUH?
UNYU UNYU
THAT'S ODD...
SCRAMBLE SCRAMBLE
CRAWL CRAWL
FUN FUN, KOINOBORI~!
RRRIP!
NYAH?!
......
Mi~
RRRIPPED
KOINOBORI-SAN IS...

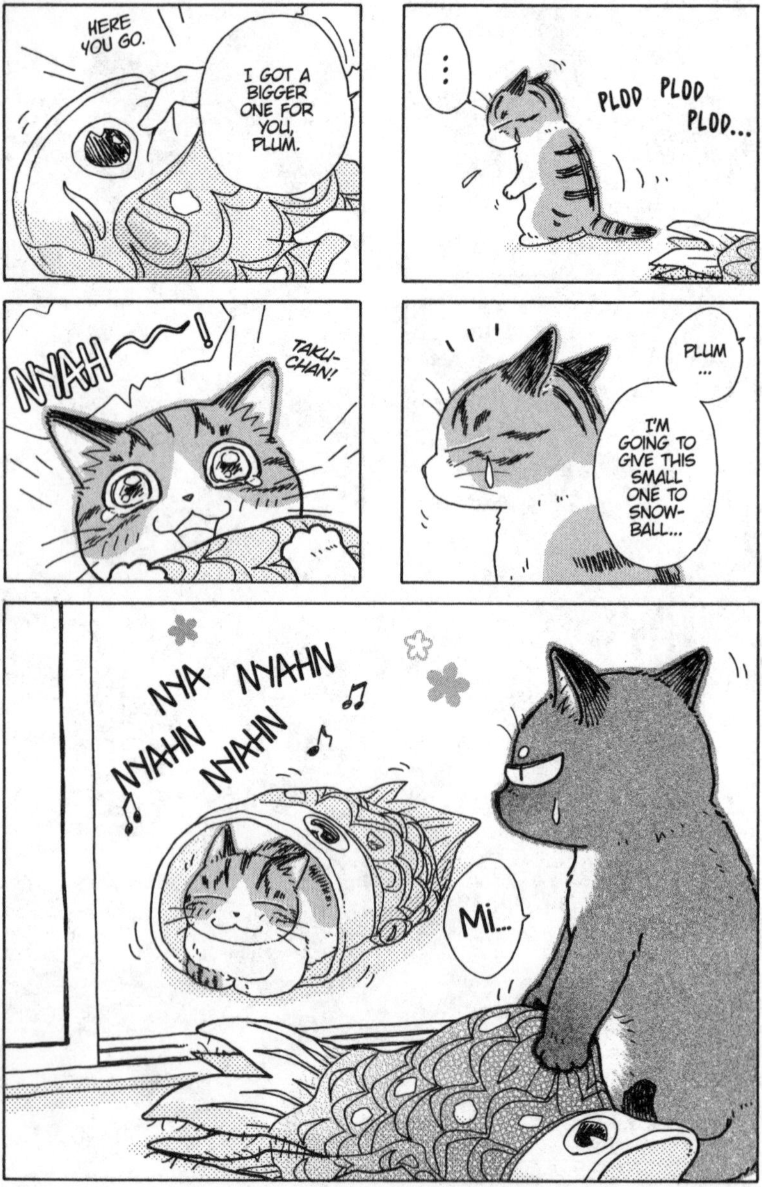

...
PLOD PLOD PLOD...
HERE YOU GO.
I GOT A BIGGER ONE FOR YOU, PLUM.
PLUM...
I'M GOING TO GIVE THIS SMALL ONE TO SNOW-BALL...
TAKU-CHAN!
NYAH~~~!
Mi...
NYA NYAHN
NYAHN NYAHN

THE SHAVED EYEBROW
CAT SNOWBALL

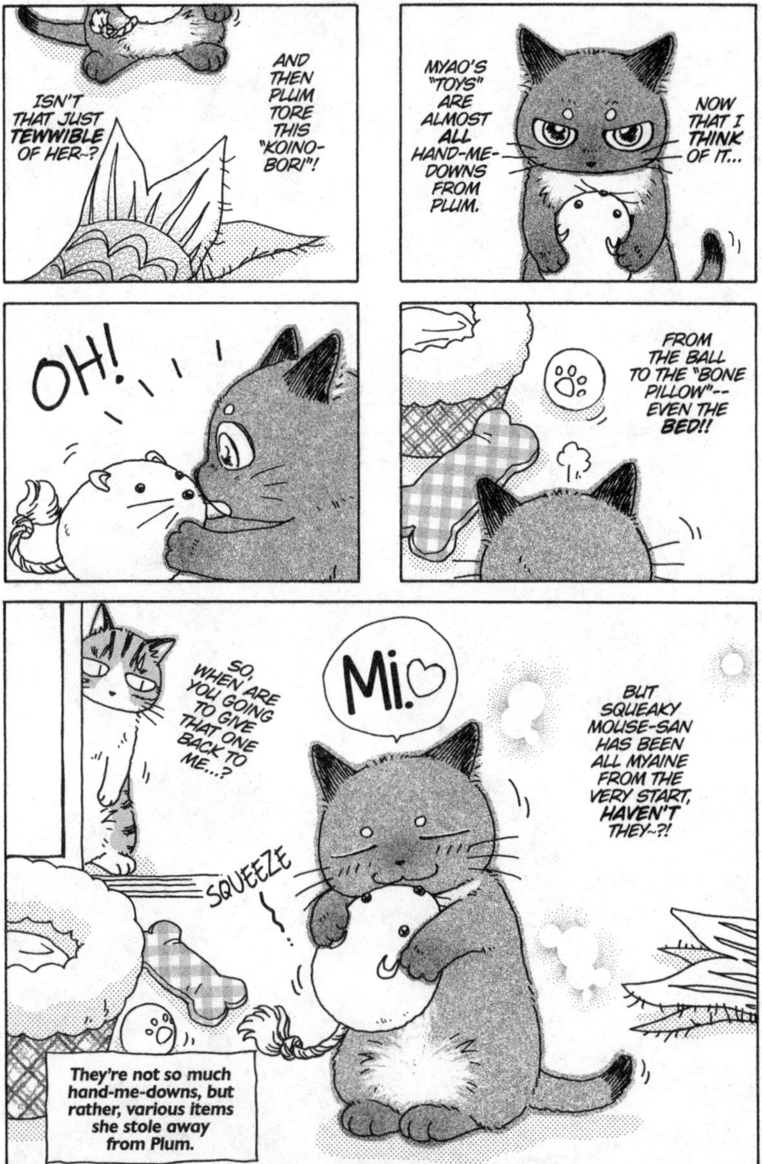
NOW THAT I THINK OF IT...
MYAO'S "TOYS" ARE ALMOST ALL HAND-ME-DOWNS FROM PLUM.
AND THEN PLUM TORE THIS "KOINOBORI"!
ISN'T THAT JUST TEWWIBLE OF HER~?
FROM THE BALL TO THE "BONE PILLOW"-- EVEN THE BED!!
OH!
BUT SQUEAKY MOUSE-SAN HAS BEEN ALL MYAINE FROM THE VERY START, HAVEN'T THEY~?!
Mi.♡
SO, WHEN ARE YOU GOING TO GIVE THAT ONE BACK TO ME...?
SQUEEZE
They're not so much hand-me-downs, but rather, various items she stole away from Plum.

THE END

CHAPTER 14
SNOWBALL'S DEBUT

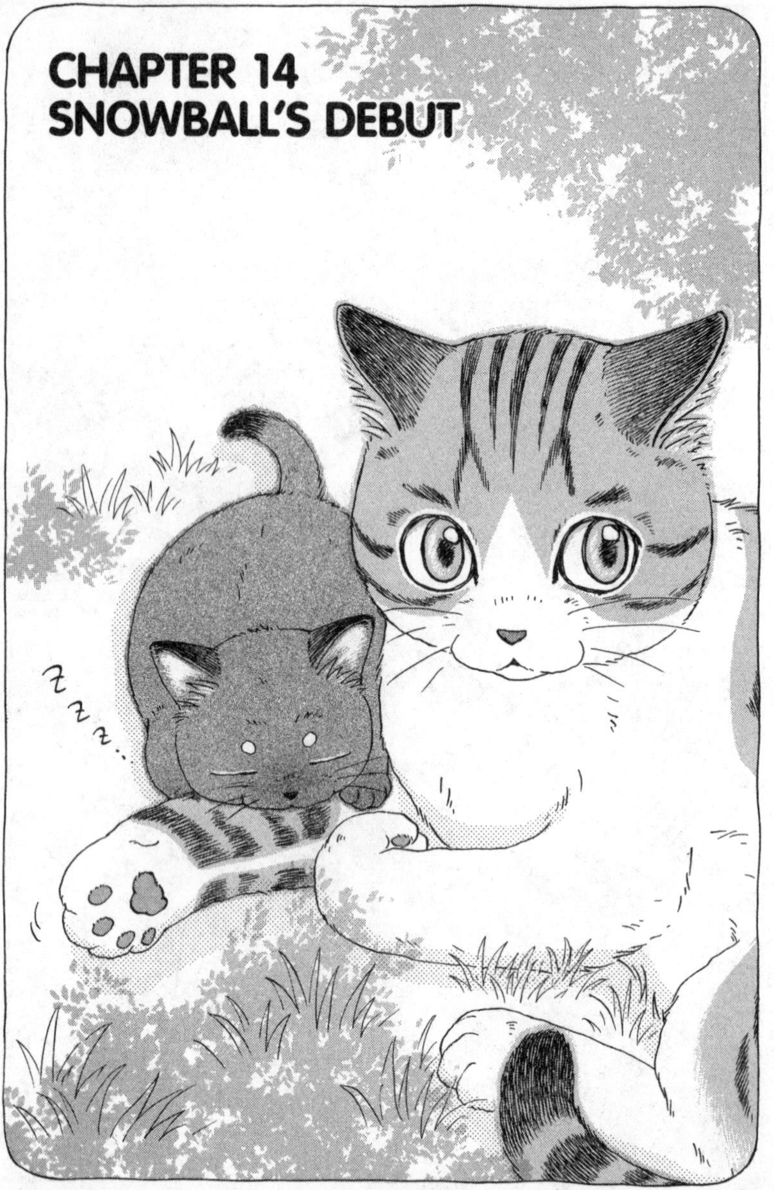
Z Z Z..

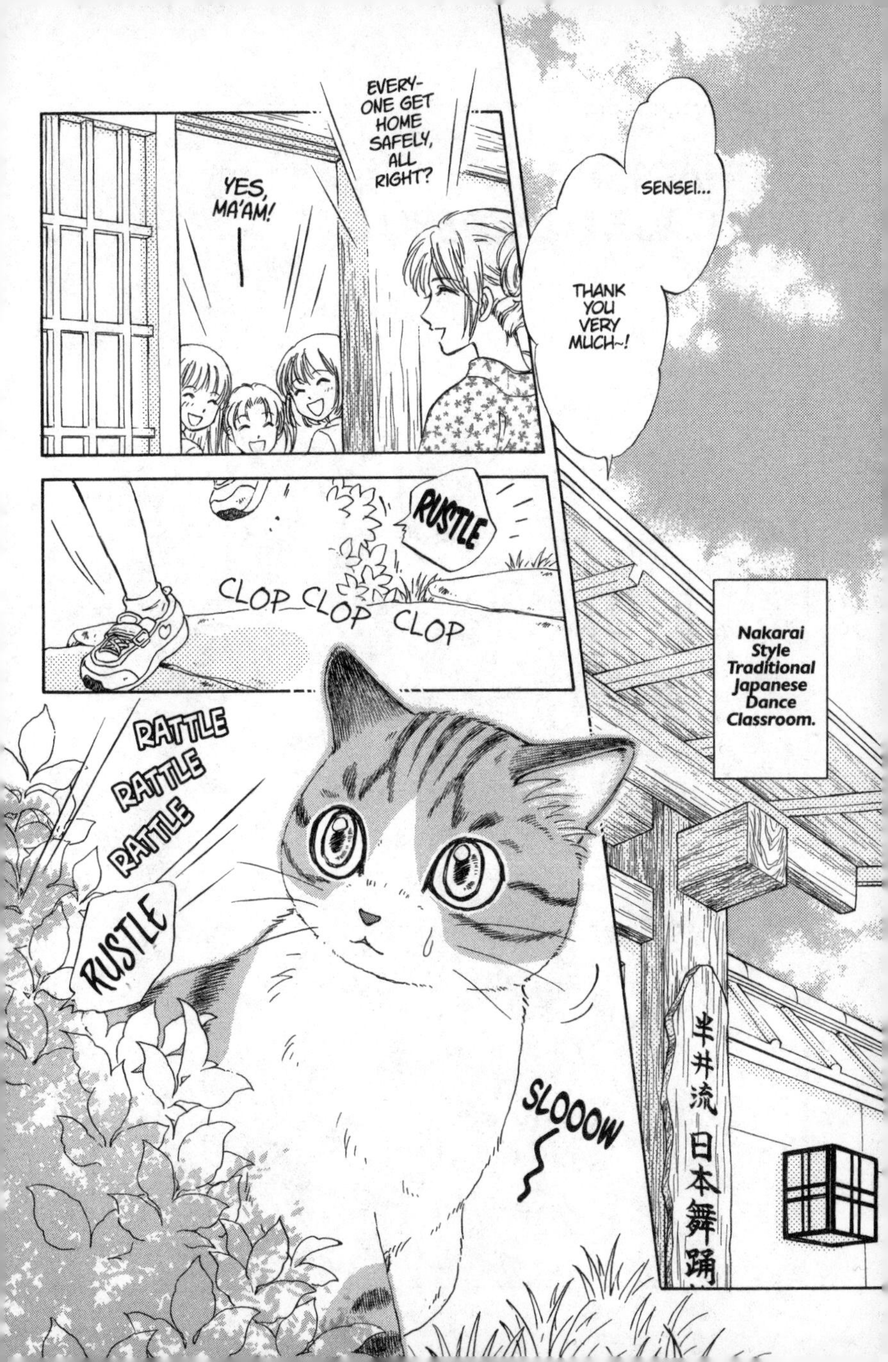
EVERY-ONE GET HOME SAFELY, ALL RIGHT?
YES, MA'AM!
SENSEI...
THANK YOU VERY MUCH~!
RUSTLE
CLOP CLOP CLOP
Nakarai Style Traditional Japanese Dance Classroom.
半井流 日本舞踊
RATTLE RATTLE RATTLE
RUSTLE
SLOOOW

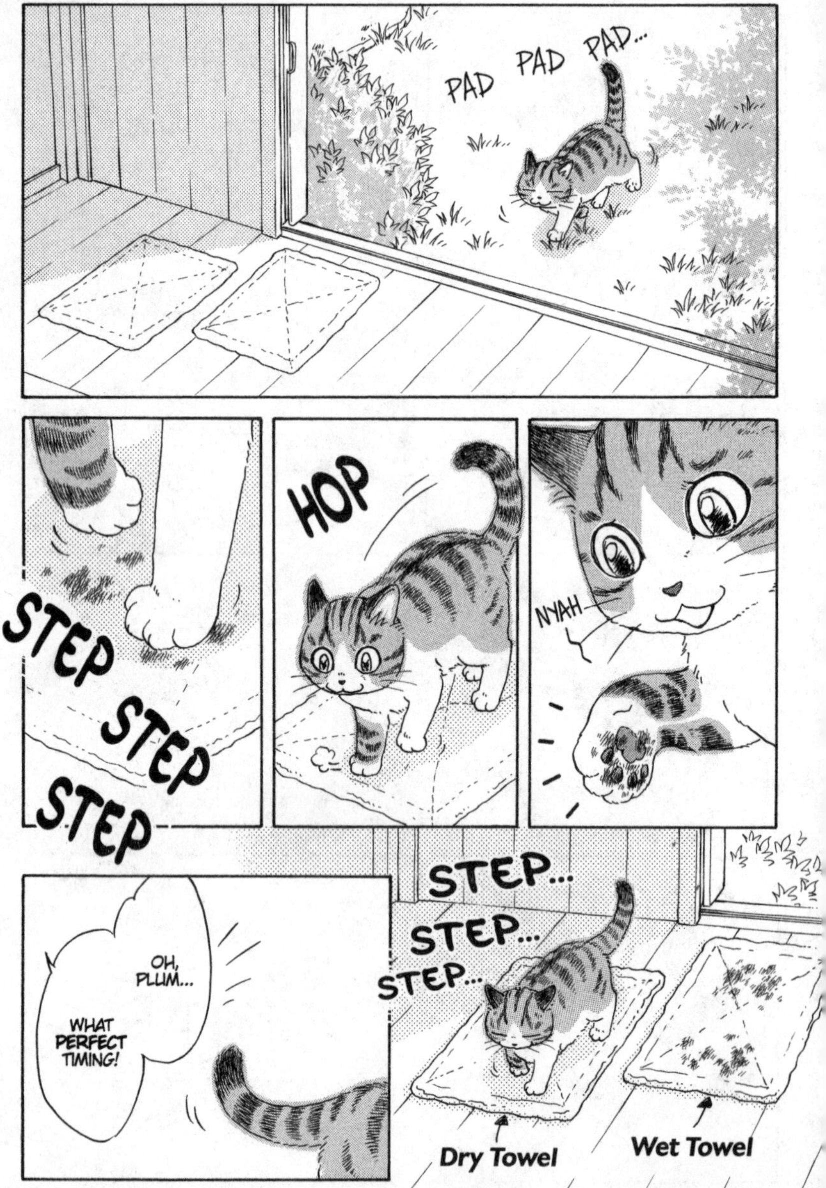
PAD PAD PAD...
NYAH
HOP
STEP
STEP
STEP
STEP...
STEP...
STEP...
Wet Towel
Dry Towel
OH, PLUM...
WHAT PERFECT TIMING!

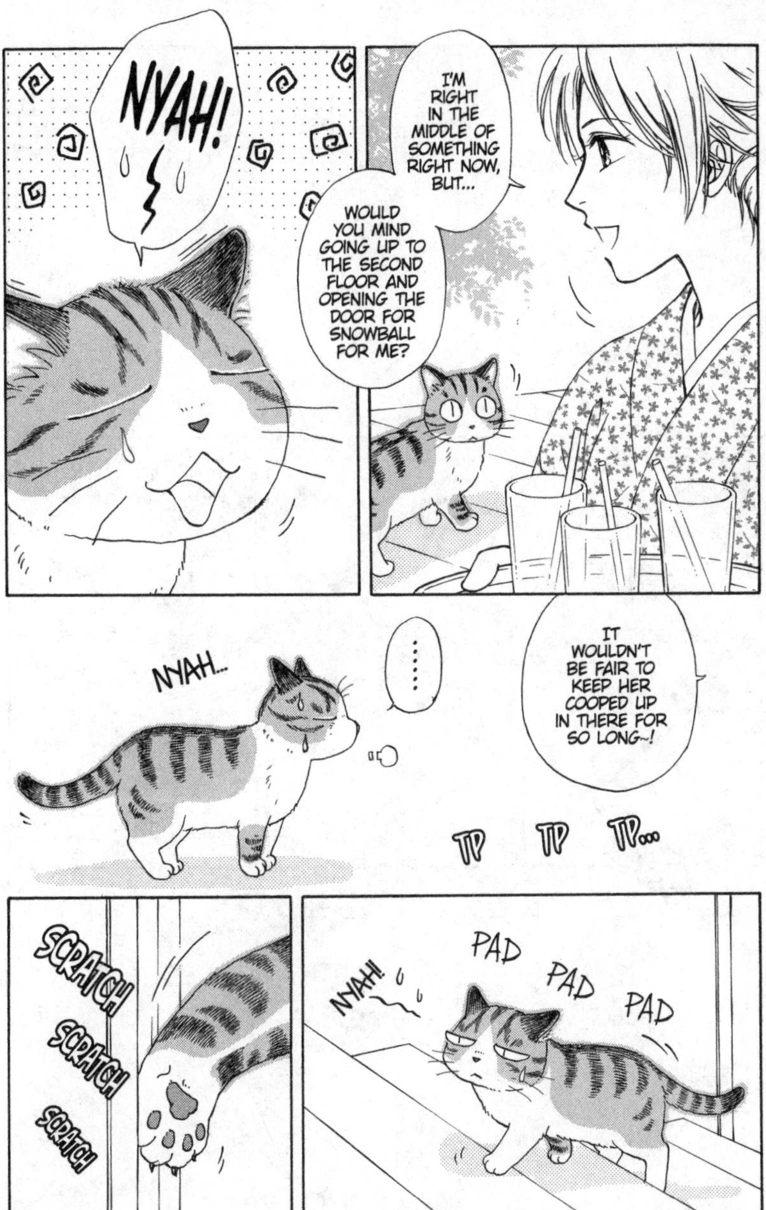
I'M RIGHT IN THE MIDDLE OF SOMETHING RIGHT NOW, BUT...
WOULD YOU MIND GOING UP TO THE SECOND FLOOR AND OPENING THE DOOR FOR SNOWBALL FOR ME?
NYAH!
IT WOULDN'T BE FAIR TO KEEP HER COOPED UP IN THERE FOR SO LONG~!
......
NYAH...
TP TP TP...
PAD PAD PAD
NYAH!
SCRATCH
SCRATCH
SCRATCH

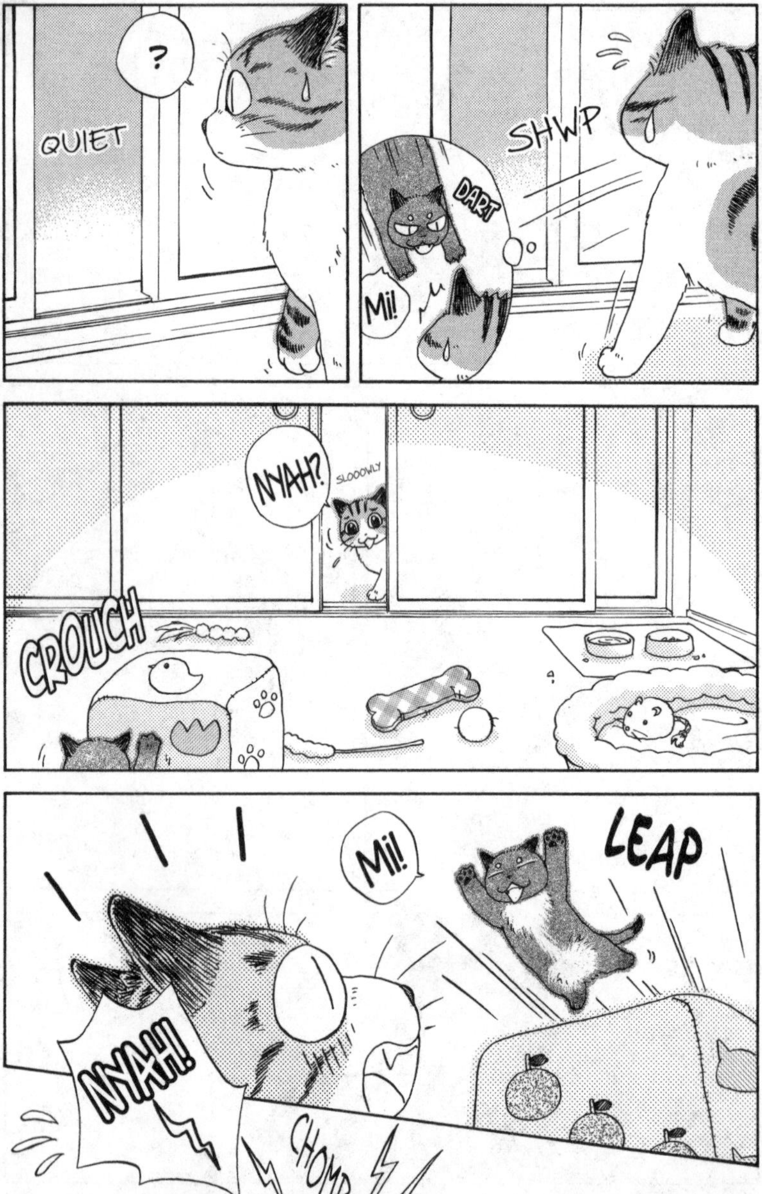
SHWP
DART
Mi!
?
QUIET
NYAH?
SLOOOWLY
CROUCH
LEAP
Mi!
NYAH!
CHOMP

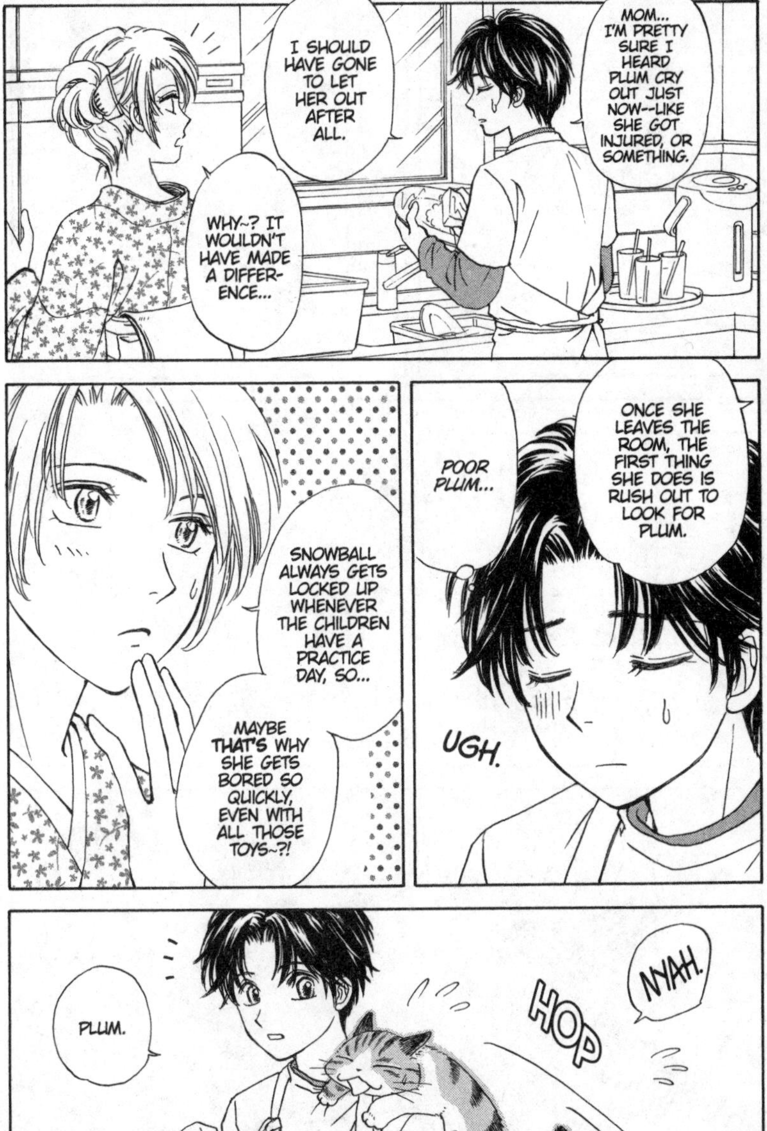
MOM... I'M PRETTY SURE I HEARD PLUM CRY OUT JUST NOW--LIKE SHE GOT INJURED, OR SOMETHING.
I SHOULD HAVE GONE TO LET HER OUT AFTER ALL.
WHY~? IT WOULDN'T HAVE MADE A DIFFERENCE...
ONCE SHE LEAVES THE ROOM, THE FIRST THING SHE DOES IS RUSH OUT TO LOOK FOR PLUM.
POOR PLUM...
UGH.
SNOWBALL ALWAYS GETS LOCKED UP WHENEVER THE CHILDREN HAVE A PRACTICE DAY, SO...
MAYBE **THAT'S** WHY SHE GETS BORED SO QUICKLY, EVEN WITH ALL THOSE TOYS~?!
NYAH.
HOP
PLUM.

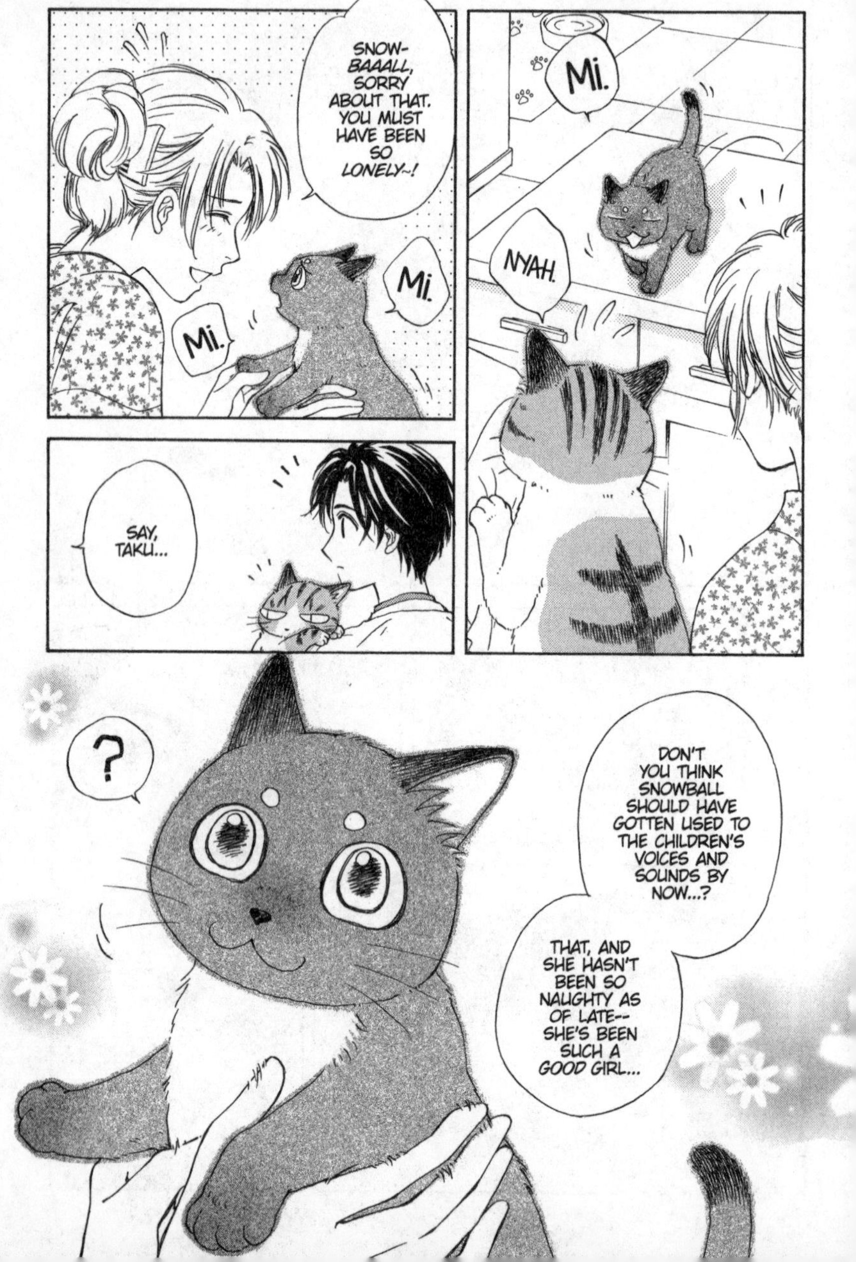
Mi.
NYAH.
SNOW-BAAALL, SORRY ABOUT THAT. YOU MUST HAVE BEEN SO *LONELY~!*
Mi.
Mi.
SAY, TAKU...
DON'T YOU THINK SNOWBALL SHOULD HAVE GOTTEN USED TO THE CHILDREN'S VOICES AND SOUNDS BY NOW...?
THAT, AND SHE HASN'T BEEN SO NAUGHTY AS OF LATE--SHE'S BEEN SUCH A *GOOD* GIRL...
?

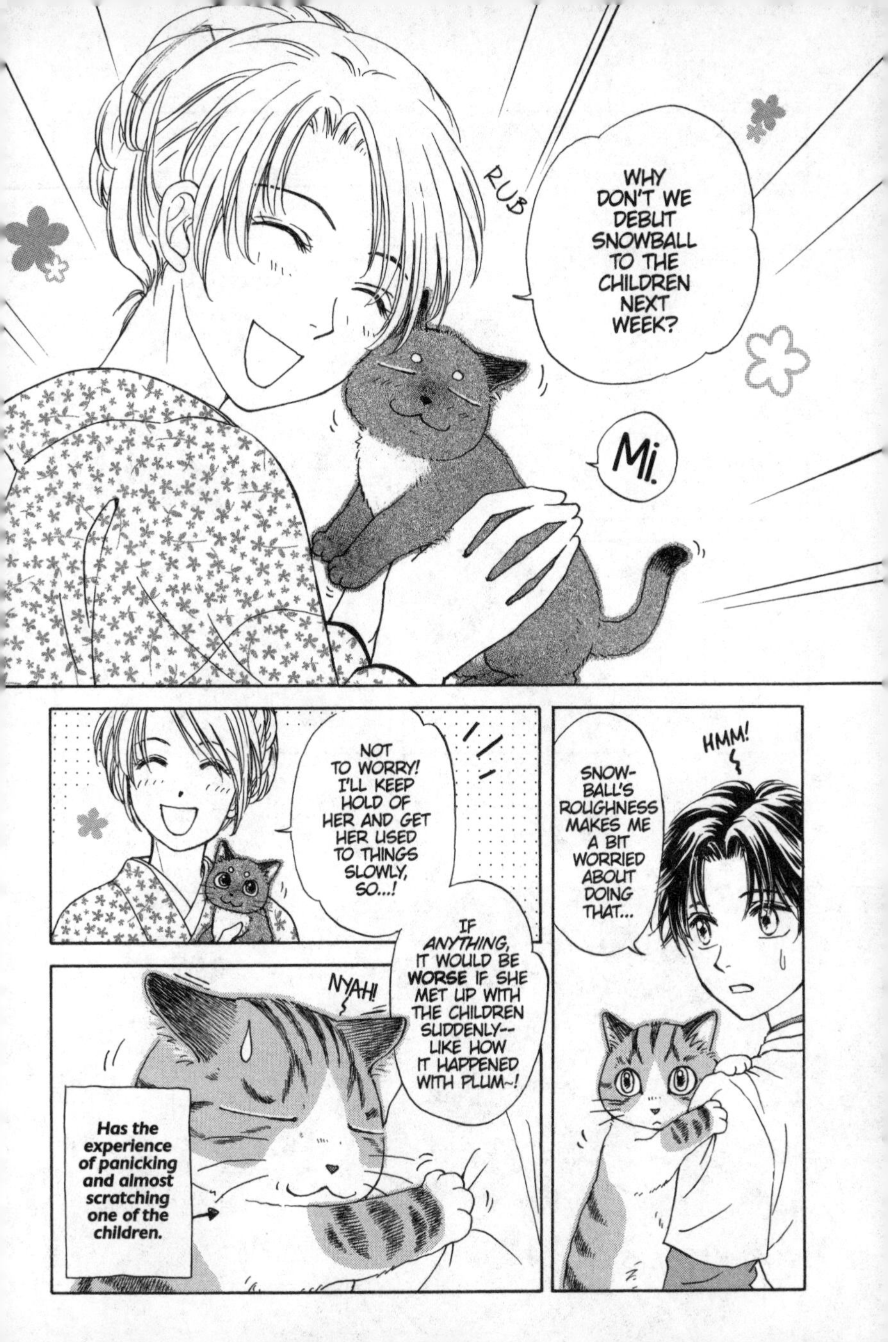
RUB
WHY DON'T WE DEBUT SNOWBALL TO THE CHILDREN NEXT WEEK?
Mi.
HMM!
SNOW-BALL'S ROUGHNESS MAKES ME A BIT WORRIED ABOUT DOING THAT...
NOT TO WORRY! I'LL KEEP HOLD OF HER AND GET HER USED TO THINGS SLOWLY, SO...!
IF *ANYTHING*, IT WOULD BE **WORSE** IF SHE MET UP WITH THE CHILDREN SUDDENLY-- LIKE HOW IT HAPPENED WITH PLUM~!
NYAH!
Has the experience of panicking and almost scratching one of the children.

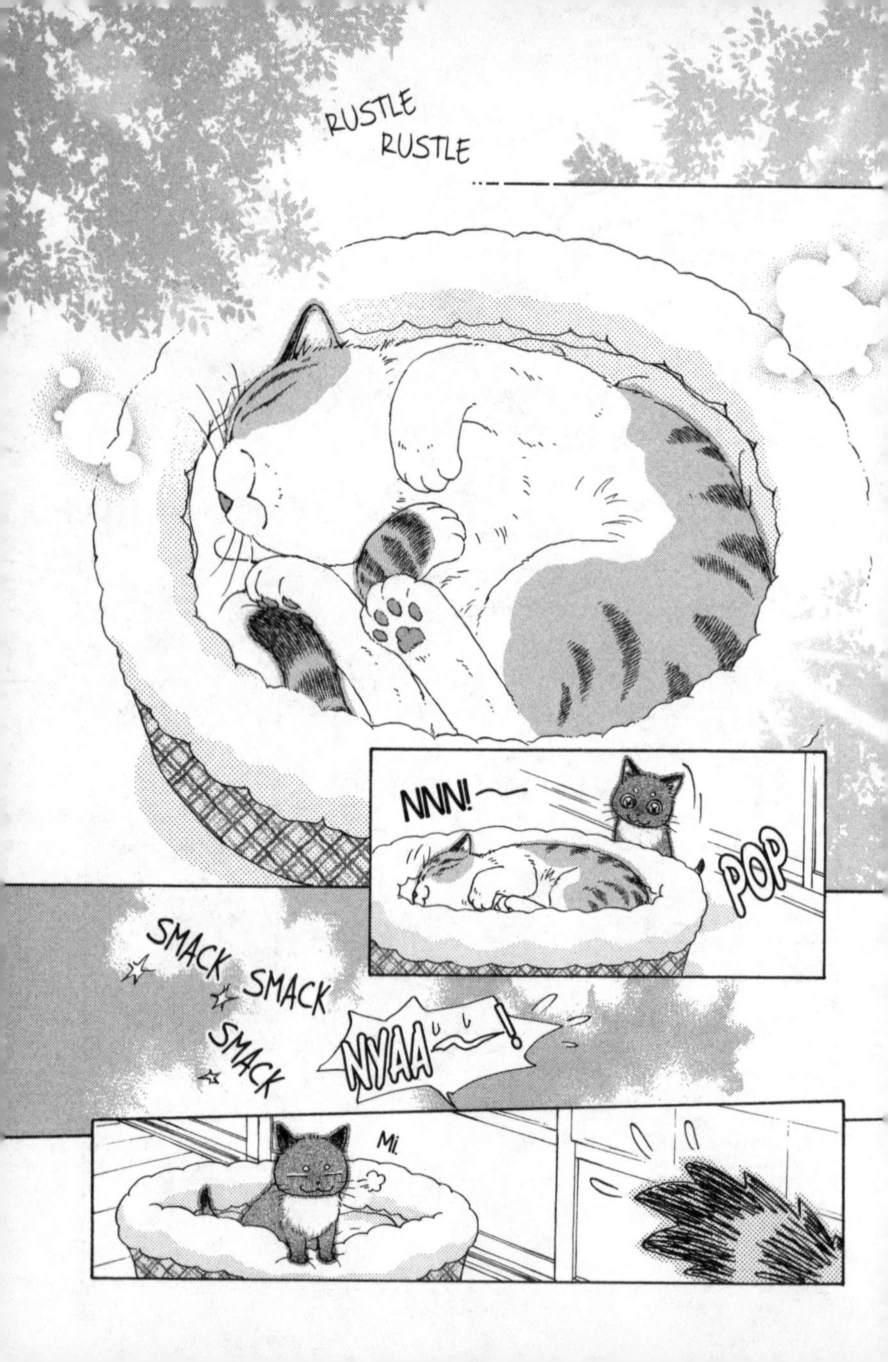
RUSTLE
RUSTLE
NNN!~
POP
SMACK
SMACK
SMACK
NYAA~!
Mi.

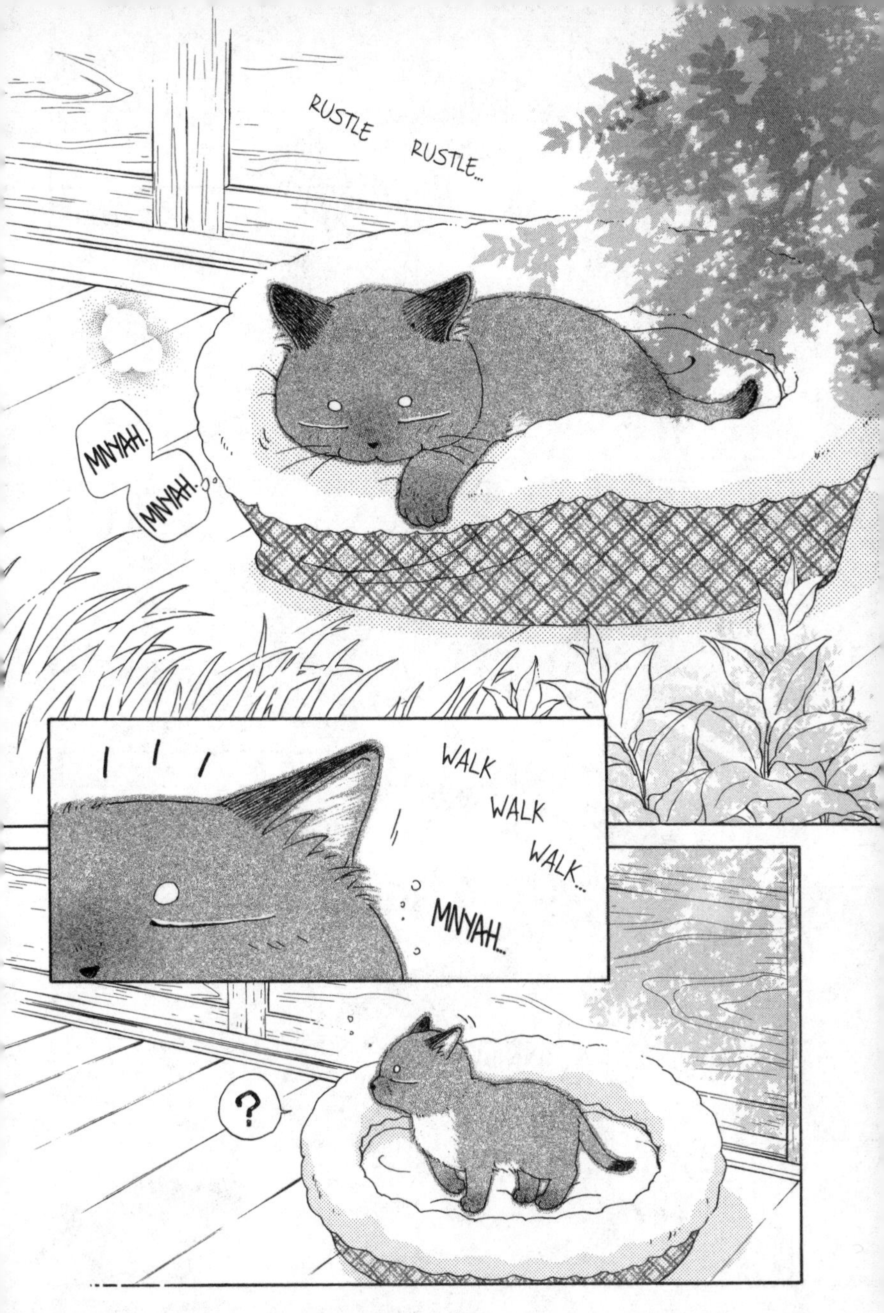
RUSTLE
RUSTLE...
MNYAH.
MNYAH.
WALK
WALK
WALK...
MNYAH...
?

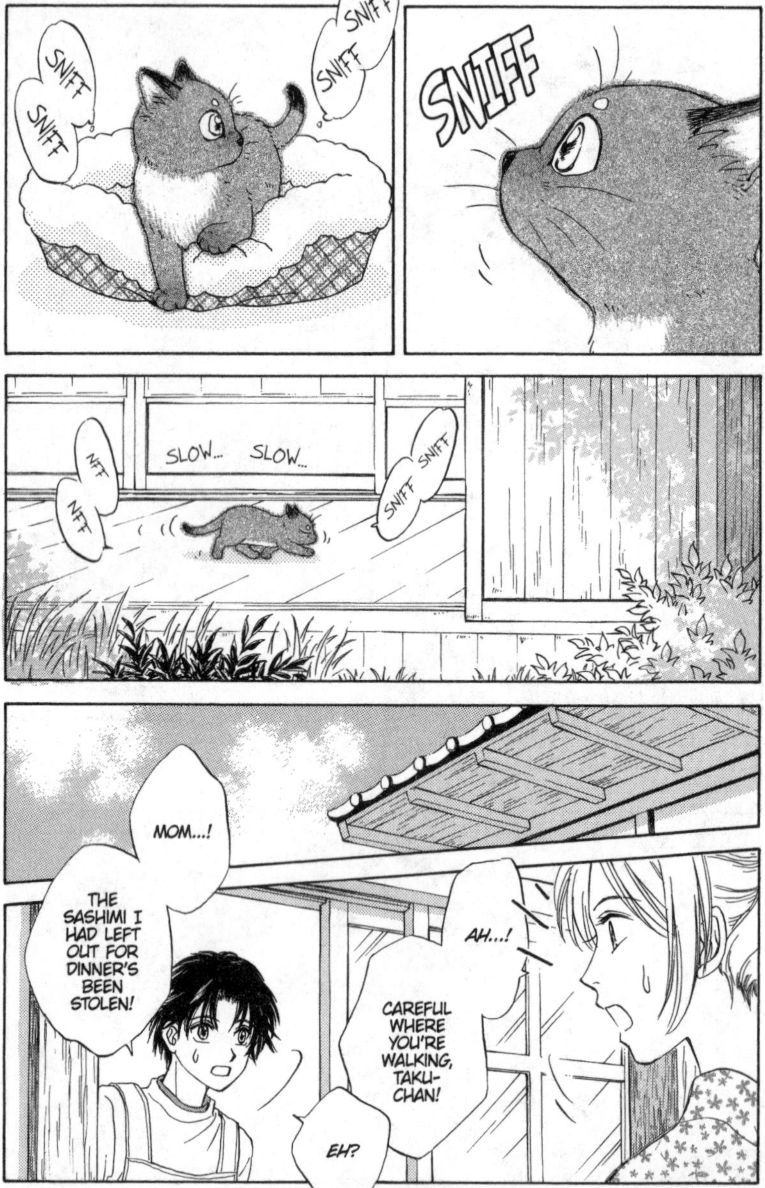
SNIFF
SNIFF SNIFF
SNIFF SNIFF
SNIFF SNIFF
SLOW... SLOW...
NFF NFF
MOM...!
THE SASHIMI I HAD LEFT OUT FOR DINNER'S BEEN STOLEN!
AH...!
CAREFUL WHERE YOU'RE WALKING, TAKU-CHAN!
EH?

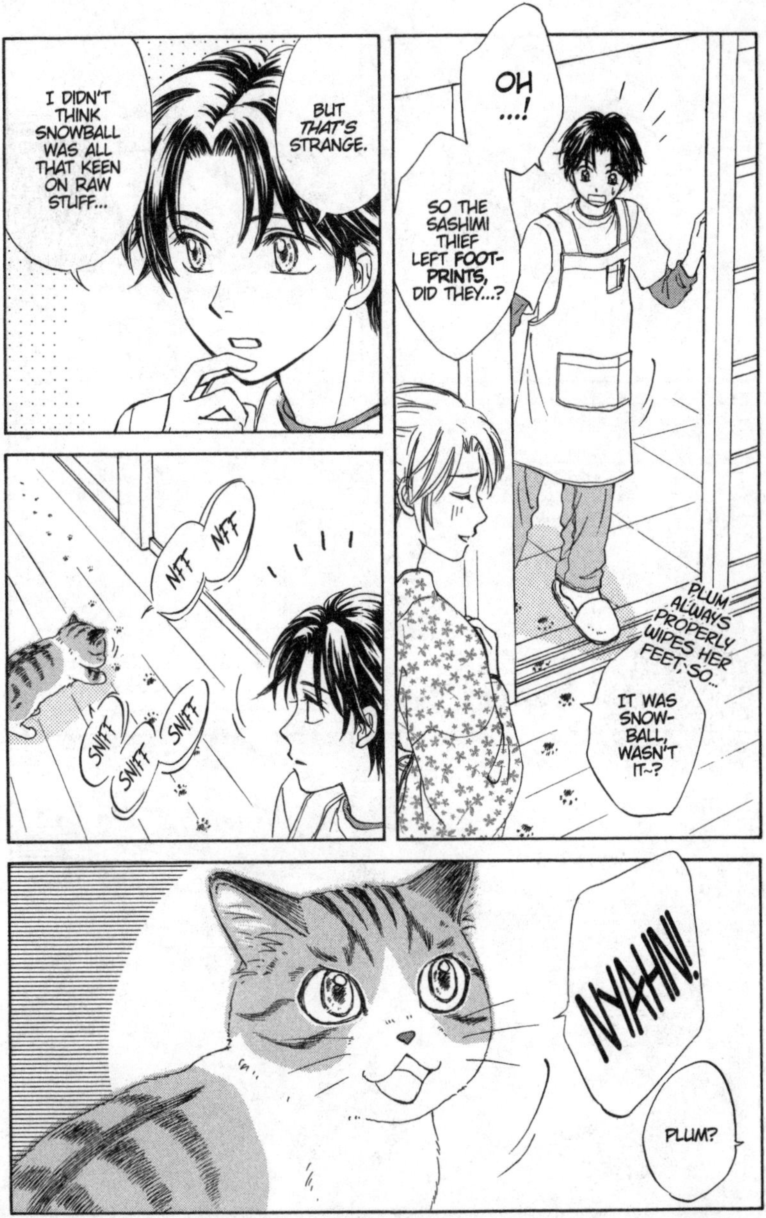
OH ...!
SO THE SASHIMI THIEF LEFT FOOT-PRINTS, DID THEY...?
PLUM ALWAYS PROPERLY WIPES HER FEET, SO...
IT WAS SNOW-BALL, WASN'T IT~?
BUT THAT'S STRANGE.
I DIDN'T THINK SNOWBALL WAS ALL THAT KEEN ON RAW STUFF...
NFF NFF NFF
SNIFF SNIFF SNIFF
NYAHN!
PLUM?

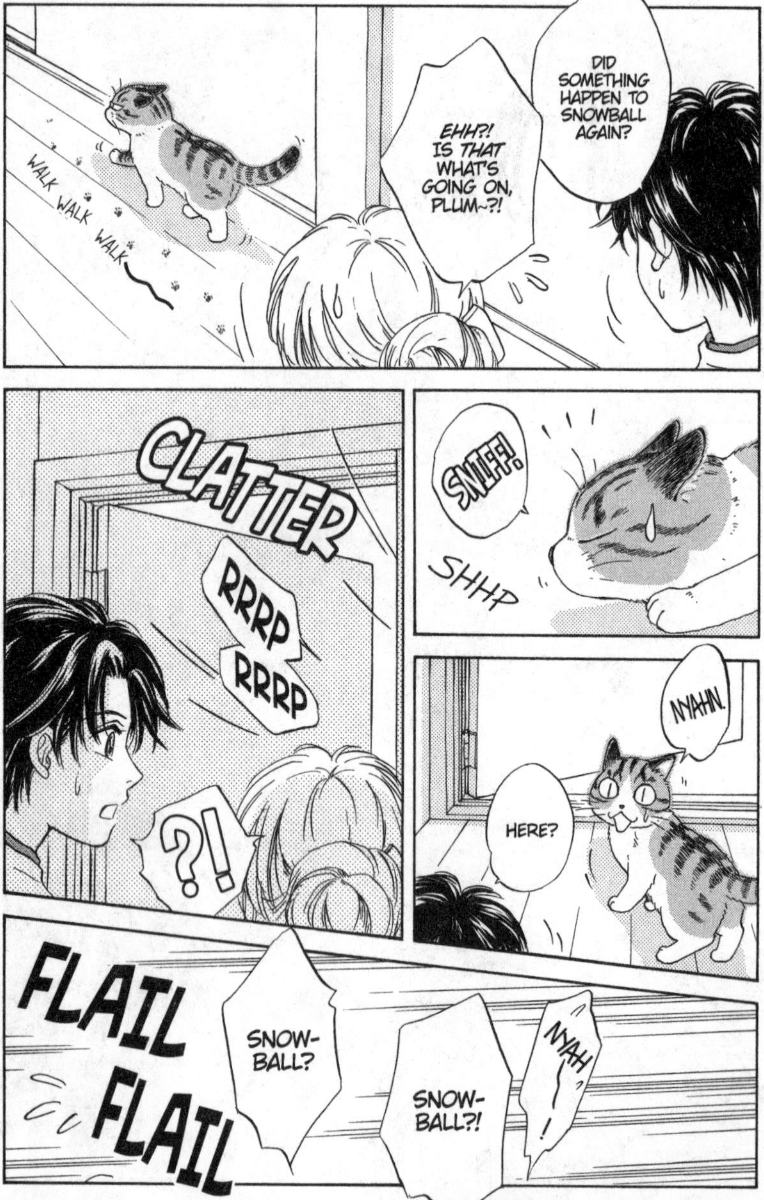
DID SOMETHING HAPPEN TO SNOWBALL AGAIN?
EHH?! IS THAT WHAT'S GOING ON, PLUM~?!
WALK WALK WALK
SNIFF?!
SHHP
NYAHN.
HERE?
CLATTER
RRRP RRRP
?!
NYAH!
SNOW-BALL?!
SNOW-BALL?
FLAIL FLAIL

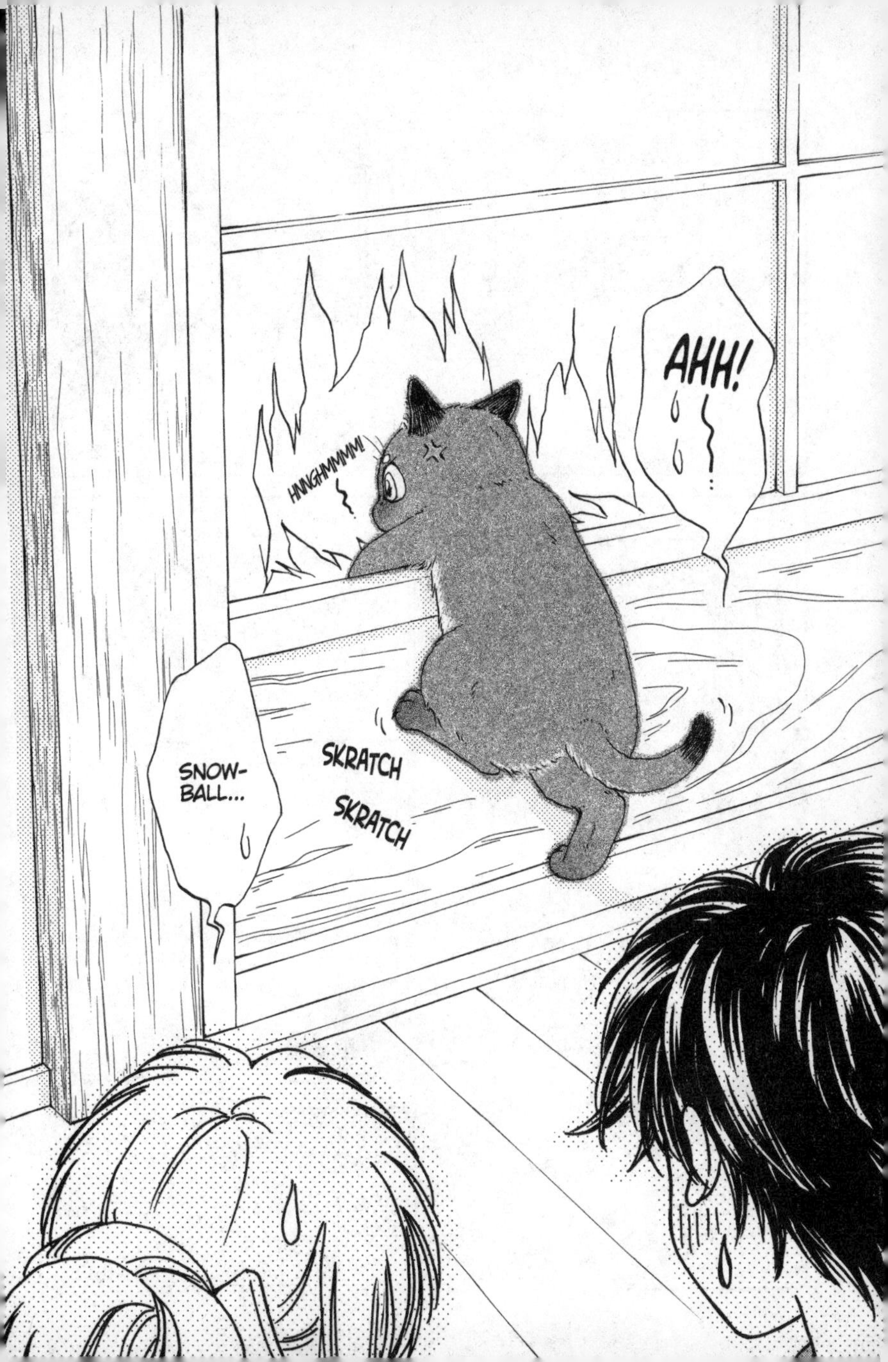
AHH!
HNNGHMMMM!
SKRATCH
SKRATCH
SNOW-BALL...

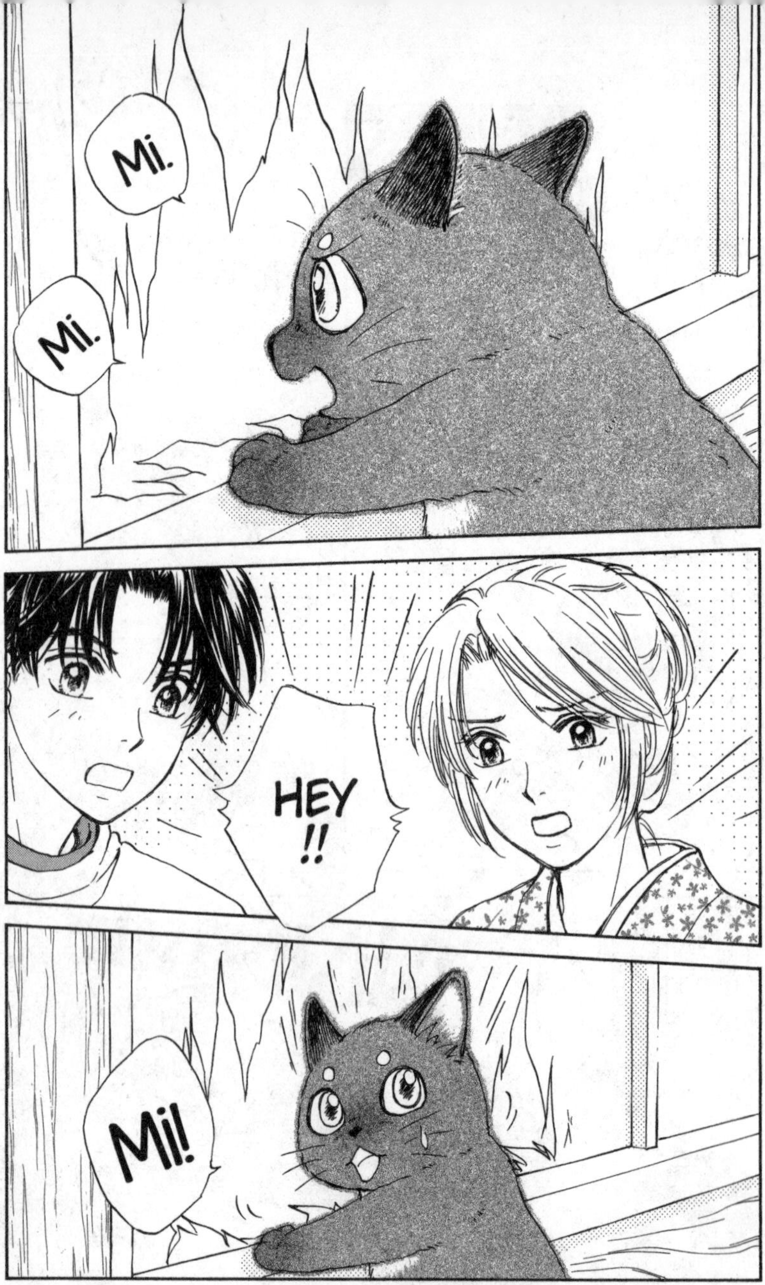
Mi.
Mi.
HEY !!
Mi!

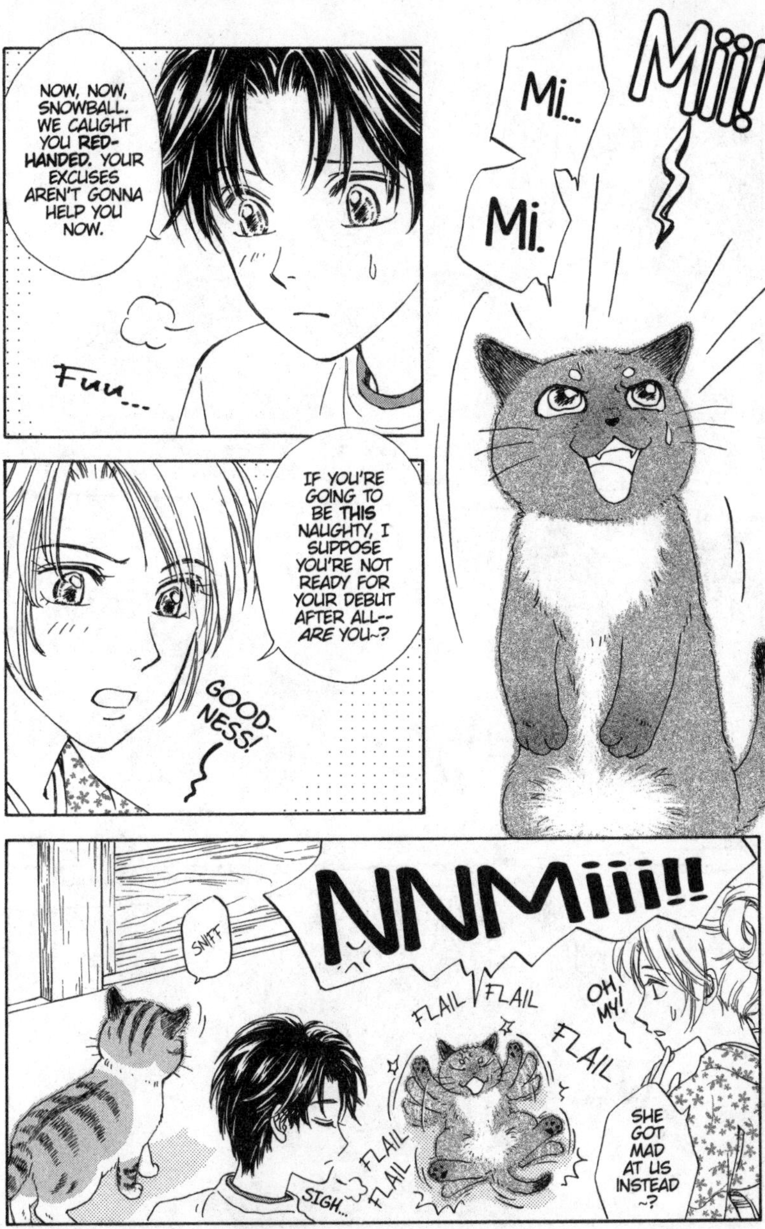
Mii!
Mi...
Mi.
NOW, NOW, SNOWBALL. WE CAUGHT YOU RED-HANDED. YOUR EXCUSES AREN'T GONNA HELP YOU NOW.
Fuu...
IF YOU'RE GOING TO BE THIS NAUGHTY, I SUPPOSE YOU'RE NOT READY FOR YOUR DEBUT AFTER ALL-- ARE YOU~?
GOOD-NESS!
NNMiiii!!
OH MY!
SHE GOT MAD AT US INSTEAD ~?
FLAIL
FLAIL
FLAIL
SNIFF
FLAIL
FLAIL
SIGH...

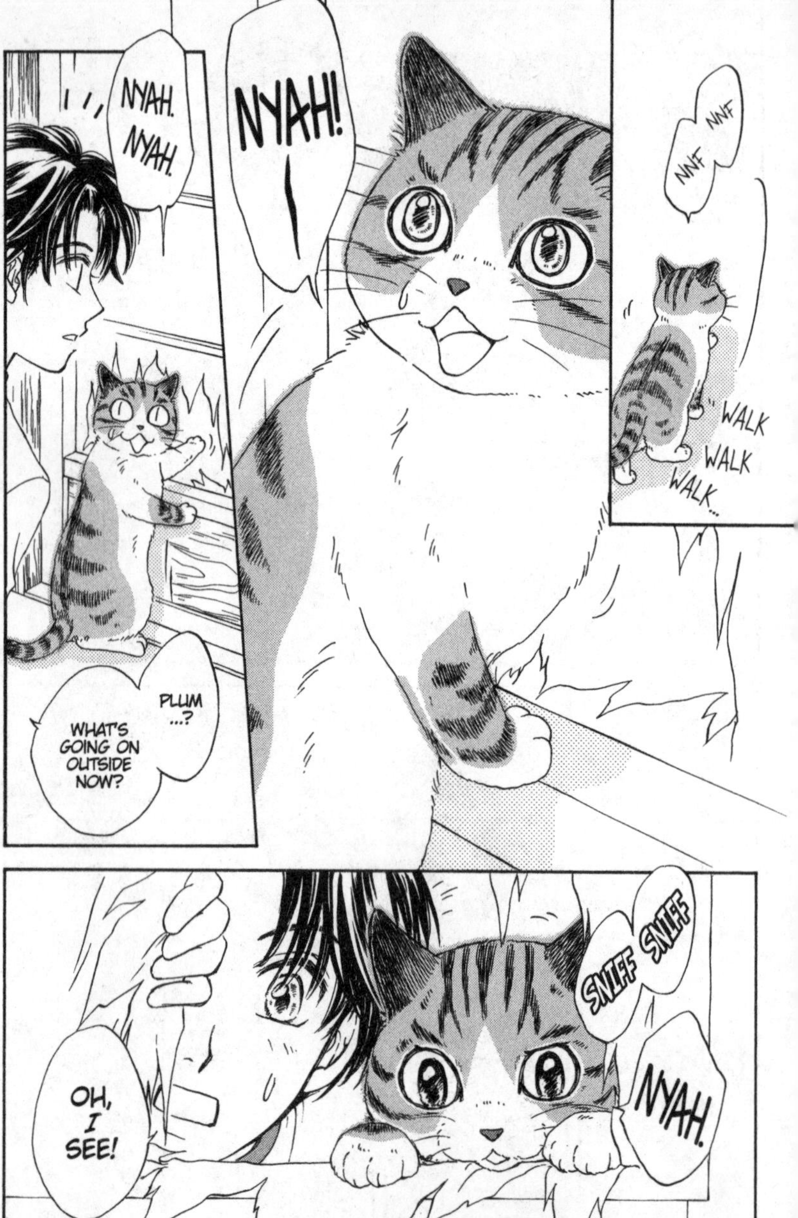
NNF NNF
WALK WALK WALK...
NYAH!
NYAH. NYAH.
PLUM ...?
WHAT'S GOING ON OUTSIDE NOW?
SNIFF SNIFF
NYAH.
OH, I SEE!

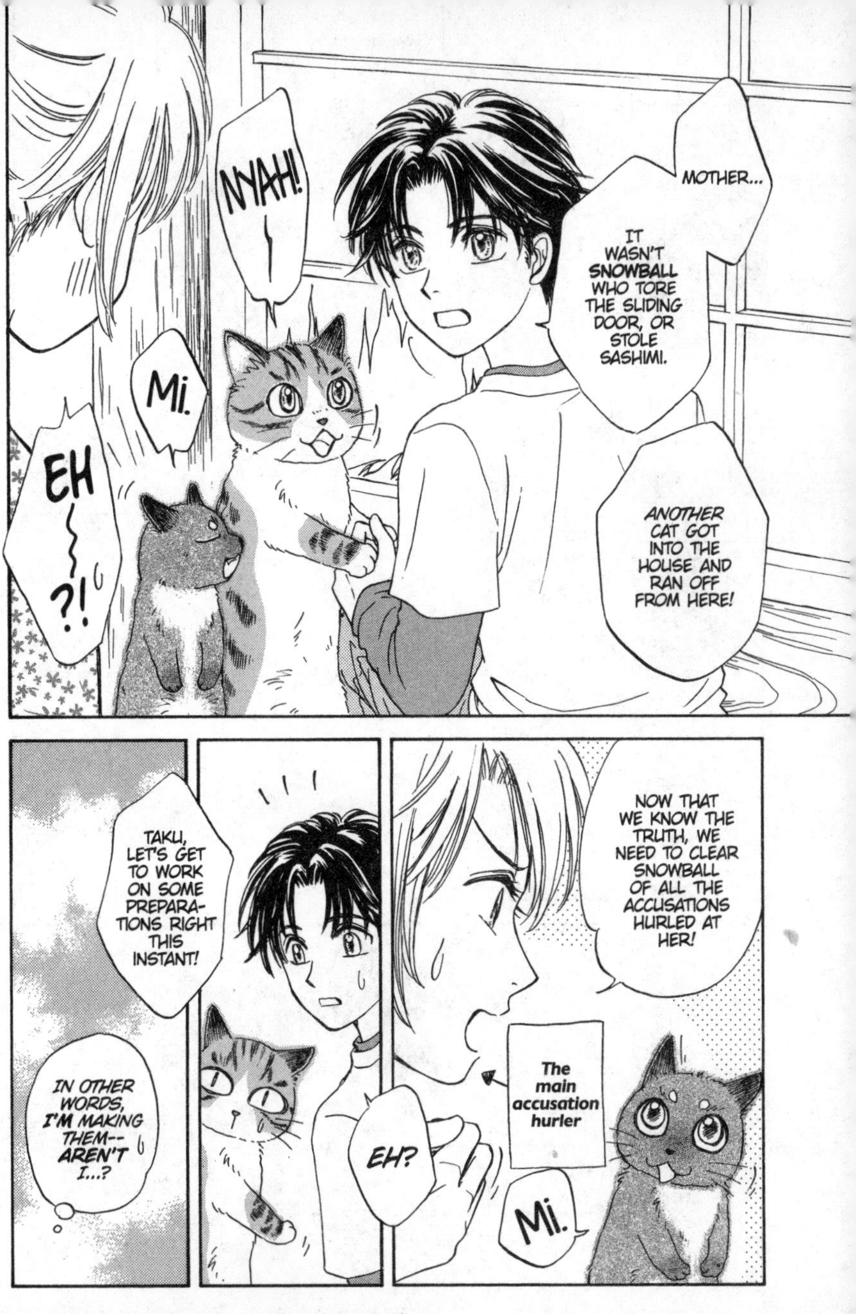
MOTHER...
IT WASN'T SNOWBALL WHO TORE THE SLIDING DOOR, OR STOLE SASHIMI.
ANOTHER CAT GOT INTO THE HOUSE AND RAN OFF FROM HERE!
NYAH!
Mi.
EH~~?!
NOW THAT WE KNOW THE TRUTH, WE NEED TO CLEAR SNOWBALL OF ALL THE ACCUSATIONS HURLED AT HER!
The main accusation hurler
Mi.
TAKU, LET'S GET TO WORK ON SOME PREPARATIONS RIGHT THIS INSTANT!
EH?
IN OTHER WORDS, I'M MAKING THEM--AREN'T I...?

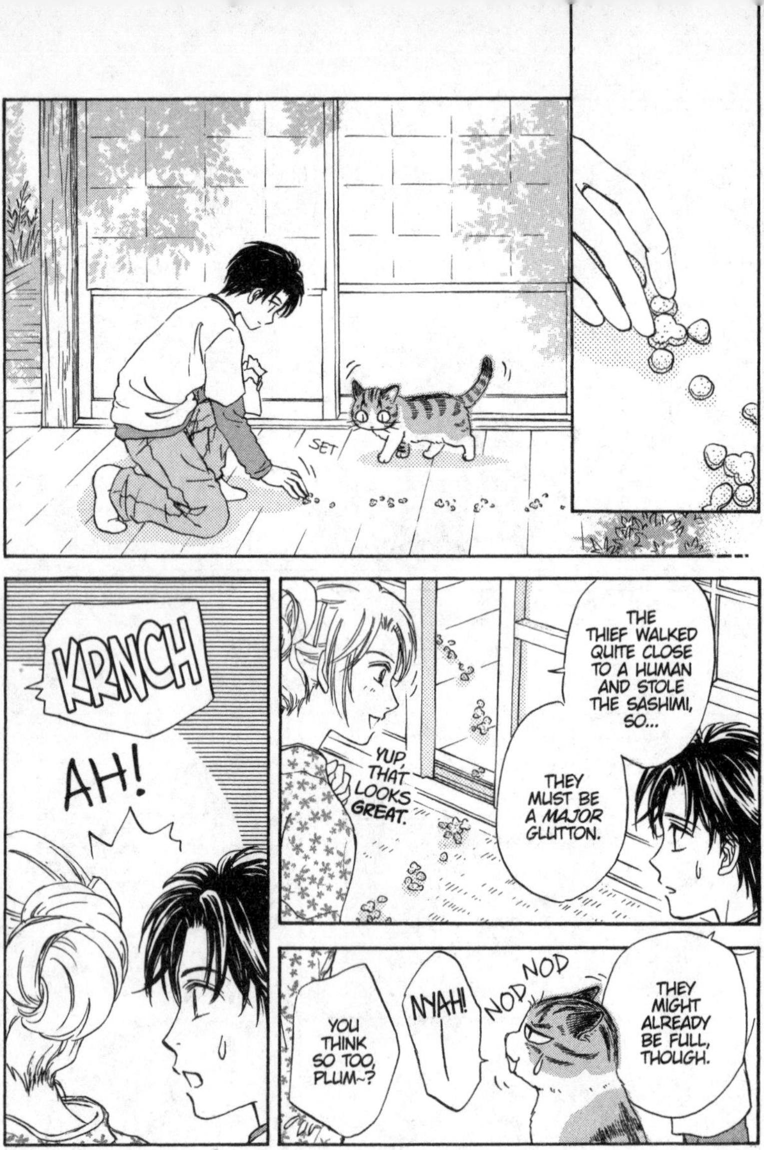
SET
THE THIEF WALKED QUITE CLOSE TO A HUMAN AND STOLE THE SASHIMI, SO...
THEY MUST BE A *MAJOR* GLUTTON.
YUP, THAT LOOKS GREAT.
THEY MIGHT ALREADY BE FULL, THOUGH.
NOD NOD
NOD
NYAH!
YOU THINK SO TOO, PLUM~?
KRNCH
AH!
KRNCH KRNCH
WALK WALK WALK...

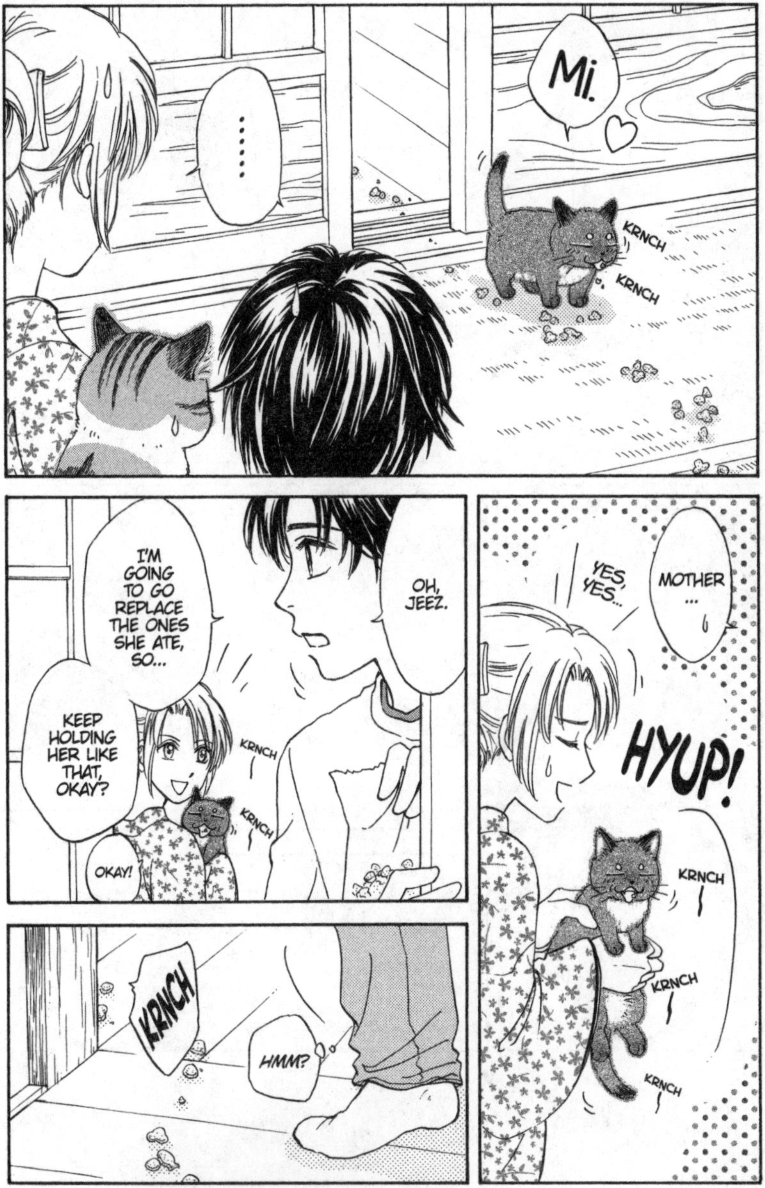
Mi.
KRNCH
KRNCH
......
MOTHER ...
YES, YES...
HYUP!
KRNCH
KRNCH
KRNCH
OH, JEEZ.
I'M GOING TO GO REPLACE THE ONES SHE ATE, SO...
KEEP HOLDING HER LIKE THAT, OKAY?
KRNCH
KRNCH
OKAY!
HMM?
KRNCH

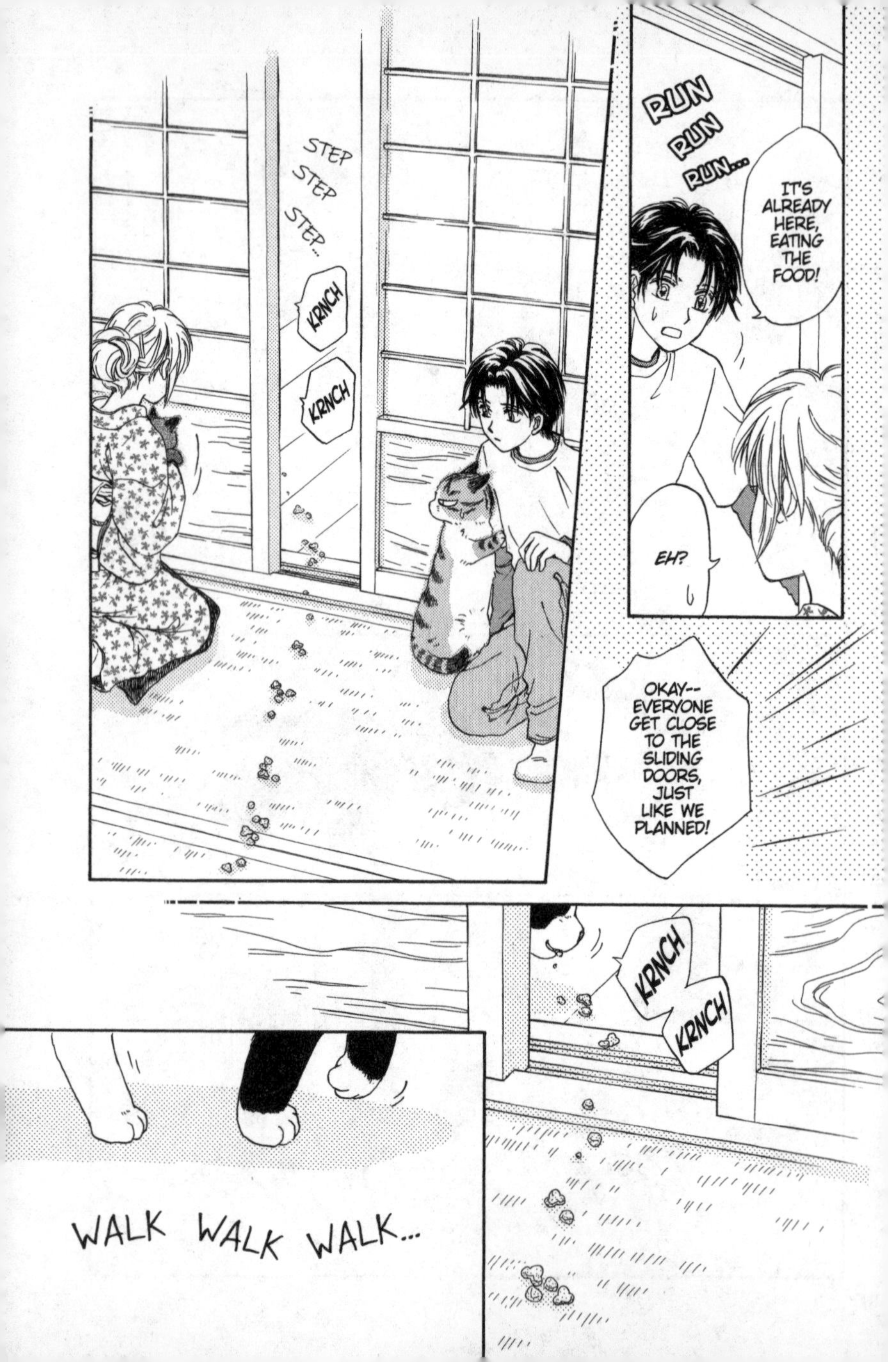
RUN
RUN
RUN...
IT'S ALREADY HERE, EATING THE FOOD!
EH?
OKAY-- EVERYONE GET CLOSE TO THE SLIDING DOORS, JUST LIKE WE PLANNED!
STEP
STEP
STEP...
KRNCH
KRNCH
KRNCH
KRNCH
WALK WALK WALK...

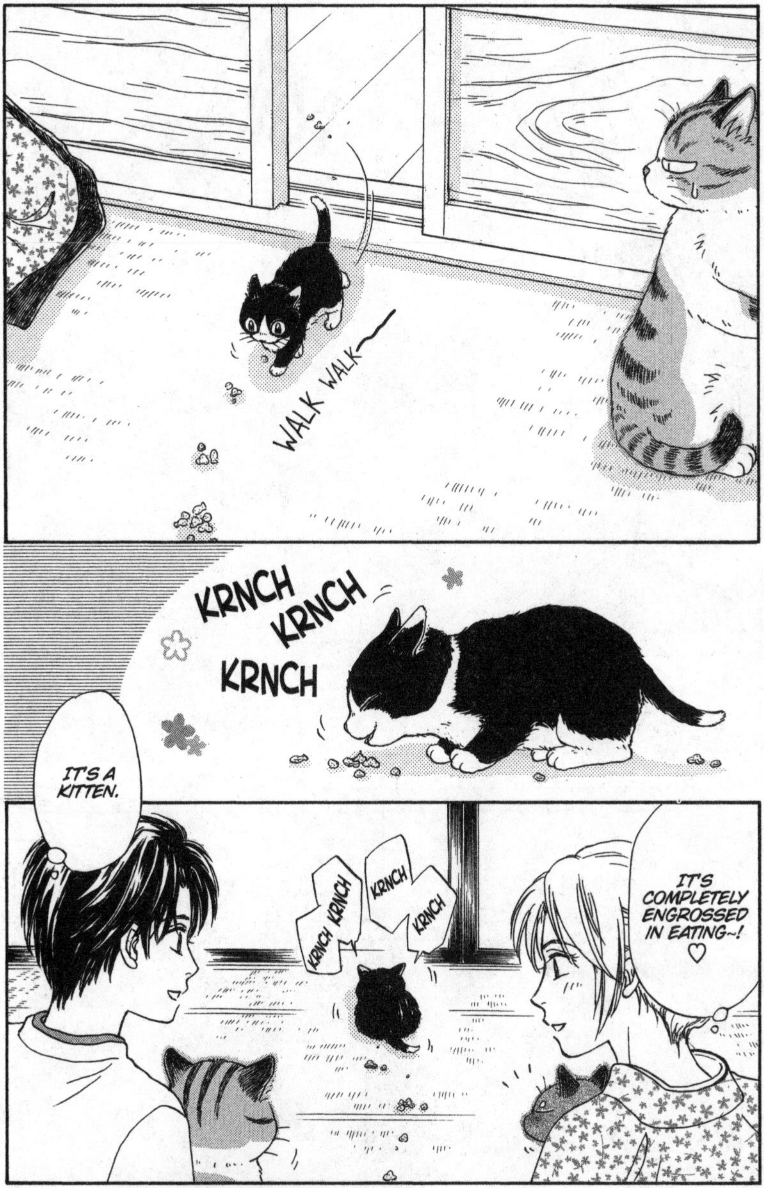
WALK WALK~
KRNCH
KRNCH
KRNCH
IT'S A KITTEN.
KRNCH KRNCH
KRNCH KRNCH
KRNCH
IT'S COMPLETELY ENGROSSED IN EATING~! ♡

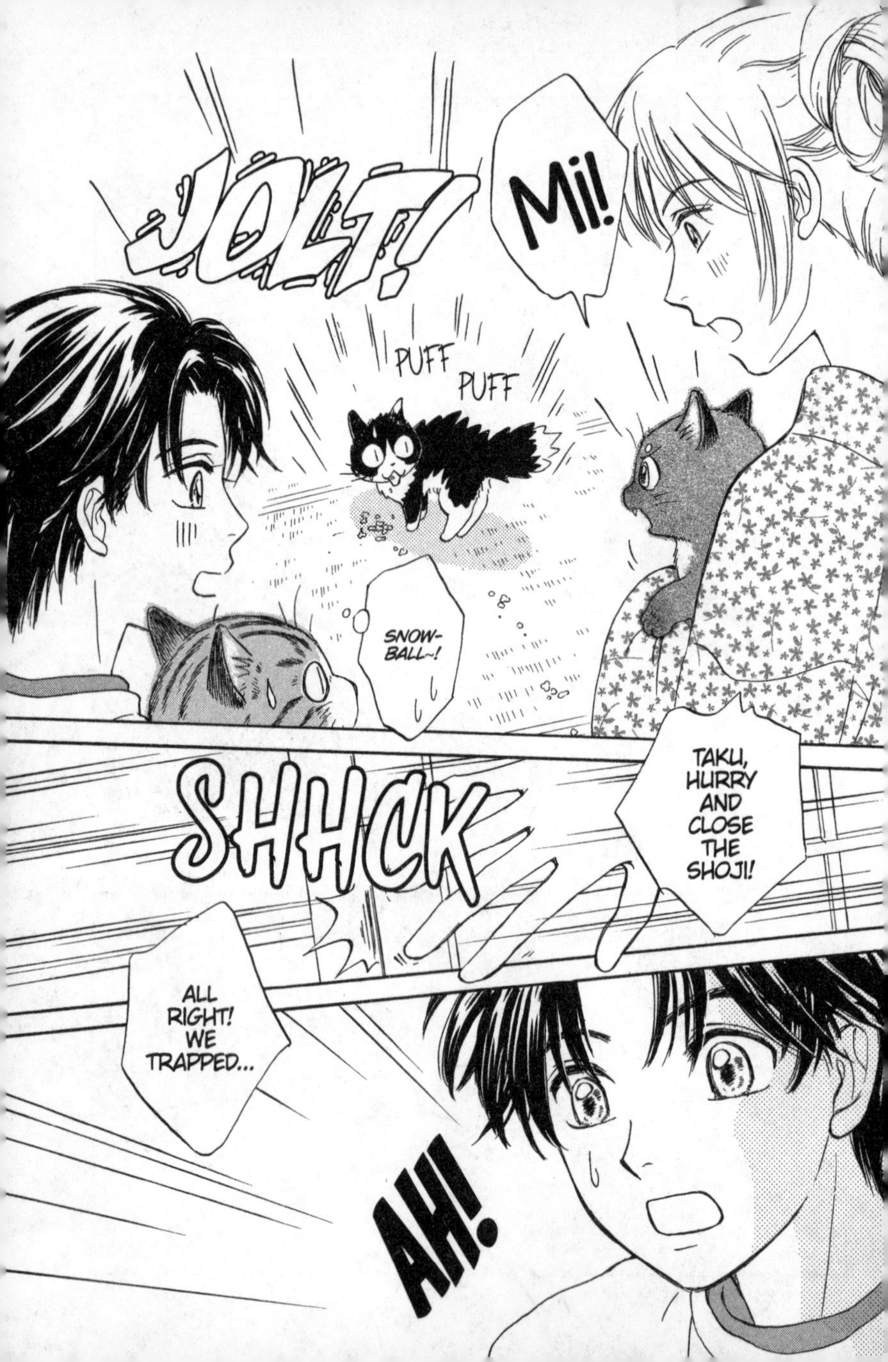
Mi!
JOLT!
PUFF PUFF
SNOW-BALL~!
TAKU, HURRY AND CLOSE THE SHOJI!
SHHCK
ALL RIGHT! WE TRAPPED...
AH!

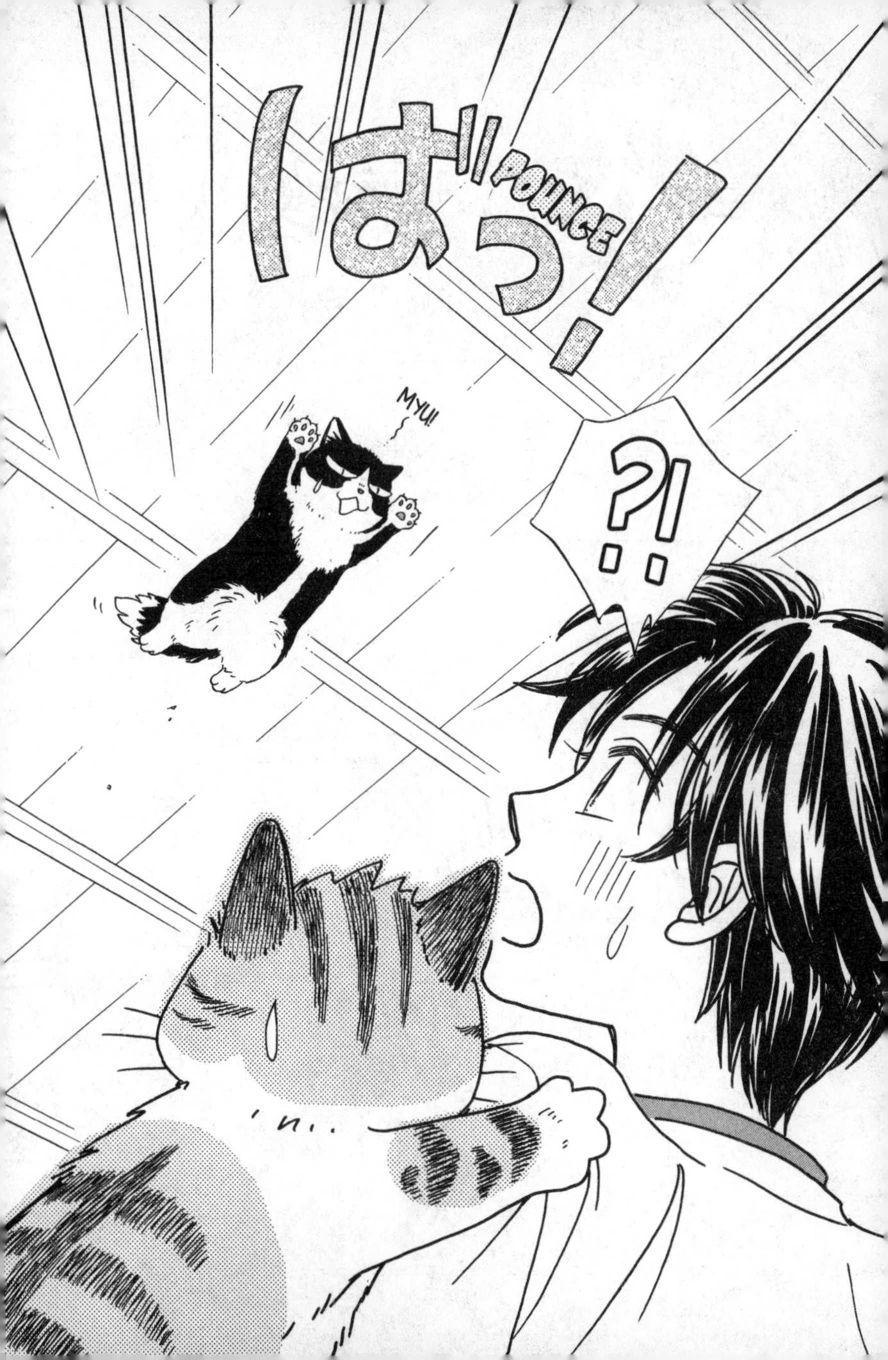
ばっ!
POUNCE
?!
MYU!

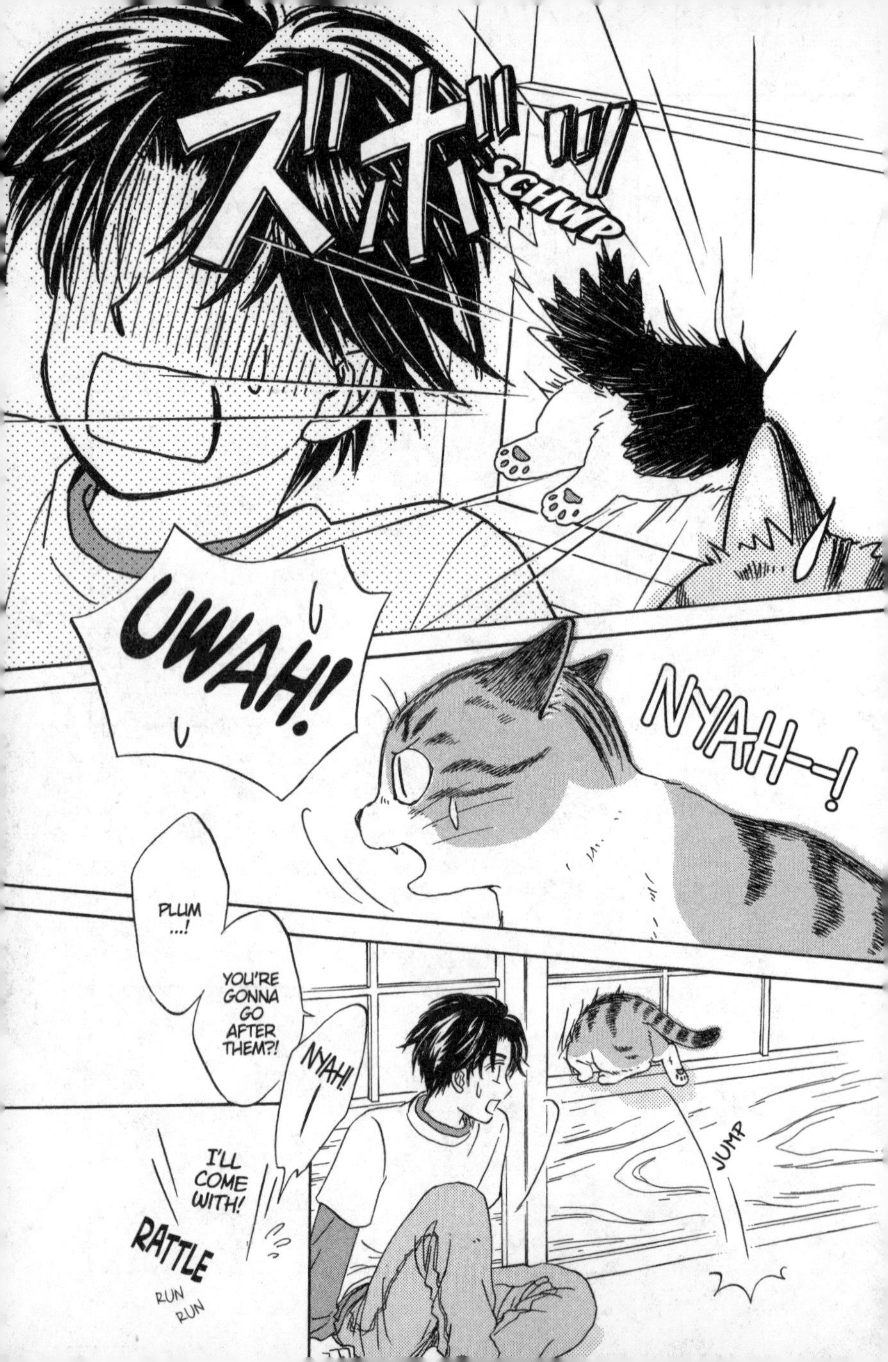

スッ
SCHWP
UWAH!
NYAH--!
PLUM ...!
YOU'RE GONNA GO AFTER THEM?!
NYAH!
JUMP
I'LL COME WITH!
RATTLE
RUN RUN

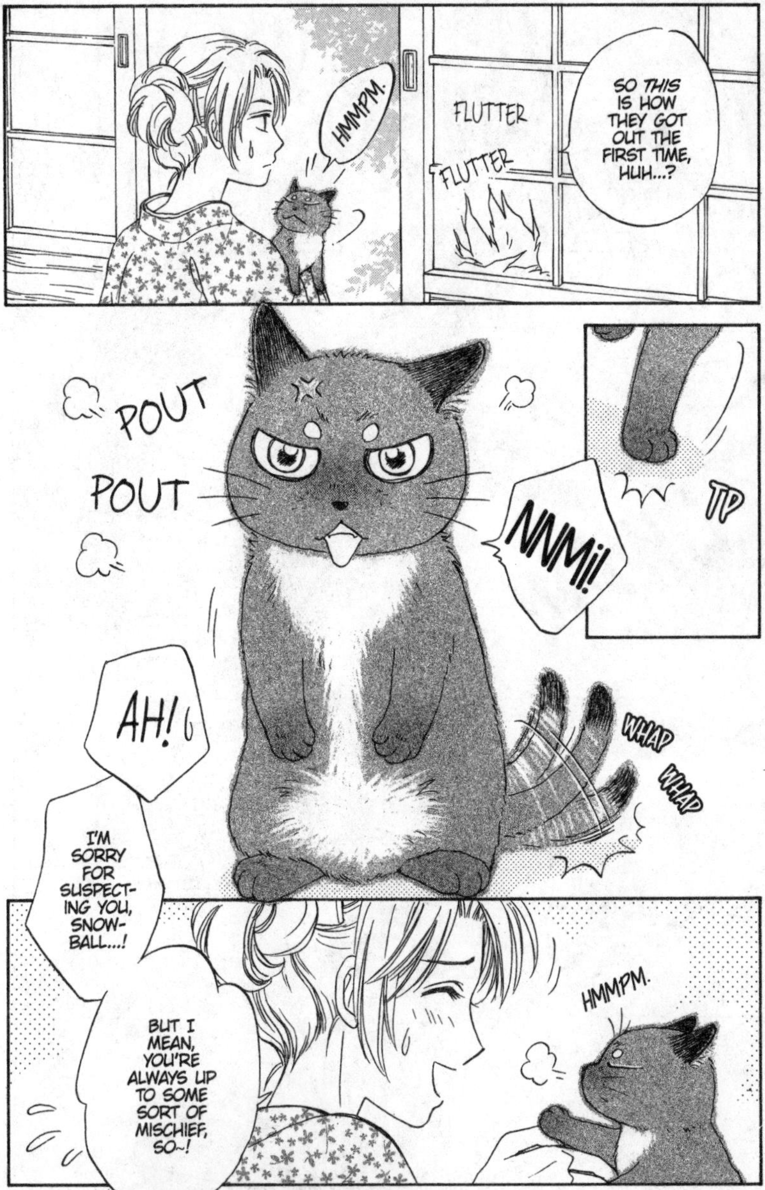
SO THIS IS HOW THEY GOT OUT THE FIRST TIME, HUH...?
FLUTTER
FLUTTER
HMMPM.
TP
NNMi!
POUT
POUT
WHAP
WHAP
AH!
I'M SORRY FOR SUSPECTING YOU, SNOWBALL...!
BUT I MEAN, YOU'RE ALWAYS UP TO SOME SORT OF MISCHIEF, SO~!
HMMPM.

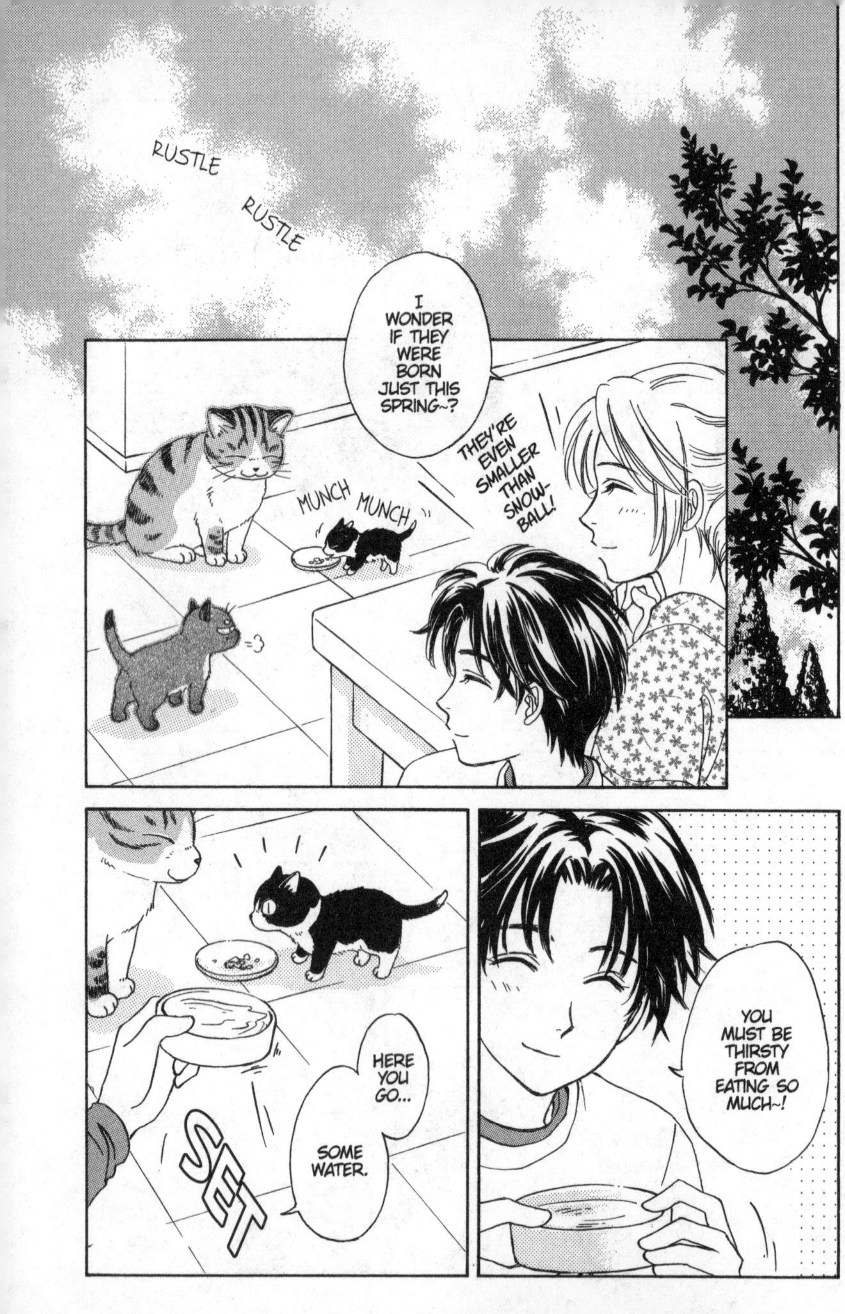
RUSTLE
RUSTLE
I WONDER IF THEY WERE BORN JUST THIS SPRING~?
THEY'RE EVEN SMALLER THAN SNOW-BALL!
MUNCH MUNCH
YOU MUST BE THIRSTY FROM EATING SO MUCH~!
HERE YOU GO...
SOME WATER.
SET

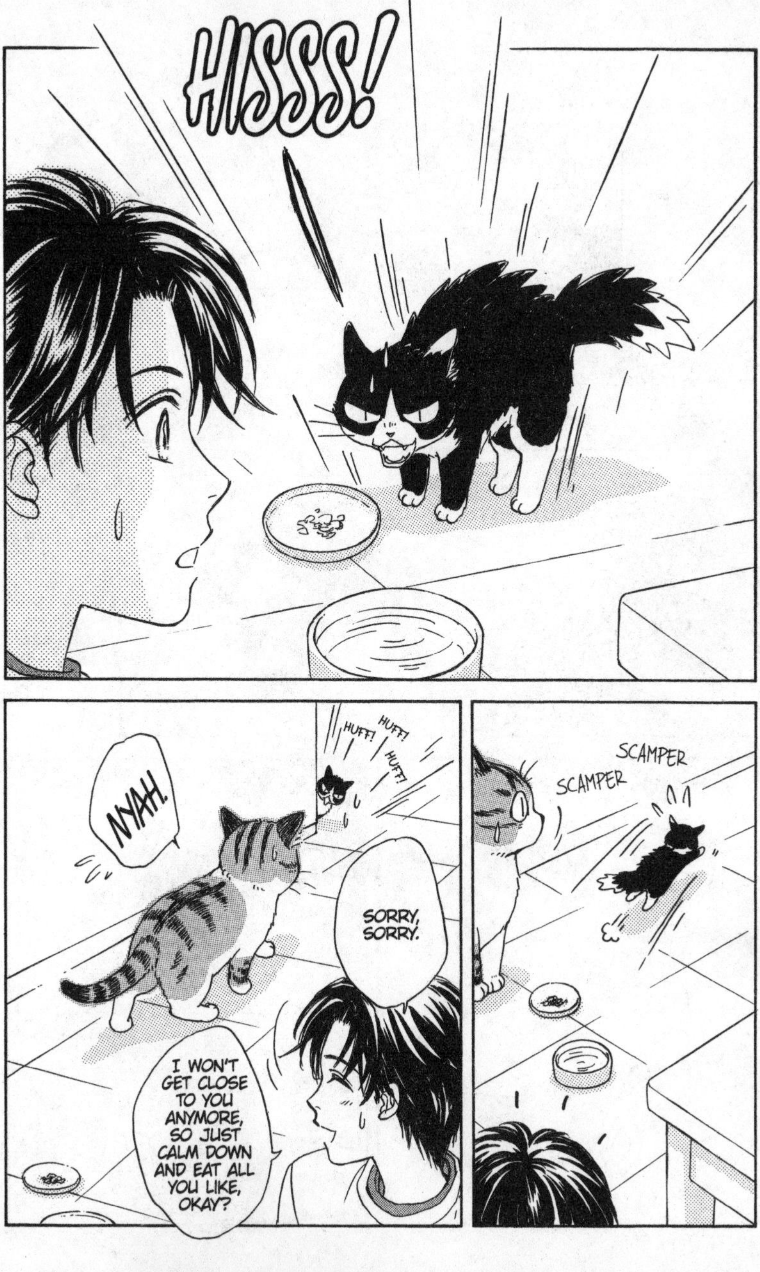
HISSS!
SCAMPER
SCAMPER
HUFF!
HUFF!
HUFF!
NYAH.
SORRY, SORRY.
I WON'T GET CLOSE TO YOU ANYMORE, SO JUST CALM DOWN AND EAT ALL YOU LIKE, OKAY?

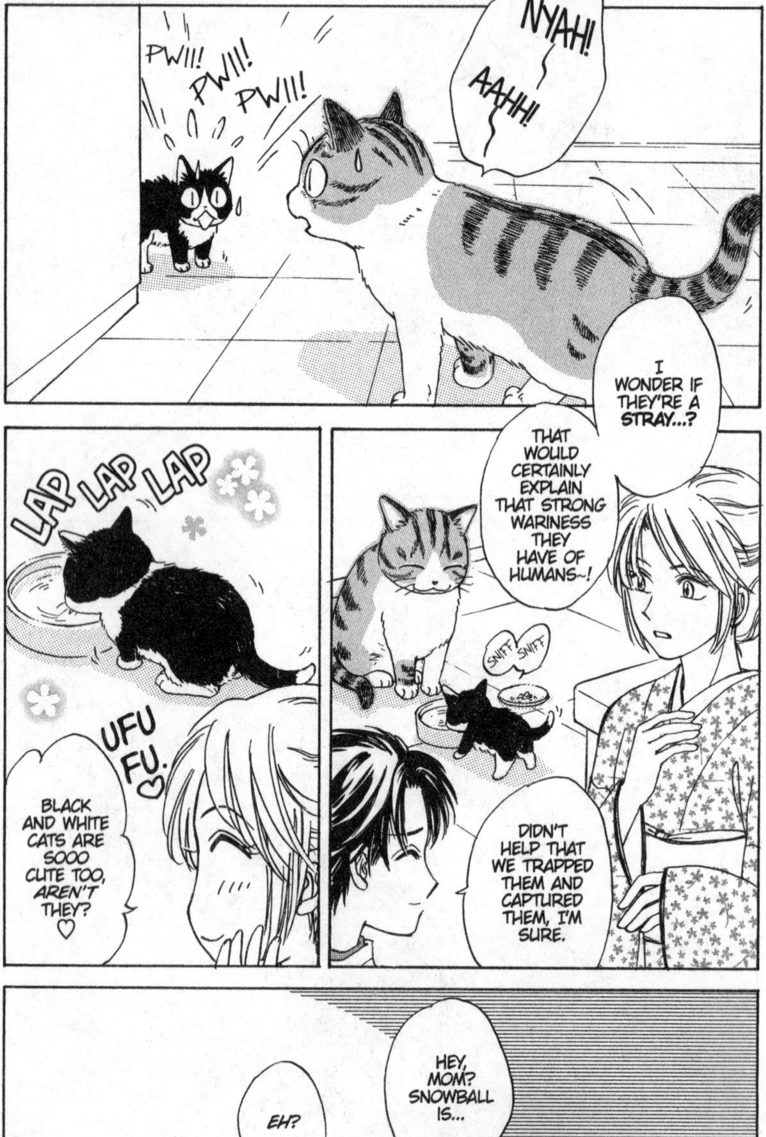
NYAH!
AAHH!
PWII! PWII! PWII!
I WONDER IF THEY'RE A STRAY...?
THAT WOULD CERTAINLY EXPLAIN THAT STRONG WARINESS THEY HAVE OF HUMANS~!
SNIFF SNIFF
DIDN'T HELP THAT WE TRAPPED THEM AND CAPTURED THEM, I'M SURE.
LAP LAP LAP
UFU FU. ♡
BLACK AND WHITE CATS ARE SOOO CUTE TOO, AREN'T THEY? ♡
HEY, MOM? SNOWBALL IS...
EH?

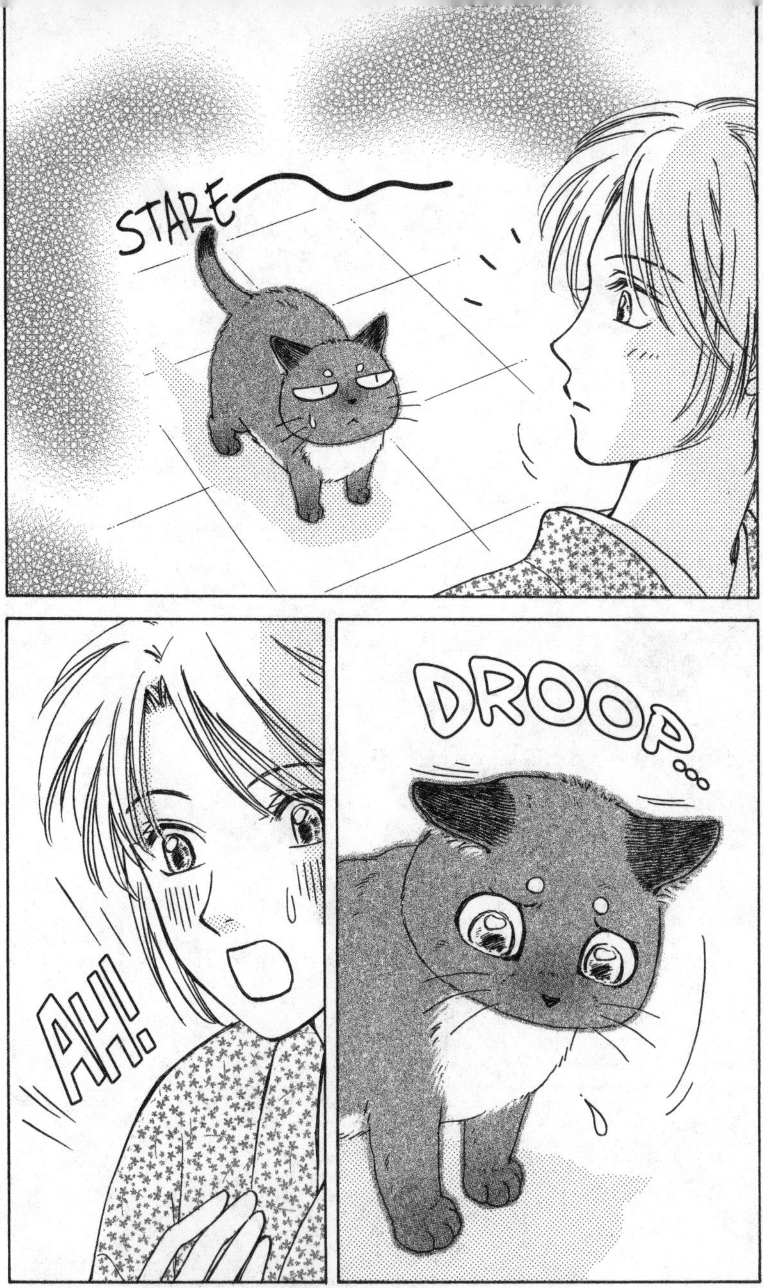
STARE
DROOP...
AH!

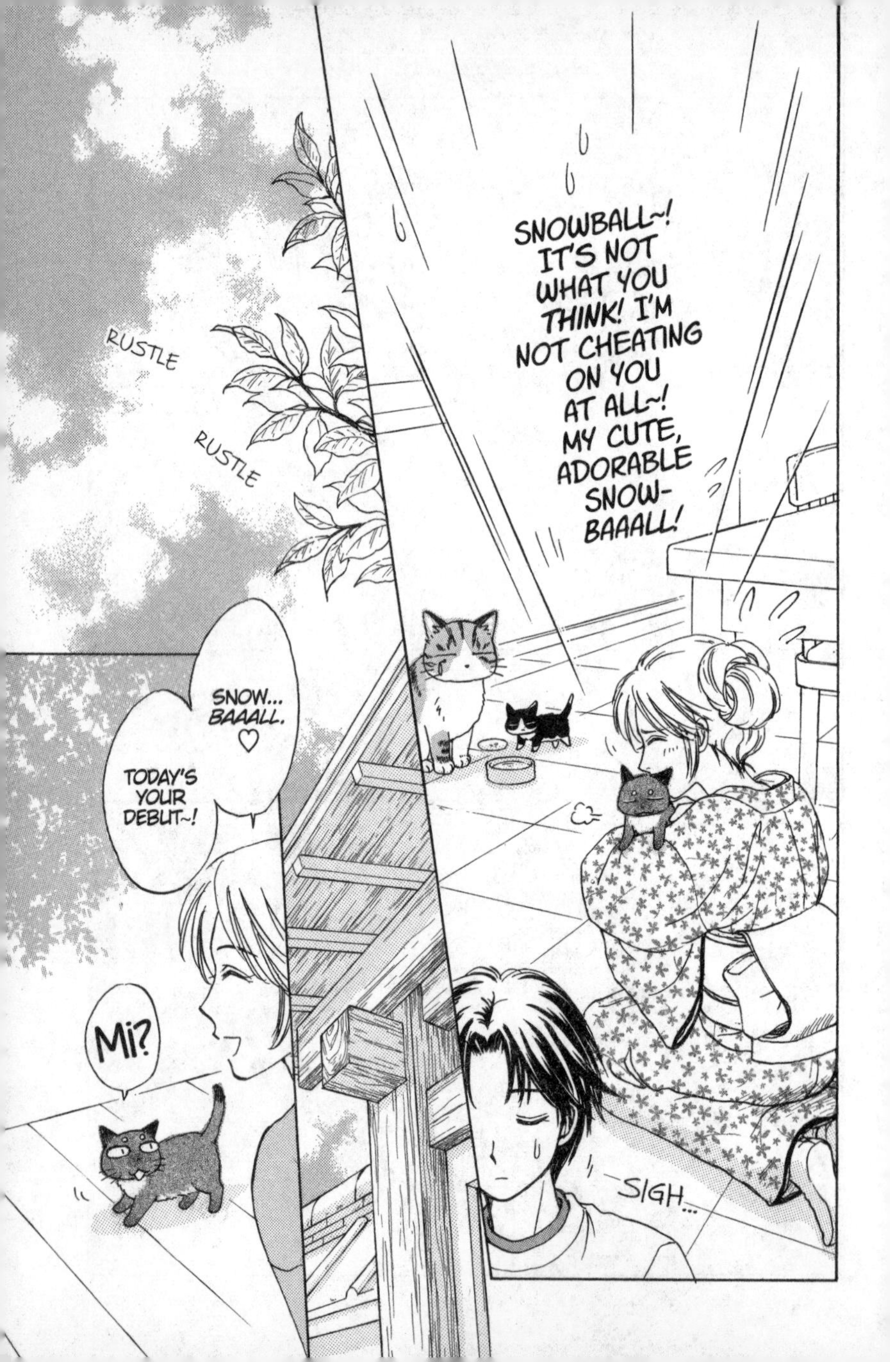
SNOWBALL~! IT'S NOT WHAT YOU THINK! I'M NOT CHEATING ON YOU AT ALL~! MY CUTE, ADORABLE SNOW-BAAALL!
SIGH...
RUSTLE
RUSTLE
SNOW... BAAALL. ♡
TODAY'S YOUR DEBUT~!
Mi?

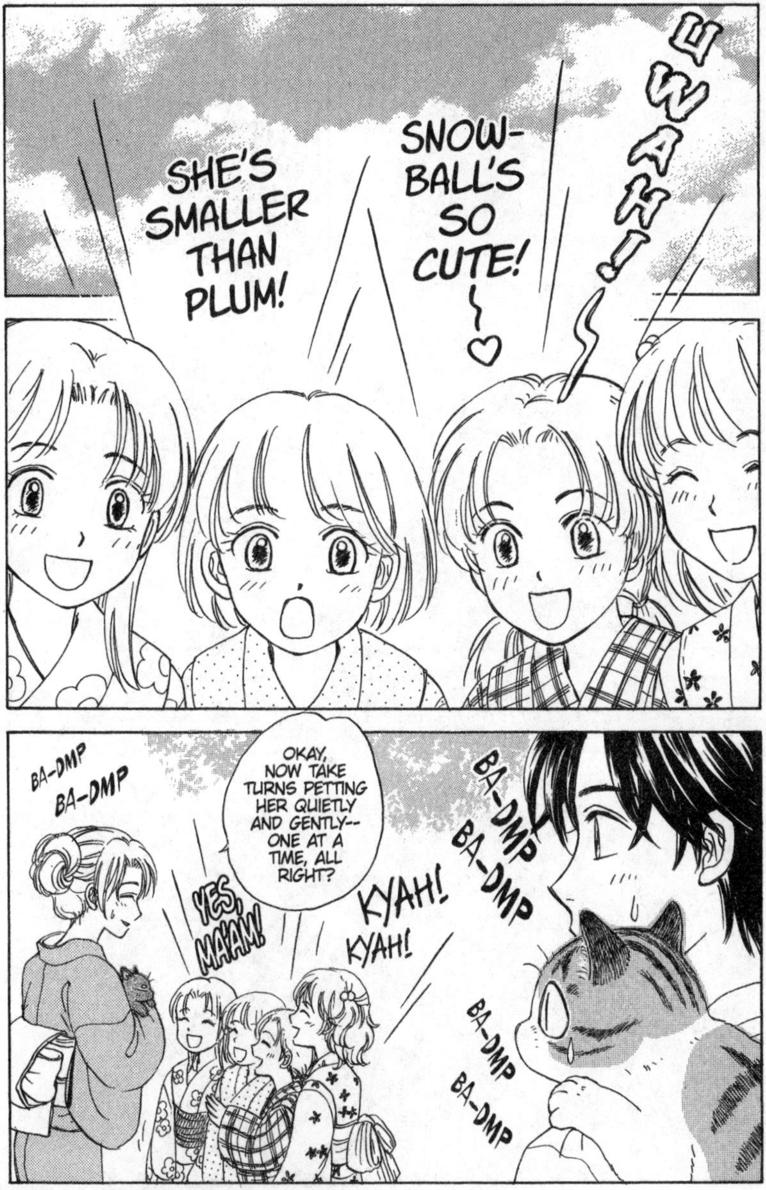
UWAH!!
SNOW-BALL'S SO CUTE! ~♥
SHE'S SMALLER THAN PLUM!
BA-DMP BA-DMP
BA-DMP BA-DMP
OKAY, NOW TAKE TURNS PETTING HER QUIETLY AND GENTLY-- ONE AT A TIME, ALL RIGHT?
KYAH! KYAH!
YES, MA'AM!
BA-DMP BA-DMP

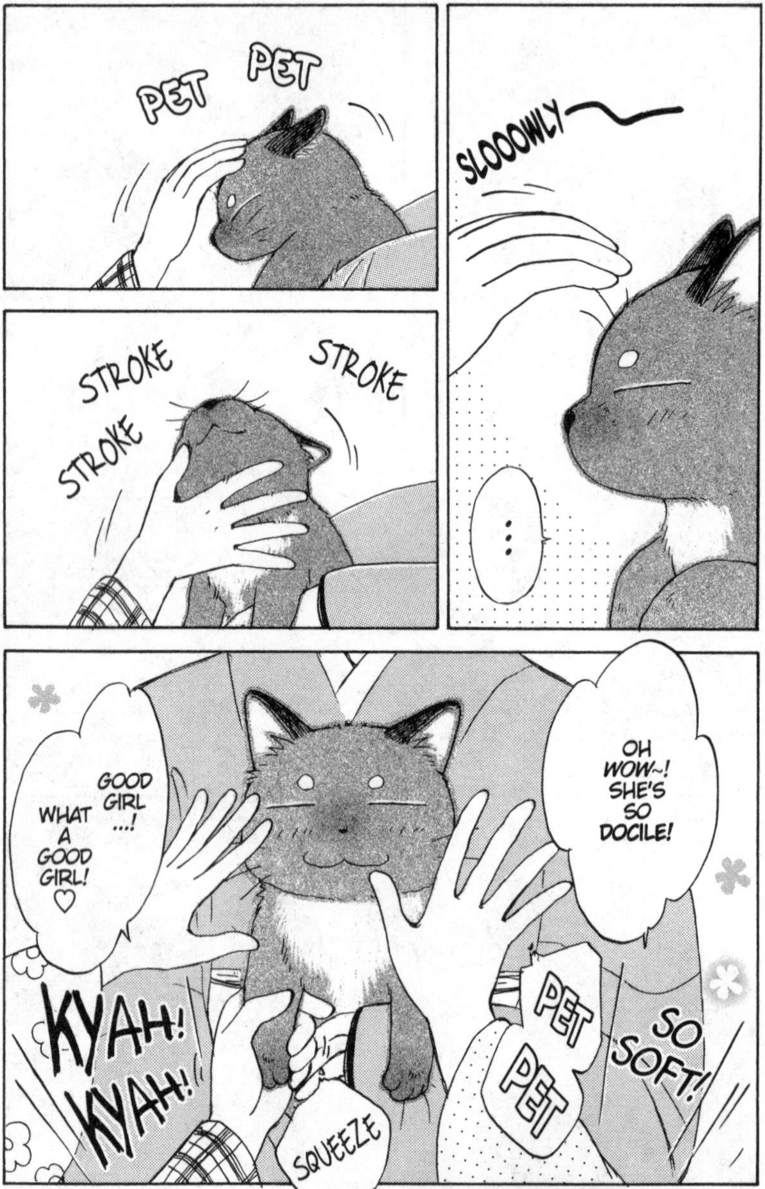
SLOOOWLY~
...
PET PET
STROKE STROKE
STROKE
OH WOW~! SHE'S SO DOCILE!
SO SOFT!
PET PET
GOOD GIRL ...!
WHAT A GOOD GIRL! ♡
KYAH! KYAH!
SQUEEZE

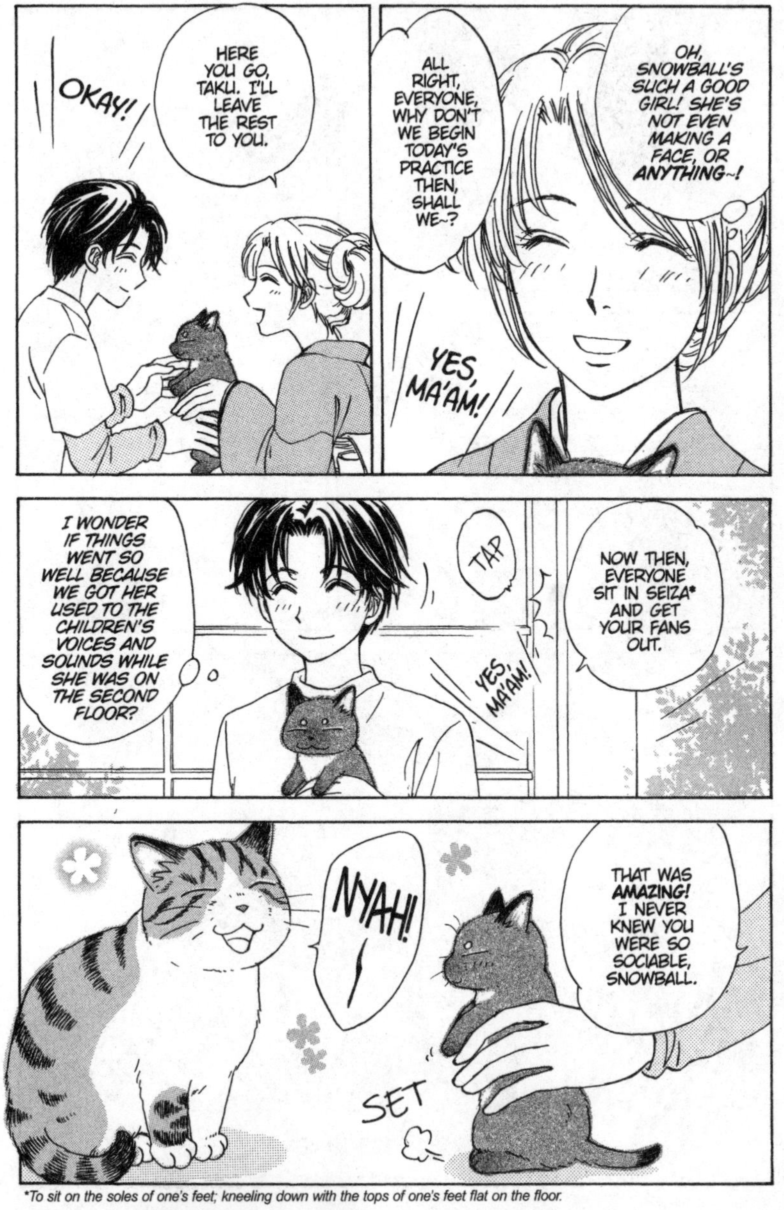
OH, SNOWBALL'S SUCH A GOOD GIRL! SHE'S NOT EVEN MAKING A FACE, OR ANYTHING~!
ALL RIGHT, EVERYONE, WHY DON'T WE BEGIN TODAY'S PRACTICE THEN, SHALL WE~?
YES, MA'AM!
HERE YOU GO, TAKU. I'LL LEAVE THE REST TO YOU.
OKAY!
NOW THEN, EVERYONE SIT IN SEIZA* AND GET YOUR FANS OUT.
YES, MA'AM!
TAP
I WONDER IF THINGS WENT SO WELL BECAUSE WE GOT HER USED TO THE CHILDREN'S VOICES AND SOUNDS WHILE SHE WAS ON THE SECOND FLOOR?
THAT WAS AMAZING! I NEVER KNEW YOU WERE SO SOCIABLE, SNOWBALL.
SET
NYAH!

*To sit on the soles of one's feet; kneeling down with the tops of one's feet flat on the floor.

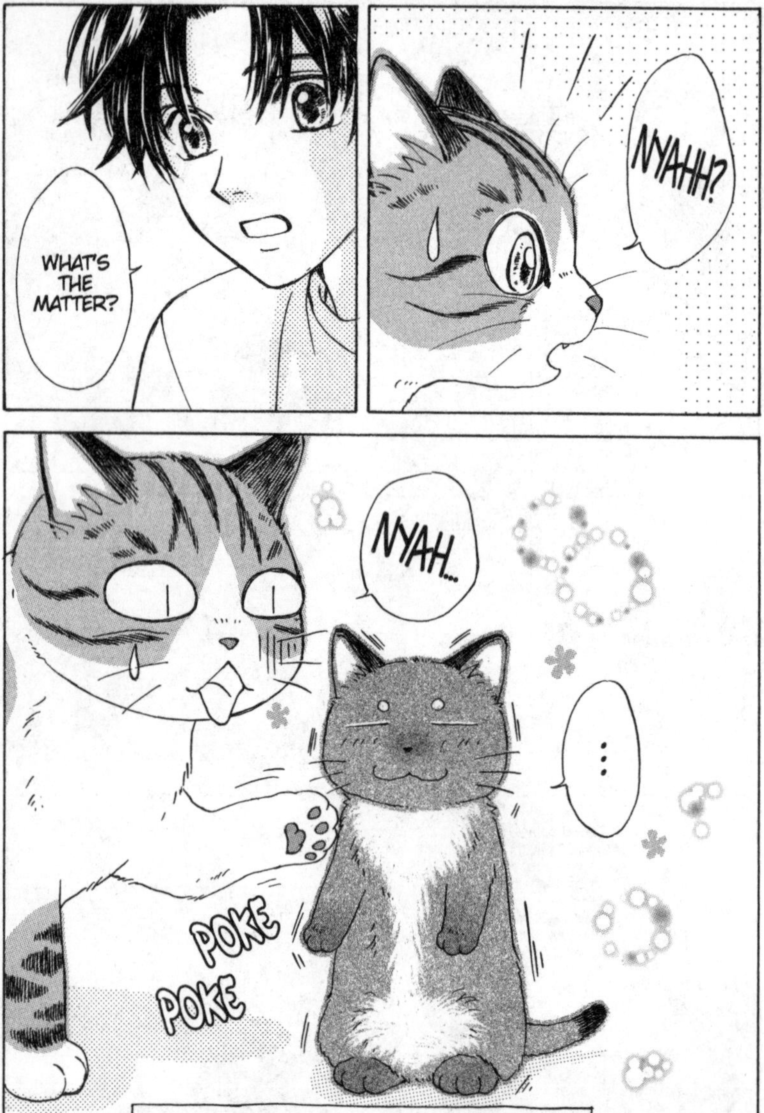
NYAHH?
WHAT'S THE MATTER?
...
NYAH...
POKE
POKE
Completely frozen up

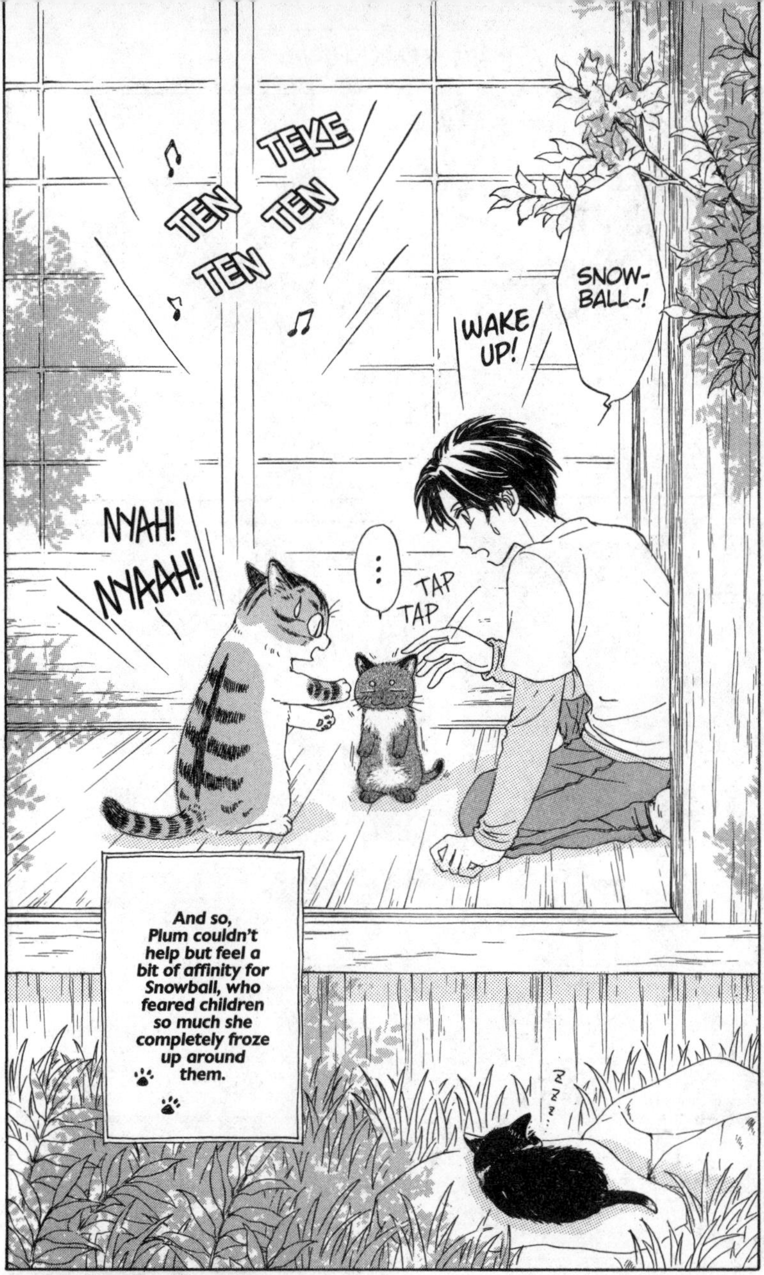
SNOW-BALL~!
WAKE UP!
TEKE TEN TEN TEN TEN
...
TAP TAP
NYAH! NYAAH!
And so, Plum couldn't help but feel a bit of affinity for Snowball, who feared children so much she completely froze up around them.
z z z...

THE END

SHORT.9 PLUM AND SNOWBALL

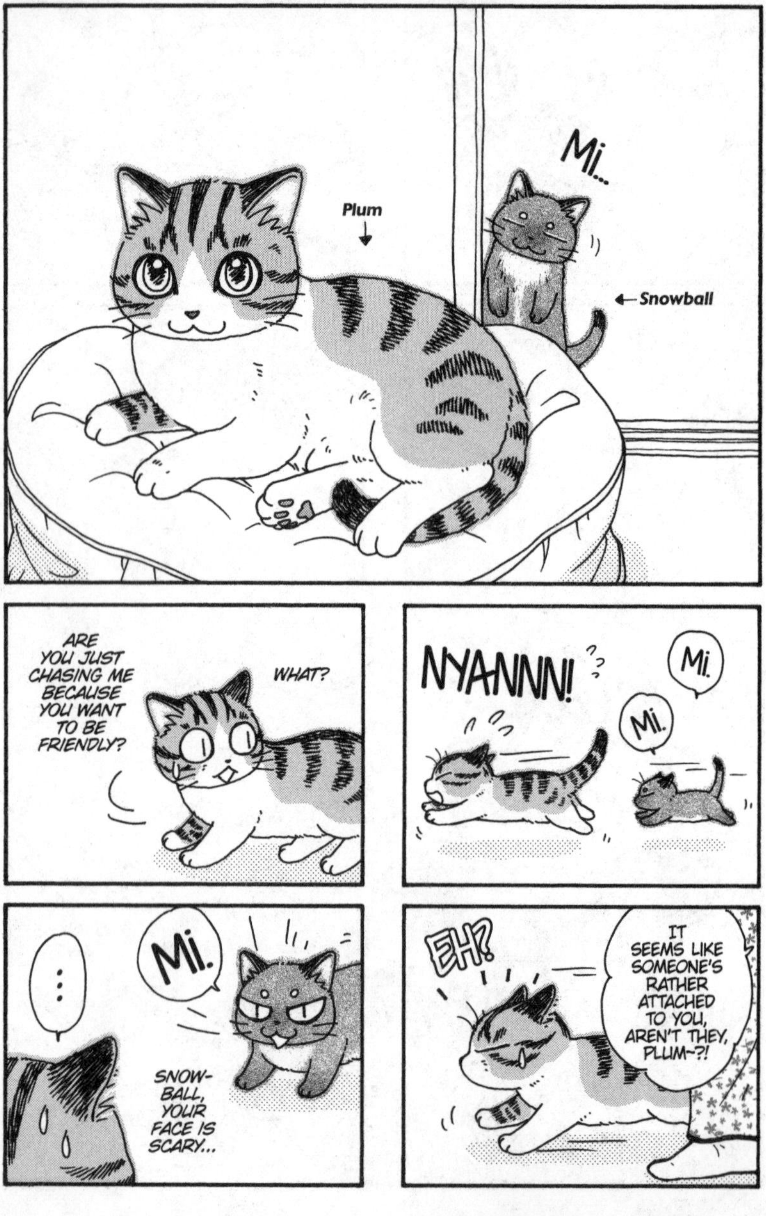
Mi...
Snowball
Plum
NYANNN!
Mi.
Mi.
WHAT?
ARE YOU JUST CHASING ME BECAUSE YOU WANT TO BE FRIENDLY?
EH?
IT SEEMS LIKE SOMEONE'S RATHER ATTACHED TO YOU, AREN'T THEY, PLUM~?!
Mi.
...
SNOW-BALL, YOUR FACE IS SCARY...

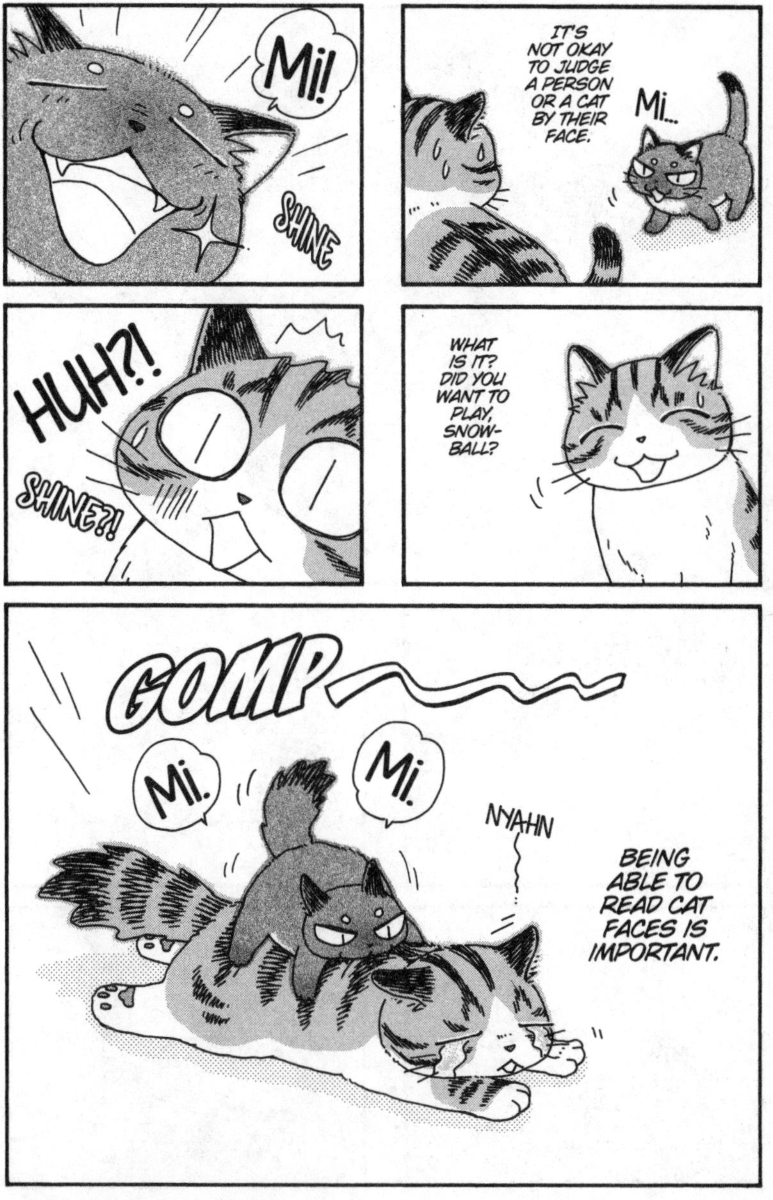
IT'S NOT OKAY TO JUDGE A PERSON OR A CAT BY THEIR FACE.
Mi...
Mi!
SHINE
WHAT IS IT? DID YOU WANT TO PLAY, SNOW-BALL?
HUH?!
SHINE?!
GOMP
Mi.
Mi.
NYAHN
BEING ABLE TO READ CAT FACES IS IMPORTANT.

SNOWBALL STYLE: HOW TO FIND A WARM BED

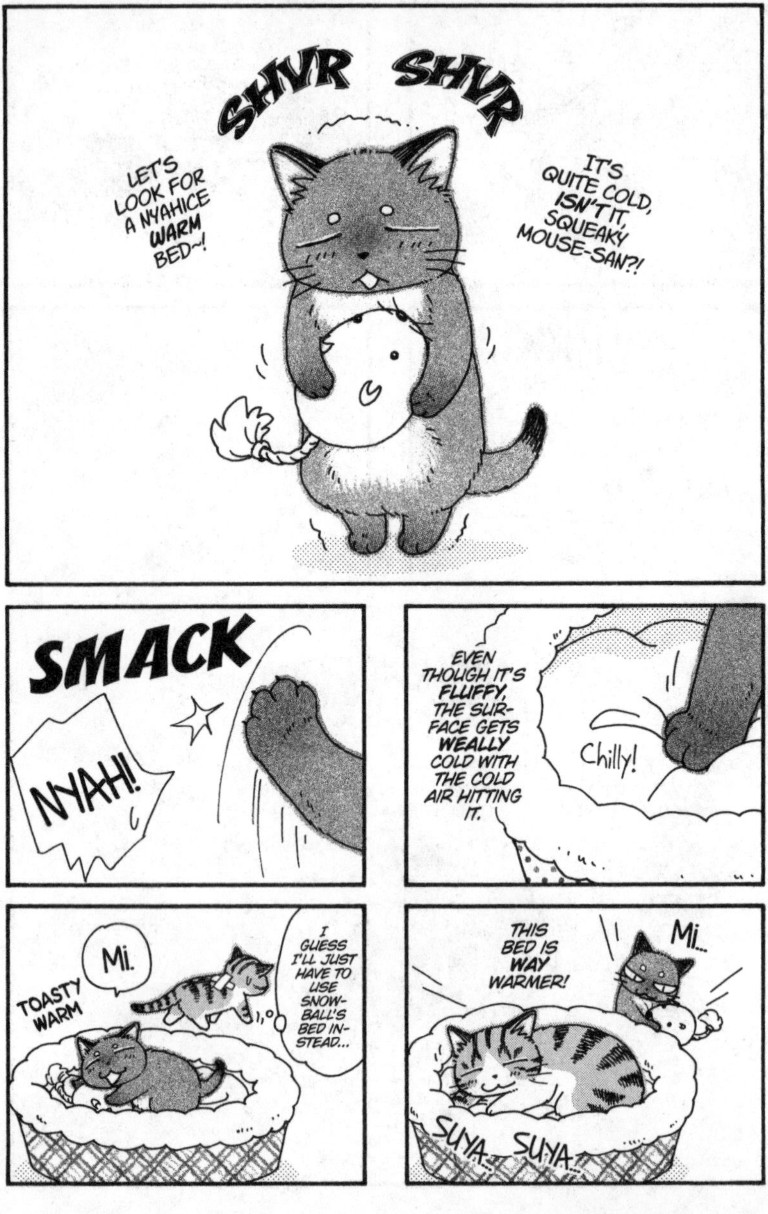
SHVR SHVR
IT'S QUITE COLD, ISN'T IT, SQUEAKY MOUSE-SAN?!
LET'S LOOK FOR A NYAHICE WARM BED~!
EVEN THOUGH IT'S FLUFFY, THE SUR-FACE GETS WEALLY COLD WITH THE COLD AIR HITTING IT.
Chilly!
SMACK
NYAH!
THIS BED IS WAY WARMER!
Mi...
SUYA... SUYA...
I GUESS I'LL JUST HAVE TO USE SNOW-BALL'S BED IN-STEAD...
Mi.
TOASTY WARM

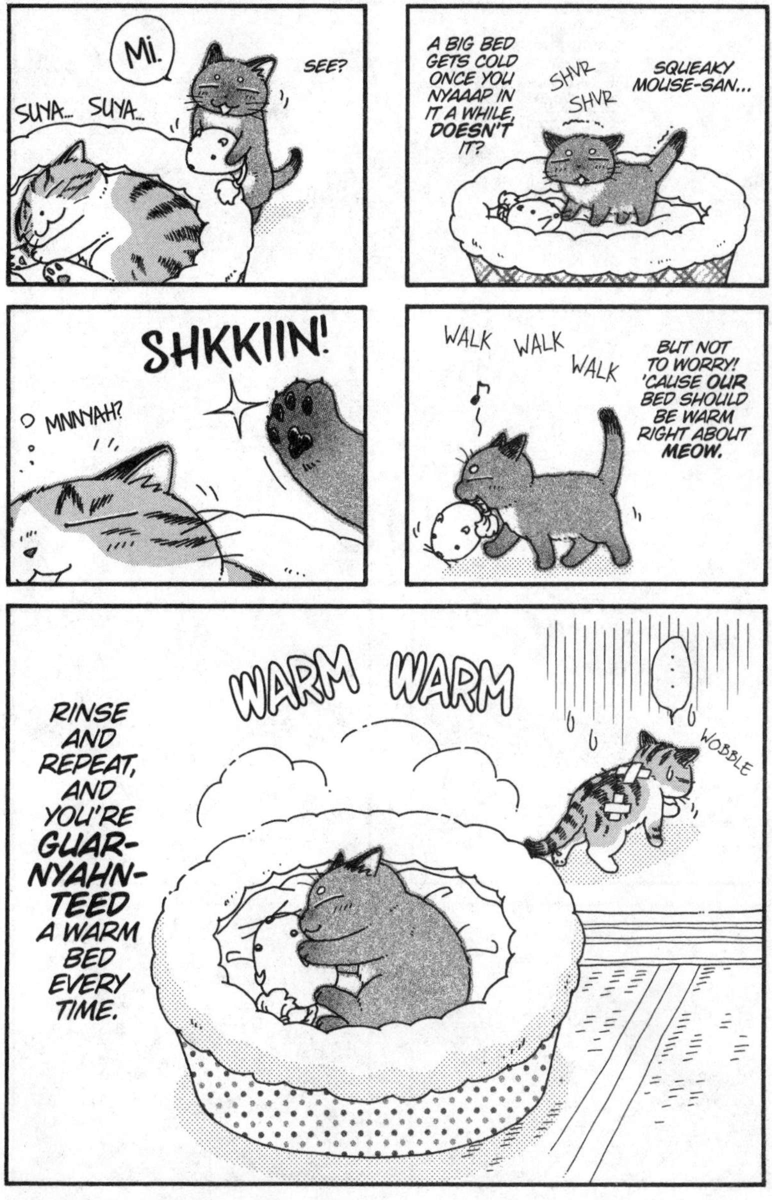
SQUEAKY MOUSE-SAN...
SHVR SHVR
A BIG BED GETS COLD ONCE YOU NYAAAP IN IT A WHILE, DOESN'T IT?
SEE?
Mi.
SUYA... SUYA...
BUT NOT TO WORRY! 'CAUSE OUR BED SHOULD BE WARM RIGHT ABOUT MEOW.
WALK WALK WALK
SHKKIIN!
MNNYAH?
WOBBLE
...
WARM WARM
RINSE AND REPEAT, AND YOU'RE GUAR-NYAHN-TEED A WARM BED EVERY TIME.

SNOWBALL RETURNS THE FAVOR

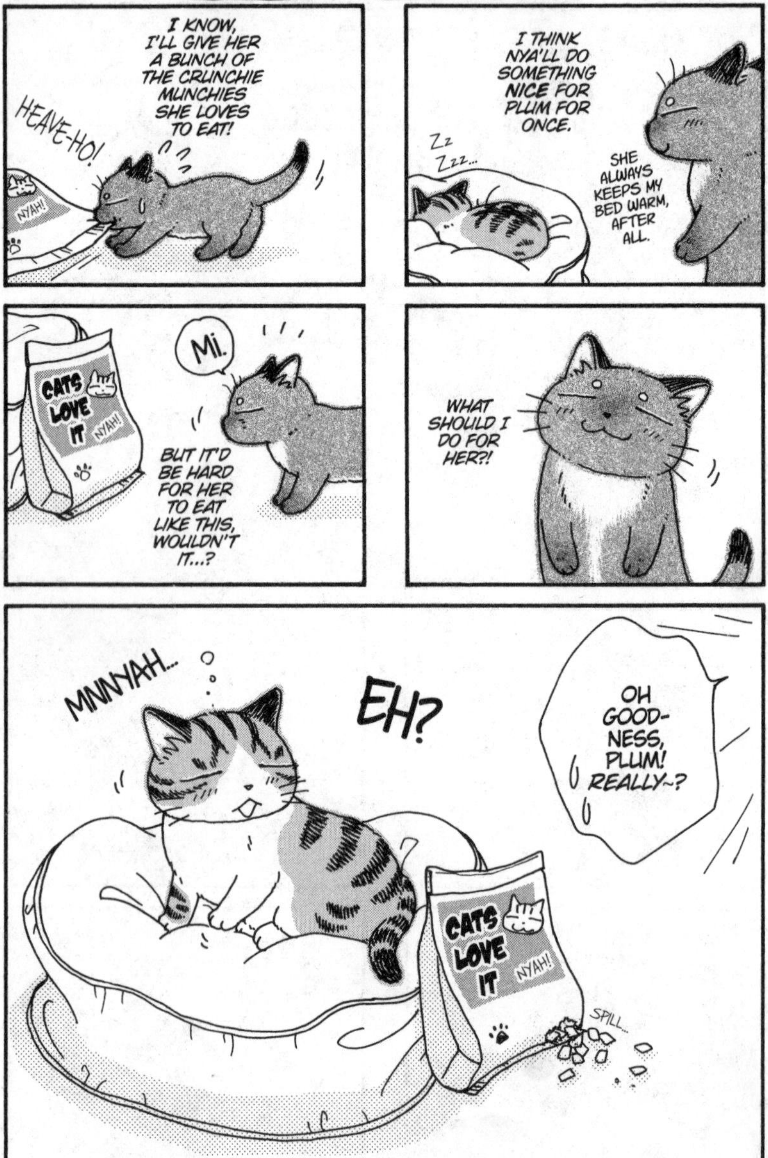
I THINK NYA'LL DO SOMETHING NICE FOR PLUM FOR ONCE.
SHE ALWAYS KEEPS MY BED WARM, AFTER ALL.
Zz Zzz...
I KNOW, I'LL GIVE HER A BUNCH OF THE CRUNCHIE MUNCHIES SHE LOVES TO EAT!
HEAVE-HO!
NYAH!
WHAT SHOULD I DO FOR HER?!
Mi.
BUT IT'D BE HARD FOR HER TO EAT LIKE THIS, WOULDN'T IT...?
CATS LOVE IT
NYAH!
OH GOOD-NESS, PLUM! REALLY~?
EH?
MNNYAH...
CATS LOVE IT
NYAH!
SPILL...

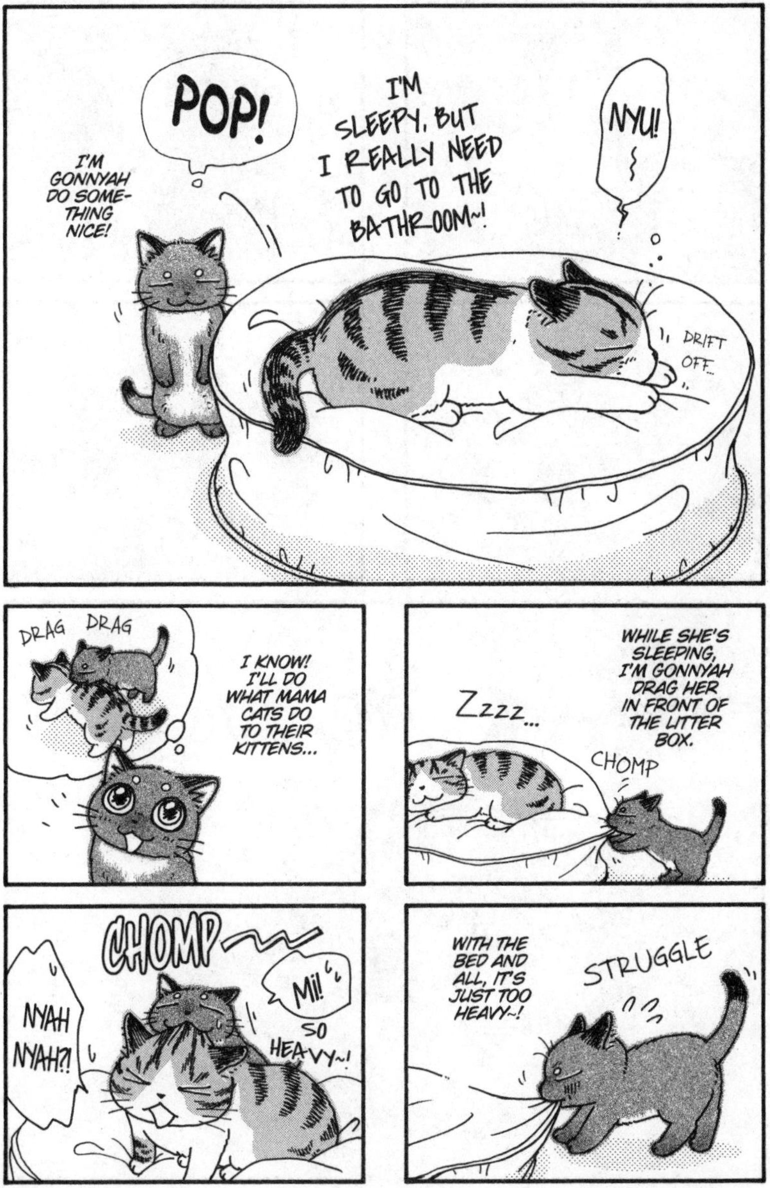
NYU!
DRIFT OFF...
I'M SLEEPY, BUT I REALLY NEED TO GO TO THE BATHROOM~!
POP!
I'M GONNYAH DO SOMETHING NICE!
WHILE SHE'S SLEEPING, I'M GONNYAH DRAG HER IN FRONT OF THE LITTER BOX.
Zzzz...
CHOMP
I KNOW! I'LL DO WHAT MAMA CATS DO TO THEIR KITTENS...
DRAG DRAG
STRUGGLE
WITH THE BED AND ALL, IT'S JUST TOO HEAVY~!
Mi!
SO HEAVY~!
CHOMP
NYAH NYAH?!

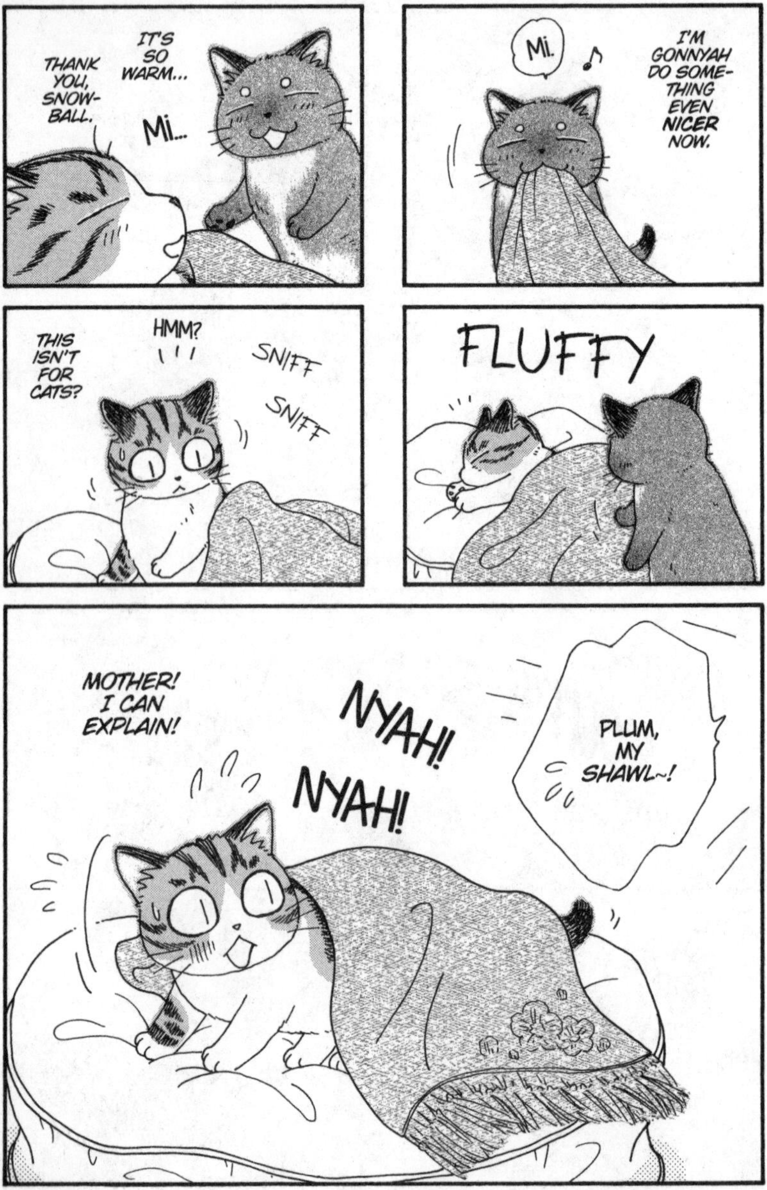
I'M GONNYAH DO SOME-THING EVEN NICER NOW.
Mi.
IT'S SO WARM...
THANK YOU, SNOW-BALL.
Mi...
FLUFFY
SNIFF
SNIFF
HMM?
THIS ISN'T FOR CATS?
PLUM, MY SHAWL~!
NYAH!
NYAH!
MOTHER! I CAN EXPLAIN!

Plum's Revenge

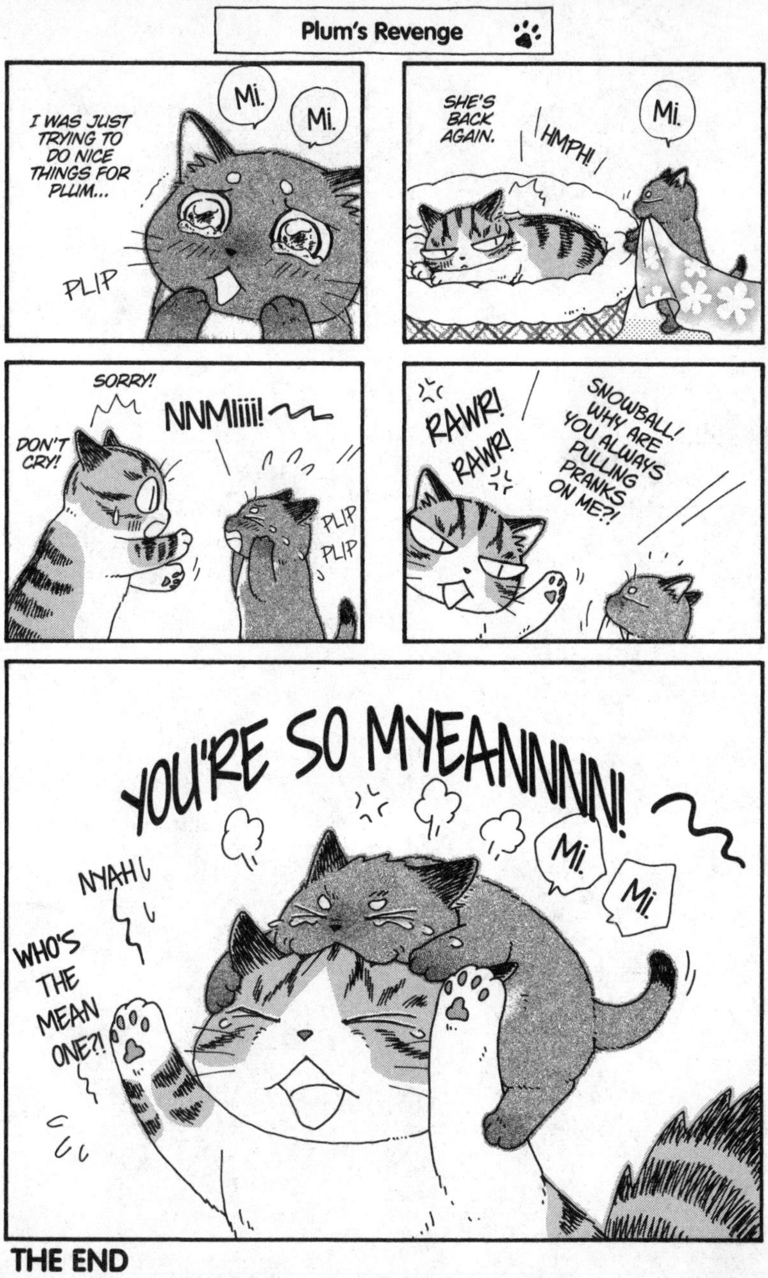

Mi.
SHE'S BACK AGAIN.
HMPH!
Mi.
Mi.
I WAS JUST TRYING TO DO NICE THINGS FOR PLUM...
PLIP
SNOWBALL! WHY ARE YOU ALWAYS PULLING PRANKS ON ME?!
RAWR!
RAWR!
NNMIiiii!
SORRY!
DON'T CRY!
PLIP
PLIP
Mi.
Mi.
YOU'RE SO MYEANNNNN!
NYAH
WHO'S THE MEAN ONE?!

THE END

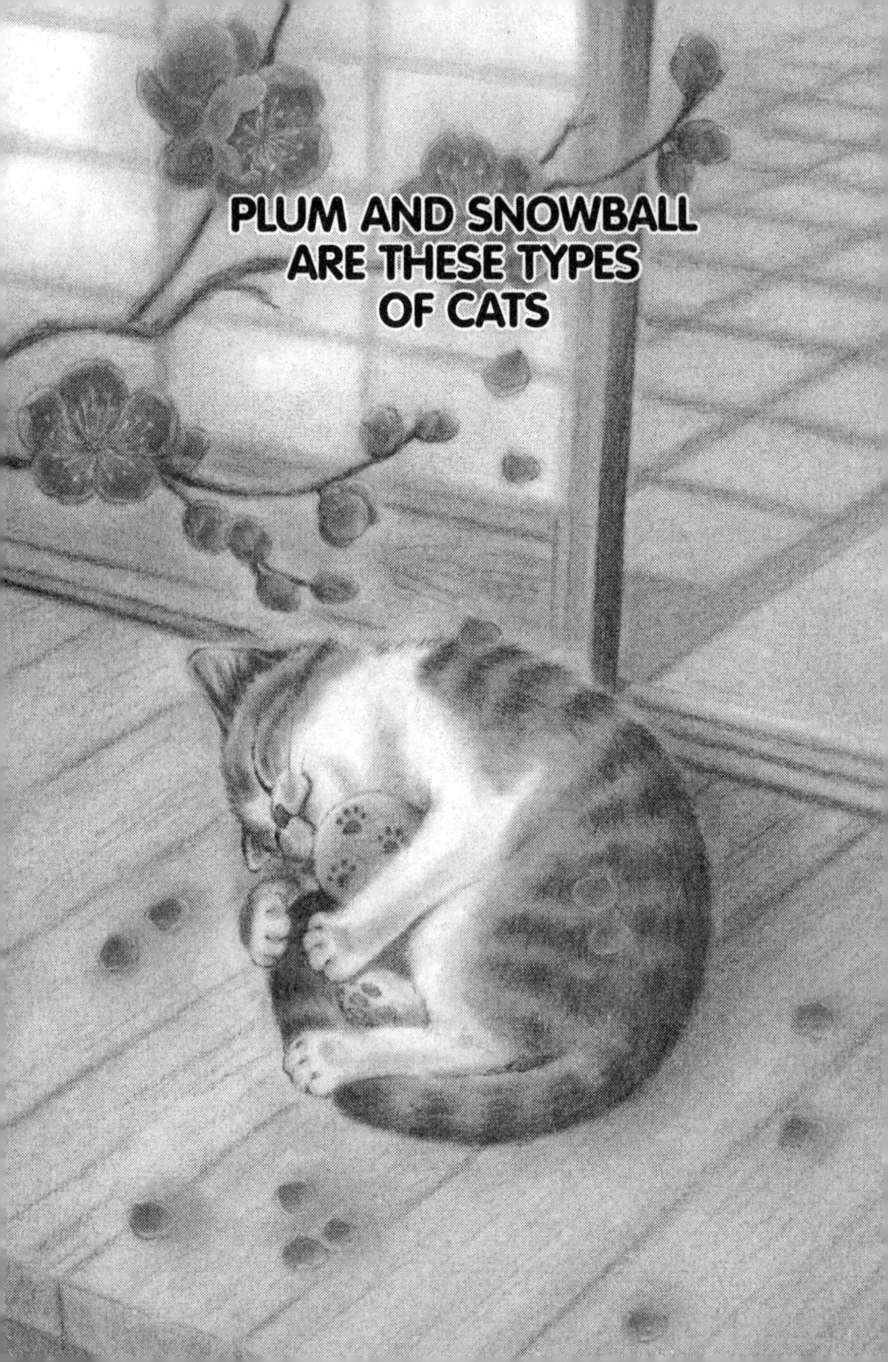
PLUM AND SNOWBALL
ARE THESE TYPES
OF CATS

PLUM

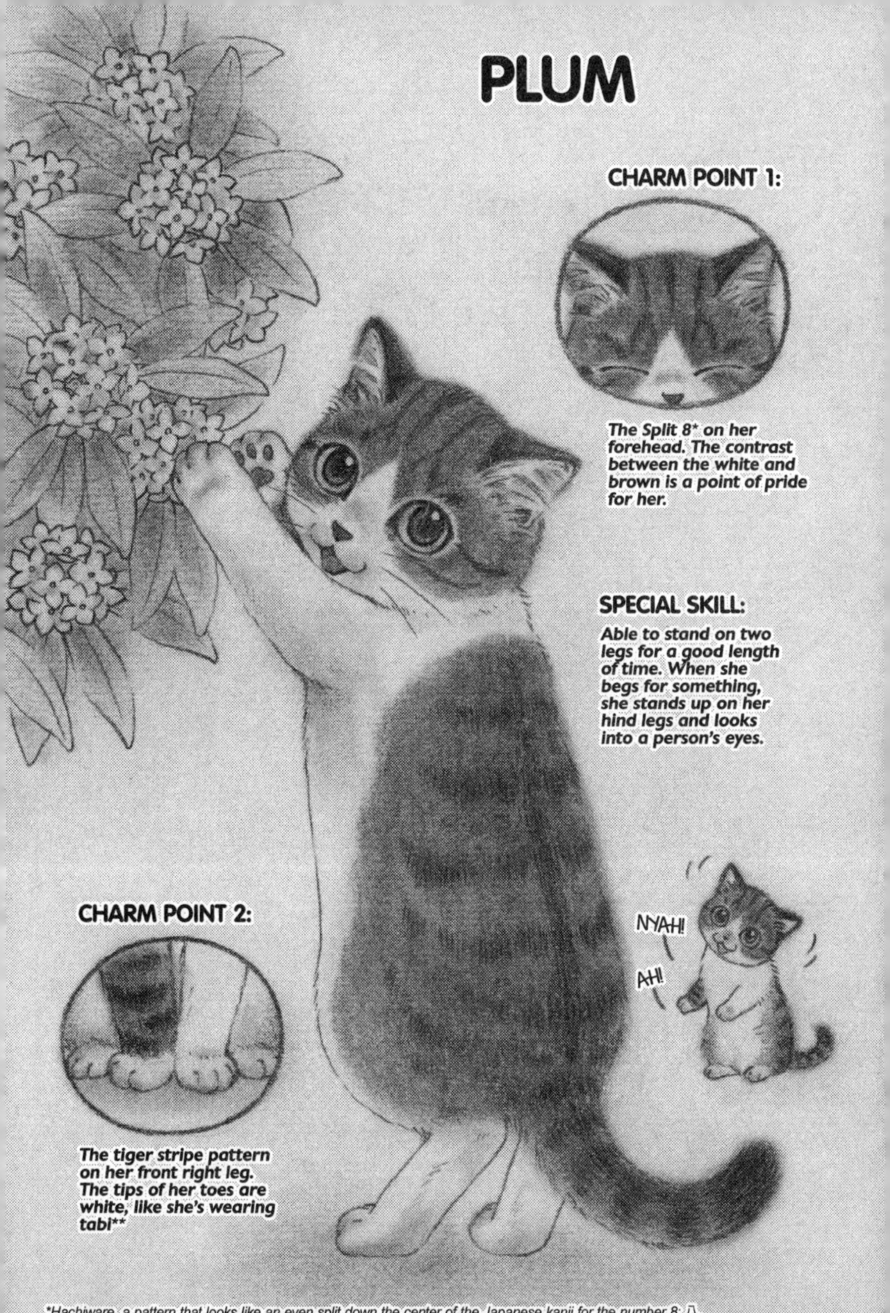

NYAH!
AH!

CHARM POINT 1:

The Split 8 on her forehead. The contrast between the white and brown is a point of pride for her.*

SPECIAL SKILL:

Able to stand on two legs for a good length of time. When she begs for something, she stands up on her hind legs and looks into a person's eyes.

CHARM POINT 2:

The tiger stripe pattern on her front right leg. The tips of her toes are white, like she's wearing tabi**

*Hachiware, a pattern that looks like an even split down the center of the Japanese kanji for the number 8: 八.

**Japanese split-toe socks.

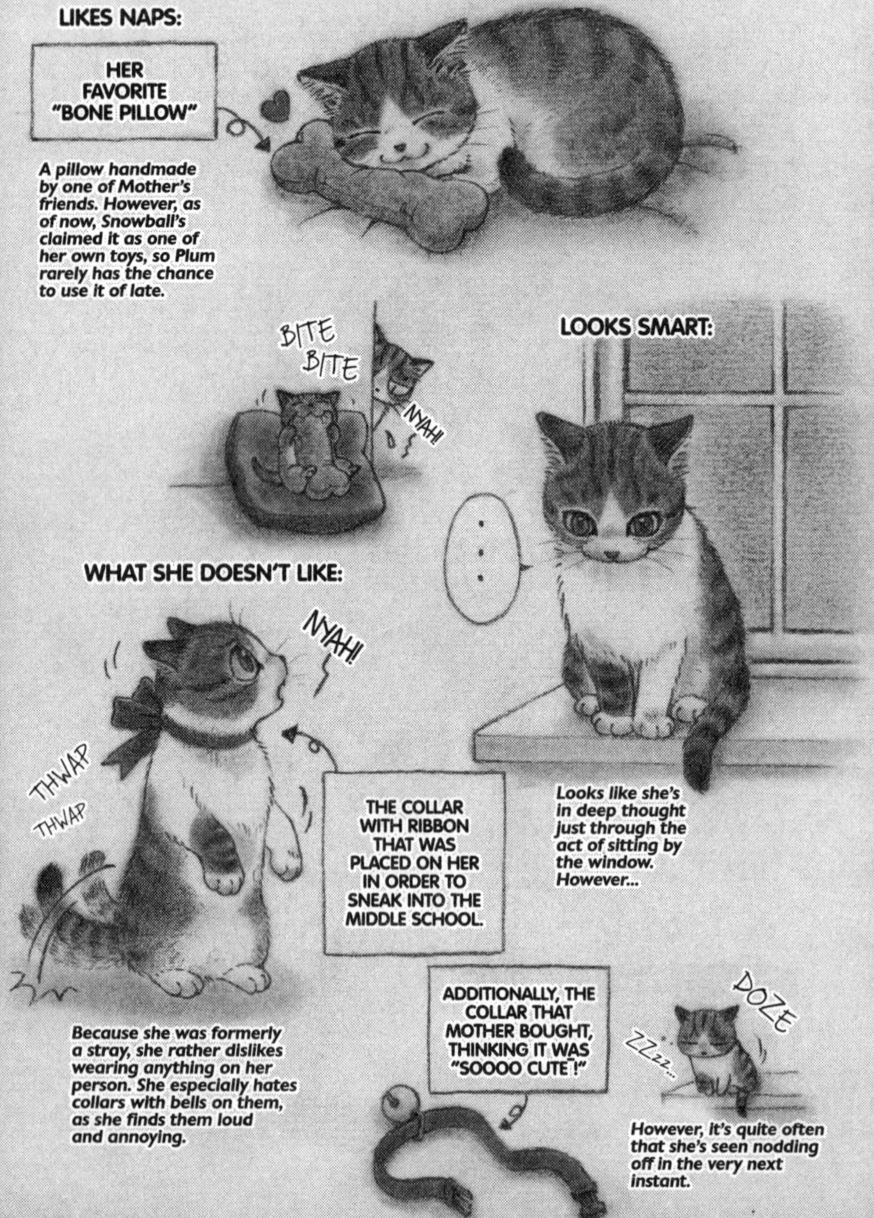
LIKES NAPS:
HER FAVORITE "BONE PILLOW"
A pillow handmade by one of Mother's friends. However, as of now, Snowball's claimed it as one of her own toys, so Plum rarely has the chance to use it of late.
BITE BITE
NYAH!
LOOKS SMART:
...
Looks like she's in deep thought just through the act of sitting by the window. However...
WHAT SHE DOESN'T LIKE:
NYAH!
THWAP THWAP
THE COLLAR WITH RIBBON THAT WAS PLACED ON HER IN ORDER TO SNEAK INTO THE MIDDLE SCHOOL.
Because she was formerly a stray, she rather dislikes wearing anything on her person. She especially hates collars with bells on them, as she finds them loud and annoying.
ADDITIONALLY, THE COLLAR THAT MOTHER BOUGHT, THINKING IT WAS "SOOOO CUTE!"
DOZE
ZZzz...
However, it's quite often that she's seen nodding off in the very next instant.

CATNIP FOR CATS:

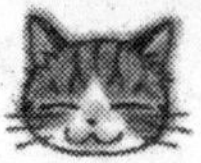

The "Catnip Ball" she favors. Strings of catnip woven into a ball. Has a catnip rod inside as well.

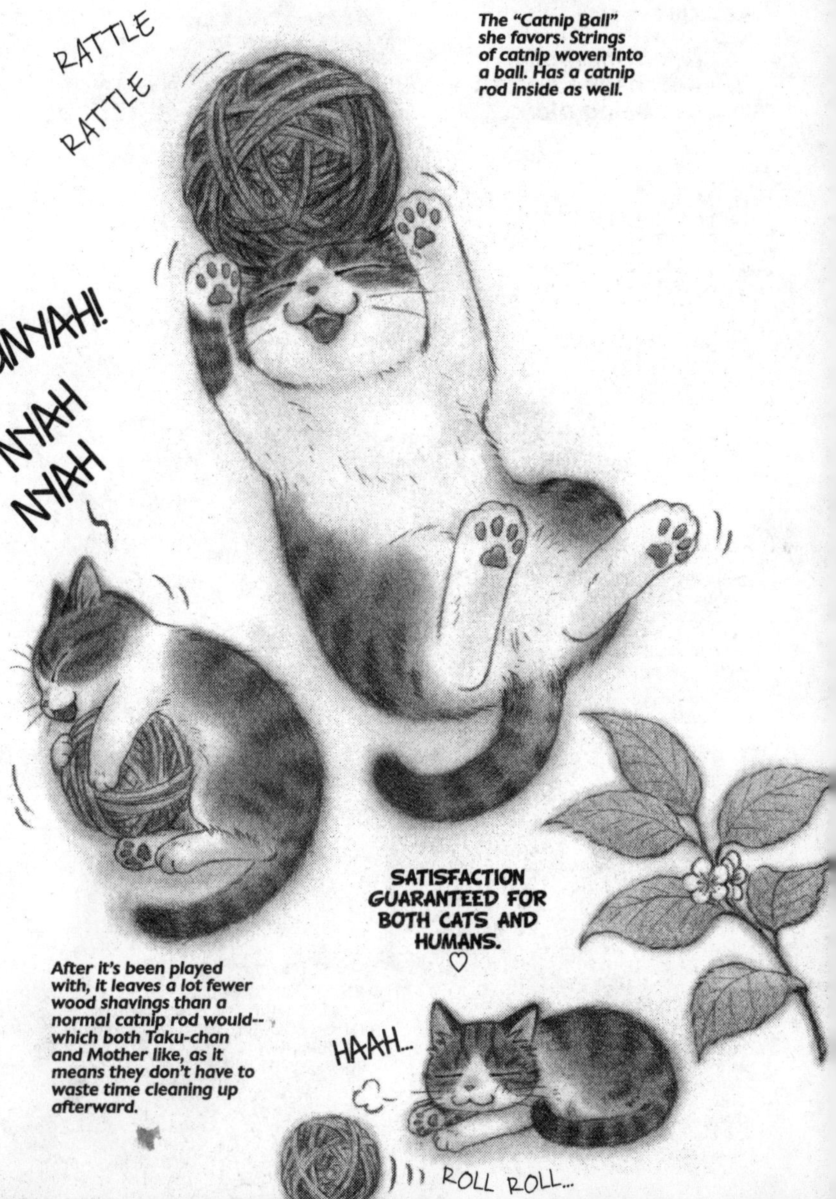
RATTLE
RATTLE
UNYAH!
NYAH NYAH
SATISFACTION GUARANTEED FOR BOTH CATS AND HUMANS. ♡
HAAH...
ROLL ROLL...

After it's been played with, it leaves a lot fewer wood shavings than a normal catnip rod would--which both Taku-chan and Mother like, as it means they don't have to waste time cleaning up afterward.

SNOWBALL

A selfish, spoiled kitten who doesn't like being alone.

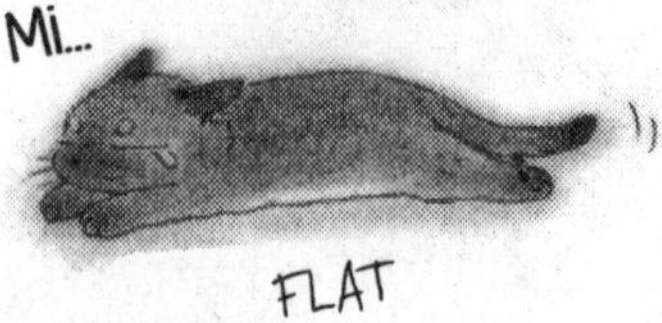

Mi...
FLAT

CHARM POINT 1:

The small white dots sitting daintily right above her eyes.

CHARM POINT 2:

Her white chest, which makes it look like she's wearing an apron.

CHARM POINT 3:

The coloring behind her ears, the tips of her toes, and her tail are all slightly darker than the rest of her body.

SQUEAKY MOUSE-SAN:

Though the feel of the material it's made of is a far cry from that of a real mouse, it's still one of her most favored things.

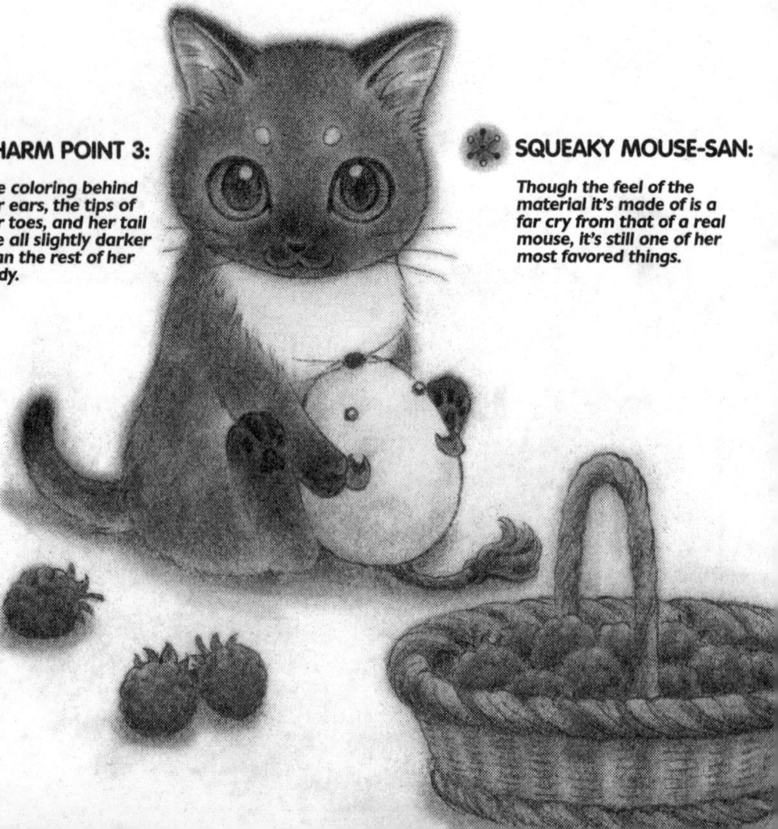

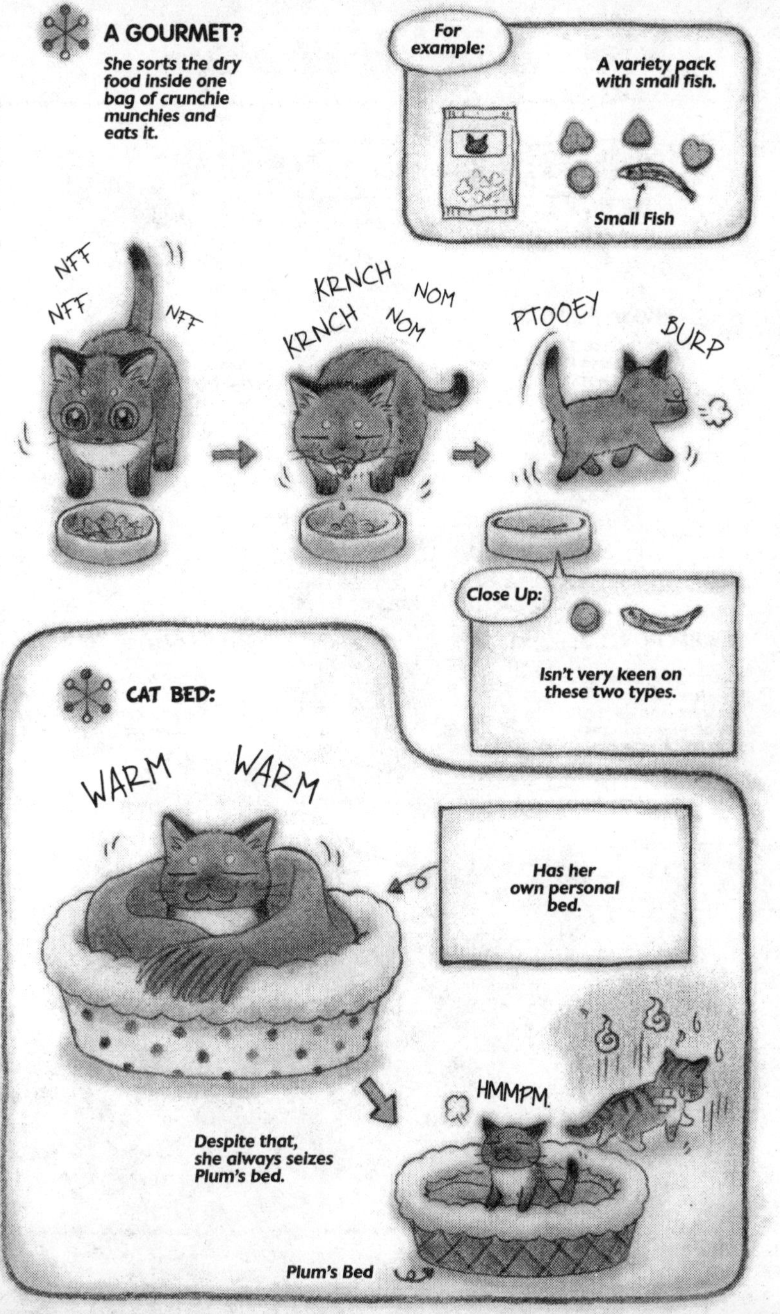
A GOURMET?
She sorts the dry food inside one bag of crunchie munchies and eats it.
For example:
A variety pack with small fish.
Small Fish
NFF
NFF
NFF
KRNCH
KRNCH
NOM
NOM
PTOOEY
BURP
Close Up:
Isn't very keen on these two types.
CAT BED:
WARM
WARM
Has her own personal bed.
Despite that, she always seizes Plum's bed.
HMMPM.
Plum's Bed

STORIES ABOUT MY CATS

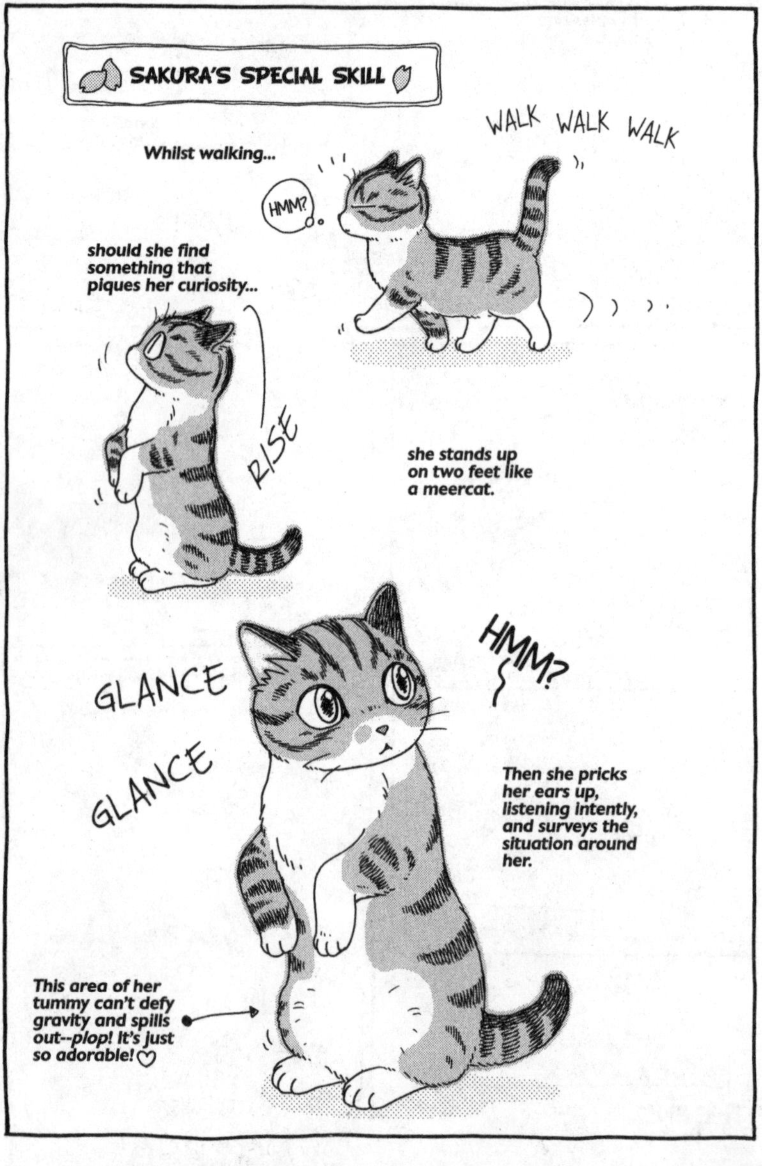
SAKURA'S SPECIAL SKILL
WALK WALK WALK
Whilst walking...
HMM?
should she find something that piques her curiosity...
RISE
she stands up on two feet like a meercat.
HMM?
GLANCE
GLANCE
Then she pricks her ears up, listening intently, and surveys the situation around her.
This area of her tummy can't defy gravity and spills out--*plop!* It's just so adorable! ♡

STORIES ABOUT MY CATS

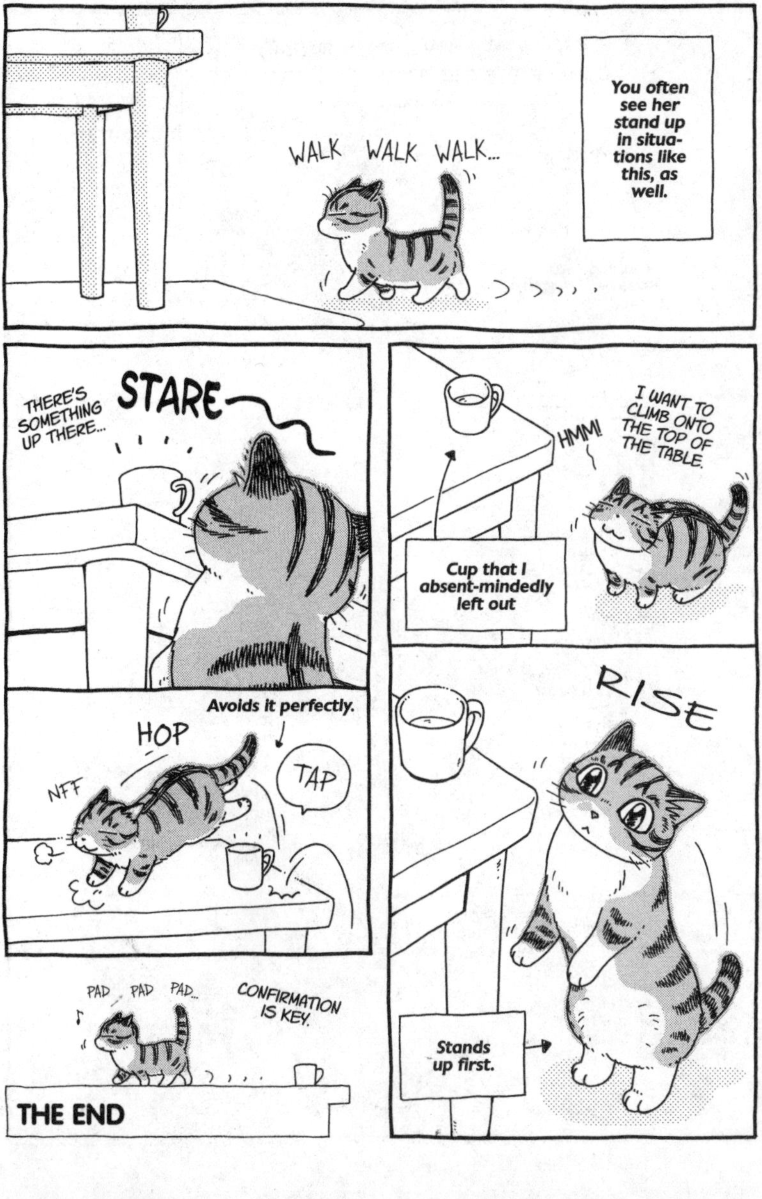
You often see her stand up in situations like this, as well.
WALK WALK WALK...
I WANT TO CLIMB ONTO THE TOP OF THE TABLE.
HMM!
Cup that I absent-mindedly left out
THERE'S SOMETHING UP THERE...
STARE
RISE
Stands up first.
Avoids it perfectly.
TAP
HOP
NFF
CONFIRMATION IS KEY.
PAD PAD PAD...
THE END

STORIES ABOUT MY CATS

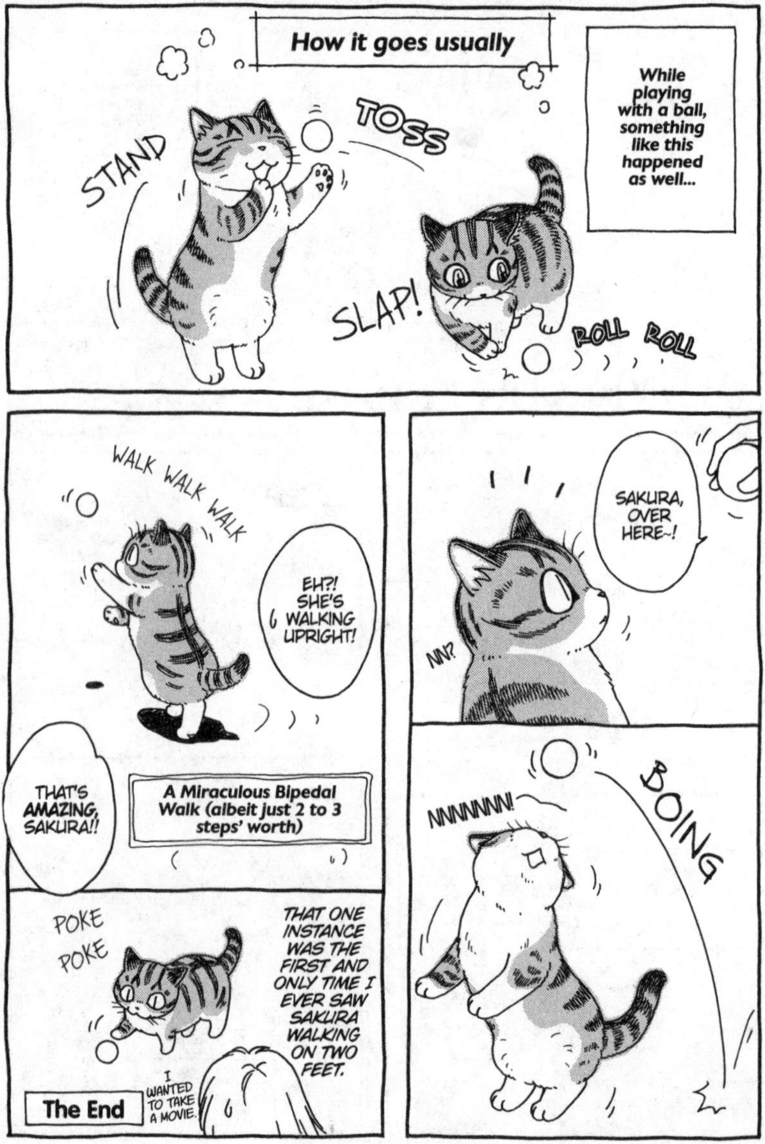
While playing with a ball, something like this happened as well...
How it goes usually
TOSS
STAND
SLAP!
ROLL ROLL
SAKURA, OVER HERE~!
NN?
BOING
NNNNNNN!
WALK WALK WALK
EH?! SHE'S WALKING UPRIGHT!
A Miraculous Bipedal Walk (albeit just 2 to 3 steps' worth)
THAT'S AMAZING, SAKURA!!
THAT ONE INSTANCE WAS THE FIRST AND ONLY TIME I EVER SAW SAKURA WALKING ON TWO FEET.
POKE
POKE
I WANTED TO TAKE A MOVIE.
The End

STORIES ABOUT MY CATS

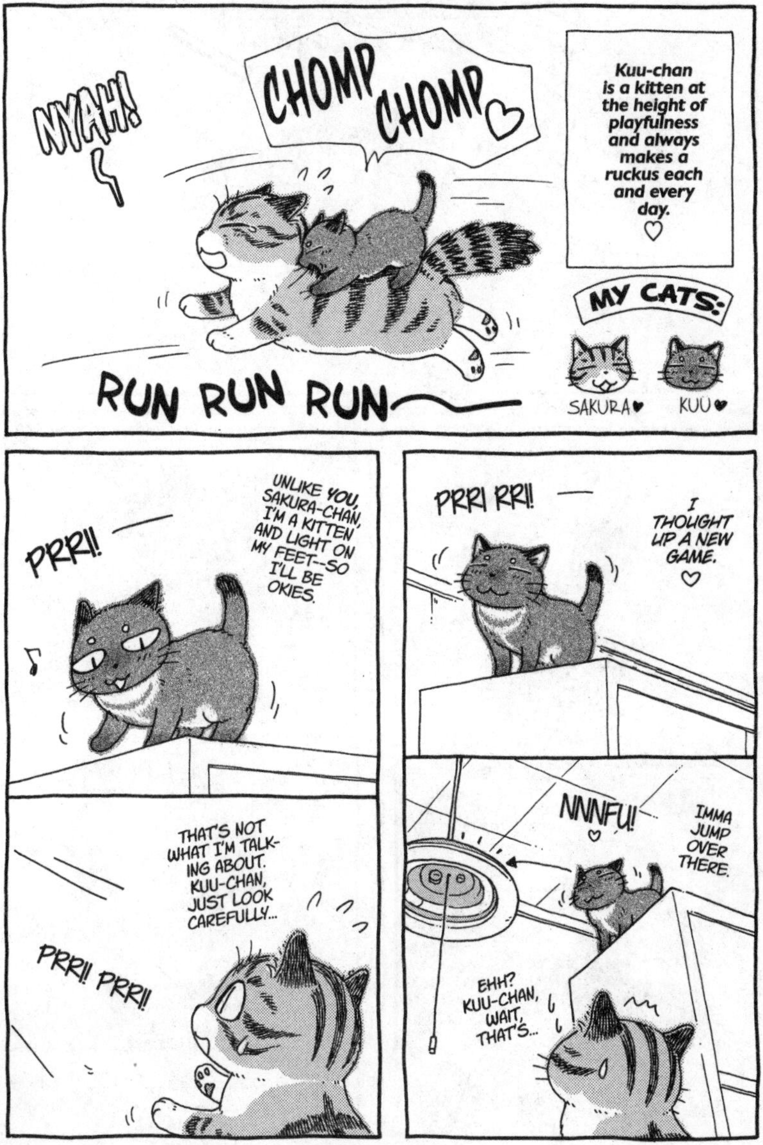

Kuu-chan is a kitten at the height of playfulness and always makes a ruckus each and every day. ♡
MY CATS:
SAKURA♥
KUU♥
CHOMP CHOMP ♡
NYAH!
RUN RUN RUN
I THOUGHT UP A NEW GAME. ♡
PRRI RRI!
UNLIKE YOU, SAKURA-CHAN, I'M A KITTEN AND LIGHT ON MY FEET--SO I'LL BE OKIES.
PRR!
IMMA JUMP OVER THERE.
NNNFU! ♡
EHH? KUU-CHAN, WAIT, THAT'S...
THAT'S NOT WHAT I'M TALKING ABOUT. KUU-CHAN, JUST LOOK CAREFULLY...
PRR!! PRR!!

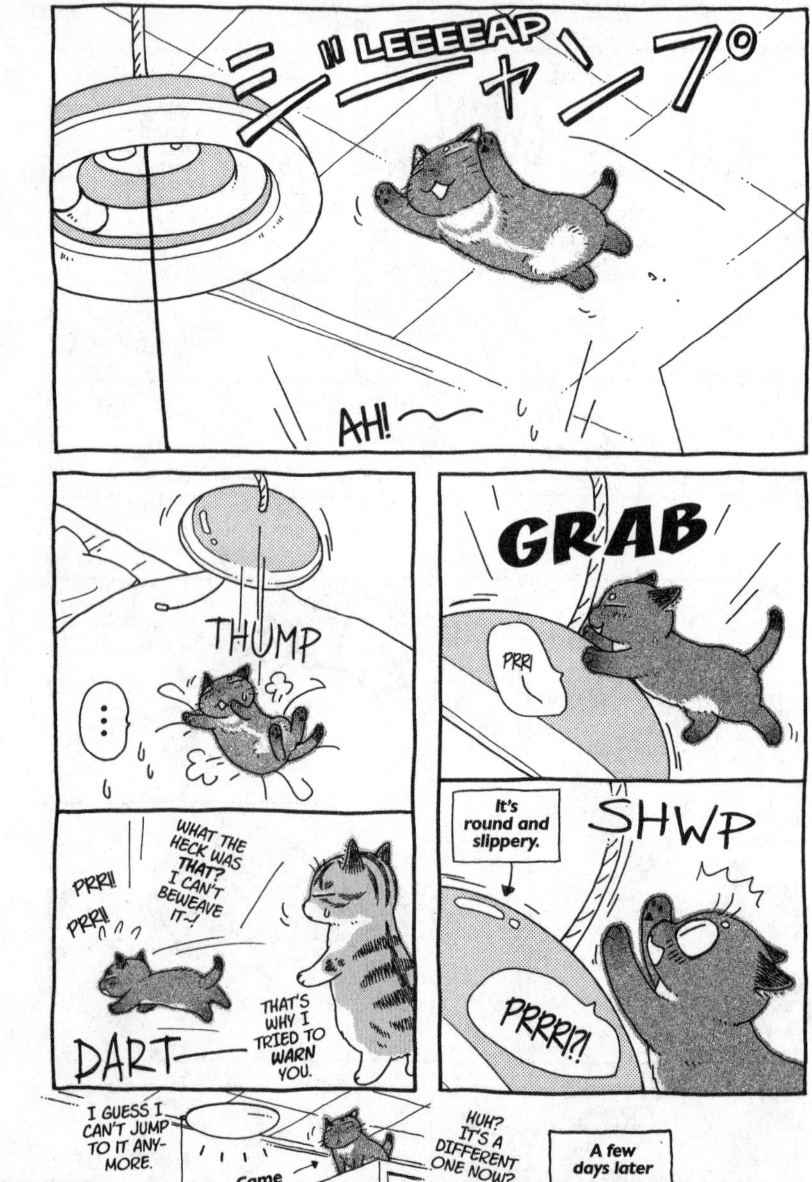
LEEEEAP
ジャンプ
AH!~~
GRAB
PRR!
THUMP
...
It's round and slippery.
SHWP
PRRR!?!
WHAT THE HECK WAS THAT? I CAN'T BEWEAVE IT~!
PRR!
PRR!
THAT'S WHY I TRIED TO WARN YOU.
DART—
A few days later
HUH? IT'S A DIFFERENT ONE NOW?
Came for revenge
I GUESS I CAN'T JUMP TO IT ANYMORE.
THE END

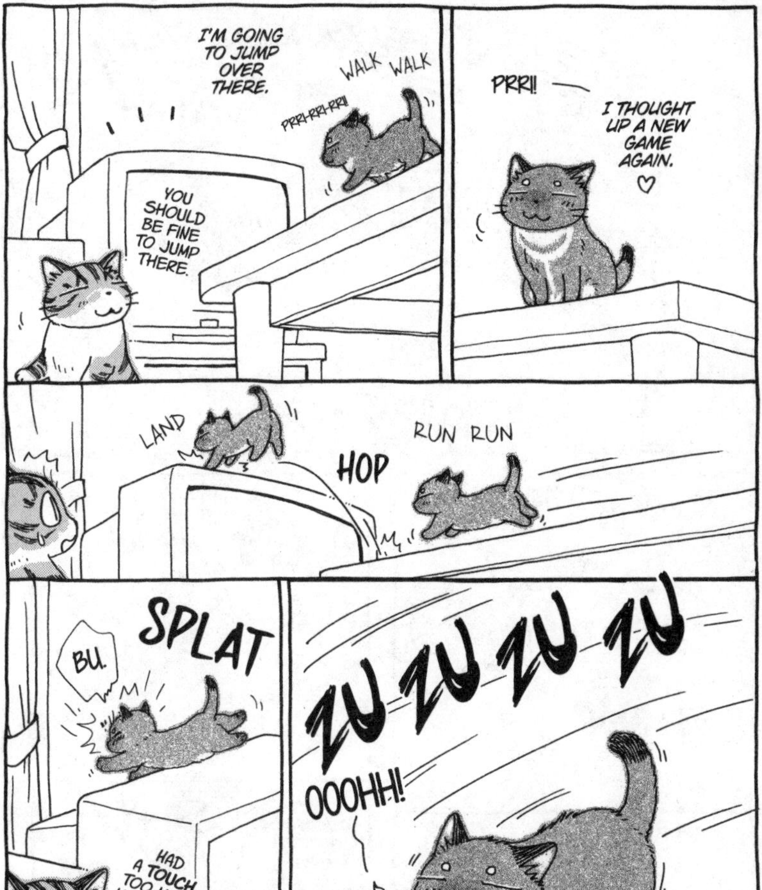
PRR!!
I THOUGHT UP A NEW GAME AGAIN.
I'M GOING TO JUMP OVER THERE.
WALK WALK
PRRI-RRI-RRI!
YOU SHOULD BE FINE TO JUMP THERE.
RUN RUN
HOP
LAND
ZU ZU ZU ZU
OOOHH!
IT'S SWIPPERY~!
SPLAT
BU.
HAD A TOUCH TOO MUCH MOMENTUM THERE...
The End

TO EVERYONE WHO HELPED WORK ON THIS BOOK AND TO MY READERS, THANK YOU VERY MUCH. ♡

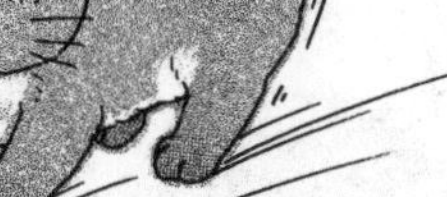
NYAHN!
MI!

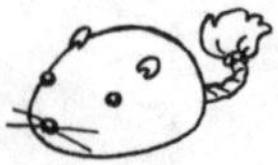

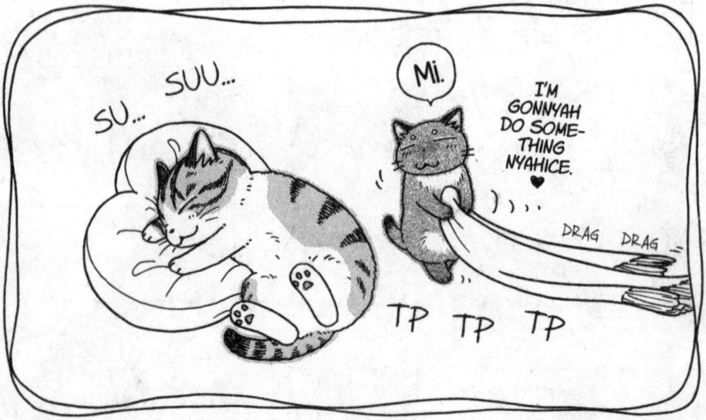
I'M GONNYAH DO SOME-THING NYAHICE. ♥
Mi.
DRAG DRAG
TP TP TP
SUU...
SU...

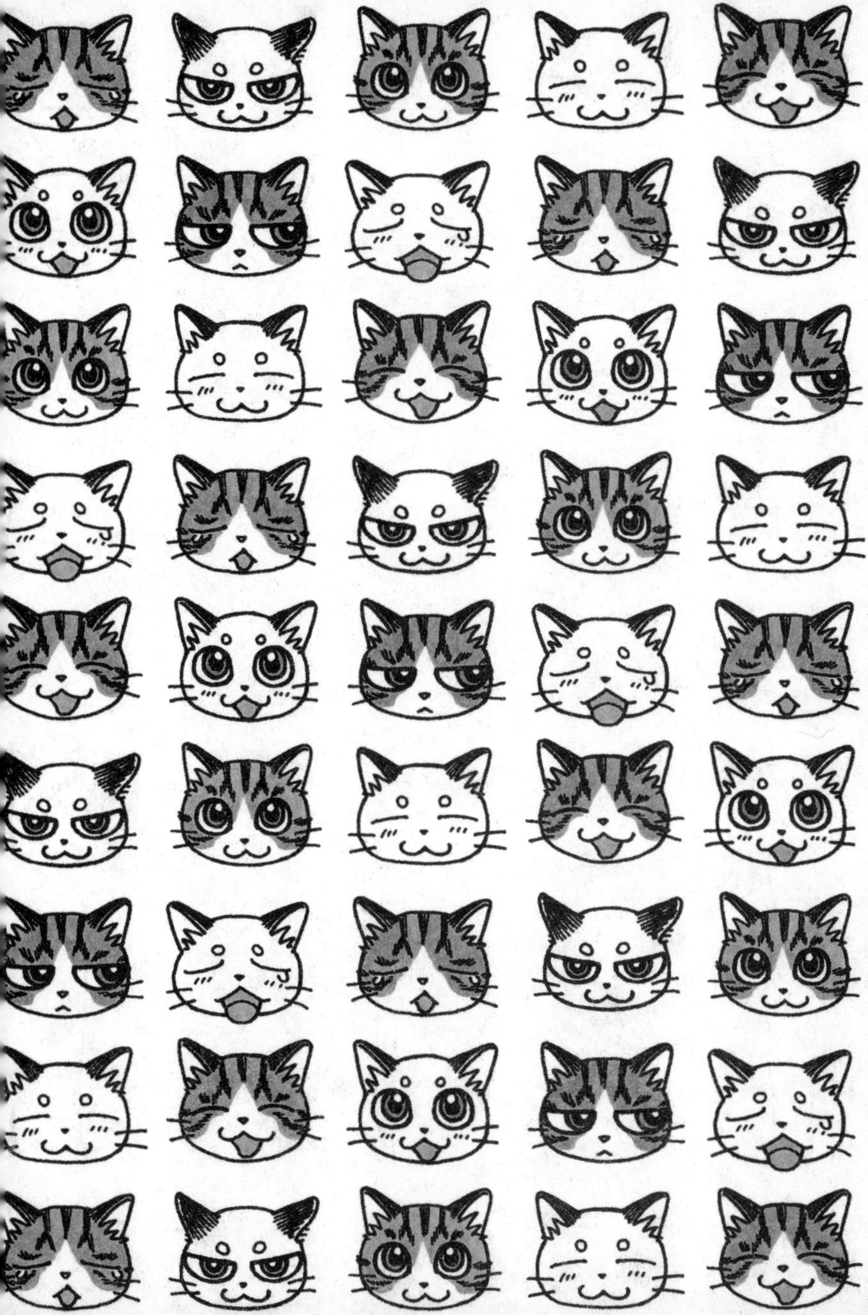

Plum Crazy!
tales of a
tiger-striped cat

story & art by
HOSHINO NATSUMI

2

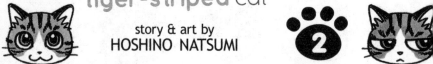

plum Crazy!
tales of a
tiger-striped cat